W9-BXU-115

The Writer's World
Sentences and Paragraphs

FOURTH EDITION

Lynne Gaetz
Lionel Groulx College

Suneeti Phadke
St. Jerome College

PEARSON

Boston   Columbus   Indianapolis   New York   San Francisco   Upper Saddle River
Amsterdam   Cape Town   Dubai   London   Madrid   Milan   Munich   Paris   Montreal   Toronto
Delhi   Mexico City   Sao Paulo   Sydney   Hong Kong   Seoul   Singapore   Taipei   Tokyo

Executive Editor: Matthew Wright
Editorial Assistant: Laura Marenghi
Senior Development Editor: Marion Castellucci
Development Editor: Erica Nikolaidis
Senior Supplements Editor: Donna Campion
Executive Digital Producer: Stefanie Snajder
Content Specialist: Erin Jenkins
Digital Editor: Sara Gordus
Executive Marketing Manager: Roxanne McCarley
Production Manager: Denise Phillip Grant

Project Coordination, Text Design, and Electronic
    Page Makeup: Laserwords Private Limited
Cover Designer/Manager: Wendy Ann Fredericks
Cover Photo: © Shutterstock
Text Permissions: Aptara
Photo Researcher: Integra
Senior Manufacturing Buyer: Dennis Para
Printer/Binder: Courier/Kendallville
Cover Printer: Lehigh-Phoenix Color Hagerstown

Credits and acknowledgments borrowed from other sources and reproduced, with permission, in this textbook appear on the appropriate page within text and on pages 451–452.

Library of Congress Cataloging-in-Publication Data

Gaetz, Lynne, 1960–
    The writer's world : sentences and paragraphs / Lynne Gaetz, Lionel Groulx College ; Suneeti Phadke, St. Jerome College. — Fourth Edition.
        pages cm.
    ISBN 978-0-321-89514-1 (alk. paper)
    1. English language—Sentences—Problems, exercises, etc. 2. English language—Paragraphs—Problems, exercises, etc.
I. Phadke, Suneeti, 1961– II. Title.
    PE1441.G34 2014
    808'.042—dc23

                                                                    2013028567

10 9 8 7 6 5 4 3—CRK—17 16 15 14

PEARSON

Student Edition ISBN-13:   978-0-321-89514-1
Student Edition ISBN-10:   0-321-89514-2

A la Carte Edition ISBN-13: 978-0-321-90799-8
A la Carte Edition ISBN-10:   0-321-90799-X

Contents

Preface

Thank you for making the third edition of *The Writer's World* a resounding success; we are delighted that the book has been able to help so many students across the country. This fourth edition, too, can help your students produce writing that is technically correct and richly detailed whether your classes are filled with students who have varying skill levels, whether students are native or nonnative speakers of English, or whether they learn better through the use of visuals.

When we started the first edition, we set out to develop practical and pedagogically sound approaches to these challenges, and we are pleased to hear that the book has been helping students succeed in their writing courses. We began with the idea that this project should be a collaboration with other developmental writing teachers. So we met with more than forty-five instructors from around the country, asking for their opinions and insights regarding (1) the challenges posed by the course, (2) the needs of today's ever-changing student population, and (3) the ideas and features we were proposing to provide them and you with a more effective teaching and learning tool. Pearson also commissioned dozens of detailed manuscript reviews from instructors, asking them to analyze and evaluate each draft of the manuscript. These reviewers identified numerous ways in which we could refine and enhance our key features. Their invaluable feedback was incorporated throughout *The Writer's World*. The text you are seeing is truly the product of a successful partnership between the authors, publisher, and well over one hundred developmental writing instructors.

What's New in the Fourth Edition?
Deeper MyWritingLab Integration

New to this edition, resources and assessments designed specifically for *The Writer's World* are in MyWritingLab along with the eText and all the diagnostic, practice, and assessment resources of MyWritingLab. Students can use MyWritingLab to access media resources, practice, and assessment for each chapter of *The Writer's World*. When they see MyWritingLab™ in the text, students have the option of completing the practice online right in MyWritingLab. Most practice assessments will flow to your instructor gradebook in MyWritingLab, reducing grading time and allowing you to focus attention on those students who may need extra help and practice.

- All Writer's Room activities can be completed in MyWritingLab, giving students access to a wide range of customizable instruction, practice, and assessment.
- Students can now answer additional reading comprehension questions for readings in Chapter 30 in MyWritingLab, offering extra practice and assessment and helping students strengthen their grasp of the readings.

A New Look

A new clean and modern design streamlines instruction and increases usability, allowing students to more effectively find and retain the information covered.

New Grammar Practices

Most of the grammar practices in Part II: The Editing Handbook are new, providing updated grammar instruction through the lens of topical and culturally relevant content.

New and More Images

This edition presents new dynamic and vibrant images—photos of colorful ethnic celebrations, pop culture icons, and a Banksy mural—that will engage students and prompt critical thinking.

New Readings

In Chapter 30, five new readings relate to the grammar themes. Thought-provoking essays from Touré, Josh Freed, Katrina Onstad, Bill Bryson, and Tom Spears discuss Internet privacy, modern notions of multiculturalism, and celebrity philanthropy.

Updated Film Writing Prompts

The film writing prompts in Chapter 30 have been updated to include newer and more recent movies, as well as a range of independent and mainstream selections, such as *The Hunger Games*, *Silver Linings Playbook*, and *Dredd*.

How *The Writer's World* Meets Students' Diverse Needs

We created *The Writer's World* to meet your students' diverse needs. To accomplish this goal, we asked both the instructors in our focus groups and the reviewers at every stage not only to critique our ideas but also to offer their suggestions and recommendations for features that would enhance the learning process of their students. The result has been the integration of many elements that are not found in other textbooks, including our visual program, coverage of nonnative speaker material, and strategies for addressing the varying skill levels students bring to the course.

The Visual Program

A stimulating full-color book, *The Writer's World* recognizes that today's world is a visual one, and it encourages students to become better communicators by responding to images. **Chapter-opening visuals in Part I** help students think about the chapters' key concepts in new ways. For example, in the Chapter 5 opener, a photograph of a skyscraper sets the stage for essay writing. Both the skyscraper and an essay need specific types of support to make them sturdy structures.

Each chapter in Part II opens with a photo to help illustrate the theme of the examples and exercises in that chapter and section.

The visuals in Part III provide students with further opportunities to write in response to images. Students get additional writing practice through different activities such as looking at photos and watching films. These visual aids inspire students and give them varied and engaging topics for writing.

Seamless Coverage for Nonnative Speakers

Instructors in our focus groups noted the growing number of nonnative/ESL speakers enrolling in their developmental writing courses. Although some of these students have special needs relating to the writing process, many of you still have a large portion of native speakers in your courses whose more traditional needs must also be satisfied. To meet the challenge of this rapidly changing dynamic, we have carefully implemented and integrated content throughout to assist these students. *The Writer's World* does not have separate ESL boxes, ESL chapters, or tacked-on ESL appendices. Instead, information that traditionally poses challenges to nonnative speakers is woven seamlessly throughout the book. In our extensive experience teaching writing to both native and nonnative speakers of English, we have learned that both groups learn best when they are not distracted by ESL labels. With the seamless approach, nonnative speakers do not feel self-conscious and segregated, and native speakers do not tune out detailed explanations that may also benefit them. Many of these traditional problem areas receive more coverage than you would find in other textbooks, arming the instructor with the material to effectively meet the needs of nonnative speakers. Moreover, the *Annotated Instructor's Edition* provides more than seventy-five ESL Teaching Tips designed specifically to help instructors better meet the needs of their nonnative speakers.

Issue-Focused Thematic Grammar

In our survey of instructors' needs, many of you indicated that one of the primary challenges in teaching your course is finding materials that are engaging to students in a contemporary context. This is especially true in grammar instruction. **Students come to the course with varying skill levels**, and many students are simply not interested in grammar. To address this challenge, we have introduced **issue-focused thematic grammar** in *The Writer's World*.

Each section in Part II revolves around a common theme. These themes include Lifestyles, Entertainment and Culture, Beliefs, Trades and Technology, The Earth and Beyond, Relationships, Creatures Large and Small, and The Business World. Each chapter within a section includes issues related to the theme. The thematic approach enables students to broaden their awareness of important subjects, allowing them to infuse their writing with reflection and insight. Also, we believe (and our reviewers concurred) that it makes grammar more engaging. And the more engaging grammar is, the more likely students are to retain key concepts—raising their skill level in these important building blocks of writing.

We also feel that it is important not to isolate grammar from the writing process. Therefore, The Writer's Room feature at the end of each grammar section contains writing topics that are related to the theme of the section and that follow different writing patterns. To help students appreciate the relevance of their writing tasks, **each grammar chapter begins with a grammar snapshot**—a sample taken from an authentic piece of writing that highlights the grammar concept. There is also an editing checklist that is specific to the grammar concepts covered in that chapter. Finally, at the end of each grammar section, there is The Writers' Circle, a collaborative activity that is particularly helpful to nonnative speakers.

Learning Aids to Help Students Get the Most from *The Writer's World*

Overwhelmingly, focus group participants and reviewers asked that both a larger number and a greater diversity of exercises and activities be incorporated into the text. In response to this feedback, we have developed and tested the following items in *The Writer's World*. We are confident they will help your students become better writers.

Hints In each chapter, Hint boxes highlight important writing and grammar points. Hints are useful for all students, but many will be particularly helpful for nonnative speakers. For example, in Chapter 3 (page 35) there is a hint about being direct and avoiding circular reasoning.

HINT ◀ **Avoiding Circular Reasoning**

Circular reasoning means that a writer restates his or her main point in various ways but does not provide supporting details. The main idea goes in circles and never progresses—kind of like a dog chasing its tail. Avoid using circular reasoning by writing a concise topic sentence and by supporting the topic sentence with facts, examples, or anecdotes.

For example, the following paragraph has circular reasoning.

People should not drink and drive because it is too dangerous. They can hurt themselves. Drinking and driving causes accidents, and sometimes people die.

The Writer's Desk Part I includes The Writer's Desk exercises, which help students get used to practicing all stages and steps of the writing process. Students begin with prewriting and then progress to developing, organizing (using paragraph plans), drafting, and, finally, revising and editing to create a final draft. Turn to Chapter 3, page 40, for an example of The Writer's Desk.

THE WRITER'S DESK **Revise and Edit Your Paragraph**

Choose a paragraph that you wrote for Chapter 2, or choose one that you have written for another assignment. Carefully revise and edit your paragraph.

Checklists Each end-of-chapter checklist is a chapter review exercise. Questions prompt students to recall and review what they have learned in the chapter. Turn to Chapter 3, page 43, for an example of the Checklists feature.

Revising and Editing Checklist

When you revise and edit a paragraph, ask yourself the following questions.

☐ Does my paragraph have **unity**? Ensure that every sentence relates to the main idea.

☐ Does my paragraph have **adequate support**? Verify that there are enough details and examples to support your main point.

☐ Is my paragraph **coherent**? Try to use transitional expressions to link ideas.

☐ Does my paragraph have good **style**? Check for varied sentence patterns and exact language.

☐ Does my paragraph have any errors? **Edit** for errors in grammar, punctuation, spelling, and mechanics.

☐ Is my **final draft** error-free?

The Writer's Room   **The Writer's Room** contains writing activities that correspond to general, college, and workplace topics. Some prompts are brief to allow students to freely form ideas while others are expanded to give students more direction.

There is literally something for every student writer in this end-of-chapter feature. Students who respond well to visual cues will appreciate the photo writing exercises in **The Writer's Room** in Part II. Students who learn best by hearing through collaboration will appreciate the discussion and group work prompts in **The Writers' Circle** section of selected **The Writer's Rooms**. To help students see how grammar is not isolated from the writing process, there are also **The Writer's Room** activities at the end of sections 1–8 in Part II: The Editing Handbook. Turn to Chapter 3, page 42, to see an example of The Writer's Room. In addition, all Writer's Room exercises can be completed in MyWritingLab, giving students access to a wide range of customizable instruction, practice, and assessment.

THÈ WRITER'S ROOM   MyWritingLab

Writing Activity 1

Choose a paragraph that you have written for this course. Revise and edit that paragraph, and then write a final draft.

Writing Activity 2

Choose one of the following topics, or choose your own topic and write a paragraph. You could try exploring strategies to generate ideas. The first sentence of your paragraph should make a point about your topic. Remember to revise and edit your paragraph before you write the final draft.

General Topics	College or Work-Related Topics
1. an interesting dream	6. an unusual experience at college
2. a family story	7. computer problems
3. a wonderful view	8. reasons to stay in college
4. weddings	9. learning a new skill
5. an accident	10. a job interview

MyWritingLab™
Complete these writing assignments at mywritinglab.com

How We Organized *The Writer's World*

The Writer's World: Sentences and Paragraphs is divided into three parts for ease of use, convenience, and ultimate flexibility.

Part I: The Writing Process teaches students how to formulate ideas (Exploring); how to expand, organize, and present those ideas in a piece of writing (Developing); and how to polish their writing so that they convey their message as clearly as possible (Revising and Editing). The result is that writing becomes far less daunting because students have specific steps to follow.

Chapter 4 of Part I gives students an overview of nine patterns of development. As they work through the practices and write their own paragraphs, students begin to see how using a writing pattern can help them fulfill their purpose for writing.

Chapter 5 of Part I covers the parts of the essay and explains how students can apply what they have learned about paragraph development to essay writing.

Part II: The Editing Handbook is a thematic grammar handbook. In each chapter, the examples correspond to a section theme, such as Lifestyles, Trades and Technology, or The Business World. As students work through the chapters, they hone their grammar and editing skills while gaining knowledge about a variety of topics. In addition to helping retain interest in the grammar practices, the thematic material provides sparks that ignite new ideas that students can apply to their writing.

Part III: Reading Strategies and Selections offers tips, readings, and follow-up questions. Students learn how to write by observing and dissecting what they read. The readings are arranged by the themes that are found in Part II: The Editing Handbook, thereby providing more fodder for generating writing ideas.

Pearson Writing Resources for Instructors and Students

Book-Specific Ancillary Material

Annotated Instructor's Edition for *The Writer's World: Sentences and Paragraphs, 4/e*
ISBN 0-321-89517-7

The *AIE* offers in-text answers, marginal annotations for teaching each chapter, links to the *Instructor's Resource Manual (IRM)*, and MyWritingLab teaching tips. It is a valuable resource for experienced and first-time instructors alike.

Instructor's Resource Manual for *The Writer's World: Sentences and Paragraphs, 4/e*
ISBN 0-321-89520-7

The material in the *IRM* is designed to save instructors time and provide them with effective options for teaching their writing classes. It offers suggestions for setting up their course; provides lots of extra practice for students who need it; offers quizzes and grammar tests, including unit tests; furnishes grading rubrics for each rhetorical mode; and supplies answers in case instructors want to print them out and have students grade their own work. This valuable resource is exceptionally useful for adjuncts who might need advice in setting up their initial classes or who might be teaching a variety of writing classes with too many students and not enough time.

PowerPoint Presentation for *The Writer's World: Sentences and Paragraphs, 4/e*
ISBN 0-321-89518-5

PowerPoint presentations to accompany each chapter consist of classroom-ready lecture outline slides, lecture tips and classroom activities, and review questions. Available for download from the Instructor Resource Center.

Answer Key for *The Writer's World: Sentences and Paragraphs, 4/e*
ISBN 0-321-89519-3

The Answer Key contains the solutions to the exercises in the student edition of the text. Available for download from the Instructor Resource Center.

MyWritingLab MyWritingLab™

Where practice, application, and demonstration meet to improve writing

MyWritingLab, a complete online learning program, provides additional resources and effective practice exercises for developing writers. MyWritingLab accelerates learning through layered assessment and a personalized learning path utilizing the Knewton Adaptive Learning Platform™, which customizes standardized educational content to piece together the perfect personalized bundle of content for each student. With over eight thousand exercises and immediate feedback to answers, the integrated learning aids of MyWritingLab reinforce learning throughout the semester.

What makes the practice, application, and demonstration in MyWritingLab more effective?

Diagnostic Testing: MyWritingLab's diagnostic Path Builder test comprehensively assesses students' skills in grammar. Students are provided with an individualized learning path based on the diagnostic's results, identifying the areas where they most need help.

Progressive Learning: The heart of MyWritingLab is the progressive learning that takes place as students complete the Overview, Animations, Recall, Apply, and Write exercises along with the Post-test within each topic. Students move from preparation (Overview, Animation) to literal comprehension (Recall) to critical understanding (Apply) to the ability to demonstrate a skill in their own writing (Write) to total mastery (Post-test). This progression of critical thinking enables students to truly master the skills and concepts they need to become successful writers.

Online Gradebook: All student work in MyWritingLab is captured in the Online Gradebook. Instructors can see what and how many topics their students have mastered. They can also view students' individual scores on all assignments throughout MyWritingLab, as well as overviews by student and class performance by module. Students can monitor their progress in new Completed Work pages, which show them their totals, scores, time on task, and the date and time of their work by module.

eText: The eText for *The Writer's World* is accessed through MyWritingLab. Students now have the eText at their fingertips while completing the various exercises and activities within MyWritingLab. The MyWritingLab logo (MyWritingLab™) is used throughout the book to indicate exercises or writing activities that can be completed in and submitted through MyWritingLab (results flow directly to the Gradebook where appropriate).

Additional Resources

Pearson is pleased to offer a variety of support materials to help make writing instruction easier for teachers and to help students excel in their coursework. Many of our student supplements are available free or at a greatly reduced price when packaged with *The Writer's World: Sentences and Paragraphs, 4/e.* Visit www.pearsonhighereducation.com, contact your local Pearson sales representative, or review a detailed listing of the full supplements package in the *Instructor's Resource Manual* for more information.

Suneeti Phadke in the Caribbean

Lynne Gaetz in the Dominican Republic

Acknowledgments

Many people have helped us produce *The Writer's World*. First and foremost, we would like to thank our students for inspiring us and providing us with extraordinary feedback. Their words and insights pervade this book.

We also benefited greatly from the insightful comments and suggestions from over one hundred instructors across the nation, all of whom are listed in the opening pages of the *Annotated Instructor's Edition*. Our colleagues' feedback was invaluable and helped shape *The Writer's World* series content, focus, and organization.

Reviewers

The following reviewers provided insight and assistance in the latest revision of *The Writer's World* series:

Justin Bonnett, Saint Paul College
Cheryl Borman, Hillsborough Community College, Ybor City Campus
Adam Carlberg, Tallahessee Community College
Judith L. Carter, Amarillo College
Zoe Ann Cerny, Horry-Georgetown Technical College
Cathy J. Clements, State Fair Community College
Cynthia Dawes, Edgecombe Community College
Mary F. Di Stefano Diaz, Broward College
Stephanie Fischer, Southern Connecticut State University
Paul Gallagher, Red Rocks Community College
Kim Allen Gleed, Harrisburg Area Community College
Karen Hindhede, Central Arizona College
Schahara Hudelson, South Plains College
Dianna W. Hydem Jefferson State Community College
Stacy Janicki, Ridgewater College
Patrice Johnson, Dallas County Community College District
Jennifer Johnston, Hillsborough Community College
Julie Keenan, Harrisburg Area Community College
Patricia A. Lacey, Harper College
Nicole Lacroix, Red Rock Community College
Ruth K. MacDonald, Lincoln College of New England
Joy McClain, Ivy Technical Community College, Evansville
Ellen Olmstead, Montgomery College
Deborah Peterson, Blinn College
Rebecca Portis, Montgomery College
Sharon Race, South Plains College
Stephanie Sabourin, Montgomery College
Sharisse Turner, Tallahassee Community College
Jody Wheeler, Saint Paul College
Julie Yankanich, Camden County College

We are indebted to the team of dedicated professionals at Pearson who have helped make this project a reality. They have boosted our spirits and have believed in us every step of the way. Special thanks to Erica Nikolaidis for her magnificent job in polishing this book and to Matthew Wright for trusting our instincts and enthusiastically propelling us forward. We owe a deep debt of gratitude to Yolanda de Rooy, whose encouraging words helped ignite this project. Michelle Gardner's attention to detail in the production process kept us motivated and on task and made *The Writer's World* a much better resource for both instructors and students.

Finally, we would like to dedicate this book to our families who supported us and who patiently put up with our long hours on the computer. Manu and Natalia continually encouraged us. Rebeka Pelaez Gaetz, a graphic designer, provided helpful suggestions about the visual direction of the book. We especially appreciate the support and sacrifices of Diego, Rebeka, Kiran, and Meghana.

A Note to Students

Your knowledge, ideas, and opinions are important. The ability to clearly communicate those ideas is invaluable in your personal, academic, and professional life. When your writing is error-free, readers will focus on your message, and you will be able to persuade, inform, entertain, or inspire them. *The Writer's World* includes strategies that will help you improve your written communication. Quite simply, when you become a better writer, you become a better communicator. It is our greatest wish for *The Writer's World* to make you excited about writing, communicating, and learning.

Enjoy!

Lynne Gaetz and Suneeti Phadke
writingrewards@pearson.com

Call for Student Writing!

Do you want to be published in *The Writer's World*? Send your paragraphs and essays to us along with your complete contact information. If your work is selected to appear in the next edition of *The Writer's World*, you will receive credit for your work and a copy of the book!

Lynne Gaetz and Suneeti Phadke
writingrewards@pearson.com

Part I
The Writing Process

The ability to express your ideas in written form is very useful in your personal, academic, and professional life. It does not take a special talent to write well. If you are willing to practice the writing process, you will be able to produce well-written sentences, paragraphs, and essays.

The Writing Process involves formulating ideas (Exploring), expanding and organizing those ideas (Developing), and polishing your writing to clearly convey your message (Revising and Editing). Chapters 1–3 break down the steps you can follow in the Exploring, Developing, and Revising and Editing stages of the writing process. Chapter 4 presents nine patterns of paragraph development and their different purposes. Chapter 5 shows you how to apply what you've learned about paragraph development to essay writing.

CHAPTER 1
▶ **EXPLORING**

- Consider your topic.
- Consider your audience.
- Consider your purpose.
- Try exploring strategies.

CHAPTER 2
▶ **DEVELOPING**

- Narrow your topic.
- Express your main idea.
- Develop your supporting ideas.
- Make a plan.
- Write your first draft.

CHAPTER 3
▶ **REVISING AND EDITING**

- Revise for unity.
- Revise for adequate support.
- Revise for coherence.
- Revise for style.
- Edit for technical errors.

CHAPTER 4

▶ PARAGRAPH PATTERNS

- Illustration
- Narration
- Description
- Process
- Definition
- Comparison and Contrast
- Cause and Effect
- Classification
- Argument

CHAPTER 5

▶ WRITING THE ESSAY

- Thesis Statement
- Supporting Ideas
- Essay Plan
- Introduction
- Conclusion
- First Draft
- Revising and Editing the Essay
- Final Draft

MODEL PARAGRAPH

By following the writing process, you will learn to write well-constructed paragraphs. A paragraph should focus on one main idea, and it should have the following parts.

People use many parts of the body to convey information to others. Facial expressions are the most important type of body language. A smile, for instance, shows pleasure. Individuals use eye contact to invite social interaction. Avoiding someone's eye, in contrast, discourages communication. People also speak with their hands. Common hand gestures convey, among other things, an insult, a request for a ride, an invitation, or a demand that others stop in their tracks. In conclusion, body language is often as important a form of communication as spoken language.

The **topic sentence** expresses the main idea.

The **supporting sentences** provide details and examples.

The **concluding sentence** brings the paragraph to a satisfactory close.

1 Exploring

The exploring stage of the writing process is like trying out a new dish. You search for interesting recipes and ingredients.

LO 1 Define exploring.

What Is Exploring?

An explorer investigates a place to find new and interesting information. **Exploring** is also useful during the writing process. Whenever you have trouble finding a topic, you can use specific techniques to generate ideas.

There are four steps in the exploring stage of the writing process.

> **ESSAY LINK**
> When you plan an essay, you should follow the four exploring steps.

▶ EXPLORING

STEP 1 **Consider your topic.** Think about whom or what you will write about.

STEP 2 **Consider your audience.** Determine who your intended readers will be.

STEP 3 **Consider your purpose.** Think about your reasons for writing.

STEP 4 **Try exploring strategies.** Practice using various techniques to find ideas.

Understanding Your Assignment

As soon as you are given an assignment, make sure that you understand your task. Answer the following questions about the assignment.

- How many words or pages should I write?
- What is the due date for the assignment?

◆ Are there any special qualities my writing should include?

◆ Will I write in class or at home?

After you have considered your task, think about your topic, purpose, and audience.

Topic

LO 2 Identify a topic.

Your **topic** is what you are writing about. When your instructor gives you a topic for your writing, you can narrow it to suit your interests. For example, if your instructor asks you to write about relationships, you could write about marriage, divorce, children, family responsibilities, or traditions. You should focus on an aspect of the topic that you know about and find interesting.

When you think about the topic, ask yourself the following questions.

◆ What about the topic interests me?

◆ Do I have special knowledge about the topic?

◆ Does anything about the topic arouse my emotions?

Audience

LO 3 Identify your audience.

Your **audience** is your intended reader. The reader might be your instructor, other students, your boss, your coworkers, and so on. When you write, remember to adapt your language and vocabulary for each specific audience. For example, in a formal report written for your business class, you might use specialized accounting terms, and in an e-mail to your best friend, you would probably use abbreviations or slang terms.

When you consider your audience, ask yourself the following questions.

◆ Who will read my assignment? Will it be my instructor, other students, or people outside my classroom?

◆ What do my readers probably know about the subject?

◆ What information will my readers expect?

> **HINT** **Your Instructor as Your Audience**
>
> For many college assignments, your audience is your instructor. When you write for him or her, use standard English. In other words, try to use correct grammar, sentence structure, and vocabulary.
>
> Do not leave out information because you assume that your instructor knows a lot about the topic. When your instructor reads your work, he or she will expect you to reveal what you have learned or what you have understood about the topic.

Purpose

LO 4 Determine your purpose.

Your **purpose** is your reason for writing. Sometimes you may have more than one purpose. When you consider your purpose, ask yourself the following questions.

◆ Do I want to **entertain**? Is my goal to tell a story?

◆ Do I want to **persuade**? Is my goal to convince the reader that my point of view is the correct one?

◆ Do I want to **inform**? Is my goal to explain something or give information about a topic?

HINT ◀ Purposes May Overlap

Sometimes you may have more than one purpose. For example, in a paragraph about a childhood memory, your purpose could be to tell a story about your first trip to a new place. At the same time, you could inform your readers about the things to see in that area, or you could persuade readers that traveling is, or is not, worthwhile.

LO 5 Try some exploring strategies.

Exploring Strategies

After you determine your topic, audience, and purpose, try some **exploring strategies**—also known as **prewriting strategies**—to help get your ideas flowing. There are two types of prewriting strategies: general and focused. **General prewriting** will help you develop wide-ranging ideas to write about. **Focused prewriting** will help you narrow a broad topic so that the topic becomes more specific and therefore more manageable for your assignment. In this chapter, you will see examples of general prewriting.

The three most common strategies are *freewriting, brainstorming,* and *clustering.* It is not necessary to do all of the strategies explained in this chapter. Find the strategy that works best for you.

HINT ◀ When to Use Exploring Strategies

You can use the exploring strategies at any stage of the writing process.
- To find a topic
- To narrow a broad topic
- To generate ideas about your topic
- To generate supporting details

Freewriting

When you **freewrite**, you write without stopping for a limited period of time. You record whatever thoughts come into your mind without worrying about them. Even if you run out of ideas, you can just repeat a word or phrase, or you can write, "I don't know what to say."

During freewriting, do not be concerned with your grammar or spelling. If you use a computer, let your ideas flow and do not worry about typing mistakes. Remember that the point is to generate ideas and not to create a perfect sample of writing.

Alfonzo's Freewriting

College student Alfonzo Calderon jotted down some of his thoughts about addictions. He wrote for five minutes without stopping.

> There are different types of addictions, like the usual, lets see,
> addiction to alcohol, drugs of course, gambling. Some people are

addicted to food, what else, t.v. Can people be addicted to music? what about the Internet, some of my friends are always online, they are always checking out their Facebook page. I chat sometimes, mostly with my friends, I have a facebook friend in Spain, he and I chat about music—especially types of guitars, What else, one of my friends is addicted to running, he runs everyday, I don't think its healthy . . .

PRACTICE 1

Underline topics from Alfonzo's freewriting that could be expanded into complete paragraphs.

THE WRITER'S DESK Freewriting

Choose one of the following topics and do some freewriting. Remember to write without stopping.

TOPICS: Food   Travel   Family

_____

_____

_____

_____

_____

_____

_____

_____

_____

_____

_____

_____

_____

_____

_____

Brainstorming

When you **brainstorm,** you create a list of ideas. You can include opinions, details, images, questions, or anything else that comes to mind. If you need to, you can stop to think while you are creating your list. Do not worry about grammar or spelling. Remember that the point is to generate ideas.

College student Jinsuk Suh brainstormed about the topic "neighborhoods." Her audience was her instructor and other students, and her purpose was to inform.

—large versus small neighborhoods

—flea markets

—crime

—ethnic neighborhoods

—my neighbors

—markets

—neighborhood friends

PRACTICE 2

Read Jinsuk's list about neigborhoods, and underline ideas that could be developed into complete paragraphs.

THE WRITER'S DESK   Brainstorming

Choose one of the following topics and brainstorm. Let your ideas flow when you create your list.

TOPICS: Celebrations   College   Fashion trends

_____

_____

_____

_____

_____

_____

_____

_____

_____

_____

Clustering

When you **cluster**, you draw a word map. To begin, write your topic in the middle of the page. Then, think of ideas that relate to the topic. Using lines or arrows, connect each idea to the central topic or to other ideas. Keep writing, circling, and connecting ideas until you have groups, or "clusters," of them on your page. When you finish, you will have a visual image of your ideas.

Anton's Clustering

College student Anton Gromyko used clustering to explore ideas about movies.

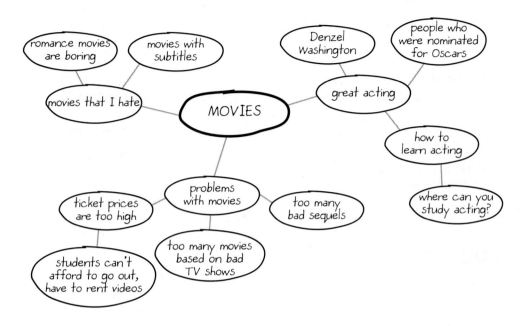

PRACTICE 3

Look at Anton's clustering. Circle one or more clusters that would make a good paragraph.

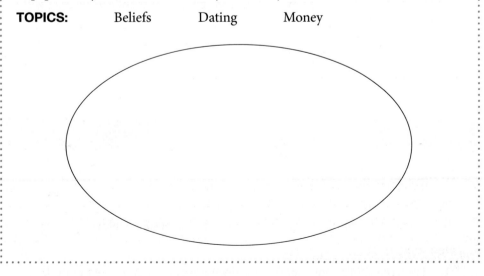

THE WRITER'S DESK Clustering

Choose one of the following topics and try clustering here or on a separate sheet of paper. Let your ideas flow when you create your cluster.

TOPICS: Beliefs   Dating   Money

HINT ◄ Questioning

Another way to generate ideas about a topic is to ask yourself a series of questions and write responses to them. The questions can help you define and narrow your topic. One common way to do this is to ask yourself *who, what, when, where, why,* and *how* questions.

Question	Possible Answers
Why do people travel?	To escape, to learn about other cultures, to enjoy good weather
How can they travel?	Flying, taking a train or bus, taking walking tours, hiking, sailing, cycling
What are inexpensive ways to travel?	Find last-minute deals, go backpacking, stay with friends or in youth hostels, share gas expenses

LO 6 Practice journal and portfolio writing.

Journal and Portfolio Writing
Keeping a Journal

American educator and writer Christina Baldwin once said, "Journal writing is like a voyage to the interior." One good way to practice your writing is to keep a journal. In a journal, you record your thoughts, opinions, ideas, and impressions. Journal writing provides you with a chance to practice your writing without worrying about the audience. It also gives you a source of material when you are asked to write about a topic of your choice.

You can write about any topic that appeals to you. Here are some suggestions.

♦ **College:** You can describe new things you have learned, express opinions about your courses, and list ideas for assignments.

♦ **Your personal life:** You can describe your feelings about your career goals. You can also write about personal problems and solutions, reflect about past and future decisions, express feelings about your job, and so on.

♦ **Controversial issues:** You can write about your reactions to controversies in the world, in your country, in your state, in your city, at your college, or even within your own family.

♦ **Interesting facts:** Perhaps you have discovered new and interesting information in a course, in a newspaper, or in some other way. You can record interesting facts in your journal.

MyWritingLab™
Complete these writing assignments at mywritinglab.com

MyWritingLab
THE WRITER'S ROOM

Writing Activity 1: Topics

Choose one of the following topics, or choose your own topic. Then generate ideas about the topic. You may want to try the suggested exploring strategy.

General Topics

1. Try freewriting about sports. Jot down any ideas that come to mind.

2. Try brainstorming about important ceremonies. List the first ideas that come to mind.

3. Try clustering about friends. Write the word *friends* in the middle of the page. Then create clusters of ideas that relate to the topic.

College or Work-Related Topics

4. Try freewriting to come up with ideas about career choices.

5. Try brainstorming about influential people. To get ideas, list anything that comes to mind when you think about people you admire.

6. Try clustering about education. Write the word *education* in the center of the page. Then create clusters of ideas that relate to the topic.

Writing Activity 2: Photo Writing

View the following cartoon. What is the topic? Who is the audience? What is the purpose? Does the cartoon achieve its purpose? Brainstorm a list of ideas about any topics that come to mind after seeing the cartoon.

NO, I DON'T HAVE A SCANNER YOU CAN BORROW.

© Ralph Hagen/www.CartoonStock.com

Exploring Checklist

When you explore a topic, ask yourself the following questions.

☐ What is my **topic**? Consider what you will write about.

☐ Who is my **audience**? Think about your intended readers.

☐ What is my **purpose**? Determine your reason for writing.

☐ Which exploring strategy will I use? You could try one of the next strategies or a combination of strategies.

Freewriting is writing without stopping for a limited period of time.

Brainstorming is making a list.

Clustering is drawing a word map.

Questioning is asking and answering questions.

2 Developing

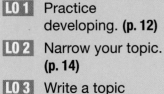

The developing stage of the writing process is like cooking a meal. Combining a variety of ingredients, you develop the recipe.

L01 Practice developing.

ESSAY LINK
You can follow similar steps when you develop an essay. See Chapter 5 for more details about essay writing.

What Is Developing?

Chapter 1 explained how you can explore ideas for writing. This chapter takes you, step by step, through the development of a paragraph. There are five key steps in the developing stage.

▶ DEVELOPING

STEP 1 **Narrow your topic.** Find an aspect of the topic that interests you.

STEP 2 **Express your main idea.** Write a topic sentence that expresses the central idea of the piece of writing.

STEP 3 **Develop your supporting ideas.** Generate ideas that support your topic sentence.

STEP 4 **Make a plan.** Organize your main and supporting ideas, and place your ideas in a plan.

STEP 5 **Write your first draft.** Communicate your ideas in a single written piece.

Reviewing Paragraph Structure

A **paragraph** is a group of sentences focusing on one central idea. Paragraphs can stand alone, or they can be part of a longer work such as an essay, a letter, or a report.

The **topic sentence** expresses the main point of the paragraph and shows the writer's attitude toward the subject.

The **body sentences** provide details that support the main point.

The **concluding sentence** brings the paragraph to a satisfactory close.

Topic sentence _____
_____. Supporting detail _____
_____
_____. Supporting detail _____
_____
_____. Supporting detail _____
_____.
Concluding sentence _____
_____.

Veena's Paragraph

College student Veena Thomas wrote the following paragraph. Read her paragraph, and then answer the questions.

> **As college students, we have a completely different culture than anyone else.** A few thousand students live together in what amounts to our own little city. Crowded into doubles and triples, we are brought together by our physical closeness, our similarities, and our differences. We share the bathrooms with strangers who soon become friends. We laugh together, cry together, and sleep through class together. Our dorm room becomes our refuge with its unmade beds, posters on the walls, and inflatable chairs. Money is a problem because we never have enough of it. When we get sick of cafeteria food, we subsist on 25-cent ramen noodles and boxes of oatmeal. We drink way too much coffee, and we order pizza at 1 a.m. We live on College Standard Time, which is about four hours behind everyone else. So while everyone else sleeps, we hang out with our music playing until the early hours of the morning. It's a different life, but it's our life, and we love it.

PRACTICE 1

Look at the structure of Veena's paragraph. The topic sentence (a statement of a main idea) is in bold. List Veena's supporting ideas. The first one has been done for you.

We live in our own little city of students crowded together. _____

_____

_____

_____

_____

_____

Paragraph Form

Your paragraphs should have the following form.

- Always indent the first word of a paragraph. Move it about 1 inch, or five spaces, from the left-hand margin.
- Leave a 1- to 1½-inch margin on each side of your paragraph.
- Begin every sentence with a capital letter, and end each sentence with the proper punctuation.
- If the last sentence of the paragraph does not go to the margin, leave the rest of the row blank.

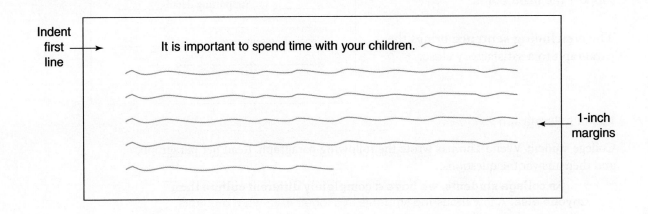

Indent first line →

It is important to spend time with your children.

← 1-inch margins

LO 2 Narrow your topic.

Narrow the Topic

Sometimes you may be given a topic that is too broad for one paragraph. In those situations, you need to make your topic fit the size of the assignment. When you **narrow your topic**, you make it more specific. To narrow your topic, you can use the exploring strategies (freewriting, brainstorming, clustering, or questioning) that you learned in Chapter 1.

Donovan's List to Narrow the Topic

College student Donovan Lynch used brainstorming to narrow his broad topic, "food."

—good restaurants
—when I ate too much junk food
—labeling genetically modified food

THE WRITER'S DESK **Narrow the Topic**

The next topics are very broad. Practice narrowing each topic.

EXAMPLE: Neighborhoods: Community center

Neighborhood markets

Neighborhood crime

1. Beliefs: _____

   _____

   _____

2. Fashion trends: _____

   _____

   _____

3. Dating: _____

   _____

   _____

4. Celebrations: _____

   _____

   _____

5. Education: _____

   _____

   _____

The Topic Sentence

LO3 Write a topic sentence.

The next step in the writing process is to write a sentence that expresses the main idea. In a paragraph, the statement of the main idea is called the **topic sentence**. The topic sentence of a paragraph has several features.

*   It introduces the topic.
*   It states the main (or controlling) idea.
*   It is the most general sentence.
*   It is supported by the other sentences.

The **controlling idea** is an essential part of the topic sentence because it makes a point about the topic. The controlling idea expresses the writer's opinion, attitude, or feeling. You can express different controlling ideas about the same topic. For example, the following topic sentences are about leaving the family home, but each sentence makes a different point about the topic.

narrowed topic   controlling idea
Leaving the family home is a difficult experience for some college students.

controlling idea   narrowed topic
The most exciting and important part of a youth's life is **leaving the family home.**

PRACTICE 2

Read each topic sentence. Underline the topic once and the controlling idea twice. To find the topic, ask yourself what the paragraph is about.

EXAMPLE: College students should take their studies seriously.

1. Homeowners can take a few easy precautions to protect their property from theft.

2. Children without siblings tend to be self-reliant.

3. The living room looked welcoming.

4. Become a better listener by following three simple steps.

5. Anton felt frustrated on his first day at work.

6. Marcus experienced several unexpected surprises when he bought his first used car.

ESSAY LINK
When you write a thesis statement for an essay, ask yourself questions 1–3 to check that your thesis statement is complete and valid.

Writing an Effective Topic Sentence

When you develop your topic sentence, avoid some common errors by asking yourself these four questions.

1. **Is my topic sentence a complete sentence?** Your topic sentence should always be a complete sentence that reveals a complete thought.

Incomplete	Living alone.
	(This is a topic but *not* a topic sentence. It does not express a complete thought.)
Topic sentence	There are many advantages to living alone.

2. **Does my topic sentence have a controlling idea?** Your topic sentence should make a point about your paragraph's topic. It should not simply announce the topic.

Announcement	I will write about nursing.
	(This sentence announces the topic but says nothing relevant about it. Do not use expressions such as *My topic is* or *I will write about.*)
Topic sentence	Nurses need to be in good physical and psychological health.

3. **Does my topic sentence make a valid and supportable point?** Your topic sentence should express a valid point that you can support with details and examples. It should not be a vaguely worded statement, and it should not be a highly questionable generalization.

Vague	Today's students are too weak.
	(How are they weak?)
Invalid point	Today's students have more responsibilities than those in the past.
	(Is this really true? This might be a hard assertion to prove.)
Topic sentence	Some of the best students in this college juggle schoolwork, children, and part-time jobs.

4. **Can I support my topic sentence in a single paragraph?** Your topic sentence should express an idea that you can support in a paragraph. It should not be too broad or too narrow.

Too broad	There are many good libraries.
	(It would be difficult to write only one paragraph about this topic.)
Too narrow	The college library is located beside the student center.
	(What more is there to say?)
Topic sentence	The college library, which is beside the student center, contains valuable resources for students.

HINT ◀ Write a Clear Topic Sentence

Your topic sentence should not express an obvious or well-known fact. Write something that will interest your readers and make them want to continue reading.

Obvious	Work is important.
	(Everybody knows this.)
Better	When looking for a job, remember that some factors are more important than having a good salary.

PRACTICE 3

Identify why each of the following topic sentences is not effective. Then, choose the word or words from the list that best describe the problem with each topic sentence. (A topic sentence may have more than one problem.) Finally, correct the problem by revising each sentence.

Incomplete	Vague	Announces
Invalid	Broad	Narrow

EXAMPLE: I am going to write about athletes.

Problem: _Announces; broad_

Revised sentence: _The salaries in professional basketball are too high._

_____

1. Privacy issues on Facebook.

Problem: _____

Revised statement: _____

_____

2. Teenagers are disrespectful.

   Problem: _____

   Revised statement: _____

   _____

3. This morning, Antonio ate toast for breakfast.

   Problem: _____

   Revised statement: _____

   _____

4. Music is important.

   Problem: _____

   Revised statement: _____

   _____

5. I will give my opinion about the influence of celebrities on society.

   Problem: _____

   Revised statement: _____

   _____

6. Diseases have killed many people.

   Problem: _____

   Revised statement: _____

   _____

HINT ◀ Placement of the Topic Sentence

Because you are developing your writing skills, it is a good idea to place your topic sentence at the beginning of your paragraph. Then, follow it with supporting details. Opening your paragraph with a topic sentence helps your readers immediately identify what your paragraph is about.

PRACTICE 4

Choose the best topic sentence for each paragraph.

1. First, physical exercise builds muscle strength and increases stamina. Aerobic activities strengthen heart muscles. Running or cycling can also improve endurance. Furthermore, physical activity greatly benefits mental health. It reduces stress and helps people to relax. Also, individuals can make new friends by joining a gym or sports class. In addition, people can learn new skills when they practice a sport or activity.

Possible topic sentences:

____ Many people join a gym or play a sport.

____ When people participate in a physical activity, they gain many advantages.

____ People should participate in sports that they like to keep their motivation.

2.   In their book *Second Chances,* Blakeslee and Wallerstein cite studies showing that boys are more likely to have external behavior problems after a marital breakup. For example, boys may become more impulsive, aggressive, and antisocial. After divorce, girls generally internalize their anger and frustration. They may become anxious and depressed.

Possible topic sentences:

____ Girls often become withdrawn after a divorce.

____ Divorce is common in the United States.

____ Research suggests that male and female children react to divorce in different ways.

3.   Whenever Americans send an e-mail, it leaves a footprint on more than one computer. The record allows employers and others to have access to employee correspondence. Also, most cities have a complex system of cameras in public places. For example, traffic cameras take pictures of drivers going through red lights or speeding. This information is automatically transmitted to the traffic police, who can then send traffic tickets to the offenders. Moreover, anytime an Internet user buys a product online, the consumer's profile is created. Profiles are often sold to marketing companies.

Possible topic sentences:

____ The Internet has changed our lives in many ways.

____ Technology gives humans the ability to control their lives.

____ Modern technology has led to a loss of our privacy.

THE WRITER'S DESK Write Topic Sentences

Narrow each topic. Then, write a topic sentence that contains a controlling idea. (You could refer to your ideas in The Writer's Desk: Narrow the Topic on pages 14–15.)

EXAMPLE: Neighborhoods

Narrowed topic: Neighborhood markets

Topic sentence: Zion Market is one of the busiest and best Korean markets.

1. Beliefs

    Narrowed topic: _____

    Topic sentence: _____

    _____

2. Fashion trends

    Narrowed topic: _____

    Topic sentence: _____

    _____

    _____

3. Dating

    Narrowed topic: _____

    Topic sentence: _____

    _____

4. Celebrations

    Narrowed topic: _____

    Topic sentence: _____

    _____

5. Education

    Narrowed topic: _____

    Topic sentence: _____

    _____

LO 4 Develop supporting details.

> **ESSAY LINK**
> In an essay, you place the thesis statement in the introduction. Then each supporting idea becomes a distinct paragraph with its own topic sentence.

The Supporting Ideas

After you have written a clear topic sentence, you can focus on **supporting details**, which are the facts and examples that provide the reader with interesting information about the subject matter. There are three steps you can take to determine your paragraph's supporting details.

1. Generate supporting ideas.
2. Choose the best supporting ideas.
3. Organize your ideas.

Generating Supporting Ideas

You can use an exploring strategy—freewriting, brainstorming, clustering, or questioning—to generate supporting ideas.

Jinsuk's Supporting Ideas

Jinsuk Suh chose one of her narrowed topics related to "neighborhoods" and wrote her topic sentence. Then she listed ideas that could support the topic sentence.

Topic Sentence: Zion Market is one of the busiest and best Korean markets.

—products are of good quality

—fruits and vegetables are fresh

—prices of products are low

—many people

—sale each weekend

—no quarrels between customers and employees

—employees are kind

—very noisy

TECHNOLOGY LINK
If you write your paragraph on a computer, put your topic sentence in bold. Then you (and your instructor) can easily identify it.

THE WRITER'S DESK List Supporting Ideas

Choose one of your topic sentences from the previous Writer's Desk, and make a list of ideas that could support it.

Topic sentence: _____

_____

Supporting ideas: _____

_____

_____

_____

_____

_____

_____

_____

_____

Choosing the Best Ideas

A paragraph should have **unity**, which means that all of its sentences relate directly to its topic sentence. To achieve unity, examine your prewriting carefully and then choose three or four ideas that are most compelling and that clearly support your topic sentence. You may notice that several items in your list are similar; therefore, you can group them together. Remove any ideas that do not support your topic sentence.

Jinsuk's Supporting Ideas

First, Jinsuk crossed out ideas that she did not want to develop. Then, she highlighted three of the most appealing ideas and labeled them A, B, and C. Finally, she regrouped other details from the list that best supported the most appealing ideas.

Topic Sentence: Zion Market is one of the busiest and best Korean markets.

- **products are of good quality**   A
- fruits and vegetables are fresh

- **prices of products are low**   B
- ~~many people~~
- sale each weekend

- no quarrels between customers and employees
- **employees are kind**   C

- ~~very noisy~~

TECHNOLOGY LINK
On a computer, you can cut (ctrl X) and paste (ctrl V) similar ideas together.
On a Mac, you can highlight and drag sentences.

HINT   Identifying the Best Ideas

There are many ways to highlight your best ideas. You can circle the best supporting points and then use lines or arrows to link them with secondary ideas. You could also use highlighter pens or asterisks (*) to identify the best supporting points.

THE WRITER'S DESK Choose the Best Ideas

For the Writer's Desk on page 21, you produced a list of ideas. Identify ideas that clearly support the topic sentence. If there are any related ideas, group them. You can cross out ideas that you do not want to develop.

ESSAY LINK
In an essay, you can also use time, space, or emphatic order to organize your ideas.

Organizing Your Ideas

The next step is to organize your ideas in a logical manner. There are three common organizational methods: time order, emphatic order, and space order. You can use **transitions**—words such as *first, then,* and *furthermore*—to guide readers from one idea to the next. You can find a more complete list of transitions on page 37 in Chapter 3, "Revising and Editing."

Time Order

When you use **time order**, you arrange the details according to the sequence in which they have occurred. Use time order to narrate a story, explain how to do something, or describe a historical event.

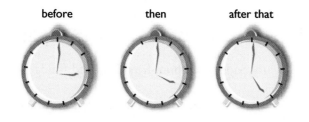

before   then   after that

Here are some transitional expressions you can use in time order paragraphs.

after that	first	later	next
eventually	in the beginning	meanwhile	then
finally	last	months after	while

The next paragraph uses time order.

> Discovering that a bird species is extinct is a big deal. In 1973, students from the University of Hawaii discovered a new species of bird on Maui. They named the bird *po'ouli*. A census in the early 1980s located about 140 birds. Since then, the number of birds has diminished sharply. In 1994, only six birds could be located, and two years later only three were found. In September 2004, a single po'ouli was captured in an effort to breed more individuals in captivity. Sadly, that bird died of malaria two months later. Despite intensive searches by dozens of professional and amateur birders, no po'ouli have since been found.

—Norm Christensen, "A Requiem for the Po'ouli" in *The Environment and You* (adapted)

PRACTICE 5

Use time order to organize the supporting details beneath each of the topic sentences. Number the details in order starting with 1.

1. If you win a large amount of money in a lottery, there are some things you should do to maintain your sanity.

   ____ Take a leave of absence from your job.

   ____ Keep enough money in your savings account to take a vacation.

   ____ Take a long vacation.

   ____ Collect the money and immediately deposit it in a secure bank fund.

   ____ Stay away until the publicity about your win dies down.

2. Sadako Sasaki is an inspiration to all who hear her story.

   ____ Sadako folded one thousand paper cranes before her death in 1955.

   ____ Sadako was born in Hiroshima, Japan, in 1943.

   ____ When she was ten years old, she developed red spots on her legs.

   ____ A year later, when she turned eleven, Sadako was diagnosed with leukemia and hospitalized.

   ____ In 1958, the city of Hiroshima erected a statue of Sadako with a paper crane, as a symbol of peace.

   ____ She was only two years old when the atomic bomb was dropped on Hiroshima.

(continued)

_____ During her hospital stay, Sadako's friend visited her and reminded her of the Japanese story in which God grants a wish to anyone who folds a thousand paper cranes.

_____ After her death, Sadako's school friends raised funds to build a memorial of her.

Emphatic Order

When you use **emphatic order**, you organize supporting details in a logical sequence. For example, you can arrange details from the least to the most important, from the best to the worst, from the least appealing to the most appealing, from general to specific, and so on. How you order the details often depends on your purpose for writing.

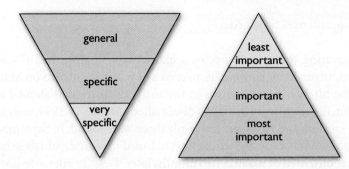

Here are some transitional expressions you can use in emphatic order paragraphs.

above all	first	moreover	particularly
clearly	furthermore	most important	principally
especially	least of all	most of all	therefore

The following paragraph uses emphatic order. The writer presents characteristics from the least to the most important.

> Psychologists have determined that people facing difficult circumstances have no single source of resilience. Rather, many factors come into play. First, those with developed social skills tend to be more resilient than other people. For example, Oprah Winfrey, a great communicator, survived traumatic events in her childhood. Furthermore, some people have a genetic predisposition toward higher self-esteem. But one character trait, above all others, seems to help people cope, and that is the ability to maintain an optimistic attitude. According to author Martin Seligman, positive thinkers tend to believe that problems are outside themselves and not permanent, and they generally rise above failure.
>
> —Suzanne Moreau, student

HINT ‹ Using Emphatic Order

When you organize details using emphatic order, use your own values and opinions to determine what is most or least important, upsetting, remarkable, and so on. Another writer may organize the same ideas in a different way.

PRACTICE 6

Use emphatic order to organize the supporting details beneath each topic sentence. Number them in order from least important (1) to most important (5).

1. Doing homework assignments can benefit schoolchildren in many ways.

   ____ Finishing homework assignments gives students a sense of accomplishment.

   ____ Children learn to follow directions.

   ____ Students learn the subject better by correcting mistakes or improving their work.

   ____ Pupils learn to manage their time.

   ____ Homework assignments allow parents to understand what their children are learning.

2. Our new mayor has made many mistakes.

   ____ He made negative comments about some religious minorities.

   ____ He wears unflattering suits that are too large.

   ____ He hired his own children as advisors.

   ____ He made a lot of money on a land flip, and citizens believe he is corrupt.

   ____ He doesn't smile for photographs.

Space Order

When you use **space order**, you describe an image in the sequence in which you see it. For example, you could describe something or someone from top to bottom or bottom to top, from left to right or right to left, or from far to near or near to far.

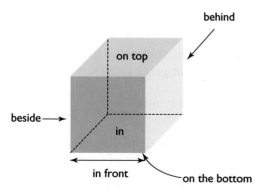

Here are some transitional expressions you can use in space order paragraphs.

above	closer in	near	on the top
at the back	farther out	next to	to the left
behind	in front	on the bottom	under

The next paragraph uses space order.

> They sat across from Mariam, Jalil and his wives, at a long, dark brown table. Between them, in the center of the table, was a crystal vase of fresh marigolds and a sweating pitcher of water. The red-haired woman who had introduced herself as Niloufar's mother, Afsoon, was sitting on Jalil's right. The other two, Khadija and Nargis, were on his left. The wives each had on a flimsy black scarf, which they wore not on their heads but tied loosely around the neck like an afterthought.
>
> —Khaled Hosseini, *A Thousand Splendid Suns*

PRACTICE 7

Read the next paragraph and answer the questions that follow.

unobstructed:
clear

crevices:
cracks

> We placed our tent in a clearing and had an **unobstructed** view of Mount Pilatus. The peak of the mountain was snow covered. Just below the snow, there were rows of pines cut by **crevices**. Under the pines there was a rocky cliff where several mountain goats wandered. At the bottom of the mountain was a village. We could see the church steeple and the red and black roofs of mining houses.
>
> —Carlo Tomasino

1. In what order does the writer describe the scene? Choose the best answer.

   a.   top to bottom   b. left to right   c. near to far

2. Underline some transitional expressions used in this paragraph to indicate space order.

PRACTICE 8

Use spatial order—moving from bottom to top—to organize the supporting details beneath the topic sentence. Number the sentences from 1 to 5.

> Tourists and architectural students gasp in delight when they see the Casa Mila, the last completed avant-garde architectural work of Antoni Gaudí.

____ Chimneys covered with broken ceramic tiles rise from the roof and seem to touch the sky.

____ The sidewalk in front of the building is decorated with blue and green ceramic tiles designed in the form of starfish.

____ The walls of the building are not straight but are in the shape of a gigantic wave.

____ The roof, dotted with small windows, is sand-colored.

____ Each balcony has curved black railings, giving a further impression of waves on the ocean.

PRACTICE 9

Read the following topic sentences. Decide what type of order you could use to develop the paragraph details. Choose time, space, or emphatic order.

EXAMPLE: College students should take their studies seriously.   _____Emphatic_____

1. Several interesting things happened when the probe landed on Mars.   _____

2. Children without siblings tend to be self-reliant.   _____

3. The bronze statue was truly original.   _____

4. Last Saturday was one of the best days of my life.   _____

5. The dorm room was an uncontrollable mess.   _____

6. High blood pressure is caused by several factors.   _____

THE WRITER'S DESK Organize Your Ideas

Look at the list of ideas that you wrote for the Writer's Desk on page 21. Organize your ideas using space, time, or emphatic order by placing numbers beside the ideas.

The Paragraph Plan

LO5 Create a paragraph plan.

A **paragraph plan**—or **outline**—is a map that shows the paragraph's main and supporting ideas. To make a plan, write your topic sentence. Then list supporting points and details in the order in which you wish to present them. You can use time, space, or emphatic order to organize the supporting points.

HINT Adding Specific Details

When you prepare your paragraph plan, ask yourself whether your supporting ideas are detailed enough. If not, then you can add details to make that supporting idea stronger. For example, in Jinsuk's list about Zion Market, one of the points was about good-quality products. She added more details to make that point stronger and more complete.

Products are of good quality
– fruits and vegetables are fresh
Added: – clear colors of fruits
– juicy and sweet

Jinsuk's Paragraph Plan

After she chose the best ideas and organized them, Jinsuk modified her topic sentence and wrote a paragraph plan.

Topic Sentence: Zion Market is a busy and popular Korean market because it has good-quality products, low prices, and kind employees.

Support 1:	I can find many products of good quality.
Details:	—fruits and vegetables are fresh
	—clear colors of fruits
	—delicious, juicy, and sweet
Support 2:	The prices of many products are low.
Details:	—better prices than in other markets
	—sales every weekend
Support 3:	Employees are kind.
Details:	—there are no quarrels between customers and employees
	—manager responds quickly to requests

THE WRITER'S DESK **Write a Paragraph Plan**

Look at the topic sentence and the organized list of supporting ideas that you created for the previous Writer's Desks. Now, fill in the following paragraph plan. Remember to include details for each supporting idea.

Topic sentence: _____

_____

Support 1: _____

Details: _____

_____

Support 2: _____

Details: _____

_____

Support 3: _____

Details: _____

_____

LO 6 Write a first draft.

The First Draft

The next step is to write the first draft. Take information from your paragraph plan and, using complete sentences, write a paragraph. Your first draft includes your topic sentence and supporting details.

Jinsuk's First Draft

Jinsuk wrote the first draft of her paragraph about Zion Market. You may notice that the paragraph contains mistakes. In Chapter 3, you will see how she revises and edits her paragraph.

Zion Market is a busy and popular Korean market because it has three characteristics: good quality, low prices, and kind employees. Shopping in Zion Market makes me excited because I can find many products of good quality. Especially, the fruits. They are all fresh. Their colors are clear. They are delicious, they are flavorful, juicy, and sweet. In addition, the prices of many products are lower than thoses in other markets. Every weekend, different kind of products are on sale. All the employees are very kind. I have never had uncomfortable situation or witnessed any quarrels between customers and employees. The manager keeps walking around the market and the head of each section respond quickly to the requests of the customers. The fruit section manager suggests which fruit is the tastiest. His happy face makes me feel good. These three characteristics make this market one of the busiest markets.

HINT ◄ Writing the Concluding Sentence

Some paragraphs end with a **concluding sentence**, which brings the paragraph to a satisfactory close. If you want to write a concluding sentence for your paragraph, here are three suggestions.

- Restate the topic sentence in a fresh, new way.
- Make an interesting final observation.
- End with a prediction, suggestion, or quotation.

ESSAY LINK
Essays end with a concluding paragraph. For more information about essay conclusions, see pages 103–105.

THE WRITER'S DESK Write Your First Draft

In the previous Writer's Desk on page 28, you created a paragraph plan. Now, on a separate sheet of paper, write your first draft of that paragraph.

THE WRITER'S ROOM   MyWritingLab

MyWritingLab™
Complete these writing assignments at mywritinglab.com

Writing Activity 1: Topics

In the Writer's Room in Chapter 1, "Exploring," you used various strategies to find ideas about the following topics. Select one of the topics and write a paragraph. Remember to follow the steps of the writing process.

General Topics

1. sports
2. YouTube
3. friends

College or Work-Related Topics

4. career choices
5. an influential person
6. uniforms

Writing Activity 2: Photo Writing

Describe your neighborhood. You could describe a person you frequently see or a place such as a park or building.

Developing Checklist

When you develop a paragraph, ask yourself the following questions.

- ☐ Does my **topic sentence** introduce the topic and state the controlling idea?
- ☐ Do I **support the topic sentence** with facts and examples?
- ☐ Do I **organize the details** using time, space, or emphatic order?
- ☐ Does my **paragraph plan** help me visualize the main and supporting ideas?
- ☐ Does my **first draft** use complete sentences?

Revising and Editing

The revising and editing stages of the writing process are like adding the finishing touches to a meal. Small improvements can help a good meal become a great one.

What Are Revising and Editing?

LO 1 Define revising and editing.

Revising and editing are effective ways to improve your writing. When you **revise**, you modify your writing to make it more convincing and precise. You do this by looking for inadequate development and poor organization, and then you make any necessary changes. When you **edit**, you proofread your final draft. You look for errors in grammar, spelling, punctuation, and mechanics.

There are five key steps in the revising and editing stages.

▶ REVISING AND EDITING

STEP 1 **Revise for unity.** Make sure that all parts of your work relate to the main idea.

STEP 2 **Revise for adequate support.** Ensure that you have enough details to effectively support the main idea.

STEP 3 **Revise for coherence.** Verify that your ideas flow smoothly and are logically linked.

STEP 4 **Revise for style.** Make sure that your sentences are varied and interesting.

STEP 5 **Edit for technical errors.** Proofread your work and correct errors in grammar, spelling, mechanics, and punctuation.

LO 2 Revise for unity.

Revise for Unity

In a paragraph, every idea should move in the same direction just like this railroad track goes straight ahead.

> **ESSAY LINK**
> When revising an essay, ensure that each body paragraph has unity.

When a paragraph has **unity**, all of the sentences support the topic sentence. If a paragraph lacks unity, then it is difficult for the reader to understand the main point. To check for unity, verify that every sentence relates to the main idea.

Devon's Paragraph Without Unity

College student Devon Washington wrote the following paragraph, and he accidentally drifted away from his main idea. If he removed the highlighted sentences, then his paragraph would have unity.

The writer took a detour here.

> Athletes who use steroids damage their reputations and their health. Young children look up to their favorite sports stars, and they want to be like those stars. When someone famous such as Barry Bonds admits to using performance-enhancing drugs, young fans begin to think that steroid usage is acceptable. Bonds and others send a message that the only way to succeed in sports is to cheat. Steroids also hurt the athletes' bodies. The substances can damage the kidneys, the liver, and the heart. I think that some young members of my gym take steroids. They lift weights, but their muscles seem to be unusually bulky. I don't think they can achieve such large muscles from only weightlifting. Nobody should use drugs to have a better performance.

PRACTICE 1

Read paragraphs A, B, and C. For each one, underline the topic sentence. Then indicate whether the paragraph has unity. If the paragraph lacks unity, remove the sentences that do not relate to the topic sentence.

A. Professional women's sports is underrepresented in news coverage. For example, most newspapers write stories about women's sports on Wednesdays when there is little going on in men's sports. Television transmits more men's professional sports than women's professional sports. Women's soccer, football, and basketball are rarely televised. According to sociology professor Michael Messner in his report "Gender in Televised Sports," televised coverage of women's sports has actually decreased from 8.7 percent in 1999 to less than 2 percent in 2009. However, there are many news stories about some women's athletic activities. Women's tennis games are televised, and newspapers and magazines feature players such as Maria Sharapova. Also, there are many magazine articles about golfer Michelle Wie. It is unfortunate that women's sports do not get the same amount of media coverage as men's sports.

Circle the correct answer. Does the paragraph have unity?

    a. yes   b. no

B. To minimize the problems associated with divorce, parents need to maintain a stable environment for their children. For example, any fighting over finances or child visitation should not occur in front of the children. Parents should try to live near each other so that the kids have easy access to both parents. To further stabilize children's lives after a divorce, many parents now opt for the "family home." The kids don't have to change houses to visit each parent; instead, the parents take turns living in the family home. If parents just remember to put children first, then the effects of divorce on the children can be minimized.

Circle the correct answer. Does the paragraph have unity?

    a. yes   b. no

C. In this computer age, electronic voting seems like a logical way to collect and count votes. However, paperless electronic voting is both unreliable and dangerous. First, the software in voting machines may be faulty. During the 2006 midterm elections, overseers in some states noted that machines switched votes from one candidate to another because of touch-screen problems. Additionally, voting machines can be easily manipulated. In 2004, Maryland hired RABA Technologies to try to hack the state's new voting machines. Computer whizzes were able to vote more than once and change voting outcomes, and they concluded that even high school students could hack the machines. In Holland, hackers using telephone lines were able to manipulate and delete votes. However, electronic voting has some good points. The elimination of paper ballots is good for the environment. Also, votes can be counted more quickly by machine than they can by hand. Certainly, governments should think twice about implementing electronic voting machines.

Circle the correct answer. Does the paragraph have unity?

    a. yes   b. no

L03 Revise for adequate support.

Revise for Adequate Support

A bridge is built using several well-placed support columns. Like a bridge, a paragraph requires adequate support to help it stand on its own.

When you revise for adequate support, ensure that your paragraph contains strong and convincing supporting details.

Jinsuk's Revision for Adequate Support

Jinsuk Suh wrote a paragraph about Zion Market, but she needed some specific examples to back up some of her points. She added some details to strengthen her paragraph.

> Zion Market is a busy and popular Korean market because it has
>
> three characteristics: good quality, low prices, and kind employees.
>
> Shopping in Zion Market makes me excited because I can find many
>
> products of good quality. Especially, the fruits. They are all fresh. Their
>
> _, and the fruits are not dried-up but moist_
> colors are clear. They are delicious, they are flavorful, juicy, and sweet.
> ^
> In addition, the prices of many products are lower than thoses in other
>
> markets. Every weekend, different kind of products are on sale.
> **There are special discounts on fresh vegetables, bags of rice,**
> **and cartons filled with brown eggs.**
> All the employees are very kind. I have never had uncomfortable
> ^
> situation or witnessed any quarrels between customers and employees.
>
> The manager keeps walking around the market and the head of each
>
> section respond quickly to the requests of the customers. The fruit section
> _, a small, chubby man who always smiles,_
> manager suggests which fruit is the tastiest. His happy face makes me
> ^
> feel good. These three characteristics make this market one of the busiest
>
> markets.

ESSAY LINK
When you revise an essay, ensure that you have adequately supported the thesis statement. Also, verify that each body paragraph has sufficient supporting details.

PRACTICE 2

The following paragraph attempts to persuade, but it does not have any specific details that make strong points.

> Our city encourages people to reduce household waste in a number of ways. Families are provided with green recycle boxes. Many different items can be recycled in this way. Households also receive compost boxes. People are encouraged to compost kitchen waste. Finally, citizens can leave electric products at recycling centers around town. By recycling, people can reduce the amount of trash they produce each year.

When the preceding paragraph is expanded with specific details and examples, it becomes more convincing. Add details on the lines provided.

Our city encourages people to reduce household waste in a number of ways. Families are provided with green recycle boxes. Many different objects can be recycled in this way. Items such as _____ _____ can be placed in the box for recycling. Households also receive compost boxes. People are encouraged to compost kitchen waste. For example, _____ . Also, garden waste like _____ make good compost. Finally, citizens can leave electric products at recycling centers around town. For instance, _____ can be recycled at specific centers. By recycling, people can reduce the amount of trash they produce each year.

When a paragraph has circular reasoning, the main idea does not progress. The writer leads the reader in circles.

HINT ◀ **Avoiding Circular Reasoning**

Circular reasoning means that a writer restates his or her main point in various ways but does not provide supporting details. The main idea goes in circles and never progresses—kind of like a dog chasing its tail. Avoid using circular reasoning by writing a concise topic sentence and by supporting the topic sentence with facts, examples, or anecdotes.

For example, the following paragraph has circular reasoning.

> People should not drink and drive because it is too dangerous. They can hurt themselves. Drinking and driving causes accidents, and sometimes people die.

PRACTICE 3

The next passages do not have sufficient supporting examples. List examples for each paragraph.

EXAMPLE: My sister's apartment is a disaster zone. The entrance and the kitchen

are messy. So is the bathroom. There are things everywhere.

Add examples: <u>The front hall is filled with shoes.</u>

<u>The kitchen sink is filled with dirty dishes.</u>

<u>There are wet towels on the bathroom floor.</u>

1.   Many people think that rock music of their youth was the best music ever. My grandfather went to college in the 1960s, and he loved the rock music of that era. When my father was a student twenty years later, he thought that his parents' music was dated. He preferred to listen to rock bands of the 1980s. Today, rock bands from this decade are really popular with my generation.

Add examples: _____

_____

_____

_____

2.   Clive and Gina won first prize for the most beautiful garden. They have many different types of flowers. They also have a small herb garden. In addition, they have planted trees at the back of their property.

Add examples: _____

_____

_____

_____

3.   Since 2000, reality television has invaded our homes. There are many types of reality shows. They all include ordinary people who participate in unusual contests. Sometimes the shows take place in unusual places.

Add examples: _____

_____

_____

_____

LO 4 Revise for coherence.

Revise for Coherence

> **ESSAY LINK**
> To create coherence in an essay, you can place transitional expressions at the beginning of each body paragraph.

Just as couplings link train cars, transitional expressions link ideas in a paragraph.

When you revise for coherence, you ensure that your reader has a smooth voyage through your paragraph. **Coherence** means that the sentences flow and are logically organized.

Transitional Expressions

Transitional expressions are linking words or phrases, and they show the reader the connections between ideas in paragraphs and essays. Here are some common transitional expressions.

Function	Transitional Word or Expression				
Addition	again	first	in addition	next	
	also	for one thing	in fact	second	
	besides	furthermore	moreover	then	
				third	
Concession of a point	certainly	indeed	no doubt	of course	to be sure
Comparison	as well	equally	likewise	similarly	
Contrast	however	instead	on the contrary		
	in contrast	nevertheless	on the other hand		
Effect or result	as a result	consequently	then	therefore	thus
Example	for example	in other words	specifically		
	for instance	namely	to illustrate		
Emphasis	above all	in fact	indeed	most important	of course
	clearly	in particular	least of all	most of all	undoubtedly
Space	above	beside	in the middle	on the left/right	
	at the back	closer in	inside	on top	
	behind	farther out	nearby	outside	
	below	in front	on the bottom	under	
Summary or conclusion	generally	in short	thus	to conclude	
	in conclusion	on the whole		to summarize	
	in other words	therefore			
Time	after that	eventually	in the future	one day	then
	at that time	first	in the past	presently	these days
	at the moment	gradually	later	second	third
	currently	immediately	meanwhile	so far	
	earlier		now	subsequently	
				suddenly	

GRAMMAR LINK
For more practice using transitions in sentences, see Chapter 15, "Compound Sentences."

HINT ◄ Use Transitional Expressions with Complete Sentences

When you add a transitional expression to a sentence, ensure that your sentence is complete. Your sentence must have a subject and a verb, and it must express a complete thought.

Incomplete   First, the price of movie tickets.

Complete   First, the price of movie tickets is too high.

PRACTICE 4

Add the following transitional expressions to the next paragraph. Use each transitional word once. There may be more than one correct answer for each space.

First	In addition	Therefore
For example	In fact	Undoubtedly

Computer technology is creating an unskilled labor force. _____, many companies are using complex mathematical models to make business decisions. _____, in most companies, managers do not decide if and when to order stock. A computer model indicates when a company needs to order a particular item. _____, many employees work in isolation. They sit in front of their computers and do not need to communicate as much with each other as in the past. _____, good verbal communication skills are being eroded. Moreover, computer technology helps companies to outsource services. _____, companies do not need to train local workers for skills that can be done elsewhere for less cost. _____, due to the influence of computer technology, labor practices are going to keep on changing in the near future.

LO 5 Revise for style.

ESSAY LINK
Revise your essays for style, ensuring that sentences are varied and that your language is exact. To learn more about sentence variety and exact language, see Chapters 17 and 23.

Revise for Style

Just as a blend of colors makes a train interior more beautiful, varied sentence style makes a paragraph more compelling.

Another important step in the revision process is to ensure that you have varied your sentences and that you have used concise wording. When you revise for sentence style, ask yourself the following questions.

- Have I used a variety of sentence patterns?
- Have I used exact language?
- Have I avoided using repetitious or vague language?

Jinsuk's Revision for Coherence and Style

Jinsuk Suh revised her paragraph about Zion Market. To show connections between ideas, she added transitional words. She also changed some language to make it more exact.

> Zion Market is a busy and popular Korean market because it has three characteristics: good quality, low prices, and kind employees. Shopping in Zion Market makes me excited because I can find many products of good quality. Especially, the fruits. They are all fresh. Their *stalks and peels of all* colors are clear, and the fruits are not dried-up but moist. ~~They~~ *Also, they* are delicious, they are flavorful, juicy, and sweet. In addition, the prices of many products are lower than thoses in other markets. Every weekend, different kind of products are on sale. There are special discounts on fresh vegetables, bags of rice, and cartons filled with brown eggs. ~~All~~ *Furthermore, all* the employees are very kind. I have never had uncomfortable situation or witnessed any quarrels between customers and employees. The manager keeps walking around the market and the head of each section respond quickly to the requests of the customers. ~~The~~ *For example, the* fruit section manager, a small, chubby man who always smiles, suggests which fruit is the tastiest. His happy face makes me feel good. These three characteristics make this market one of the busiest markets.

◄ Added exact language.

◄ Added a transition.

◄ Added a transition.

◄ Added a transition.

Edit for Errors

LO 6 Edit for errors.

When you **edit**, you reread your writing and make sure that it is free of errors. Look for mistakes in grammar, punctuation, mechanics, and spelling. The editing guide at the end of this book contains some common editing codes that your teacher may use.

HINT ◄ Spelling and Grammar Logs

It is a good idea to put your text aside for a day or two before you edit it. You could also keep a spelling and grammar log.

- **Keep a spelling log.** In a notebook or binder, keep a list of all of your spelling mistakes. Then, you can refer to your list of spelling errors when you edit your writing.
- **Keep a grammar log.** After you receive each corrected assignment, choose an error. Write down the error and a rule about it in your grammar log.

See Appendix 5 for more information about the spelling and grammar logs.

Jinsuk's Editing

Jinsuk edited her paragraph for spelling and grammar errors.

> Zion Market is a busy and popular Korean market because it has
>
> three characteristics: good quality, low prices, and kind employees.
>
> Shopping in Zion Market makes me excited because I can find many
>
> are tasty
> products of good quality. Especially, the fruits. They are all fresh. Their
>
> colors are clear, and the stalks and peels of all fruits are not dried-up but
>
> . T
> moist. Also, they are delicious, they are flavorful, juicy, and sweet. In
>
> those
> addition, the prices of many products are lower than ~~thoses~~ in other
>
> kinds
> markets. Every weekend, different ~~kind~~ of products are on sale. There are
>
> special discounts on fresh vegetables, bags of rice, milk, and cartons filled
>
> with brown eggs. Furthermore, all the employees are very kind. I have
>
> an
> never had uncomfortable situation or witnessed any quarrels between
>
> customers and employees. The manager keeps walking around the
>
> , responds
> market and the head of each section ~~respond~~ quickly to the requests of
>
> the customers. For example, the fruit section manager, a small, chubby
>
> man who always smiles, suggests which fruit is the tastiest. His happy
>
> face makes me feel good. These three characteristics make this market
>
> one of the busiest markets.

THE WRITER'S DESK Revise and Edit Your Paragraph

Choose a paragraph that you wrote for Chapter 2, or choose one that you have written for another assignment. Carefully revise and edit your paragraph.

Peer Feedback

After you write a paragraph or an essay, it is useful to get peer feedback. Ask another person such as a friend, family member, or fellow student to read your work and give you comments and suggestions on its strengths and weaknesses.

Peer Feedback Form

Written by: _____   Feedback by: _____

Date: _____

1. Your main idea is _____

   _____

   _____

2. Your best supporting ideas are _____

   _____

   _____

   _____

3. I like _____

   _____

   _____

4. Perhaps you could change _____

   _____

   _____

   _____

5. My other comments are _____

   _____

   _____

   _____

   _____

HINT   **Offer Constructive Criticism**

When you peer-edit someone else's writing, try to make constructive suggestions rather than destructive comments. Phrase your comments in a positive way. Look at the following examples.

Instead of saying . . .	You could say . . .
Your examples are dull.	Perhaps you could add more details to your examples.
Your paragraph is confusing.	Your topic sentence needs a controlling idea.

When you are editing someone else's work, try using a peer feedback form as a guideline. A sample form is on the next page.

The Final Draft

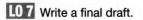
LO 7   Write a final draft.

When you have finished making revisions on the first draft of your paragraph, write the final draft. Include all of the changes that you have made during the revising and editing phases. Before you hand in your final draft, proofread it one last time to ensure that you have caught any errors.

THE WRITER'S DESK   **Writing Your Final Draft**

You have developed, revised, and edited your paragraph. Now write the final draft. Before you hand it in to your instructor, proofread it one last time to ensure that you have found all of your errors.

MyWritingLab™

Complete these writing assignments at mywritinglab.com

MyWritingLab   **THE WRITER'S ROOM**

Writing Activity 1

Choose a paragraph that you have written for this course. Revise and edit that paragraph, and then write a final draft.

Writing Activity 2

Choose one of the following topics, or choose your own topic and write a paragraph. You could try exploring strategies to generate ideas. The first sentence of your paragraph should make a point about your topic. Remember to revise and edit your paragraph before you write the final draft.

General Topics	College or Work-Related Topics
1. an interesting dream	6. an unusual experience at college
2. a family story	7. computer problems
3. a wonderful view	8. reasons to stay in college
4. weddings	9. learning a new skill
5. an accident	10. a job interview

Revising and Editing Checklist

When you revise and edit a paragraph, ask yourself the following questions.

☐ Does my paragraph have **unity**? Ensure that every sentence relates to the main idea.

☐ Does my paragraph have **adequate support**? Verify that there are enough details and examples to support your main point.

☐ Is my paragraph **coherent**? Try to use transitional expressions to link ideas.

☐ Does my paragraph have good **style**? Check for varied sentence patterns and exact language.

☐ Does my paragraph have any errors? **Edit** for errors in grammar, punctuation, spelling, and mechanics.

☐ Is my **final draft** error-free?

4 Paragraph Patterns

A fashion designer uses diverse patterns to create coats for different purposes. In this chapter, you will learn about nine writing patterns.

LO 1 Learn about paragraph patterns.

What Are Paragraph Patterns?

Paragraph patterns, or **modes**, are methods writers can use to develop a piece of writing. Each pattern has a specific purpose. For example, if you want to entertain your audience by telling a story about your recent adventure, you might write a narrative paragraph. If your purpose is to explain the steps needed to complete an activity, you might write a process paragraph. Sometimes, more than one pattern can fulfill your purpose. Take a moment to review nine different writing patterns.

Pattern	Purpose
Illustration	To illustrate or prove a point using specific examples
Narration	To narrate or tell a story about a sequence of events that happened

(continued)

Pattern	Purpose
Description	To describe using vivid details and images that appeal to the reader's senses
Process	To inform the reader about how to do something, how something works, or how something happened
Definition	To define or explain what a term or concept means by providing relevant examples
Comparison and Contrast	To present information about similarities (compare) or differences (contrast)
Cause and Effect	To explain why an event happened (the cause) or what the consequences of the event were (the effects)
Classification	To sort a topic into different categories
Argument	To argue or to take a position on an issue and offer reasons for your position

A) The Illustration Paragraph

An **illustration paragraph** uses specific examples to **illustrate** or clarify the main point. For example, if you are writing a paragraph about your most valuable possessions, you might list your grandmother's ring, your photo album, your family videos, and so on.

LO 2 Define the purpose of an illustration paragraph.

Illustration writing is a pattern that you frequently use in college because you must support your main idea with examples.

PRACTICE 1

Read the paragraph and answer the questions that follow.

> The human brain seems to be programmed for song. Physiologists have shown that a mother's lullaby does double duty by lowering a child's arousal levels while simultaneously increasing the child's ability to focus attention. Also, music therapists have found that listening to music induces the release of pleasure-producing endorphins that both lower blood pressure and ease the sensation of physical pain. Attentive listening helps us focus our ideas. Furthermore, musical training can improve a person's organizational skills and even have a positive effect on IQ. Indeed, scientists hypothesize that while performing, musicians are actually engaged in high-powered brain **calisthenics**, which can transfer to other areas of life. Finally, social scientists believe that music, by bringing people together to perform and listen, may have provided an early model for social cooperation and cohesion. Music seems to be a fundamental building block in the development of culture.

calisthenics: exercises

—Steven Cornelius and Mary Natvig, *Music: A Social Experience*

1. Underline the topic sentence of this paragraph.

2. Circle three transitional expressions.

3. What is the author's point of view about music?

4.   How does the writer support the topic sentence? List four examples.

_____

_____

_____

_____

THE WRITER'S DESK Exploring

Think about the following questions, and write down the first ideas that come to mind. Try to write two or three ideas for each topic.

EXAMPLE: What clutter do you have in your backpack or purse?

purse is a total nightmare, overflowing with tissues, lists, brush,

comb, hair elastics, gum, candies; wallet is filled with points cards

that I never use, receipts

1.   What are some examples of objects that you value?

_____

_____

2.   What are some creative gift ideas?

_____

_____

3.   What are some useless items in your home?

_____

_____

_____

The Topic Sentence

The topic sentence in an illustration paragraph controls the direction of the paragraph. It includes the topic and a controlling idea about the topic.

controlling idea   topic

<u>There are several good reasons</u> **to save money**.

THE WRITER'S DESK Write Topic Sentences

Write a topic sentence for each of the following topics. Your sentence should have a controlling idea that expresses the direction of the paragraph. Remember that the goal of the paragraph is to give examples.

EXAMPLE: Topic: My backpack or purse

Topic sentence: _My purse is a magnet for clutter._ _____

_____

1. Topic: Objects that you value
   Topic sentence: _____

   _____

2. Topic: Creative gift ideas
   Topic sentence: _____

   _____

3. Topic: Useless items
   Topic sentence: _____

   _____

The Supporting Ideas

In an illustration paragraph, the examples support the topic sentence. A paragraph plan helps you organize your topic sentence and supporting details.

An Illustration Paragraph Plan

When you write an illustration paragraph plan, make sure that your examples are valid and that they relate to the topic sentence. In the following plan, the topic sentence is supported by three examples. Then, each example is supported with details.

Topic sentence: My purse is a magnet for clutter.

Support 1:	Useless grooming products fill one entire compartment.
Details:	—old lipstick tubes and nearly empty compacts jumble together
	—hairbrush, hair elastics, and hair clips take up a lot of space
Support 2:	My wallet, bursting with items, fills an inner pocket.
Details:	—customer cards from coffee shops pile together
	—gas station points cards are rarely used
	—photos of family members spill out

Support 3:   Kleenex and notes block up the outside pockets.

Details: —tissues are stuffed in corners in case of emergencies

—restaurant receipts are crammed into various corners

—notes and old lists are crumpled in piles

THE WRITER'S DESK   Develop Supporting Ideas

Choose one of the topic sentences that you wrote for the previous Writer's Desk, and write a detailed paragraph plan. List at least three examples that could support the topic sentence, and then give details for each.

Topic sentence: _____

_____

Support 1: _____

Details: _____

_____

Support 2: _____

Details: _____

_____

Support 3: _____

Details: _____

_____

Support 4: _____

Details: _____

_____

THE WRITER'S DESK   Write an Illustration Paragraph

You have made a list of supporting ideas and details for a topic. Now write an illustration paragraph. After you finish writing, remember to revise and edit your paragraph.

THE WRITER'S ROOM
MyWritingLab

MyWritingLab™
Complete these writing assignments at mywritinglab.com

Writing Activity 1: Topics

Write an illustration paragraph about one of the following topics.

General Topics

1. unhealthy habits
2. favorite clothing
3. inexpensive decorating solutions
4. annoying sounds
5. inexpensive activities

College and Work-Related Topics

6. inappropriate workplace clothing
7. qualities that help people succeed
8. undesirable or difficult jobs
9. useful objects in my workplace
10. excuses for not finishing something

Writing Activity 2: Photo Writing

Examine the photo. As you look at it, think about things that frustrate you or drive you crazy. Then write an illustration paragraph.

WRITING LINK
See the Writer's Rooms in the following grammar chapters for more illustration writing topics.

Chapter 8, Writer's Room topic 1 (page 155)
Chapter 12, Writer's Room topic 1 (page 215)
Chapter 15, Writer's Room topic 1 (page 248)
Chapter 21, Writer's Room topic 1 (page 305)
Chapter 22, Writer's Room topic 1 (page 315)

Illustration Paragraph Checklist

As you write your illustration paragraph, review the paragraph checklist on the inside back cover. Also, ask yourself the following questions.

☐ Does my topic sentence include a controlling idea that can be supported with examples?

☐ Do my supporting ideas contain sufficient examples that clearly support the topic sentence?

☐ Are the examples smoothly and logically connected?

READING LINK
The following readings use examples to support the main idea.

"A Cultural Minefield" by William Ecenbarger (page 408)
"The Rewards of Dirty Work" by Linda L. Lindsey and Stephen Beach (page 436)

LO 3 Define the purpose of a narrative paragraph.

B) The Narrative Paragraph

A **narrative** paragraph tells a story about what happened and generally explains events in the order in which they occurred.

There are two main types of narrative writing. When you use **first-person narration**, you describe a personal experience using *I* or *we* (first-person pronouns). When you use **third-person narration**, you describe what happened to somebody else using *he, she,* or *they* (third-person pronouns). Most news reports use third-person narration. Review the following examples.

First person   When I was a child, I played a terrible prank on my sister.

Third person   The mayor denied reports that he had misappropriated funds.

PRACTICE 2

Read the paragraph and answer the questions that follow.

buffarilla: an invented word that is a combination of buffalo and gorilla

> When I was in seventh grade, one of the big ninth-grade girls began bullying me. She didn't shake me down for lunch money or even touch me. But she stalked me in the halls, on the playground, and in the girls' lavatory. The way that **buffarilla** rolled her eyes and worked her neck in my direction, I could feel her fingers yanking out every hair on my head—and I didn't have that much. In class, instead of paying attention, I began to envision the after-school crowd that would gather to watch me get stomped into the ground. Every day, my adversary seemed to grow bigger, meaner, and stronger. In my mind she evolved from a menacing older girl into a monster. By the time I realized that she wasn't really interested in fighting me—just intimidating me with dirty looks—I was already bruised from kicking my own butt.

—Bebe Moore Campbell, "Dancing with Fear"

1. What type of narration is this selection?
   a. First person   b. Third person

2. Underline the topic sentence.

3. What organizational method does the author use?
   a. Time order   b. Space order   c. Emphatic order

4. List what happens in the paragraph. (List only the main events.)

   _____

   _____

   _____

5. What did the author learn?

   _____

   _____

   _____

THE WRITER'S DESK Exploring

Think about the following questions, and write down the first ideas that come to mind. Try to write two or three ideas for each topic.

EXAMPLE: What are some bad purchases that you have made?

Bought black dress that is really too small

Bought a used car that was a lemon

Spent too much on a horrible haircut

1. In the past, what interesting place did you visit? What did you do in that place?

_____

_____

_____

_____

2. Think about a moment when you received good news. What happened?

_____

_____

_____

_____

3. What is the best time of the day? What do you do at that time every day?

_____

_____

_____

_____

The Topic Sentence

The **topic sentence** controls the direction of the paragraph and includes the topic and a controlling idea. To create a meaningful topic sentence for a narrative paragraph, you could ask yourself these questions: What did I learn? How did I change? How is the event important?

           topic   controlling idea

Our high school graduation ceremony <u>was a disaster</u>.

THE WRITER'S DESK   Write Topic Sentences

Write a topic sentence for each of the following topics. Your sentence should make a point about the topic. Remember that the goal of the paragraph is to tell a story.

EXAMPLE: Topic: A bad purchase

Topic sentence: *My problems began the moment I paid for my used car.*

1. Topic: A place I visited

   Topic sentence: _____

   _____

2. Topic: Good news that I received

   Topic sentence: _____

   _____

3. Topic: A great time of day

   Topic sentence: _____

   _____

The Supporting Ideas

A narrative paragraph should contain details that explain what happened. To be as complete as possible, a good narrative paragraph should provide answers to most of the following questions.

- *Who* is the paragraph about?
- *What* happened?
- *When* did it happen?

- *Where* did it happen?
- *Why* did it happen?
- *How* did it happen?

A Narrative Paragraph Plan

When you write a narrative paragraph plan, make sure that your details are valid and that they relate to the topic sentence. Also, think about how you can organize your ideas. In the following plan, each detail explains what happened by using time order.

WRITING LINK
For more information about organizing ideas using time, space, and emphatic order, see pages 22 to 27 of Chapter 2, "Developing."

Topic sentence: My problems began the moment I paid for my used car.

    Support 1:   When I paid the $500, the seller expressed relief.

      Details: —actually said "Whew"

               —exchanged knowing glances with his buddy

Support 2:	The drive home was filled with anxiety.
Details:	—became concerned that the car wouldn't make it
	—car seemed to gain and lose power
	—twice had to stop the car because it was overheating
Support 3:	I parked the car in my apartment parking space and noticed something dripping.
Details:	—smelled burning oil
	—black liquid dripped and stained the pavement
	—landlord, with a scowl, peered out her window at my car

THE WRITER'S DESK Develop Supporting Ideas

Choose one of the topic sentences that you wrote for the previous Writer's Desk, and write a detailed paragraph plan. List the events in the order in which they occurred.

Topic sentence: _____

_____

Support 1: _____

Details: _____

_____

_____

Support 2: _____

Details: _____

_____

_____

Support 3: _____

Details: _____

_____

_____

THE WRITER'S DESK Write a Narrative Paragraph

You have made a list of supporting ideas for a topic. Now write a narrative paragraph. After you finish writing, remember to revise and edit your paragraph.

MyWritingLab™

Complete these writing assignments at mywritinglab.com

WRITING LINK

See the Writer's Rooms in the following grammar chapters for more narrative writing topics.

Chapter 9, Writer's Room topic 1 (page 173)

Chapter 14, Writer's Room topic 1 (page 236)

Chapter 15, Writer's Room topic 2 (page 248)

Chapter 21, Writer's Room topic 2 (page 305)

Chapter 23, Writer's Room topic 1 (page 325)

READING LINK

The following readings use narrative writing.

"Birth" by Maya Angelou (page 395)

"The Reverend Evans's Universe" by Bill Bryson (page 421)

MyWritingLab

THE WRITER'S ROOM

Writing Activity 1: Topics

Write a narrative paragraph about one of the following topics.

General Topics

1. a scandal
2. a bad hair experience
3. a rebellious act
4. a good or bad financial decision
5. something you learned from a parent or relative

College and Work-Related Topics

6. a mistake at work
7. a smart career decision
8. a positive college experience
9. when you were first hired
10. when you lost or quit a job

Writing Activity 2: Photo Writing

Examine the photo. As you look at it, think about a ceremony or celebration that you participated in. Describe what happened.

Narrative Paragraph Checklist

As you write your narrative paragraph, review the paragraph checklist on the inside back cover. Also, ask yourself the following questions.

☐ Does my topic sentence clearly express the topic of the narration, and does it make a point about that topic?

☐ Does my paragraph answer most of the following questions: who, what, when, where, why, how?

☐ Do I use transitional expressions to help clarify the order of events?

☐ Do I include details to make my narration more interesting?

C) The Descriptive Paragraph

When writing a **descriptive** paragraph, use words to create a vivid impression of a subject. Descriptive writing often contains details that appeal to the five senses: seeing, smelling, hearing, tasting, and touching. Readers should be able to imagine and visualize what you are describing. For example, you might describe a frightening experience or a stunning landscape.

PRACTICE 3

Read the paragraph and answer the questions that follow.

> I was in Acapulco, Mexico, for a mini-vacation when I was literally swept off my feet. We arrived at the beach early in the morning. As I walked along, sand worked its way into my flip-flop sandals, and I could feel its warmth between my toes. The sun's rays heat up my back, shoulders, and neck. But most of all, I heard the roaring of the waves. How they called to me. A whitecap formed that was about to crash, and I decided that it was mine. With an open-mouthed smile, I ran in its direction with the illusion of breaking the water. With every step I took, the wave grew larger. I realized just how big it truly was as I ducked under it in pure fear. The wave curved over me as it would a surfer, and the world became silent. I imagined that this is how a collision with a truck would feel if the truck were made out of water. My world instantly turned black, and I tumbled and rolled at the mercy of the sea. Water invaded my nose, ears, and eyes. The taste of salty water filled my mouth. Then, just as quickly as it had arrived, the foaming wave receded—leaving me as its footprint. Crawling my way back to dry sand, I coughed up ocean water. I had been chewed up and spat out by the sea.

—Vince Rosas, student

1. Underline the topic sentence.

2. What is the main impression that the writer creates?
    a. fear   b. happiness   c. sadness   d. anger

3. Give examples of sensory details.

    a. sight _____
    _____
    _____

    b. sound _____
    _____
    _____

    c. taste _____
    _____
    _____

    d. touch _____
    _____
    _____

THE WRITER'S DESK Exploring

Think about the following questions, and write down the first ideas that come to mind. Try to write two or three ideas for each topic.

EXAMPLE: Think about some extremely busy places.

the waiting room at the hospital, the bus station, the line to buy

my college textbooks

_____

_____

1. Where do you go when you want to relax? Think of two or three places.

_____

_____

2. What did you look like in the past? What fashions did you wear? What hairstyles did you have? (You might look at old photographs for inspiration.)

_____

_____

_____

3. What are some of your prized possessions or gadgets? List some ideas.

_____

_____

_____

_____

The Topic Sentence

In the **topic sentence** of a descriptive paragraph, you should convey a dominant impression about the subject. The dominant impression is the overall mood that you wish to convey. For example, the paragraph could convey an impression of tension, joy, nervousness, or anger.

topic   controlling idea
When I arrived at the secluded cabin, I felt relieved.

THE WRITER'S DESK Write Topic Sentences

Write a topic sentence for each of the following topics. Your sentence should state what you are describing and express a dominant impression.

EXAMPLE: Topic: A busy place

Topic sentence: *After I broke my wrist while cycling, I had an uncomfortable and anxious wait at the hospital.*

1. Topic: A relaxing place
   Topic sentence: _____
   _____
   _____
   _____

2. Topic: Yourself in the past
   Topic sentence: _____
   _____
   _____
   _____

3. Topic: A prized possession or gadget
   Topic sentence: _____
   _____
   _____
   _____

The Supporting Ideas

To create a dominant impression, think about your topic and make a list of your feelings and impressions. These details can include things that you saw, heard, smelled, tasted, or touched.

HINT ◀ Use Interesting and Detailed Vocabulary

In your paragraph, use interesting descriptive vocabulary. Avoid overused words such as *nice, bad, mean*, and *hot*. For example, instead of writing "He was mean," you might write "He was as nasty as a raging pit bull." For more information about specific and vivid language, refer to Chapter 23, "Exact Language."

THE WRITER'S DESK **List Images and Impressions**

Think about images, impressions, and feelings that the following topics inspire in you. Make a list under each topic.

EXAMPLE: A busy place: _____

hospital waiting room

baby cried

little boy ran back and forth

old man coughed

hot and sweaty

stuffy air

heart pounded

1. A relaxing place: _____

2. Yourself in the past: _____

3. A prized possession: _____

WRITING LINK
For more information about organizing ideas using time, space, and emphatic order, see pages 22–27 in Chapter 2, "Developing."

A Descriptive Paragraph Plan

When you write a descriptive paragraph plan, make sure that your details are valid and that they relate to the topic sentence. You could place your details in space order, time order, or emphatic order. The order that you use depends on the topic of your paragraph. In the following plan, the details, which are in time order, appeal to the senses and develop the dominant impression.

Topic sentence: After I broke my wrist while cycling, I had an uncomfortable and anxious wait at the hospital.

> **Support 1:** The room was extremely noisy.
> **Details:** —a baby cried
> —a little boy ran back and forth
> —an old man hacked and coughed

Support 2: There was no air conditioning, so it was hot and stuffy.
Details: —sweat ran down my back

—used my newspaper as a fan

Support 3: I was concerned about my wrist.
Details: —felt a throbbing sensation

—noticed swelling at the top of my hand

—saw a growing bruise

THE WRITER'S DESK **Develop Supporting Ideas**

Choose one of the topic sentences that you developed in the previous Writer's Desks, and write a detailed paragraph plan. Remember to develop a dominant impression.

Topic sentence: _____

_____

Support 1: _____

Details: _____

_____

Support 2: _____

Details: _____

_____

Support 3: _____

Details: _____

_____

Support 4: _____

Details: _____

_____

THE WRITER'S DESK **Write a Descriptive Paragraph**

You have made a list of supporting ideas for a topic. Now write a descriptive paragraph. After you finish writing, remember to revise and edit your paragraph.

MyWritingLab™
Complete these writing assignments at mywritinglab.com

MyWritingLab

THE WRITER'S ROOM

Writing Activity 1: Topics

Write a descriptive paragraph about one of the following topics.

General Topics

1. a favorite childhood toy
2. a fad or fashion trend
3. a shocking experience
4. an eccentric family member
5. a messy place

College and Work-Related Topics

6. a friend I have made at college or at work
7. an unusual teacher from your past
8. the place where you study
9. a bad day at work
10. the style of clothing you wear to work

Writing Activity 2: Photo Writing

Examine the photo. As you look at it, think about a feast that you enjoyed. Describe the sights, sounds, odors, and tastes.

WRITING LINK
See the Writer's Rooms in the following grammar chapters for more descriptive writing topics.

Chapter 9, Writer's Room topic 2 (page 173)
Chapter 11, Writer's Room topics 1 and 2 (page 201)
Chapter 17, Writer's Room topic 1 (page 265)
Chapter 19, Writer's Room topic 1 (page 281)
Chapter 26, Writer's Room topic 1 (page 360)

READING LINK
The following readings use descriptive writing.

"Fish Cheeks" by Amy Tan (page 393)
"Skydiving" by Touré (page 402)

Descriptive Paragraph Checklist

As you write your descriptive paragraph, review the paragraph checklist on the inside back cover. Also, ask yourself the following questions.

☐ Does my topic sentence clearly show what I will describe?

☐ Does my topic sentence make a point about the topic?

☐ Does my paragraph have a dominant impression?

☐ Does each body paragraph contain supporting details that appeal to the reader's senses?

D) The Process Paragraph

LO 5 Define the purpose of a process paragraph.

A **process** is a series of steps done in chronological or emphatic order. In a **process paragraph**, you explain how to do something. For example, you might explain how to change the oil in your car, how to plan a party, or how to write a résumé. The reader should be able to follow the directions and do the process.

PRACTICE 4

Read the paragraph and answer the questions that follow.

> Safety in welding is essential. Welders need to wear the proper gear to avoid potentially dangerous events. First, they must wear gauntlet gloves to protect their hands and skin from the intense heat and the electric arc rays, which can burn skin worse than the sun in a fraction of a second. Second, they must wear a welding helmet with a filter lens, which shades their eyes from the bright rays of the electric arc or the combustible gas flame. The effect experienced after eyeball exposure, even when indirect, is called arc flash. Arc flash causes eyes to redden, burn, and itch, and it can leave a person temporarily and possibly permanently blind. Trained welders know the possibility of getting a lighter scale arc flash from simple things like reflective stripes on coveralls or from a partner welding nearby. Furthermore, welders must never wear clothing made of synthetics because it can melt and burn the skin. Also, plastic shoes and jewelry should be avoided. These items can cause serious burns, and they can smolder or ignite into flames.
>
> —Kelly Bruce, student and professional welder

1. Underline the topic sentence. Remember that the topic sentence may not be the first sentence in the paragraph.

2. In process paragraphs, the support is generally a series of steps. List the steps a person should take to be safe when welding.

   _____

   _____

   _____

   _____

3. Circle the transitional expressions that introduce each point.

4. This paragraph does not have a concluding sentence. Write a concluding sentence.

   _____

   _____

   _____

   _____

THE WRITER'S DESK Exploring

Think about the following questions, and write down the first ideas that come to mind. Try to write two or three ideas for each topic.

EXAMPLE: What are some ways to find a mate?

join a club, ask your friends, be open and receptive, don't act

desperate, be yourself, use an Internet dating service

_____

1. What are some things you should do when you prepare for a move to a new place?

   _____

   _____

   _____

2. What should you do if you want to plan a surprise party?

   _____

   _____

   _____

3. What steps can you take to impress a date?

   _____

   _____

   _____

The Topic Sentence

The topic sentence in a process paragraph includes the process you are describing and a controlling idea.

      topic (process)   controlling idea

When you make a mosaic, there are several precautions you should take.

It is also possible to make a topic sentence that contains a map, or guide, to the details that you will present in your paragraph. To guide your readers, you can mention the main steps in your topic sentence.

                topic   controlling idea

When you build a ceramic tile mosaic, have the proper safety equipment, tools, and workspace.

THE WRITER'S DESK Write Topic Sentences

Write a topic sentence for each of the following topics. Your sentence should have a controlling idea that expresses the direction of the paragraph. Remember that the goal of the paragraph is to explain how to do something.

EXAMPLE: Topic: How to find a mate

Topic sentence: _With careful preparation and screening, you can_ _find a mate on the Internet._

1. Topic: How to prepare for a move

   Topic sentence: _____

   _____

2. Topic: How to plan a surprise party

   Topic sentence: _____

   _____

3. Topic: How to impress a date

   Topic sentence: _____

   _____

The Supporting Ideas

When you write the supporting ideas, decide which steps your reader needs to take to complete the process. Explain each step in detail. Organize your steps chronologically. Remember to mention any necessary tools or supplies.

HINT ◀ Give Steps, Not Examples

When you explain how to do a process, describe each step. Do not simply list examples of the process.

How to Relax

List of Examples	Steps in the Process
Read a book.	Change into comfortable clothing.
Take a bath.	Do some deep breathing.
Go for a long walk.	Choose a good book.
Listen to soothing music.	Find a relaxing place to read.

A Process Paragraph Plan

When you write a process paragraph plan, decide how you will organize your plan, and make sure that you explain each step clearly. In the following paragraph plan, the writer uses time order to describe the process.

Topic sentence: With careful preparation and screening, you can find a mate on the Internet.

Step 1:	Prepare by finding a reliable dating site.
Details:	—Ask friends about possible sites.
	—Make sure the site targets people in your area.
Step 2:	Write an interesting profile.
Details:	—Use positive terms to describe yourself, such as *dynamic* and *energetic*.
	—Get a friend or a professional to look over your profile.
Step 3:	Screen replies carefully.
Details:	—Choose your favorite responses.
	—Invite friends to help you sort potential dates.
Step 4:	Meet only in public places.
Details:	—Consider meeting in the daytime, maybe in a coffee shop.
	—Avoid alcohol because it can cloud judgment.

THE WRITER'S DESK **Develop Supporting Ideas**

Choose one of the topic sentences that you wrote for the previous Writer's Desk, and write a detailed paragraph plan.

Topic sentence: _____

_____

Support 1: _____

Details: _____

_____

Support 2: _____

Details: _____

_____

Support 3: _____

Details: _____

_____

Support 4: _____

Details: _____

_____

THE WRITER'S DESK Write a Process Paragraph

You have made a list of supporting ideas for a topic. Now write a process paragraph. After you finish writing, remember to revise and edit your paragraph.

THE WRITER'S ROOM

MyWritingLab™

Writing Activity 1: Topics

Write a process paragraph about one of the following topics.

General Topics

1. how to play a specific sport
2. how to discipline a small child
3. how to buy a used car
4. how to make friends
5. how to make a great beverage

College and Work-Related Topics

6. how to use a particular machine
7. how to choose a college
8. how to dress for success
9. how to do a task in your workplace
10. how to keep a job

Writing Activity 2: Photo Writing

Examine the photo and think about processes that you can describe. For example, you might explain how to get along with coworkers, neighbors, or family members. Other ideas include how to make friends or how to encourage teamwork.

MyWritingLab™

Complete these writing assignments at mywritinglab.com

WRITING LINK
See the Writer's Rooms in the following grammar chapters for more process writing topics.

Chapter 6, Writer's Room topic 1 (page 125)
Chapter 10, Writer's Room topic 1 (page 190)
Chapter 22, Writer's Room topic 2 (page 315)
Chapter 28, Writer's Room topic 1 (page 381)

READING LINK
The following readings use process writing.

"How to Handle Conflict" by P. Gregory Smith (page 432)

"How to Remember Names" by Roger Seip (page 434)

┌───┐
│ *Process Paragraph Checklist* · · · · · · · · · · · · · · · · · · ·   │
│   │
│ As you write your process paragraph, review the paragraph checklist on the │
│ inside back cover. Also, ask yourself the following questions.   │
│   │
│ ☐ Does my topic sentence make a point about the process?   │
│   │
│ ☐ Does my paragraph explain how to do something?   │
│   │
│ ☐ Do I clearly explain each step in the process?   │
│   │
│ ☐ Do I mention any supplies that my reader needs to complete the process? │
│   │
│ ☐ Do I use transitions to connect the steps in the process?   │
│   │
└───┘

LO 6 Define the purpose of a definition paragraph.

E) The Definition Paragraph

A **definition** tells you what something means. When you write a **definition paragraph**, you give your personal definition of a term or concept. Although you can define most terms in a few sentences, you may need to offer extended definitions for words that are particularly complex. For example, you can write a paragraph or even an entire book about the term *happiness*. The way that you interpret the term is unique, and you would bring your own opinions, experiences, and impressions to your definition paragraph.

PRACTICE 5

Read the paragraph and answer the questions that follow.

> In all societies, people evaluate their transitions according to a social clock that determines whether they are "on time" or "off time" for their age. Cultures have different social clocks that define the right time to marry, start work, and have children. In some societies, young men and women are supposed to marry and start having children right after puberty, and work responsibilities come later. In others, a man may not marry until he has shown that he can support a family, which might not be until his thirties. When nearly everyone in a particular age group goes through the same experience or enters a new role at the same time—going to school, driving a car, voting, marrying, having a baby, retiring—adjusting to these anticipated transitions is relatively easy. Conversely, if someone is not doing things at the same pace as his or her peers, that person may feel out of step. Society's reactions to people who are "off time" vary as well, from amused tolerance ("Oh, when will he grow up?") to pity, scorn, and outright rejection.
>
> —Carole Wade and Carol Tavris, *Invitation to Psychology*

1. Underline the topic sentence.

2. What is the writer defining? _____

3. Write your own definition of the term by summarizing the information in the paragraph.

_____

_____

_____

4. Think of a specific example to support this paragraph. For example, you might explain how someone you know is "off time."

_____

_____

THE WRITER'S DESK Exploring

Think about the following questions, and write down the first ideas that come to mind. Try to write two or three ideas for each topic.

EXAMPLE: What is *leet speak*?

Computer language; uses numbers; hackers use it _____

1. What is peer pressure? _____

_____

2. What is a slob? _____

_____

3. What is charisma? _____

_____

The Topic Sentence

In your **topic sentence**, indicate what you are defining and include a definition of the term. Look at the three ways to define a term.

◆ **Definition by synonym.** You can give a word that means the same thing as the term.

term + synonyms
Gratuitous means unnecessary or uncalled for.

◆ **Definition by negation.** Explain what the term is not, and then explain what it is.

term + what it is not + what it is
Sexual harassment is not harmless banter; it is intimidating and unwanted sexual attention.

◆ **Definition by category.** Decide what larger group the term belongs to, and then determine the unique characteristics that set the term apart from others in that category.

term + category + detail
A blogger is a writer who expresses his or her opinions in an Internet journal.

THE WRITER'S DESK Write Topic Sentences

Write a topic sentence for each of the following topics. Your sentence should have a controlling idea that expresses the direction of the paragraph. Remember that the goal of the paragraph is to define something.

EXAMPLE: Topic: Leet speak

Topic sentence: _Leet speak is not just a passing fad; it is a unique_
language used by computer users.

1. Topic: Peer pressure
   Topic sentence: _____

   _____

2. Topic: A slob
   Topic sentence: _____

   _____

3. Topic: Charisma
   Topic sentence: _____

   _____

The Supporting Ideas

A definition paragraph should include a complete definition of a term, and it should have adequate examples that support the definition. Remember to provide various types of support. Do not simply repeat the definition.

A Definition Paragraph Plan

When you write a definition paragraph plan, make sure that your details are valid and that they relate to the topic sentence.

Topic sentence: Leet speak is not just a passing fad; it is a unique language used by computer users.

Support 1:	Leet speak is not a traditional language.
Details:	—not spoken or handwritten
	—needs a keyboard
Support 2:	Like all languages, leet speak reflects the culture of the user.
Details:	—created by hackers to avoid detection
	—replaces letters with numbers
	—makes communicating online faster

Support 3:   Leet speak has pervaded cyberspace.

Details: —A Web comic, *Megatokyo*, popularized leet speak.

         —Web site communities use leet speak to express excitement.

         —Web sites have dictionaries to translate between normal script and leet speak.

THE WRITER'S DESK   Develop Supporting Ideas

Choose one of the topic sentences that you wrote for the previous Writer's Desk, and write a detailed paragraph plan.

Topic sentence: _____

_____

Support 1: _____

_____

Details: _____

_____

_____

Support 2: _____

_____

Details: _____

_____

_____

Support 3: _____

_____

Details: _____

_____

_____

THE WRITER'S DESK   Write a Definition Paragraph

You have made a list of supporting ideas for a topic. Now write a definition paragraph. After you finish writing, remember to revise and edit your paragraph.

MyWritingLab

THE WRITER'S ROOM

Writing Activity 1: Topics

Write a definition paragraph about one of the following topics.

General Topics

1. common sense
2. a gambler
3. a nest egg
4. a mouse potato
5. a drama queen

College and Work-Related Topics

6. a golden handshake
7. hero worship
8. burnout
9. materialistic
10. an effective boss

Writing Activity 2: Photo Writing

What is road rage? Write a paragraph explaining the term. Provide specific examples in your supporting ideas.

WRITING LINK
See the Writer's Rooms in the following grammar chapters for more definition writing topics.

Chapter 6, Writer's Room topic 2 (page 125)
Chapter 10, Writer's Room topic 2 (page 190)
Chapter 16, Writer's Room topic 1 (page 260)
Chapter 19, Writer's Room topic 2 (page 281)
Chapter 24, Writer's Room topic 2 (page 337)
Chapter 27, Writer's Room topic 2 (page 369)

READING LINK
The following readings use definition writing.

"Celanthropists" by Katrina Onstad (page 411)
"The Allure of Apple" by Juan Rodriguez (page 429)

Definition Paragraph Checklist

As you write your definition paragraph, review the paragraph checklist on the inside back cover. Also, ask yourself the following questions.

☐ Does my topic sentence contain a definition by synonym, negation, or category?

☐ Do all of my supporting sentences relate to the topic sentence?

☐ Do I use concise language in my definition?

☐ Do I include enough examples to help define the term?

F) The Comparison and Contrast Paragraph

LO 7 Define the purpose of a comparison and contrast paragraph.

You **compare** when you want to find similarities, and you **contrast** when you want to find differences. When writing a comparison and contrast paragraph, you prove a specific point by explaining how people, places, things, or ideas are the same or different. For example, you might compare two jobs that you have had, two different ways of disciplining, or two ideas about how to stimulate the national economy.

Before you write, you must make a decision about whether you will focus on similarities, differences, or both. As you explore your topic, it is a good idea to make a list of both similarities and differences. Later, you can use some of the ideas in your paragraph plan.

PRACTICE 6

Read the paragraph and answer the questions that follow.

> In the restaurant business, cooks and servers have the main positions, and some people say that cooks have a difficult job. However, cooks have several advantages over servers. First, cooks can get paid up to $15 an hour whereas servers earn the minimum wage and must depend on tips. If the cook has a bad day, he or she can snap at others. The server, on the other hand, has to remain polite and make sure that the guests are welcomed and treated warmly. When cooks mess up, their checks won't suffer, but servers cannot show stress or impatience because it directly affects their tips. Furthermore, the cleaning schedule is easier for a cook. At the end of the shift, the chef has to clean up only his or her work station. The server has to wait until the customers have all left and then clean the section and the side station. Sometimes the server has to clean a shelving area, which can take up to an hour. Most of the time, the silverware has to be rolled in a special napkin for the next day, which is the server's responsibility. Finally, after a long shift, cooks can keep their entire income and do not have to share with the others who helped them accomplish their job. Servers, however, have to give a percentage of their tips to the bartender and the busboy or busgirl. So although the cook is considered to be the harder worker in the restaurant business, it is the server who really deserves respect.
>
> —Tiffany Hines, student

1. Underline the topic sentence. Be careful because it may not be the first sentence.

2. List the key differences between the job of a cook and a server.

Cook	Server
_____	_____
_____	_____
_____	_____
_____	_____
_____	_____

Think about the following questions, and write down the first ideas that come to mind. Try to write two or three ideas for each topic.

EXAMPLE: Compare two beautiful seasons.

Autumn

red and gold colors

days get shorter

trees lose leaves

Spring

budding leaves and flowers

days get longer

trees turn green

1. Compare two friends or family members.

Type 1: _____   Type 2: _____

_____   _____

_____   _____

_____   _____

2. Compare two different jobs that you have had.

Job 1: _____   Job 2: _____

_____   _____

_____   _____

_____   _____

3. Compare what you do on two different holidays. For example, you could compare Thanksgiving and Halloween.

Holiday 1: _____   Holiday 2: _____

_____   _____

_____   _____

_____   _____

The Topic Sentence

The topic sentence in a comparison and contrast paragraph indicates whether you are making comparisons, contrasts, or both. When you write a topic sentence, indicate what you are comparing or contrasting, and express a controlling idea. The following are examples of topic sentences for comparison and contrast paragraphs.

My brother and father argue a lot, but they have very similar personalities.

Topic (what is being compared)	father and brother
Controlling idea	similar personalities

A cat is much easier to care for than a dog.

Topic	cats and dogs
Controlling idea	cats are easier to care for

THE WRITER'S DESK **Write Topic Sentences**

Write a topic sentence for each of the following topics. Your sentence should have a controlling idea that expresses the direction of the paragraph.

EXAMPLE: Topic: Two seasons

Topic sentence: _Although both seasons are beautiful, the spring_
is a more hopeful time than the fall.

1. Topic: Two friends or family members

    Topic sentence: _____

    _____

2. Topic: Two jobs

    Topic sentence: _____

    _____

3. Topic: Two holidays

    Topic sentence: _____

    _____

The Supporting Ideas

In a comparison and contrast paragraph, you can develop your supporting ideas in two different ways.

Point-by-Point Development

To develop a topic point by point, you look at similarities or differences by going back and forth from one side to the other.

Topic-by-Topic Development

To develop your ideas topic by topic, you discuss one topic in detail, and then you discuss the other topic in detail. The next plans are for a paragraph comparing two coworkers.

Topic sentence: My two coworkers are different in every way.

Point-by-Point Comparison		**Topic-by-Topic Comparison**	
Support 1:	Appearance —Coworker A —Coworker B	**Coworker A:**	—Appearance —Skills —Temperament
Support 2:	Skills —Coworker A —Coworker B	**Coworker B:**	—Appearance —Skills —Temperament
Support 3:	Temperament —Coworker A —Coworker B		

A Comparison and Contrast Paragraph Plan

When you write a comparison and contrast paragraph plan, decide which pattern you will follow: point by point or topic by topic. Then add some details.

Topic sentence: Although both seasons are beautiful, spring is a more hopeful time than fall.

Support 1:	Fall is beautiful.
Details:	—crisp fresh air
	—gold, orange, and red leaves
Support 2:	Autumn becomes a depressing period.
Details:	—colder winds and bare tree branches
	—awareness of winter's arrival
Support 3:	Spring is also a lovely time.
Details:	—budding flowers and leaves
	—squirrels and birds return
Support 4:	Spring is a time of hope and renewal.
Details:	—nature comes back to life
	—knowledge of warmer days to come

THE WRITER'S DESK **Develop Supporting Ideas**

Choose one of the topic sentences that you wrote for the previous Writer's Desk, and write a detailed paragraph plan.

Topic sentence: _____

_____

Support 1: _____

Details: _____

_____

Support 2: _____

Details: _____

_____

Support 3: _____

Details: _____

_____

Support 4: _____

Details: _____

_____

THE WRITER'S DESK Write a Comparison and Contrast Paragraph

You have made a list of supporting ideas for a topic. Now write a comparison and contrast paragraph. After you finish writing, remember to revise and edit your paragraph.

THE WRITER'S ROOM
MyWritingLab

MyWritingLab™
Complete these writing assignments at mywritinglab.com

Writing Activity 1: Topics

Write a comparison and contrast paragraph about one of the following topics.

General Topics

1. a street vendor and a restaurant
2. two television shows
3. two neighborhoods
4. a friend and an acquaintance
5. two youth subcultures

College and Work-Related Topics

6. expectations about college and the reality of college
7. a small school or college and a large school or college
8. two different coworkers
9. working alone and working with others
10. two different bosses

Writing Activity 2: Photo Writing

Examine the photo and think about things that you can compare and contrast. Some ideas might be two positions on a team, two types of sports, a sport and a board game, or two athletes.

> **WRITING LINK**
> See the Writer's Rooms in the following grammar chapters for more comparison and contrast writing topics.
>
> Chapter 8, Writer's Room topic 2 (page 155)
> Chapter 12, Writer's Room topic 2 (page 215)
> Chapter 14, Writer's Room topic 2 (page 236)
> Chapter 18, Writer's Room topic 1 (page 275)
> Chapter 20, Writer's Room topic 1 (page 290)
> Chapter 28, Writer's Room topic 2 (page 381)

> **READING LINK**
> The following readings use comparison and contrast writing.
>
> "Your World's a Stage" by Josh Freed (page 397)
> "Saving Animals" by Tom Spears (page 423)

┌───┐
Comparison and Contrast Paragraph Checklist

As you write your comparison and contrast paragraph, review the paragraph checklist on the inside back cover. Also, ask yourself the following questions.

☐ Does my topic sentence explain what I am comparing or contrasting?

☐ Does my paragraph focus on either similarities or differences?

☐ Does my paragraph include a point-by-point or topic-by-topic pattern?

☐ Do all of my supporting examples clearly relate to the topics that are being compared or contrasted?
└───┘

LO 8 Define the purpose of a cause and effect paragraph.

G) The Cause and Effect Paragraph

Cause and effect writing explains why an event happened or what the consequences of such an event were. You often analyze the causes or effects of something. You may worry about what causes your mate to behave in a certain manner, or you may wonder about the effects of fast food on your health.

Because a paragraph is not very long, it is best to focus on either causes or effects. If you do decide to focus on both causes and effects, make sure that your topic sentence expresses your purpose to the reader.

PRACTICE 7

Read the paragraph and answer the questions that follow.

It is quite common to find university students who wait until the last minute to write a term paper or to study for an exam. However, procrastination should be avoided because it has detrimental effects on students' health and well-being. First, students who procrastinate are doomed to suffer lower marks. Instead of taking the time to carefully research the subject, go over written notes, draft an outline, write a draft, and revise and edit it, students do **cursory** research and do not bother preparing an outline. The draft that results from this process is sloppy and filled with logical and grammatical errors, which can lead to a poor grade. Furthermore, there are emotional **hindrances** generated by the pressured nature of rushed work. The sense of a looming deadline causes increased feelings of stress in the procrastinating student, which affects his or her ability to concentrate. Consistent procrastinating over schoolwork combined with other everyday stresses can cause a student to break down. Finally, procrastinating students can damage their physical health. For example, many students stay up all night cramming for exams. They do not get adequate sleep, which impairs judgment and harms the body. Therefore, procrastinating can diminish a student's work, physical condition, mental condition, and academic future.

—Arthur Carlyle, student

cursory: superficial, brief

hindrances: obstacles

1. Underline the topic sentence. Be careful as it may not be the first sentence in the paragraph.

2. Does the paragraph focus on causes or effects? _____

3. Who is the audience? _____

4. Circle three transitional words or phrases that lead the reader from one point to the next.

5. Using your own words, list the three causes or effects.

   _____

   _____

   _____

THE WRITER'S DESK **Exploring**

Write some possible causes and effects for the following topics. Think of two or three ideas for each topic. Then choose whether you would rather write about causes or effects.

EXAMPLE: Why do some parents spoil their children, and how does being spoiled affect the children?

Causes	**Effects**
want child to like them	children become greedy
don't have parenting skills	hurts parent-child relationship
can't say no	children have no patience

Focus on: Causes

1. What are the causes and effects of doing shift work?

Causes	**Effects**
_____	_____
_____	_____
_____	_____
_____	_____

Focus on: _____

2. What are some of the causes and effects of credit card debt?

Causes	**Effects**
_____	_____
_____	_____
_____	_____
_____	_____

Focus on: _____

3. What are the causes and effects of moving to a new place?

Causes	Effects
_____	_____
_____	_____
_____	_____
_____	_____

Focus on: _____

The Topic Sentence

The topic sentence in a cause and effect paragraph must clearly demonstrate whether the focus is on causes, effects, or both.

topic   controlling idea (causes)
I buy fast food <u>for many reasons.</u>

topic   controlling idea (effects)
Fast food <u>has had negative effects on my health.</u>

topic   controlling idea (causes and effects)
Fast food, <u>which I eat for many reasons,</u> <u>has had some negative effects on my health.</u>

HINT ◀ **Do Not Confuse *Affect* and *Effect***

Affect is a verb, and *effect* is a noun. *Affect* (verb) means "to influence or change," and *effect* (noun) means "the result."

verb
Secondhand smoke can <u>affect</u> children's health.

noun
Secondhand smoke has many negative <u>effects</u> on children's health.

THE WRITER'S DESK **Write Topic Sentences**

Write a topic sentence for each of the following topics. Your sentence should have a controlling idea that expresses the direction of the paragraph.

EXAMPLE: Topic: Spoiled children

Topic sentence: <u>*Parents spoil their children for several reasons.*</u>

1. Topic: Doing shift work

Topic sentence: _____

_____

2. Topic: Having credit card debt

Topic sentence: _____

_____

3. Topic: Moving to a new place

Topic sentence: _____

_____

The Supporting Ideas

After you have developed an effective topic sentence, generate supporting ideas. For a cause and effect paragraph, think of examples that clearly show the causes or effects. Then arrange your examples in emphatic order. Emphatic order means that you can place your examples from the most to the least important or from the least to the most important.

A Cause and Effect Paragraph Plan

When you write a cause and effect paragraph plan, think about the order of your ideas. List details under each supporting idea.

Topic sentence: Parents spoil their children for many reasons.

Support 1:   People are not educated about good parenting skills.

    Details: —Schools do not teach how to be a good parent.

              —Some people may follow the habits of their own parents.

Support 2:   They want to be the child's friend instead of an authority figure.

    Details: —Parents won't say no.

              —Parents want to be liked.

Support 3:   They believe that children should have the best things in life.

    Details: —Parents think they are doing their children a favor by buying toys, video games, and so on.

              —They feel that there is nothing wrong with instant gratification.

Support 4:   Some parents are motivated by guilt to overspend on their children.

    Details: —They spend very little time with their children.

              —Parents buy gifts, unnecessary clothing, and so on.

THE WRITER'S DESK **Develop Supporting Ideas**

Choose one of the topic sentences that you wrote for the previous Writer's Desk, and write a detailed paragraph plan.

Topic sentence: _____

_____

Support 1: _____

Details: _____

_____

Support 2: _____

Details: _____

_____

Support 3: _____

Details: _____

_____

Support 4: _____

Details: _____

_____

THE WRITER'S DESK **Write a Cause and Effect Paragraph**

You have made a list of supporting ideas for a topic. Now write a cause and effect paragraph. After you finish writing, remember to revise and edit your paragraph.

MyWritingLab™

Complete these writing assignments at mywritinglab.com

MyWritingLab
THE WRITER'S ROOM

Writing Activity 1: Topics

Write a cause and effect paragraph about one of the following topics. As you consider each topic, think about both causes and effects.

General Topics

1. sleep deprivation
2. an addiction to fast food
3. having a pet
4. having plastic surgery
5. moving to a new country

College and Work-Related Topics

6. participating in team sports
7. having workplace stress
8. high tuition fees
9. working with a friend, mate, or spouse
10. working nights

WRITING LINK
See the Writer's Rooms in the following grammar chapters for more cause and effect writing topics.

Chapter 7, Writer's Room topic 1 (page 143)
Chapter 13, Writer's Room topic 1 (page 229)
Chapter 22, Writer's Room topic 3 (page 315)
Chapter 24, Writer's Room topic 1 (page 337)
Chapter 25, Writer's Room topic 1 (page 346)

Writing Activity 2: Photo Writing

Examine the photo. Consider how clothing choices affect the way that people are judged.

READING LINK
The following readings use cause and effect writing.
"Fat Chance" by Dorothy Nixon (page 399)
"Is It Love or a Trick?" by Jon Katz (page 425)

Cause and Effect Paragraph Checklist

As you write your cause and effect paragraph, review the paragraph checklist on the inside back cover. Also, ask yourself the following questions.

☐ Does my topic sentence indicate clearly that my paragraph focuses on causes, effects, or both?

☐ Do I have adequate supporting examples for causes and/or effects?

☐ Do I make logical and valid points?

☐ Do I use the terms *effect* and *affect* correctly?

LO 9 Define the purpose of a classification paragraph.

H) The Classification Paragraph

In a **classification paragraph**, you sort a subject into more understandable categories. Each of the categories must be part of a larger group, yet they must also be distinct. For example, you might write a paragraph about different categories of housework that must be done in the kitchen, bathroom, and living room, or you could divide the topic into chores done by the children, parents, and grandparents.

To find a topic for a classification paragraph, think of something that can be sorted into different groups. Also, determine a reason for classifying the items. When you are planning your ideas for a classification paragraph, remember two points:

1. **Use a common classification principle.** A **classification principle** is the overall method that you use to sort the subject into categories. To find the classification principle, think about one common characteristic that unites the different

categories. For example, if your subject is "relationships," your classification principle might be any of the following:

- ◆ Types of annoying dates
- ◆ Ways to meet people
- ◆ Dating alone, with another couple, or in groups
- ◆ Types of couples

2. **Sort the subject into distinct categories.** A classification paragraph should have two or more categories.

Topic: Types of couples

Classification principle: Annoying couples

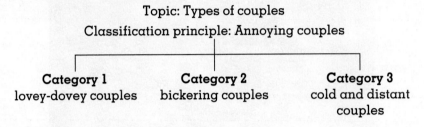

| **Category 1** | **Category 2** | **Category 3** |
| lovey-dovey couples | bickering couples | cold and distant couples |

PRACTICE 8

Read the paragraph and answer the questions that follow.

Violations of the criminal law can be of many different types and can vary in severity. Felonies are the most serious crimes. This category includes acts such as murder, rape, aggravated assault, robbery involving a weapon, and arson. Felons can be sentenced to death or have their property confiscated. A misdemeanor is a less serious crime and consists of an offense such as petty theft, disorderly conduct, or disturbing the peace. It also includes simple assault, in which the victim suffers no serious injury and in which none was intended. In general, misdemeanors can be thought of as a crime punishable by a year or less in prison. A third category of crime is the inchoate offense. Inchoate means "incomplete or partial," so inchoate offenses are those that have not yet been fully carried out. Sometimes an offender is not able to complete a crime. A burglar, for instance, may drop his tools and run if interrupted. Conspiracies are another type of inchoate offense. For example, a woman who intends to kill her husband may make a phone call to find a hit man. The call is evidence of her intent and can result in her imprisonment.

—Frank Schmalleger, excerpt from *Criminal Justice Today*

1. Underline the topic sentence.

2. What are the three categories?

_____   _____   _____

3. What is the classification principle? In other words, how are the three categories of crime distinct?

_____

4. The writer uses emphatic order. How are the crimes listed?

    a. most to least serious   b. least to most serious

    Explain your answer. _____

_____

THE WRITER'S DESK Exploring

Think about the following questions, and write down the first ideas that come to mind. Try to write two or three ideas for each topic.

EXAMPLE: What are some types of financial personalities?

cheapskates, binge spenders, sensible spenders, and squanderers

1. What are some types of pleasant smells?

_____

_____

2. What are some categories of eaters?

_____

_____

3. What are some different types of service workers?

_____

_____

The Topic Sentence

The topic sentence in a classification paragraph clearly indicates what a writer will classify. It also includes the controlling idea, which is the classification principle that the writer will use.

Several types of reality shows try to manipulate viewers.

Topic	reality shows
Classification principle	types that manipulate viewers

You can also mention the types of categories in your topic sentence.

The most beautiful scenes in nature are waterfalls, pine forests, and desert landscapes.

Topic	scenes in nature
Classification principle	types of beautiful scenes

THE WRITER'S DESK Write Topic Sentences

Write a topic sentence for each of the following topics (on page 84). Your sentence should have a controlling idea that expresses the categories you will develop.

EXAMPLE: Topic: Financial personalities

Topic sentence: The three types of people with irrational spending habits are cheapskates, binge spenders, and squanderers.

---

1. Topic: Pleasant smells

    Topic sentence: _____

    _____

2. Topic: Eaters

    Topic sentence: _____

    _____

3. Topic: Service workers

    Topic sentence: _____

    _____

The Supporting Ideas

After you have developed an effective topic sentence, generate supporting ideas. In a classification paragraph, you can list details about each of your categories.

HINT ◄ **Categories Should Not Overlap**

When sorting a topic into categories, make sure that the categories do not overlap. For example, you would not classify *healthy snacks* into vegetables, cheese, and carrots because carrots fall into the vegetable category. Each category should be distinct.

A Classification Paragraph Plan

When you write a classification plan, think of how you will organize your categories. Include different examples in each category.

Topic sentence: Three types of people with irrational spending habits are cheapskates, binge spenders, and squanderers.

Support 1: Cheapskates deprive themselves and others.

Details: —never buy nice clothing

—skimp on quality of food

—never treat others

Support 2: Binge spenders save most of the time but then overspend on crazy items.

Details: —don't make logical choices

—might skimp on meals but then pay a lot for a car

—buy cheap suits but spend too much on shoes

Support 3: The most self-destructive spender is the squanderer.

Details: —might use up entire paycheck on entertainment

—can't make it to the end of the month without going broke

—constantly pays interest on loans and credit cards

Make a Classification Chart

Another way to visualize your categories and your supporting ideas is to make a detailed classification chart. Break down the main topic into several categories, and then give details about each category. A classification chart is a visual representation of your plan.

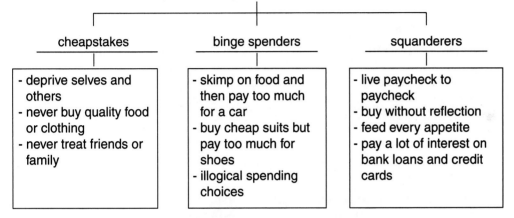

Topic sentence: Three types of people with irriational spending habits are cheapskates, binge spenders, and squanderers.

cheapstakes	binge spenders	squanderers
- deprive selves and others - never buy quality food or clothing - never treat friends or family	- skimp on food and then pay too much for a car - buy cheap suits but pay too much for shoes - illogical spending choices	- live paycheck to paycheck - buy without reflection - feed every appetite - pay a lot of interest on bank loans and credit cards

---

THE WRITER'S DESK **Develop Supporting Ideas**

Choose one of the topic sentences that you wrote for the previous Writer's Desk, and write a detailed paragraph plan. Or, if you prefer, you could make a visual classification chart on a separate sheet of paper.

Topic sentence: _____

_____

Support 1: _____

Details: _____

_____

Support 2: _____

Details: _____

_____

Support 3: _____

Details: _____

_____

MyWritingLab™
**Complete these
writing assignments at**
mywritinglab.com

MyWritingLab

THE WRITER'S ROOM

Writing Activity 1: Topics

Choose any of the following topics, or choose your own topic, and write a classification paragraph.

General Topics

Types of . . .

1. collectors
2. problems in a relationship
3. unhealthy foods
4. video games
5. inexpensive hobbies

College and Work-Related Topics

Types of . . .

6. uniforms
7. college students
8. workplaces
9. communicators
10. stress-coping strategies

Writing Activity 2: Photo Writing

Examine this photo, and think about some classification topics. For example, you might discuss types of pets, types of pet owners, or types of entertainment involving animals. Then write a classification paragraph.

WRITING LINK
See the Writer's Room
in the following grammar
chapters for more
classification writing topics.
Chapter 26, Writer's Room
    topic 2 (page 360)
Chapter 27, Writer's Room
    topic 1 (page 369)

READING LINK
The following reading uses
classification writing.
"What's Your Humor
    Style?" by Louise
    Dobson (page 405)

Classification Paragraph Checklist

As you write your classification paragraph, review the checklist on the inside back cover. Also, ask yourself the following questions.

☐ Does my topic sentence explain the categories that will be discussed?

☐ Do I use a common classification principle to unite the various items?

☐ Do I offer sufficient details to explain each category?

☐ Do I arrange the categories in a logical manner?

☐ Does all of the supporting information relate to the categories that are being discussed?

☐ Do I include categories that do not overlap?

I) The Argument Paragraph

LO 10 Define the purpose of an argument paragraph.

In an **argument paragraph**, you take a position on an issue, and you try to defend your position. For example, you might argue that taxes are too high, that a restaurant is excellent, or that a certain breed of dog should be banned.

Although some people may disagree with you, try to be direct in argument writing. State your point of view clearly and unapologetically.

PRACTICE 9

Read the next paragraph and answer the questions that follow.

Under current Texas law, people with concealed handgun licenses are not permitted to carry their weapons on college campuses, and that law is a good one. Of course, many disagree. The group Students for Concealed Carry (SCC) wants students to have the right to carry guns to college, arguing that responsible, licensed gun-carrying students could prevent an attack such as the one at Virginia Tech, when thirty-six students were killed. However, if a gun-carrying student had opened fire on the shooter at Virginia Tech, how many more students might have died in the crossfire? There could have been multiple students shooting each other, with nobody knowing who the original gunman was. Furthermore, how would police have been able to tell the difference between the "good" shooter and the "bad" shooter? In the event of a sweeping, thoughtless killing spree, more gunfire can only lead to more confusion, more chaos, more injuries, and more deaths. Although we have the right to own weapons, we shouldn't depend on gun-carrying vigilante students to protect us. Finally, college campuses are often at high risk for volatility. Binge drinking is quite common, so factor alcohol use with students carrying weapons around campus, and that could become a deadly recipe. Something should be done about gun violence on college campuses, but arming students is the wrong approach.

—Kyle Cage, student

1. Underline the topic sentence.

2. What are the three main arguments?

   _____

   _____

   _____

3. What transitional expressions does the writer use?

   _____

4. Is the student's argument convincing? Explain why or why not.

_____

_____

THE WRITER'S DESK Exploring

Think about the following questions, and write down the first ideas that come to mind. Try to write two or three ideas for each topic.

EXAMPLE: What are the benefits or disadvantages of youth centers?

I don't know. Youth centers have organized activities such as sports. But they might not provide reliable supervision for vulnerable children.

1. Should the custom of tipping for service be abolished? Why or why not?

_____

_____

_____

2. Did your high school have adequate supplies and equipment? Evaluate a school that you went to.

_____

_____

_____

3. Are social networking sites helpful or harmful? Explain your answer.

_____

_____

_____

The Topic Sentence

The **topic sentence** in an argument paragraph mentions the subject and a debatable point of view about the subject. You can use *should, must,* or *ought to* in your topic sentence.

controlling idea   topic (issue)

Our police forces should not use **racial profiling.**

Your topic sentence can further guide your readers by listing the specific arguments you will make in the paragraph.

controlling idea topic (issue)   argument 1

Parents should not **spank their children** because spanking is a violent act,

argument 2   argument 3

it scares children, and it teaches children to become violent.

HINT ◄ **Write a Debatable Topic Sentence**

Your topic sentence should be a debatable statement. It should not be a fact or a statement of opinion.

Fact	Some breeds of dogs can be aggressive.
	(Who can argue with that point?)
Opinion	I think that pit bulls should be banned.
	(This is a statement of opinion. Nobody can deny that you want pit bulls to be banned. Do not use phrases such as *In my opinion*, *I think*, or *I believe* in your topic sentence.)
Argument	Pit bulls should be banned.
	(This statement is debatable.)

THE WRITER'S DESK **Write Topic Sentences**

Write a topic sentence for each of the following topics. Your sentence should have a controlling idea that expresses the direction of the paragraph. Remember that the goal of the paragraph is to express your viewpoint.

EXAMPLE: Topic: Value of youth centers

Topic sentence: *Our neighborhood needs a youth center.*

1. Topic: Tipping for service

   Topic sentence: _____

   _____

2. Topic: Your high school's resources

   Topic sentence: _____

   _____

3. Topic: The value of social networking sites

   Topic sentence: _____

   _____

The Supporting Ideas

In the body of your paragraph, give convincing supporting arguments. Try to use several types of supporting evidence such as anecdotes, facts and statistics, and answers to the opposition.

◆ **Anecdotes** are specific experiences or stories that support your point of view.

◆ **Facts** are statements that can be verified in some way. **Statistics** are a type of fact. When you use a fact, make sure that your source is reliable.

◆ Think about your opponents' arguments, and provide **answers to the opposition** in response to their arguments.

HINT ◀ Avoid Circular Reasoning

Circular reasoning means that a paragraph restates its main point in various ways but does not provide supporting details. Avoid it by offering separate supporting ideas and precise examples.

Circular

Film actors, who lead decadent lives, should not earn huge salaries because so many average people struggle. Many ordinary folks work long hours and have trouble making ends meet. Some actors work only a few months, earn millions, and then buy ridiculous luxury items. They lose touch with reality. Film studios should cut actors' high salaries and then disburse the remaining amount to people who really need the money.

Improved

Film actors, who often lead decadent lives, should not earn huge salaries while so many average people struggle. Many ordinary folks, such as teachers and nurses, work long hours and have trouble making ends meet. **Yet, the actor Brad Pitt's $20-million-per-movie salary is more than the combined wages of a small city's police department.** Also, some actors lose touch with reality. **Consider the difference between John Travolta, who flies a private jet, and a caregiver like Luisa Moreno, who spends $18.40 a day commuting on public buses. And, in a nation with so much homelessness, the actor Johnny Depp owns an entire island in addition to several houses.** Film studios should cut actors' high salaries and then disburse the remaining amount to people who really need the money.

An Argument Paragraph Plan

When you write an argument paragraph plan, think about how you will organize your arguments. If possible, include different types of supporting evidence: facts, statistics, anecdotes, and answers to the opposition.

Topic sentence: Our neighborhood needs a youth center.

Support 1:	Local teens are bored and get into trouble.
Details:	—gangs hang out in parks
	—teens get involved in the drug trade
	—no activities for local youths
Support 2:	A youth center can provide teens with activities.
Details:	—my old neighborhood had a vibrant youth center
	—we played pool and card games and rapped
	—skateboarding park next to the center attracts people
Support 3:	A youth center will improve our community.
Details:	—make the area more attractive for new residents
	—lower the crime rate
	—provide jobs for local people who build and run the center

THE WRITER'S DESK Develop Supporting Ideas

Choose one of the topic sentences that you wrote for the previous Writer's Desk, and write a paragraph plan. Include supporting arguments, and list a detail for each argument.

Topic sentence: _____

_____

Support 1: _____

   Details: _____

_____

Support 2: _____

   Details: _____

_____

Support 3: _____

   Details: _____

_____

Support 4: _____

   Details: _____

_____

THE WRITER'S DESK Write an Argument Paragraph

You have made a list of supporting ideas for a topic. Now write an argument paragraph. After you finish writing, remember to revise and edit your paragraph.

THE WRITER'S ROOM MyWritingLab

MyWritingLab™
Complete these
writing assignments at
mywritinglab.com

Writing Activity 1: Topics

Write an argument paragraph about one of the following topics. Agree or disagree with the statement. Remember to narrow your topic and to follow the writing process.

WRITING LINK

See the Writer's Rooms in the following grammar chapters for more argument writing topics.

Chapter 7, Writer's Room topic 2 (page 143)
Chapter 13, Writer's Room topic 2 (page 229)
Chapter 16, Writer's Room topic 2 (page 260)
Chapter 17, Writer's Room topic 2 (page 265)
Chapter 18, Writer's Room topic 2 (page 275)
Chapter 20, Writer's Room topic 2 (page 290)
Chapter 23, Writer's Room topic 2 (page 325)
Chapter 25, Writer's Room topic 2 (page 346)

READING LINK

The following readings use argument writing.

"The Cult of Emaciation" by Ben Barry (page 414)
"Shopping for Religion" by Ellen Goodman (page 417)

General Topics

Should

1. the drinking age be lowered?
2. schools abolish homework?
3. teens have a curfew?
4. smoking become illegal?
5. children learn to shoot guns?

College and Work-Related Topics

Should

6. college education be free?
7. [a specific job] be more appreciated?
8. colleges have compulsory art classes?
9. schools have vending machines?
10. all students take a gap year?

Writing Activity 2: Photo Writing

Write an argument paragraph explaining your views about dieting.

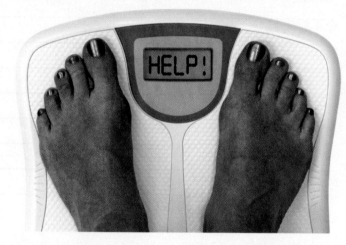

Argument Paragraph Checklist

As you write your argument paragraph, review the paragraph checklist on the inside back cover. Also, ask yourself the following questions.

☐ Does my topic sentence clearly state my position on the issue?

☐ Do I support my position with facts, statistics, anecdotes, or answers to the opposition?

☐ Do my supporting arguments provide evidence that directly supports the topic sentence?

Writing the Essay 5

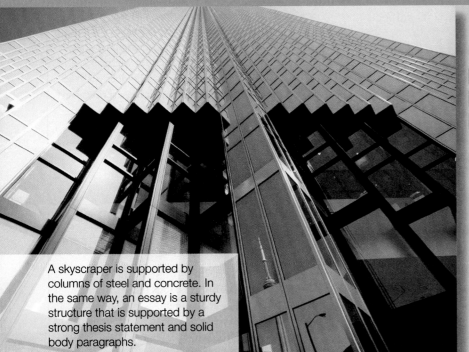

LEARNING OBJECTIVES

LO 1 Explore the essay. **(p. 93)**

LO 2 Explore essay topics. **(p. 96)**

LO 3 Determine the thesis statement. **(p. 97)**

LO 4 Identify supporting ideas. **(p. 100)**

LO 5 Write an essay plan. **(p. 101)**

LO 6 Develop the introduction. **(p. 102)**

LO 7 Develop the conclusion. **(p. 103)**

LO 8 Write a first draft. **(p. 105)**

LO 9 Revise and edit the essay. **(p. 105)**

LO 10 Write a final draft. **(p. 106)**

A skyscraper is supported by columns of steel and concrete. In the same way, an essay is a sturdy structure that is supported by a strong thesis statement and solid body paragraphs.

EXPLORING

Exploring the Essay

LO 1 Explore the essay.

An **essay** is a series of paragraphs that supports one central idea. It is divided into three parts: an **introduction**, a **body**, and a **conclusion**. There is no perfect length for an essay. Some instructors prefer five-paragraph essays, and others may ask for two- or three-page essays. The important thing to remember is that all essays, regardless of length, have certain features: the introductory paragraph introduces the essay's thesis, the body paragraphs provide support for the thesis, and the concluding paragraph brings the essay to a satisfactory close.

Review the examples on pages 94 and 95 to see how different types of sentences and paragraphs can form an essay.

The Sentence

A **sentence** always has a subject and a verb and expresses a complete thought.

> People with bad habits make a negative impression on others.

The Paragraph

A **topic sentence** introduces the subject of a paragraph and shows the writer's attitude toward its subject.

The **body** of a paragraph contains details that support its topic sentence.

A paragraph ends with a **concluding sentence**.

People with bad habits make a negative impression on others. Some individuals display bad habits when interacting with others, such as swearing constantly. Moreover, a person with bad personal hygiene does not win many friends. Also, a person who does not take care of his or her health has a serious bad habit. Everybody should work toward a little self-improvement.

The Essay

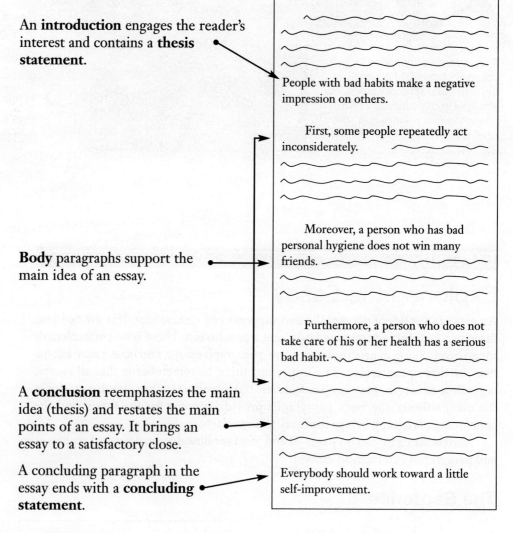

An **introduction** engages the reader's interest and contains a **thesis statement**.

People with bad habits make a negative impression on others.

First, some people repeatedly act inconsiderately.

Body paragraphs support the main idea of an essay.

Moreover, a person who has bad personal hygiene does not win many friends.

Furthermore, a person who does not take care of his or her health has a serious bad habit.

A **conclusion** reemphasizes the main idea (thesis) and restates the main points of an essay. It brings an essay to a satisfactory close.

A concluding paragraph in the essay ends with a **concluding statement**.

Everybody should work toward a little self-improvement.

The Essay's Structure

Each body paragraph begins with a topic sentence.

The introductory paragraph presents the essay's topic and contains its thesis statement.

The title gives a hint about the essay's topic.

The thesis statement contains the essay's topic and its controlling idea.

Bad Habits

Who in the world doesn't have any bad habits? It is part of every human being in the world. Habits are actions that people are so used to doing that they keep on doing them again and again, sometimes without noticing. Bad habits are automatic actions that are undesirable; people should avoid doing them. People with bad habits make a negative impression on others.

First, some people repeatedly act inconsiderately. For instance, those who constantly swear do not think about the effects of their words on others. My brother Mike uses four-letter words, which make me uncomfortable. Also, those who interrupt are disrespectful. They do not value the opinions of others. Finally, people who are late for appointments show a lack of consideration. My best friend Terrel often makes me wait for him, and it hurts our relationship. By being discourteous, a person can lose friends.

Moreover, a person who has bad personal hygiene does not win many friends. People who never wash their hands after going to the bathroom are a good case in point. A person who drinks directly from the milk or juice carton instead of using a glass sets a poor example. It is also very unpleasant to be around people who do not shower regularly or brush their teeth twice a day. For example, my brother needs to shower more often.

Furthermore, a person who does not take care of his or her health has a serious bad habit. Many teenagers spend too much time in front of their computer screen; they don't move. They certainly don't practice sports. Some people don't take care of their bodies because they smoke or take drugs. Also, some people don't eat nutritious foods or get enough sleep, both of which are essential for good health.

The more people display bad habits, the more they create a negative image of themselves. They also set a bad example for family and friends. Of course, nobody is perfect. But that does not mean that people should maintain negative characteristics. The best way to get rid of a bad habit is to have the will to make a change in lifestyle. Everybody should work toward a little self-improvement.

—*Renaud Allard, student*

The concluding paragraph brings the essay to a satisfactory close.

Each body paragraph contains details that support the thesis statement.

Explore Topics

When you are planning your essay, consider your topic, audience, and purpose. Your **topic** is whom or what you are writing about. Your **audience** is your intended reader, and your **purpose** is your reason for writing. Do you hope to entertain, inform, or persuade the reader?

Narrowing the Topic

You may need to narrow your topic (make it more specific) to ensure that it suits your purpose for writing and fits the size of the assignment. To narrow your topic, you can use some exploring methods, such as questioning (asking and answering questions) or brainstorming (jotting a rough list of ideas that come to mind). These strategies are explained in more detail in Chapter 1.

Lester's List to Narrow the Topic

Student writer Lester Robinson used brainstorming and questioning to narrow his broad topic "the Internet."

　　—Types of advertising on the Internet
　　—Should I be concerned about privacy?
　　—Downloading / file sharing
　　—How do I make a Web site?
　　—Problems with Facebook
　　—Internet hackers
　　—Internet bullying
　　—Is Internet addiction on the rise?
　　—e-crime

THE WRITER'S DESK **Narrow the Topic**

Each of the following topics is very broad. Practice narrowing each topic.

EXAMPLE:　Foreign cultures:　traveling to another country

　　　　　　　　　　　　　　learning a foreign language

　　　　　　　　　　　　　　multiculturalism in the United States

1. Work: _____

_____

_____

_____

2. Entertainment: _____

_____

_____

_____

---

3. Housing: _____

_____

_____

_____

DEVELOPING

The Thesis Statement

LO 3 Determine the thesis statement.

Once you have narrowed the topic of your essay, it is important to state your topic clearly in one sentence. Like the topic sentence in a paragraph, the **thesis statement** introduces what the essay is about and arouses the interest of the reader by making a point about the topic.

Characteristics of a Good Thesis Statement

A thesis statement has the following characteristics.

- It expresses the main topic of the essay.
- It contains a controlling idea.
- It is a complete sentence that usually appears in an essay's introductory paragraph.

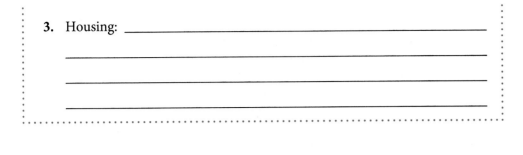

topic   controlling idea

Credit card fraud is a serious problem.

controlling idea   topic

The public has the right to know about **the scandalous private lives of politicians.**

Writing an Effective Thesis Statement

When you develop your thesis statement, ask yourself the following questions.

1. **Is my thesis statement a complete statement that has a controlling idea?**

   Your thesis statement should always reveal a complete thought and make a point about the topic. It should not simply announce the topic.

Incomplete	Campus drinking.
	(This is not a complete statement. A complete sentence has both a subject and a verb.)
Announcement	I will write about campus drinking.
	(This announces the topic but says nothing relevant about the topic. Do not use expressions such as *I will write about* or *My topic is.*)
Thesis statement	Binge drinking is a serious problem on college campuses.

2. **Does my thesis statement make a valid and supportable point?**

Your thesis statement should express a valid point that you can support with details. It should not be a vaguely worded statement, and it should not be a highly questionable generalization.

Vague	Politicians spend too much money.
	(Which politicians? What do they spend it on?)
Invalid point	Politicians are liars.
	(Is this really true for all politicians? This generalization might be difficult to prove.)
Thesis statement	Our mayor has been involved in three serious spending scandals.

HINT   ◀ **Give Specific Details**

Make sure that your thesis statement is very clear. You should give enough details to make it interesting. Your instructor may want you to guide the reader through your main points. You can do this by including specific points that you will later argue in the body of your essay.

My years in high school taught me <u>to stand up for myself</u>, <u>to focus on my goals</u>, and <u>to be an open-minded person</u>.

PRACTICE 1

Identify why each of the following thesis statements is not effective. There may be more than one reason. Then revise each statement.

Announces   Incomplete   Invalid   Vague

EXAMPLE: In this essay, I will discuss hazing in colleges.

Problem:	*Announces*
Revised sentence:	*Colleges should severely punish students who organize or participate in hazing events.*

1. Children today lack discipline.

   Problem: _____

   Revised statement: _____

   _____

2. The problems with online dating.

   Problem: _____

   Revised statement: _____

   _____

3. I am going to discuss the election process.

Problem: _____

Revised statement: _____

_____

4. Everybody is overly dependent on computers.

Problem: _____

Revised statement: _____

_____

5. Saving money.

Problem: _____

Revised statement: _____

_____

_____

THE WRITER'S DESK Write Thesis Statements

For each item, choose a narrowed topic from the previous Writer's Desk on pages 96–97. Then write an interesting thesis statement. Remember that each thesis statement should contain a controlling idea.

EXAMPLE: Topic: **Foreign cultures**

Narrowed topic: Learning a foreign language

Thesis statement: People have many advantages when they learn a

foreign language.

1. Topic: Work

Narrowed topic: _____

Thesis statement: _____

2. Topic: Entertainment

Narrowed topic: _____

Thesis statement: _____

_____

3. Topic: Housing

Narrowed topic: _____

Thesis statement: _____

_____

LO 4 Identify supporting ideas.

The Supporting Ideas

The thesis statement expresses the main idea of the entire essay. In the illustration below, you can see how topic sentences relate to the thesis statement and how details support the topic sentences. Every idea in the essay is unified and supports the thesis.

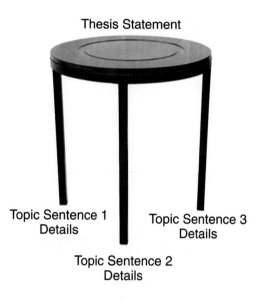

Thesis Statement

Topic Sentence 1
Details

Topic Sentence 3
Details

Topic Sentence 2
Details

Generating Supporting Ideas

To generate ideas for the body paragraphs, you can use exploring strategies such as brainstorming, clustering, or freewriting. Come up with any ideas that can support your thesis statement.

Beatrice's Supporting Ideas

Student writer Beatrice Hammond created a list to support her thesis statement. Then she reread her supporting points and removed ideas that she did not want to develop in her essay.

Thesis statement: People have many advantages when they learn a foreign language.

Supporting points:

—feel comfortable in another country
—easier to develop friendships
—work in different places
—communicate with international clients
—increases flexibility
—creates tolerance for different cultures
—easier to travel
—able to read menus and signs
—~~increases understanding of your own language~~
—~~increases vocabulary~~

THE WRITER'S DESK List Supporting Ideas

Choose one of your thesis statements from the previous Writer's Desk, and create a list of possible supporting ideas. Then review your supporting points and select the best ideas.

Thesis statement: _____

_____

Supporting ideas: _____

_____

_____

_____

_____

_____

_____

_____

_____

_____

_____

The Essay Plan

LO 5 Write an essay plan.

When you write an **essay plan** or **outline**, organize your ideas logically by using time, space, or emphatic order. To create an essay plan, do the following:

- Look at your list of ideas and identify the best supporting ideas.
- Write topic sentences that express the main supporting ideas.
- Add details under each topic sentence.

WRITING LINK
For more information about organizing ideas using time, space, and emphatic order, see pages 22–26 in Chapter 2, "Developing."

Beatrice's Essay Plan

Beatrice wrote topic sentences and supporting examples and organized her ideas into a plan. Notice that her plan begins with a thesis statement, and she indents her supporting ideas.

Thesis statement: People have many advantages when they learn a foreign language.

    I.   People who speak a foreign language find it very useful in the workplace.

          —They can work in a foreign country.

          —They can communicate with international clients.

    II.   Understanding another language makes it easier for people who like to travel.

          —They find it easier to develop friendships while traveling.

          —They can read menus and signs in a foreign country.

III. People who speak another language improve their understanding of different cultures.

—They can analyze cultural values firsthand.

—They get valuable insight into cultural differences by seeing or reading original versions of films or literature.

THE WRITER'S DESK **Write an Essay Plan**

Write an essay plan using your thesis statement and topic sentences that express the supporting details you came up with in the previous Writer's Desk. Organize those ideas, and then write them in the essay plan below.

Thesis statement: _____

_____

I. _____

_____

Details: _____

_____

II. _____

_____

Details: _____

_____

III. _____

_____

Details: _____

_____

Concluding idea: _____

_____

LO 6 Develop the introduction.

The Introduction

After you have made an essay plan, develop the sections of your essay by creating an effective introduction, linking body paragraphs, and forming a conclusion.

The **introductory paragraph** presents the subject of your essay and contains the thesis statement. A strong introduction will capture the reader's attention and make him or her want to read on.

Introduction Styles

You can develop the sentences in the introduction in several different ways. To attract the reader's attention, your introduction can include various types of material.

- General background information
- Historical background information
- An interesting anecdote or a vivid description
- A contrasting position (an idea that is the opposite of the one you will develop)

HINT ◄ Placement of the Thesis Statement

Most introductions begin with sentences that present the topic and lead the reader to the main point of the essay. Generally, the thesis statement is the last sentence in the introduction.

PRACTICE 2

In the following introductions, the thesis statements are in bold print. Read each introduction, and circle the letter of the introduction style that each writer has used.

Beatrice's Introduction

In the era of globalization, the world is getting smaller. People travel more, businesses expand internationally, and many citizens emigrate to a different country. In today's world, groups of people are no longer isolated. They come into contact with many different cultures. **Thus, people have many advantages if they learn a foreign language.**

Style: a. Anecdote   b. General   c. Historical   d. Contrasting Position

1. A few years ago, Brazilian police arrested an illegal alien. When they questioned him, he started speaking in a foreign language, so they hired Ziad Fazah to translate what the man was saying. Fazah claims to be the world's greatest polyglot. Fazah was born in Liberia but now lives in Brazil. He states that he is fluent in fifty-nine different languages. Fazah uses his linguistic abilities to communicate with people from around the world. **Like Fazah, people see that it is advantageous in the modern world to know many languages.**

    Style: a. Anecdote   b. General   c. Historical   d. Contrasting Position

2. Everybody speaks English. It is the international language of communication. Why should an English speaker go to all the trouble of learning a foreign language? Learning another language takes a lot of time and effort. So is the effort really worth it? Of course it is. **People gain many advantages when they learn a foreign language.**

    Style: a. Anecdote   b. General   c. Historical   d. Contrasting Position

3. The origins of human language are controversial. However, scholars have been studying the origins of languages spoken today. There are more than five thousand living languages in the world. Linguists group them into families of languages, each with a common ancestor. **People have many advantages when they learn different languages.**

    Style: a. Anecdote   b. General   c. Historical   d. Contrasting Position

The Conclusion

LO7 Develop the conclusion.

Every essay ends with a **conclusion**. The concluding paragraph rephrases the thesis statement and summarizes the main points in the essay.

Beatrice's Conclusion

Beatrice concluded her essay by restating her main points.

> People who speak another language find it advantageous in the workplace. Being able to communicate in a foreign language makes it easier for people to travel. Becoming proficient in a second language also helps people to understand different cultures.

To make her conclusion more interesting and original, Beatrice could incorporate a prediction, a suggestion, or a quotation.

Prediction	As the world becomes smaller through increased technological communication, people will clearly see the advantages of learning a foreign language.
Suggestion	To gain all the advantages of learning a foreign language, sign up for a language course now.
Quotation	As American modernist poet Ezra Pound stated, "The sum of human wisdom is not contained in any one language."

HINT ◄ **Avoiding Problems in the Conclusion**

In your conclusion, do not contradict your main point, and do not introduce new or irrelevant information.

PRACTICE 3

The following student essay by Véronique Bénard-Jiménez is missing an introduction and a conclusion. Read the essay's body paragraphs, and underline the topic sentence in each. Then, on a separate sheet of paper, write an interesting introduction and an effective conclusion to make this a complete essay.

Write an Introduction

Body Paragraph 1

Start investing as early as possible. College is a good time to start investing, but high school is even better. Open up a savings account. Immediately put any money you receive for your birthday or on holidays in the bank. If you work part time, a good way of increasing your savings is to put at least 10 percent of your earnings into your bank account. You will get compound interest, and your money will grow into a small nest egg over the years.

Body Paragraph 2

Sell something big. You do not necessarily have to be smarter than everyone else to be rich; you need to be extremely persuasive. Bill Gates, Richard Branson, Donald Trump, and many others did not become the wealthiest people in the world only through their intelligence; they became rich through their powers of persuasion. They

sold an idea or a lifestyle. If you have any power of persuasion, you may want to start by selling something.

Body Paragraph 3

Reinvest your profits. When people make money, they are tempted to spend it. Don't do it. The best way to get rich is by not spending your money but by reinvesting your profits. Warren Buffett follows this strategy. When Buffett was in high school, he and a friend bought a pinball machine, which they placed in a barbershop. With their initial profits, the friends bought more pinball machines instead of spending their money. Buffett later used his profits to start a small investment business. By the time he was twenty-six years old, Buffett had amassed almost $200,000. Thus, reinvesting profits is a great idea.

Write a Conclusion

THE WRITER'S DESK **Write an Introduction and a Conclusion**

In previous Writer's Desks in this chapter, you wrote an essay plan. Now write an introduction and a conclusion for your essay on a separate sheet of paper.

The First Draft

LO 8 Write a first draft.

After creating an introduction and conclusion, and after arranging the supporting ideas in a logical order, you are ready to write your first draft. The first draft includes your introduction, several body paragraphs, and your concluding paragraph. Also, think of a title for your first draft.

THE WRITER'S DESK **Write the First Draft**

Using the introduction, conclusion, and essay plan that you created in the previous Writer's Desk exercises, write the first draft of your essay.

REVISING AND EDITING

Revising and Editing the Essay

LO 9 Revise and edit the essay.

Revising and editing are extremely important steps in the writing process. When you revise your essay, you modify it to make it stronger and more convincing. You do this by reading the essay critically, looking for faulty logic, poor organization, or poor sentence style. Then you reorganize and rewrite it, making any necessary changes.

* **Revise for unity.** Verify that all of your body paragraphs support the essay's thesis statement. Also look carefully at each body paragraph to make sure that the sentences support the topic sentence.

* **Revise for adequate support.** Make sure that there are enough details and examples to make your essay strong and convincing.

WRITING LINK
For more information about revising, you may wish to review Chapter 3.

◆ **Revise for coherence.** Make sure that your paragraphs flow smoothly and logically. To guide the reader from one idea to the next, or from one paragraph to the next, try using transitional words or expressions. Here are some examples.

finally	first	furthermore
in conclusion	moreover	second

GRAMMAR LINK
To practice your editing skills, try the exercises in Chapter 29, "Editing Practice."

◆ **Edit for errors.** Proofread your essay to check for errors in punctuation, spelling, grammar, and mechanics. There is an editing guide at the end of this book. It contains some common editing codes that your instructor may use.

THE WRITER'S DESK Revising and Editing Your Essay

In previous Writer's Desks, you developed an essay and wrote the first draft. Now revise and edit your essay.

LO 10 Write a final draft.

The Final Draft

When you have finished revising the first draft of your essay, write the final version. This version should include all the changes that you have made during the revision phase of your work. You should proofread the final copy of your work to check for mistakes in grammar, spelling, mechanics, and punctuation.

THE WRITER'S DESK Writing Your Final Draft

You have developed, revised, and edited your essay. Now write the final draft. Before you give it to your instructor, proofread it one last time to ensure that you have found as many errors as possible.

MyWritingLab™
Complete these writing assignments at mywritinglab.com

MyWritingLab **THE WRITER'S ROOM**

Writing Activity 1: Topics

Choose any of the following topics, or choose your own topic. Then, write an essay. Remember to follow the writing process.

General Topics

1. a family holiday
2. role models
3. reasons to stay single
4. financial mistakes
5. superstitions

College and Work-Related Topics

6. college politics
7. community service
8. feeling pressure
9. future goals
10. positive thinking

Writing Activity 2: Photo Writing

How are traditional parenting roles changing in contemporary times? Use specific examples to support your point of view.

Essay Checklist

Exploring

☐ Think about your topic, audience, and purpose.

☐ Try exploring strategies such as brainstorming or clustering to find and narrow your topic.

Developing

☐ Write a thesis statement that introduces the topic and states the controlling idea.

☐ Support the thesis statement with facts and examples.

☐ Organize your ideas using time, space, or emphatic order.

☐ Write an essay plan to help you visualize the main and supporting ideas.

☐ Write the first draft.

Revising and Editing

☐ Revise for unity.

☐ Revise for adequate support.

☐ Revise for coherence. Use transitional expressions to link ideas.

☐ Edit for errors in spelling, punctuation, grammar, and mechanics.

☐ Write the final draft.

Part II

The Editing Handbook

Why Grammar Is Important Clear writing begins with a well-developed sentence. At the very least, a sentence needs a noun or pronoun and a verb. However, a sentence can become richer when it also includes adjectives, adverbs, conjunctions, interjections, or prepositions.

Clear writing also requires grammatically correct sentences. If your writing contains errors in grammar, you may distract readers from your message, and they may focus, instead, on your inability to communicate clearly. To improve your writing skills, it is useful to understand how the English language works. As your knowledge of grammar conventions increases, you will be more and more able to identify and correct errors in your writing.

In the Editing Handbook, you will learn to spot errors, and you will also learn about the underlying rule that applies to each error.

SECTION 1 Some Parts of Speech
THEME: Lifestyles

 6 Nouns, Determiners, and Prepositions 110

 7 Pronouns 126

SECTION 2 Problems with Verbs
THEME: Entertainment and Culture

 8 Identifying Subjects and Verbs in Simple Sentences 145

 9 Present and Past Tenses 157

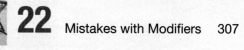

6 Nouns, Determiners, and Prepositions

SECTION THEME: Lifestyles

LEARNING OBJECTIVES

LO 1 Identify nouns. (p. 111)

LO 2 Distinguish count nouns from noncount nouns. (p. 115)

LO 3 Identify determiners. (p. 116)

LO 4 Define prepositions. (p. 120)

In this chapter, you will read about topics related to lifestyles.

GRAMMAR SNAPSHOT

Looking at Nouns, Determiners, and Prepositions

In her essay, "Yoga Y'all," Elizabeth Gilbert recounts her experiences in her yoga class. Certain parts of speech are in bold or are underlined. Identify which words are nouns, determiners, and prepositions.

> While it is true that I have had <u>some</u> fancy yoga **experiences**
> lately (including <u>a</u> recent **period** <u>in</u> <u>an</u> ancient **ashram** <u>in</u> **India**),
> my yoga **background** is actually quite long and gritty. My **mom**
> taught **yoga** <u>in</u> <u>the</u> early 1970s <u>to</u> **housewives** <u>at</u> <u>the</u> **Y.M.C.A.** <u>in</u>
> our blue-collar New England **town**.

In this chapter, you will identify and write about nouns, determiners, and prepositions.

Nouns

LO 1 Identify nouns.

Nouns are words that refer to people, places, or things. Nouns are divided into common nouns and proper nouns.

- **Common nouns** refer to general people, places, or things. Each begins with a lowercase letter. For example, *books, computer*, and *village* are common nouns.
- **Proper nouns** refer to particular people, places, or things. Each begins with a capital letter. For example, *Margaret Mead, the Amazon*, and *Thanksgiving* are proper nouns.

Singular and Plural Nouns

Nouns are either singular or plural. A **singular noun** refers to one of something, while a **plural noun** refers to more than one of something. Regular plural nouns end in *-s* or *-es*.

	Singular	**Plural**
People:	father	fathers
	sister	sisters
Places:	town	towns
	room	rooms
Things:	dish	dishes
	chair	chairs

HINT ◀ Adding *-es*

When a noun ends in *-s, -x, -ch, -sh*, or *-z*, add *-es* to form the plural.

wish–wish**es**   box–box**es**   batch–batch**es**

Irregular Plural Nouns

Irregular plural nouns do not end in *-s* or *-es*. Here are some common irregular nouns.

Singular	**Plural**	**Singular**	**Plural**
child	children	mouse	mice
foot	feet	person	people
goose	geese	tooth	teeth
man	men	woman	women

Other Plural Noun Forms

Some nouns use other rules to form the plural. It is a good idea to memorize both the rules and the exceptions.

1. For nouns ending in *f* or *fe*, change the *f* to *v* and add *-es*.

Singular	**Plural**	**Singular**	**Plural**
life	lives	self	selves
thief	thieves	shelf	shelves

Some exceptions: belief, beliefs; roof, roofs.

2. For nouns ending in a consonant + *y*, change the *y* to *i* and add *-es*.

Singular	Plural	Singular	Plural
baby	bab**ies**	cherry	cherr**ies**
berry	berr**ies**	lady	lad**ies**

If a vowel comes before the final *y*, simply add *-s*.

Singular	Plural	Singular	Plural
boy	boys	key	keys

3. Some nouns remain the same in both singular and plural forms.

Singular	Plural	Singular	Plural
deer	deer	moose	moose
fish	fish	sheep	sheep

4. Some nouns are thought of as being only plural and therefore have no singular form.

Only Plural

clothes	goods	proceeds	scissors
eyeglasses	pants	savings	tweezers

5. Some nouns are **compound nouns**, or nouns with two or more words. To form the plural of compound nouns, add *-s* or *-es* to the last word of the compound noun.

Singular	Plural	Singular	Plural
graphic art	graphic arts	test tube	test tubes
human being	human beings	water pump	water pumps

If the first word in a hyphenated compound noun is a noun, add *-s* to the noun.

Singular	Plural	Singular	Plural
attorney-at-law	attorneys-at-law	passer-by	passers-by
brother-in-law	brothers-in-law	runner-up	runners-up

6. Some nouns that are borrowed from other languages keep the plural form of the original language.

Singular	Plural	Singular	Plural
alumnus	alumni	medium	media
datum	data	phenomenon	phenomena

HINT ◀ *Persons* Versus *People*

There are two plural forms of *person*. *People* is the common plural form.

> Some **people** go to spas to relax. Many **people** like to get a massage.

Persons is used only in a legal or official context.

> The Green Water Spa was broken into by **persons** unknown.

PRACTICE 1

Fill in each blank with either the singular or plural form of the noun. If both the singular and the plural forms are the same, put an *X* in the space.

Singular	Plural
EXAMPLES:	
lottery	*lotteries*
X	pants
1. child	
2. shelf	
3. _____	phenomena
4. sister-in-law	
5. community	
6. _____	media
7. _____	goggles
8. tooth	
9. _____	wives
10. _____	sunglasses
11. high school	
12. credit card	
13. factory	
14. _____	scarves
15. person	

PRACTICE 2

Each sentence contains an incorrect plural noun form. Correct the errors.

bookshelves
EXAMPLE: Bookstores stock many eco-lifestyle books on ~~bookshelfs~~.

1. Lifestyle is defined by how peoples live.

2. It is determined by how human beings view themselfs and others.

3. Personal believes and behaviors reflect lifestyle choices.

4. Green lifestyle supporters choose activitys that do not harm the environment.

5. Such proponents walk their childs to school and recycle garbage.

6. Sociologists conduct many studys of lifestyles in different cultures.

7. Advertisers target mens and women to promote products for different lifestyles.

8. Nowadays, there is a lot of discussion in the medias about healthy habits.

HINT ◄ Key Words for Singular and Plural Nouns

- Use a singular noun after words such as *a, an, one, each, every,* and *another*.

  A <u>person</u> should exercise <u>each</u> **day**.

- Use a plural noun after words such as *two, all, both, many, few, several,* and *some*.

  <u>Some</u> **people** do <u>many</u> different **exercises**.

PRACTICE 3

Underline the key words that help to determine whether the noun in each sentence is singular or plural. Then, correct the errors in singular and plural nouns.

                     customers   dresses
EXAMPLE: <u>Several</u> ~~customer~~ bought <u>ten</u> ~~dress~~.

1. Many person only buy certain brands of consumer goods.

2. Advertisers look for numerous strategy to create an image for a specific product.

3. Publicists want every shoppers to make an emotional connection with a product.

4. Few consumer will buy a specific brand if it does not project their values.

5. Many business have created extremely successful brands.

6. One major companies that has created a recognizable brand is Apple Inc.

7. Apple's logo—an apple with a bite taken out of it—suggests a healthy lifestyles.

HINT ◄ Plural Nouns Follow *"of the"* Expressions

Use a plural noun after expressions such as *one of the, all of the, each of the,* and so on.

Martha Stewart hosts <u>one of the</u> most popular television **shows** about home and lifestyle.

PRACTICE 4

Correct eight errors with singular and plural nouns.

newspapers
EXAMPLE: Many ~~newspaper~~ have a section on lifestyle.

Many Americans are searching for a change in their daily lifes. According to

most experts, there are several actions individuals can take if they want to improve

their lifestyles. One of the most important steps people should take is to analyze what

e

they want out of life. For example, do they want more free time to spend with their

childs, or do they want to start a new business with their brothers-in-laws? If people

a little

slowly make ~~a few~~ small changes each days, they will see a great improvement in the

quality of their lives.

Count Nouns and Noncount Nouns

LO 2 Distinguish count nouns from noncount nouns.

In English, nouns are grouped into two types: count nouns and noncount nouns.

- **Count nouns** refer to people or things that can be counted, such as *car, book*, or *boy*. Count nouns have both a singular and a plural form.

    There is <u>one</u> **spa** in our town but <u>three</u> **spas** in the city.

- **Noncount nouns** refer to things that cannot be counted because they cannot be <u>divided</u>, such as *education* or *paint*. Noncount nouns generally have only the singular form.

ex) **Music** can often lead to a feeling of **serenity**.

    To express a noncount noun as a count noun, you would have to refer to it in terms of *types, varieties,* or *amounts.*

ex) People can practice different <u>types of</u> **meditation**.

    The next table shows some <u>common noncount nouns.</u>

Common Noncount Nouns

Categories of Objects		Food	Nature	Substances
clothing	machinery	bread	dust	chalk
equipment	mail	honey	electricity	charcoal
furniture	money	meat	energy	hair
homework	music	milk	pollution	ink
jewelry	postage	fish	water	paint
luggage	software	rice	wind	paper

Abstract Nouns

advice	effort	information	peace	research
attention	evidence	knowledge	progress	serenity
behavior	health	luck	proof	violence

PRACTICE 5

Change each word in italics to the plural form, if necessary. If you cannot use the plural form, write an *X* in the space.

EXAMPLE: Today's modern spa originated in ancient *society* ___ies___.

1. Since the earliest times, people have believed that bathing in hot spring *water* _____ is a means of attaining good *health* _____.

2. In the Roman Empire, soldiers marched long distances carrying heavy *equipment* _____.

3. After long *march* _____, they bathed in mineral springs to heal aching *muscle* _____.

4. Throughout the empire, bathing became a popular *ritual* _____ for all social *class* _____.

5. Romans would go to the public baths for several *hour* _____ to exercise and socialize.

6. The baths would include *library* _____, *restaurant* _____, and *garden* _____.

7. Each *room* _____ would have comfortable *furniture* _____ and soft *music* _____ to help bathers relax.

8. The ruling class could gather important *information* _____ at the public baths.

9. Archaeological *evidence* _____ shows that in the year 300, the Romans had built more than nine hundred *bath* _____.

10. In subsequent *century* _____, people continued to visit the Roman baths to treat different types of *illness* _____ and maintain a healthy *lifestyle* _____.

 Identify determiners.

Determiners

Determiners are words that identify whether a noun is specific or general.

<u>The</u> motivational **speaker**, Leo Buscaglia, was also <u>an</u> **author**.

You can use many words from different parts of speech as determiners.

Articles	a, an, the
Indefinite pronouns	any, all, both, each, either, every, few, little, many, several
Demonstrative pronouns	this, that, these, those
Numbers	one, two, three

A, An, The

Some determiners can be confusing because you can use them only in specific circumstances. *A* and *an* are general determiners, and *the* is a specific determiner.

general   specific

I want to watch a new film. The films in that collection are fascinating.

◆ Use *a* and *an* before singular count nouns but not before plural or noncount nouns.

singular count noun   noncount noun

Buscaglia wrote a **book** on love. His clients made quick **progress** to overcome their fears.

HINT ◀ A or An

- Use *a* before words that begin with a consonant (*a* man, *a* house).
  Exception: When *u* sounds like *you*, put *a* before it (*a* uniform, *a* university).
- Use *an* before words that begin with a vowel (*an* exhibit, *an* umbrella.)
  Exception: When *h* is silent, put *an* before it (*an* hour, *an* honest man).

◆ Use *the* before nouns that refer to a specific person, place, or thing.

The **writer** Zack Bugovsky also started the **company** Lovelife.

HINT ◀ Avoid Overusing *The*

Do not use *the* before nouns that refer to certain types of things or places.

Languages	He studies ~~the~~ Swahili.
Sports	We played ~~the~~ football.
Most cities and countries	Leo lived near ~~the~~ Lake Tahoe.
Exceptions:	*the* United States, *the* Netherlands

PRACTICE 6

Write either *a*, *an*, or *the* in the space provided. If no determiner is necessary, write *X* in the space.

EXAMPLE: There are many different types of ____X____ yoga positions.

1. Yoga is _____ spiritual way of life that combines mental and physical disciplines. It originated in _____ India more than 5,000 years ago. _____ earliest written descriptions of yoga are found in _____ ancient text. _____ text is called *Yoga Sutras of Patanjali*.

Chapter 6

2. The West became acquainted with yoga initially in _____ nineteenth century. At that time, British scholars translated many Indian books into _____ English. In 1893, _____ Hindu missionary traveled to _____ America. Swami Vivekananda attended _____ religious conference in _____ Chicago. In _____ following years, he journeyed around _____ country lecturing on Hinduism and yoga. In the early 1900s, more yoga masters came to _____ United States and attracted numerous disciples.

3. Today, yoga is extremely popular in _____ Western countries, but it has become _____ commodity. Many people practice yoga only as part of _____ regime of physical exercise. They do not think of it as _____ spiritual way of life.

Many, Few, Much, Little

Use *many* and *few* with (count nouns.)

> <u>Many</u> **writers** have produced self-help books, but <u>few</u> **readers** have completely changed their lives.

Use *much* and *little* with (noncount nouns.)

> Dr. Meghana Kale spent <u>much</u> **time** but very <u>little</u> **money** doing important research.

This, That, These, Those

this → single
these → plural

Both *this* and *these* refer to things that are physically close to the speaker in time or place. Use <u>*this*</u> before <u>singular nouns</u> and <u>*these*</u> before <u>plural nouns</u>.

> <u>These</u> **days**, many articles are written about theories of self-improvement. <u>This</u> **article** on my desk is on the power of positive thinking.

★
distant *{ that → single*
these → plural
from
the speaker in p/t

Use <u>*that*</u> and <u>*those*</u> to refer to things that are <u>physically distant from the speaker in time</u> or place. Use <u>*that*</u> before <u>singular nouns</u> and <u>*those*</u> before <u>plural nouns</u>.

> In the 1970s, many psychologists did research on happiness. In <u>those</u> **years**, scientists tried to develop useful tests to evaluate happiness. In <u>that</u> **building**, there is a library with many books on happiness.

Near the speaker:
this (singular)
these (plural)

Far from the speaker:
that (singular)
those (plural)

PRACTICE 7

Underline the best determiner in each set of parentheses. If no determiner is needed, underline the *X*.

EXAMPLE: (<u>Many</u> / Much) physical activities increase fitness.

1. (Many / Much) people exercise regularly, but (few / little) individuals know about the man who popularized aerobic activities. Dr. Kenneth H. Cooper worked for (the / X) Air Force in (the / X) 1960s. In (these / those) days, scientists did not know why some Air Force recruits had strong muscles but no stamina. (Few / Little) research had been done on (a / the) cardiovascular system. Dr. Cooper found (a / X) link between (a / an) individual's athletic performance and his or her body's ability to use oxygen.

2. Cooper wrote (a / the) book in (the / X) 1968. It was called *Aerobics*. At (this / that) time, the public was becoming interested in (the / X) information about diet and exercise. Dr. Cooper's book revealed how (the / X) individuals could become physically fit. His method became (the / X) basis for modern aerobic programs.

3. (These / Those) days, people complain that they do not have (many / much) time for exercise. Doctors recommend regular (a / the / X) physical activity to maintain (the / X) good health.

PRACTICE 8

Correct fifteen errors with singular nouns, plural nouns, and determiners.

                   attorneys-at-law
EXAMPLE: Many ~~attorney-at-laws~~ were astonished by the result.

1. One of the most interesting study published recently was by two researcher. Jonathan Levy of Stanford University and Shai Danziger of Ben-Gurion University looked at many decision made by a panel of judges. The researchers noticed a phenomena, which they labeled decision fatigue. The study showed that the judges had granted release to prisoners more often during the morning hearings. Little prisoners received a positive judgment if they appeared before the judges in the late afternoon.

2. Psychologists believe that most person may make poorer choices if they have too much options and are tired. For example, Melanie got married last year.

She remembers organizing every details for a wedding. But on the evening she had to make her bridal registry, she developed decision fatigue. This evening, she had spent so many time looking at houseware catalogues that eventually she paid few attention to her choices.

3. Those days, many businesses are taking into consideration the effects of decision fatigue. For instance, companys do not schedule long meetings at the end of the day. Shoppers could probably benefit from the similar strategy. They should not go shopping at the end of a long day.

LO 4 Define prepositions.

Prepositions

Prepositions are words that show concepts such as time, place, direction, and manner. They show connections or relationships between ideas. Some common prepositions are *about, around, at, before, behind, beside, between, for, in, of, on, to, toward,* and *with.*

People go **to** many different spas **for** rest and relaxation.

In the spring, my sister will go **to** a spiritual retreat.

Prepositions of Time and Place

Generally, as a description of a place or time becomes more precise, you move from *in* to *on* to *at.*

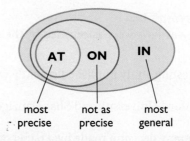

Preposition	Prepositions of Time	Prepositions of Place
in	in a year (in 2011) in a month (in October) in the morning, afternoon, evening in the spring, summer, fall, winter	in a city, country, etc. (in New Orleans, in China, in Central America)
on	on a day of the week (on Tuesday) on a specific date (on March 19) on a specific holiday (on Memorial Day) on my birthday on time ("punctual")	on a specific street (on Main Street) on a planet (on Venus) on certain technological devices (on TV, on the radio, on the phone, on the computer) on top

Preposition	Prepositions of Time	Prepositions of Place
at	at a specific time of day (at 1:30) at night at breakfast, lunch, dinner	at a specific address (at 32 Cardinal Crescent) at a specific building (at the hotel)
from . . . to	from one time to another (from 10 AM to 6 PM)	from one place to another (from New York to Miami)
for	for a period of time (for two hours)	for a distance (for five miles)

HINT ◀ To Versus At

- Use *to* after verbs that indicate movement from one place to another.

  go to   walk to   run to   move to   return to

  Exception: Do not put *to* directly before *home*.

  I'll go ~~to~~ home with you. I won't go to his home.

- Use *at* after verbs that indicate being in one place (and not moving from one place to another).

  wait at   stay at   sit at   look at   work at

PRACTICE 9

Underline the correct prepositions in the parentheses.

EXAMPLE: I take Pilates classes (on / <u>at</u>) my school.

1. Joseph Pilates was born (in / at / X) Germany (in / on) 1880.

2. As a boy, Pilates mostly stayed (at / on) home because he had asthma.

3. (In / On /At) his fourteenth birthday, Pilates started to practice yoga to build up his strength.

4. (In / On) 1925, (in / on) November 2, he moved (from / in) Germany (at / to) England.

5. One day, while walking (at / in / X) home, he got an idea for an exercise method.

6. Eventually, Pilates moved (at / to) New York and opened an exercise studio (in / at) Manhattan (in / on) Eighth Avenue.

7. Pilates and his wife taught classes early (at/ in / on) the morning (at / in / on) 10 a.m.

8. Initially, dancers went (at / in / to) the Pilates Studio to train (for / in) a couple of hours every week.

9. (In / At) 1960, the method started to become popular among celebrities.

10. Presently, there are exercise programs (in / on) television that teach audiences the Pilates method.

HINT ◀ *for, during, since*

Sometimes people confuse the prepositions *for*, *during*, and *since*. Use *during* to explain when something happens, *for* to explain how long it takes to happen, and *since* to indicate the start of an activity.

During the blackout, the meditation center closed **for** two hours.

Since 2008, I have been going to the meditation center.

PRACTICE 10

Correct six errors with prepositions.

        During   for
EXAMPLE: ~~In~~ my vacation, I went swimming ~~since~~ two hours each day.

Recently, I attended a conference on work–life balance. The keynote speech lasted during two hours. One of the experts reported that many Americans do not take their annual vacation. My company encourages employees to take holidays during a few weeks each year to avoid burnout. Last year, on the winter, I went at Hawaii during ten days, and I practiced tai chi. Since three years, I have been taking tai chi lessons.

Common Prepositional Expressions

Many common expressions contain prepositions. A preposition can follow an adjective or a verb. These types of expressions usually express a particular meaning.

This morning, I <u>listened **to**</u> the radio.

The next list contains some of the most common prepositional expressions.

accuse (somebody) of	approve of	care for
acquainted with	argue with	commit to
add to	ask for	comply with
afraid of	associate with	concerned about
agree with	aware of	confronted with
angry about	believe in	consist of
angry with	belong to	count on
apologize for	capable of	deal with
apply for	care about	decide on

decide to	interested in	rely on
depend on	introduce to	rescue from
disappointed about	jealous of	responsible for
disappointed with	keep from	sad about
dream of	located in	satisfied with
escape from	long for	scared of
excited about	look forward to	search for
familiar with	opposed to	similar to
feel like	participate in	specialize in
fond of	patient with	stop (something) from
forget about	pay attention to	succeed in
forgive (someone) for	pay for	take advantage of
friendly with	pray for	take care of
good for	prepared for	thank (someone) for
grateful for	prevent (someone) from	think about
happy about	protect (someone) from	think of
hear about	proud of	tired of
hope for	provide (someone) with	upset about
hopeful about	qualify for	upset with
innocent of	realistic about	willing to
insist on	refer to	wish for
insulted by	related to	worry about

PRACTICE 11

Write the correct prepositions in the following sentences. Use the preceding list of common prepositional expressions to help you.

EXAMPLE: Some people hope ____*for*____ good energy by following the tradition of Feng Shui.

1. Many people are familiar _____ Feng Shui. The method teaches individuals how to live in harmony with nature. Feng Shui complies _____ ancient Chinese laws to help improve a person's quality of life.

2. Feng Shui developed from Taoist philosophy. Followers believe _____ the idea that nature is filled with Qi, or energy. The ancient Chinese wished _____ favorable Qi to ensure their good fortune. They felt that Qi was responsible _____ the flow of positive energy. They insisted _____ building cities using Feng Shui principles.

3. In the West, people became acquainted _____ the essentials of Feng Shui when China encouraged tourism. Americans developed an interest _____ Chinese culture. Since the 1970s, Feng Shui masters have specialized _____ arranging living environments for followers in the West. Critics say that Westerners are not practicing the entire tradition of Feng Shui but are only paying attention _____ parts of the philosophy.

Chapter 6

FINAL REVIEW

A. Correct fourteen errors in singular and plural nouns and determiners.

EXAMPLE: Bottled water is one of the fastest growing commercial ~~beverage~~ beverages in the world.

1. One of the latest trends in American culture is drinking bottled waters. *[water]* Americans bring bottled water to football matches, *[es]* put it in their lunch boxs, *[boxes]* and drink it during business meetings. Many familys choose to drink bottled *[ies]* water rather than tap water. They don't have many confidence in tap water. *[much]* In fact, in the United States, people spend more than $15 billion on bottled *[the]* water every year.

2. Americans consume bottled water for ~~much~~ many reasons. *[many]* *[s]* First, it is very convenient because it can be transported everywhere. Second, ~~a~~ an individual may believe that *[an]* bottled water is safer to drink than tap water. (Those) days, marketers bombard *[These]* consumers with the message that bottled water is a healthier product than tap water. Some companys add unnecessary vitamins or flavors to it. Most *[ies]* importantly, the industry influences ~~persons~~ to believe that buying ~~the~~ bottled *[people]* water is a good lifestyle choice.

B. Correct six preposition errors.

EXAMPLE: Activists worry ~~of~~ about the effects of bottled water on the environment.

3. Activists participated on a discussion about bottled water. Americans should *[in]* be concerned of the environmental effects of bottled water. On one year, *[about]* *[In]* Americans use about 50 billion plastic bottles. To manufacture plastic bottles, companies require billions of gallons of oil. Moreover, around 85 percent of plastic bottles are not recycled. Since twenty years, they have filled up landfills and leaked pollutants into the ground water. Also, people should be aware at *[of]* the expense of transporting bottled water over long distances. For example, bringing water from Fiji at the United States uses fossil fuels. *[to]*

Chapter 6

THE WRITER'S ROOM

MyWritingLab

MyWritingLab™
**Complete these
writing assignments at
mywritinglab.com**

Write about one of the following topics. After you finish writing, circle any plural nouns and underline any determiners.

1. What do you do to reduce stress? Explain some steps you take.

2. What does the term *healthy lifestyle* mean to you? Write a paragraph defining this term.

Checklist: Nouns, Determiners, and Prepositions

When you edit your writing, ask yourself the next set of questions.

☐ Do I use the correct singular or plural form of nouns? Check for errors with the following:

  –spelling of regular plurals
  –count and noncount nouns
  –spelling of irregular plurals

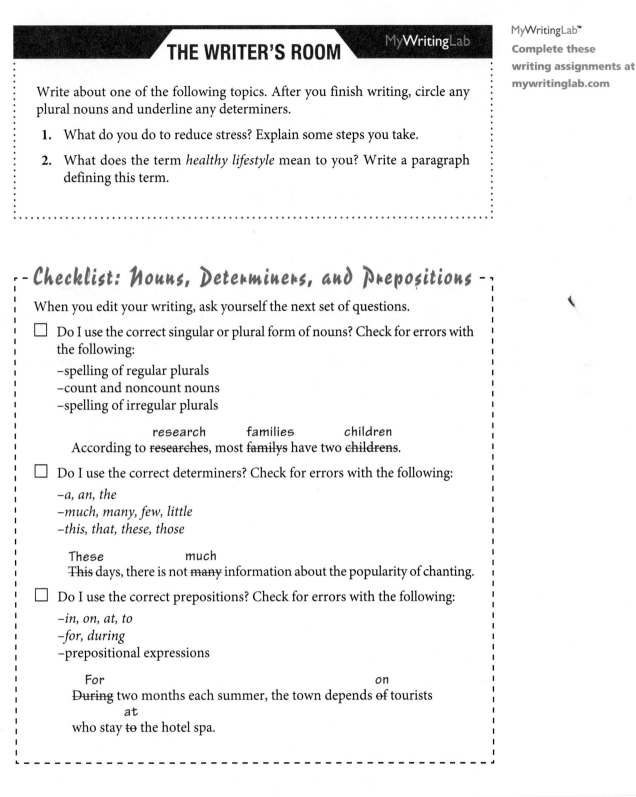

>   research   families   children
> According to ~~researches~~, most ~~familys~~ have two ~~childrens~~.

☐ Do I use the correct determiners? Check for errors with the following:

–*a, an, the*
–*much, many, few, little*
–*this, that, these, those*

>   These   much
> ~~This~~ days, there is not ~~many~~ information about the popularity of chanting.

☐ Do I use the correct prepositions? Check for errors with the following:

–*in, on, at, to*
–*for, during*
–*prepositional expressions*

>   For   on
> ~~During~~ two months each summer, the town depends ~~of~~ tourists
>   at
> who stay ~~to~~ the hotel spa.

7 Pronouns

SECTION THEME: Lifestyles

LEARNING OBJECTIVES

LO 1 Define pronoun–antecedent agreement. (p. 127)

LO 2 Identify indefinite antecedents. (p. 128)

LO 3 Avoid vague pronouns. (p. 130)

LO 4 Avoid pronoun shifts. (p. 131)

LO 5 Define pronoun case. (p. 133)

LO 6 Define possessive pronouns. (p. 134)

LO 7 Identify relative pronouns. (p. 138)

LO 8 Identify reflexive pronouns. (p. 140)

In this chapter, you will read about issues related to food.

GRAMMAR SNAPSHOT

Looking at Pronouns

Catherine Pigott is a freelance writer. In this excerpt, Pigott shows how Western societies' attitude toward food differs from that of African societies. The pronouns are underlined.

I tried desperately, but I could not eat enough to please them. It was hard for me to explain that I come from a culture in which it is almost unseemly for a woman to eat too heartily. It's considered unattractive. It was even harder to explain that to me thin is beautiful, and in my country, we deny ourselves food in our pursuit of perfect slenderness.

In this chapter, you will identify and write pronouns.

Pronoun–Antecedent Agreement

LO 1 Define pronoun–antecedent agreement.

Pronouns are words that replace nouns (people, places, or things), other pronouns, and phrases. A pronoun must agree with its **antecedent**, which is the word to which the pronoun refers. Pronouns must agree in person and number with their antecedents.

> The <u>nutritionist</u> was frustrated because **she** did not receive enough recognition for **her** work.
>
> (*Nutritionist* is the antecedent of *she* and *her*.)

> <u>Farmers</u> are lobbying the government. **They** want better prices for crops.
>
> (*Farmers* is the antecedent of *they*.)

HINT ◢ **Compound Antecedents**

Compound antecedents consist of two or more nouns joined by *and* or *or*. When the nouns are joined by *and*, you must use a plural pronoun to refer to them.

> <u>Susan Brown and Alan Booth</u> published **their** book in 1997.

When the nouns are joined by *or*, you may need a singular or plural pronoun. If both nouns are singular, then use a singular pronoun. If both nouns are plural, use a plural pronoun.

> Does <u>California or Florida</u> have **its** own farming association?

> Have more <u>men or women</u> completed **their** degrees in agriculture?

PRACTICE 1

The pronouns in the following sentences are in bold print. Underline each antecedent.

EXAMPLE: Many European <u>nations</u> wanted a monopoly over the spice trade, so **they** fought wars and established colonies.

1. Since ancient times, Arab merchants established a trade route to India because **they** wanted Eastern spices to sell.

2. Before the Middle Ages, Arabs monopolized the spice trade, and **it** made them fabulously wealthy.

3. Europeans paid high prices for any exotic spice because **they** did not have access to Eastern markets.

4. In the fourteenth century, nutmeg was rarely available, and **its** value was more than the amount of gold.

5. Queen Isabella of Spain funded early sailing expeditions because **she** wanted Spain to control the spice trade.

6. Christopher Columbus decided to sail west because **he** was searching for a shorter route to India.

Chapter 7

7. Some historians believe that the spice trade was important because **it** started the modern globalization movement.

8. Did Portugal or Spain have **its** own trading post in India?

GRAMMAR LINK
For a list of collective nouns, see page 225 in Chapter 13.

HINT ◂ Using Collective Nouns

Collective nouns refer to a group of people or things. The group acts as a unit; therefore, it is singular. For example, *family*, *army*, *crowd*, *audience*, and *organization* are collective nouns.

> The food <u>company</u> advertises **its** products.
>
> The <u>club</u> meets every Thursday. **It** is for overeaters.

PRACTICE 2

Underline the antecedents and write the appropriate pronouns in each blank.

EXAMPLE: Most <u>farmers</u> rise early in the morning, so _____they_____ go to sleep early.

1. In 2009, filmmaker Robert Kenner introduced _____ documentary, *Food, Inc.*, at various film festivals.

2. The documentary examined the food production industry, and _____ conclusions were shocking.

3. Most American farmers sell to big business, and _____ must follow company guidelines for farming methods.

4. For example, Karen Thomas buys seeds from a large company, and _____ sells the crop back to the same company.

5. The company tells Karen how much acreage of seeds to plant, and _____ also sells Karen the pesticides needed for the crop.

6. According to the documentary, corporate farming practices not only harm the environment, but _____ also lead to mistreatment of farm animals.

7. The audience enjoyed the documentary, and _____ clapped loudly when the film finished.

LO 2 Identify indefinite antecedents.

Indefinite Pronouns

Most pronouns refer to a specific person, place, or thing. You can use **indefinite pronouns** when you talk about people or things whose identity is not known or is unimportant. The following table shows some common singular and plural indefinite pronouns.

Indefinite Pronouns

Singular	another	each	nobody	other
	anybody	everybody	no one	somebody
	anyone	everyone	nothing	someone
	anything	everything	one	something
Plural	both, few, many, others, several			
Either singular or plural	all, any, some, half (and other fractions), more, most, none			

Singular Pronouns

When you use a singular indefinite antecedent, also use a singular pronoun to refer to it.

Everyone wonders if **he** or **she** should eat better.

No one wants to reduce **his** or **her** quality of life.

Plural Pronouns

When you use a plural indefinite antecedent, also use a plural pronoun to refer to it.

refers to ✓ *Pronoun*

Our town has many economic problems, and several of **them** are difficult to overcome.

Although small farmers contribute to the economy, many must sell **their** farms.

Pronouns That Can Be Singular or Plural

Some indefinite pronouns can be either singular or plural, depending on the noun to which they refer.

Many food inspectors came to the conference. All were experts in **their** fields.

(*All* refers to food inspectors; therefore, the pronoun is plural.)

Singular pronoun

We read all of the report and agreed with **its** recommendations.

(*All* refers to the report; therefore, the pronoun is singular.)

HINT ◀ Using "of the" Expressions

The subject of a sentence appears before the words *of the*. For example, in sentences containing the expression *one of the* or *each of the*, the subject is the indefinite pronoun *one* or *each*. You must use a singular pronoun to refer to the subject.

One of the cookbooks is missing **its** cover.

If the subject could be either male or female, then use *his or her* to refer to it.

Each of the students has **his or her** own copy of the book.

PRACTICE 3

Underline the correct pronouns.

EXAMPLE: Everybody is concerned about (<u>his or her</u> / their) health.

1.   Almost everyone at some point has eaten (his or her / their) lunch at a fast-food restaurant. But fast food is not only a modern American phenomenon. Every culture has (his or her / its / their) own examples of fast food. In Italy, most people eat (his or her / their) pizza slices at food stalls. In India, fast food is very popular. Few can avoid the temptation of eating (his or her / their) papri chaat or bhelpuri at food stands. In China, no one can resist buying (his or her / their) dumplings while cycling by the food vendors. Lebanon has contributed (its / their) great gift of fast food—the falafel sandwich—to North American cuisine.

2.   Fast food is popular with North Americans. McDonald's and (its /their) competitors are very successful businesses. For example, McDonald's is the largest fast-food chain in the world. Presently, health care workers and (his or her / its / their) government colleagues are closely scrutinizing the effects of fast food on North Americans. Health care workers believe that the popularity of fast food and (its / their) reliance on high-calorie ingredients is one reason for the growing obesity among young people. Each of the fast-food companies has made (its / their) own response to this criticism by offering lower-calorie choices such as salads. However, critics do not think the response is adequate.

LO 3 Avoid vague pronouns.

Vague Pronouns

Avoid using pronouns that could refer to more than one antecedent.

Whatever the pronoun is taking about

Vague	Manolo introduced me to his friend and <u>his</u> sister.
	(Whose sister is it: Manolo's or his friend's?)
Clearer	Manolo introduced me to his friend and **his friend's** sister.

Avoid using the pronouns *it* and *they* if the word has no clear antecedent.

Vague	<u>They</u> say that farmers should receive more tax breaks.
	(Who are *they*?)
Clearer	**Critics of government policy** say that farmers should receive more tax breaks.
Vague	<u>It</u> stated in the newspaper that many farmers are declaring bankruptcy.
	(Who or what is *it*?)
Clearer	**The newspaper article** stated that many farmers are declaring bankruptcy.

indicated that Americans would rather have one's food be tasty than nutritious. The food industry has responded to this consumer preference by adding flavors to packaged foods.

2.   The average American family eats approximately 25 percent of it's meals at restaurants. Fast food contains a lot of artificial flavors, but so does food at other types of restaurants. Macy Robards is a chef at an expensive restaurant in Chicago. Although clients eat fresh ingredients at her restaurant, their also getting a dose of artificial flavors. For example, just as a fast-food chain may use artificial flavor for it's sauces and dressings, she also uses such flavoring in her's.

3.   In his book, *Fast Food Nation*, Eric Schlosser writes that approximately ten thousand new processed food products are marketed every year. Most packaged food contains added flavors and colors. Schlosser is a well-known personality, although some people find he a controversial figure. My friend Lindsey is more influenced by Schlosser's book than me. Lindsey and me discuss his book a lot.

LO 7 Identify relative pronouns.

Relative Pronouns

Relative pronouns can join two short sentences. Here is a list of relative pronouns.

who	whom	whose	which	that
whoever	whomever			

- *Who* (or *whoever*) and *whom* (or *whomever*) always refer to people. *Who* is the subject of the clause, and *whom* is the object of the clause.

    The <u>chef</u> **who** specializes in Japanese cuisine is speaking today.

    The <u>restaurant critic</u> **whom** you met is my sister.
- *Which* always refers to things. *Which* clauses are set off with commas.

    The Irish potato <u>famine</u>, **which** led to mass emigration, was caused by a disease.
- *That* refers to things.

    The history <u>book</u> **that** was about the Irish potato famine was a bestseller.

HINT ◀ Finding the Correct Case

An easy way to determine that your case is correct is to say the sentence with just one pronoun.

The teacher asked her and (**I, me**) to do the presentation.

Possible choices   The teacher asked **I** . . . *or* The teacher asked **me** . . .

Correct answer   The teacher asked her and **me** to do the presentation.

PRACTICE 8

Correct any errors with pronoun case. Write *C* in the space if the sentence is correct.

EXAMPLE: My friend likes this course more than ~~me~~.   _____I (do)_____

1. Sanjay and me are in the same economics class.   _____

2. Him and I have to write a paper on the Green Revolution, a term applied to agriculture changes in the Third World in the 1960s.   _____

3. Professor King informed our class that the term Green Revolution described the export of American farming techniques to third-world nations.   _____

4. My professor told we students that the Green Revolution increased agricultural productivity in the Third World.   _____

5. Sanjay told my friend Gael and I that the Green Revolution also had negative effects.   _____

6. The US government supplied seeds to third-world farmers, but they encountered problems when they planted the seeds.   _____

7. Prakash Gosh was a poor farmer, and wealthier farmers benefited more than him.   _____

8. Him and his wife could not afford to buy seeds because they were too expensive.   _____

9. Also, poorer farmers could not afford to buy expensive farm machinery, so them and their families suffered.   _____

10. Between you and I, I think I might change my major from agricultural economics to computer science.   _____

PRACTICE 9

Correct ten pronoun errors in the next paragraphs.

EXAMPLE: Consumers should read food labels when they buy ~~they're~~ groceries.
their

1.   Everyone wants his or hers food to taste good. But are consumers equally

concerned about the nutritional quality of they're food? A recent focus group

6. _____ Joseph says that he knows that food aid is only a short-term solution to a difficult problem.

7. _____ Politicians must discuss the causes of famine, so you can create conditions to solve this serious problem.

Pronoun Case

LO 5 Define pronoun case.

Pronouns are formed according to the role they play in a sentence. A pronoun can be the subject or object of the sentence, or it can show possession. This chart shows the three main pronoun cases: subjective, objective, and possessive.

Pronoun Case

Singular	Subjective	Objective	Possessive Possessive Adjective	Possessive Pronoun
First person	I	me	my	mine
Second person	you	you	your	yours
Third person	he, she, it, who, whoever	him, her, it, whom, whomever	his, her, its, whose	his, hers
Plural				
First person	we	us	our	ours
Second person	you	you	your	yours
Third person	they	them	their	theirs

Subjective Case

A **subject** performs an action in a sentence. When a pronoun is the subject of the sentence, use the subjective form of the pronoun. In the following sentences, *she* and *we* are the subjects.

> **She** was a chef for about twenty-five years.

> **We** listened to a lecture on food safety yesterday.

Objective Case

An **object** receives an action in a sentence. When a pronoun is the object in the sentence, use the objective form of the pronoun. In the following sentences, *him* and *us* are objects.

> My horticulture class sent **him** an invitation to speak at the ceremony.

> My sister told **us** about the farmer's market.

Possessive Case

A possessive pronoun shows ownership.

♦ **Possessive adjectives** are always placed before the noun that they modify. In the next sentences, *his* and *her* are possessive adjectives.

> He finished **his** <u>essay</u> about fast food, but she did not finish **her** <u>essay</u>.

◆ **Possessive pronouns** replace the possessive adjective and noun. In the next sentence, *her* is a possessive adjective and *theirs* is a possessive pronoun.

She finished **her** <u>essay</u> about fast food, but they did not finish **theirs**.

PRACTICE 6

Underline the pronouns in each sentence. Then identify the case of each pronoun. Write *S* for subjective case, *O* for objective case, and *P* for possessive case.

P

EXAMPLE: Celebrity chef Rachel Ray has <u>her</u> own television show.

1. Recently, celebrity chefs have acquired cult status, and they can influence many people.

2. Some chefs have acquired multimillion-dollar empires by promoting their own cookbooks, television shows, and kitchen products.

3. Julia Child learned how to cook when she moved to Paris with her husband.

4. Child became the first celebrity chef when she showed Americans the secret of French cuisine on her television show.

5. Child wrote easy-to-follow recipes, and her fans gained the self-confidence to cook French food in their homes.

6. Martha Stewart, another celebrity chef, is popular with fans because she gives them tips on how to improve their lifestyle.

7. More recently, Jamie Oliver has become famous, and the public admires him for improving menus in school cafeterias.

8. Nigella Lawson flirts while cooking on television, and many people enjoy watching her.

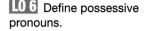 Define possessive pronouns.

Problems with Possessive Pronouns

When using the possessive pronouns *hers* and *theirs*, be careful that you do not add an apostrophe before the *-s*.

hers   theirs
The recipe book is ~~her's~~. The food magazine is ~~their's~~.

Some possessive adjectives sound like certain contractions. Review these examples of commonly confused words.

Possessive adjective	**Their** field trip was canceled.
Contraction	**They're** going to go next week. *(They're = they are.)*

Possessive adjective	**Your** nutritionist will help you choose the right food.
Contraction	**You're** going to enjoy the trip to the agricultural fair. *(You're = you are.)*
Possessive adjective	**Its** theme is about the influence of technology on farming practices.
Contraction	**It's** a book that you should read. *(It's = it is.)*

GRAMMAR LINK
See Chapter 27 for more detailed information about apostrophes.

HINT — *His* or *Her*?

To choose the correct possessive adjective, think about the possessor, *not* the object that is possessed.

• If something belongs to or is a relative of a female, use *her* + noun.

Allison and **her** father both work as chefs.

• If something belongs to or is a relative of a male, use *his* + noun.

John Deere wanted **his** workers to build solid plows.

PRACTICE 7

Underline the correct word in each set of parentheses.

EXAMPLE: The tomatoes are (her / hers), but the corn is (my / mine).

1. Wycliffe Brown has been a farmer since (his / her / their) father retired and gave (he / him) the family farm. He and (his / her) wife, Michelle, grow organic vegetables on (they're / their / theirs) farm. Michelle also grows organic herbs on (his / her / hers) own plot of land. The herd of sheep is also (they're / their / theirs). The farm is quite successful, but (they're / their / theirs) worried about (they're / their / theirs) competitors. In the United States, more and more large corporations are involved in agricultural production.

2. Critics say that corporate farming concentrates agriculture production, distribution, and sales in one business source. As a result, the family farm is losing (it's / its / his) competitive edge and often goes bankrupt. A small farmer may be forced into doing business with a corporation. Proponents of corporate farming claim that mass food production is positive because of (it's / its) cost efficiency. The corporate farm is beneficial for everybody because (it's / its) able to provide cheaper food to more people year round.

3.   My sister and I grew up on a farm where (our / ours) parents practiced organic farming methods, and (we / us) grew up eating only organic produce. My sister and I now have completely different shopping habits. I buy (my / mine) groceries anywhere convenient, but (my / mine) sister buys (her / hers) only at an organic market. Where do (you / your) buy (you / your / you're) food? Maybe (you / your / you're) also an organic food lover?

Pronouns in Comparisons with *Than* or *As*

Avoid making errors in pronoun case when the pronoun follows *than* or *as*. If the pronoun is a subject, use the subjective case. If the pronoun is an object, use the objective case.

If you use the incorrect case, your sentence may have a meaning that you do not intend it to have. Look at the differences in the meanings of the next sentences.

Objective case   I like pizza as much as **him**.

(I like pizza as much as I like him.)

Subjective case   I like pizza as much as **he**.

(I like pizza as much as he likes pizza or I like pizza as much as he does.)

HINT ◀ Complete the Thought

If you are unsure which pronoun case to use, test by completing the thought.

He likes salty snacks more than **I** [like salty snacks].

He likes salty snacks more than [he likes] **me**.

Pronouns in Prepositional Phrases

A **prepositional phrase** is made up of a preposition and its object. Therefore, always use the objective case of the pronoun after a preposition.

To **him**, Will Kellogg was a man with great ideas.

Between **you** and **me**, that breakfast cereal is too sweet.

Pronouns with *And* or *Or*

Use the correct case when nouns and pronouns are joined by *and* or *or*. If the pronouns are the subject, use the subjective case. If the pronouns are the object, use the objective case.

He or I
~~Him or me~~ had to do a presentation on fusion cuisine.

him or me
The instructor asked ~~he or I~~ to present first.

Making Pronouns Consistent in Number

Pronouns and antecedents must agree in **number**. If the antecedent is singular, then the pronoun must be singular. If the antecedent is plural, then the pronoun must be plural.

his or her
Each nutritionist encouraged ~~their~~ clients to talk openly.

he or she
If a chef wants to reduce a restaurant's carbon footprint, ~~they~~ should buy locally grown food.

HINT ◀ **Avoiding Pronoun Shifts in Paragraphs**

Sometimes it is easier to use pronouns consistently in individual sentences than in larger paragraphs or essays. When you write paragraphs and essays, always check that the pronouns agree with the antecedents in person.

In the next example, the pronouns are consistent in the first two sentences. However, they shift in person in the third sentence.

I am studying food sciences, and **I** want to be a nutritionist. In **my**
_I_
program, there are so many courses that **you** cannot decide which ones to take.

PRACTICE 5

Correct the sentences that have pronoun shift errors. Write _C_ beside any sentences that are correct.

they
EXAMPLE: People donate to international food aid, but ~~you~~ never know what percentage of money actually goes to feed the hungry.

1. _____ We went to hear a debate on giving food aid to developing countries, and you couldn't believe what was discussed.

2. _____ International aid workers stated that they provide food to desperate people in famine-stricken areas.

3. _____ Aid worker Joseph Pittman explained that he worked in Somalia for three years, and one met people who had walked for miles to get food.

4. _____ We listened to Joseph talk about his experiences in Somalia, and you were shocked by the stories.

5. _____ I know that there are many causes of famine, and you get especially upset about man-made factors like war or deforestation.

Use *this*, *that*, and *which* only to refer to a specific antecedent.

Vague	The price of cattle feed was raised. <u>This</u> caused many ranchers to panic. (What is *this*?)
Clearer	The price of cattle feed was raised. **This information** caused many ranchers to panic.

HINT ◄ **Avoid Repeating the Subject**

When you clearly mention a subject, do not repeat the subject in pronoun form.

Dr. MacKenzie, he is more than eighty years old.

His course on food science, it is really interesting.

PRACTICE 4

Correct any vague pronoun or repeated subject errors.

                Doctors say
EXAMPLE: ~~They say~~ that people should eat food from all food groups.

1. It says that some Americans are following a raw food diet.

2. The raw food diet it is supposed to have health benefits.

3. Sara told Roxanne that her energy level seemed to increase since starting the diet.

4. They say that cooking food destroys many enzymes.

5. Followers of the diet they eat at least 75 percent of their food raw.

6. I could never try this.

7. It says that some foods, like kidney beans, should never be consumed raw.

8. This can cause food poisoning when eaten.

Pronoun Shifts
Making Pronouns Consistent in Person

LO 4 Avoid pronoun shifts.

Person is the writer's perspective. In some writing assignments, you may use the first person (*I, we*). For other assignments, you may use the second person (*you*) or the third person (*he, she, it, they*). Make sure that your pronouns are consistent in person. Therefore, if you begin writing from one point of view, do not shift unnecessarily to another point of view.

               we
If we had studied, ~~one~~ would have passed the exam.

                  we
We visited every library, but ~~you~~ could not find the book.

◆ *Whose* always shows that something belongs to or is connected with someone or something. It usually replaces the possessive pronoun *his*, *her*, or *their*. Do not confuse *whose* with *who's*, which means "who is."

The food activist was selling fair trade coffee when <u>his</u> car got towed.

The food activist, **whose** car got towed, was selling fair trade coffee.

GRAMMAR LINK
Clauses with *which* are set off with commas. For more information, see Chapter 25, "Commas."

HINT ◀ *Who* or *Whom*?

If you are unsure whether to use *who* or *whom*, test yourself in the following way. Replace *who* or *whom* with another pronoun. If the replacement is a subject such as *he* or *she*, use *who*. If the replacement is an object such as *her* or *him*, use *whom*.

I know a pastry chef **who** makes excellent croissants.
(<u>He</u> makes excellent croissants.)

The man to **whom** you gave a recipe is a restaurant critic.
(You gave your recipe to <u>him</u>.)

PRACTICE 10

Underline the correct relative pronoun in each set of parentheses.

EXAMPLE: Shoppers (<u>who</u> / which) are concerned about food sources buy organically grown produce.

1. People (who / whom) are concerned about the state of the world have a new method of expressing their views.

2. They can influence economic policy by buying food products (who / that) promote social equity.

3. Xing Feng and his wife are consumers for (who / whom) equitable trade is an important issue.

4. Therefore, they buy food (who / that) is labeled "fair trade."

5. Like the Fengs, other food activists (who / whom) believe in social causes also make political statements through consumer choices.

6. The food activism movement, (which / that) is growing rapidly, is a relatively new phenomenon.

7. In the past, consumers would boycott products of companies (which / that) used unfair business practices.

8. Nowadays, businesspeople, for (who / whom) profits are important, look at customer buying trends.

9. Hugo Ricci, (who / whose) company sells fair trade products, says that his business is thriving.

10. The organic food and fair trade industry, (which / that) consumers are heartily supporting, made a profit of more than $30 billion last year.

PRACTICE 11

Write the correct relative pronoun from the list below in each blank. Remember that you cannot use *which* unless the clause is set off with commas.

who   whom   whose   which   that

EXAMPLE: Consumers _____*who*_____ strongly support environmental causes often buy organic food.

1. Organic food has many definitions. Food _____ has been grown using little or no synthetic pesticide or fertilizer is generally labeled organic. Farmers _____ crops are labeled organic do not use genetically modified seeds. Many people _____ buy organic food think that such food is better for their health. However, food _____ has been grown organically is not nutritionally superior to non-organically grown food.

2. Most consumers _____ buy organic food also believe that it is better for the environment. However, not everyone agrees. Dr. Norman Borlaug is considered to be the father of the Green Revolution. He believes that organic farming produces lower crop yields, requiring more land use. Synthetic fertilizers _____ contribute to greater crop production help the environment significantly more than organic methods.

3. Consumers for _____ health and environment are important should consider both sides of the issue. Certainly, the organic food industry, _____ is very profitable, will continue to grow in popularity in the near future.

LO 8 Identify reflexive pronouns.

Reflexive Pronouns (-*self*, -*selves*)

Use **reflexive pronouns** when you want to emphasize that the subject does an action to him- or herself.

> <u>We</u> ask **ourselves** many questions.

> The <u>book</u> sells **itself** because it is so good.

It is not typical to use reflexive pronouns for personal care activities, such as washing or shaving. However, you can use reflexive pronouns to draw attention to a surprising or an unusual action.

> My three-year-old **sister** fed **herself**.

> (The girl probably could not feed herself at a previous time.)

The next chart shows subjective pronouns and the reflexive pronouns that relate to them.

Pronouns That End with *-self* or *-selves*

Singular	Antecedent	Reflexive Pronouns
First person	I	myself
Second person	you	yourself
Third person	he, she, it	himself, herself, itself
Plural		
First person	we	ourselves
Second person	you	yourselves
Third person	they	themselves

HINT ◀ **Common Errors with Reflexive Pronouns**

Hisself and *theirselves* do not exist in English. These are incorrect ways to say *himself* and *themselves*.

themselves
The students went by ~~theirselves~~ to the lecture.

himself
The pastry chef worked by ~~hisself~~.

PRACTICE 12

Fill in the blanks with the correct reflexive pronouns.

EXAMPLE: I do not like to eat by _____ myself _____ .

1. Many times I wish that our dinner would get ready by

    _____ .

2. I often cook meals by _____ .

3. Sometimes my children start preparing dinner by _____ .

4. My son Alex goes grocery shopping by _____ .

5. My daughter plans some meals by _____ .

6. When my children make a fabulous dinner, I always say, "Congratulate

    _____ on a job well done."

7. If my husband is late coming home from work, my children and I eat by

    _____ .

8. On such occasions, he humbly offers to clean the kitchen by

    _____ .

9. Do you eat dinner with others or by _____ ?

Chapter 7

FINAL REVIEW

Read the following paragraphs and correct twenty pronoun errors.

My friend and I
EXAMPLE: ~~Me and my friend~~ enjoy eating different types of food.

1. Mark Ruttoli is a chef which loves cooking for his family. However, Mark's four-year-old daughter, Rachel, loves fast food. Every day, she begs his father to take her to McDonald's. One evening, Mark caved in to Rachel's request. Him and Rachel went to the restaurant where she ordered a Happy Meal. It came with a toy dog. The next day, Rachel saw a McDonald's commercial promoting twelve different Happy Meal toys. Of course, she wanted to go back to McDonald's so she could collect all twelve.

2. Americans they are facing a rising rate of obesity among young people. It says that over 17 percent of children are obese. Politicians and health workers are worried. Each group is expressing their opinions about this.

3. Advertising food to children might be one cause for increasing obesity rates. They say that food companies spend over $1 billion on marketing food to children. Industry executives, for who profits are important, use different strategies to promote products. For example, I watch cartoons with my daughter, and you cannot believe the large number of food commercials during the programs. In addition, food companies use interactive Web sites to target children. Young people make videos about how good the food product is. Then, children send in they're videos to the Web site. A government committee has promised that they will develop guidelines on advertising food to children.

4. Mark, whose interested in food and nutrition, is concerned. He is more knowledgeable about the effects of advertising than me. He thinks that food companies try to create an emotional link between the food product and

children. Between you and I, I think he is correct. Mark, for who health is an

important issue, is going to start a blog with advice about nutrition. He told

my friend and I that he is also starting cooking classes for teens. The cooking

class who Mark is giving will focus on healthy eating habits. My teenage son

likes to cook. Each Saturday, he makes a meal for the family by hisself. I will

ask my son to take the course. Will you tell you're children about

Mark's course?

MyWritingLab™
**Complete these
writing assignments at
mywritinglab.com**

THE WRITER'S ROOM MyWritingLab

Write about one of the following topics. After you finish writing, circle any
pronouns and check for pronoun–antecedent agreement, pronoun case, and
pronoun shift.

1. What causes people to eat junk food?

2. Should fast-food companies be held responsible for some of the health
problems in our society? Explain your point of view.

Checklist: Pronouns

When you edit your writing, ask yourself the next set of questions.

☐ Do I use the correct pronoun case? Check for errors with the following:
   –subjective, objective, and possessive case
   –comparisons with *than* or *as*
   –prepositional phrases
   –pronouns after *and* or *or*

                       me   me
   Between you and I, my parents were stricter with my brother than I.

☐ Do I use the correct relative pronouns? Check for errors with *who, whom,*
or *whose.*

             whom
   My husband, ~~who~~ you have met, is a coffee salesman.

☐ Do my pronouns and antecedents agree in number and person? Check for errors with indefinite pronouns and collective nouns.

                                     its

The government announced ~~their~~ new policy: everyone will have
his or her
~~their~~ own identity card.

☐ Are my pronoun references clear? Check for vague pronouns and inconsistent points of view.

Policymakers   I

~~They~~ say that family farms are suffering. I read the report, and ~~you~~

could not believe what it said.

READING LINK

To read more about issues related to lifestyles, see the next essays.

"Fish Cheeks" by Amy Tan (page 393)

"Your World's a Stage" by Josh Freed (page 397)

"Fat Chance" by Dorothy Nixon (page 399)

THE WRITER'S CIRCLE   Collaborative Activity

Work with a partner to write a short paragraph about what your partner has in his or her purse, backpack, pencil case, or locker. Describe the items and what the person does with those items. Then exchange paragraphs with your partner and check that nouns and pronouns are used correctly.

Identifying Subjects and Verbs in Simple Sentences

8

SECTION THEME: Entertainment and Culture

In this chapter, you will read about music and musicians.

LEARNING OBJECTIVES

LO 1 Identify simple and compound subjects. **(p. 146)**

LO 2 Identify prepositional phrases. **(p. 149)**

LO 3 Identify complete verbs, compound verbs, linking verbs, and helping verbs. **(p. 150)**

GRAMMAR SNAPSHOT

Looking at Subjects and Verbs

Sonia Margossian teaches singing. In the next excerpt from a speech, she discusses proper breathing techniques. Notice that subjects are in bold type and the verbs are underlined. Also observe that some sentences have no visible subjects.

Stand straight, and place your hands on your stomach, just below the ribs. Then take a long, deep breath, and carry the air to the bottom of your lungs. Your **shoulders** should not move as you breathe. As **you** continue to inhale, your **chest** will inflate.

In this chapter, you will identify subjects and verbs in simple sentences.

145

LO 1 Identify simple and compound subjects.

Identifying Subjects

A **sentence** has a subject and a verb, and it expresses a complete thought. The **subject** tells you who or what the sentence is about. The **verb** expresses an action or state. If a sentence is missing a subject or a verb, it is incomplete.

> subject verb
> Prehistoric **humans** banged on hollow logs to make music.

Singular or Plural Subjects

Subjects may be singular or plural. To determine the subject of a sentence, ask yourself who or what the sentence is about.

A **singular subject** is one person, place, or thing.

> **Lady Gaga** learned to play piano at an early age.
>
> The **violin** is difficult to master.

A **plural subject** is more than one person, place, or thing.

> **People** still listen to Mozart's music.
>
> Some **instruments** are easy to learn.

Pronouns as Subjects

A **subject pronoun** (*he, she, it, you, we, they*) can act as the subject of a sentence.

> That piano is beautiful, but **it** is very expensive.
>
> Louisa has a great voice. **She** should sing more often.

Gerunds (*-ing* Words) as Subjects

Sometimes a **gerund** (the *-ing* form of a verb, acting as a noun) is the subject of a sentence.

> **Listening** is an important skill.
>
> **Dancing** can improve your cardiovascular health.

HINT ◀ **Simple Versus Complete Subject**

In a sentence, the **simple subject** is the noun or pronoun. The complete name of a person, place, or organization is a simple subject.

> she   guitar   Kendrick Lamar   Sony Music Corporation

The **complete subject** is the noun, plus the words that describe the noun. In these examples, the descriptive words are underlined.

> new acoustic guitar   Jazmine's upright piano   the tiny microphone

> simple subject
> The expensive old **violin** is very fragile.
> complete subject

PRACTICE 1

Underline the complete subject in each sentence. (Remember to underline the subject and the words that describe the subject.) Then circle the simple subject.

EXAMPLE: <u>A famous recording (artist)</u> is Adele.

1. Adele Laurie Blue Adkins was born on May 5, 1988.
2. Her supportive family was not musical.
3. The aspiring young singer entered a performing arts school.
4. Singing became her greatest talent.
5. Her best friend posted a video of Adele on MySpace in 2006.
6. A record company executive saw the video and contacted Adele.
7. Shingai Shoniwa lived next door.
8. The Noisettes vocalist influenced Adele.
9. Writing songs became a priority for the British singer.
10. Many young fans attempt to sing "Rolling in the Deep."

Compound Subjects

Many sentences have more than one subject. These are called compound subjects. Notice that *and* is not part of the compound subject.

> **Guitars**, **lutes**, and **banjos** are stringed instruments.

> **Reporters** and **photographers** crowded around the singer.

PRACTICE 2

Complete each sentence by adding one or more logical subjects.

EXAMPLE: _____Rihanna_____ sings and dances.

1. In my opinion, _____ is the most interesting type of music.

2. _____ is not one of my greatest talents.

3. _____, _____, and _____ are great musicians.

4. The _____ is missing a string.

5. The _____ and _____ are my least favorite instruments.

Chapter 8

Chapter 8

Special Subject Problems

Unstated Subjects (Commands)

In a sentence that expresses a command, the subject is unstated, but it is still understood. The unstated subject is *you*. (The word *should* is implied.)

> Practice every day.

> Do not judge the musician harshly.

Here, There

Here and *there* are not subjects. In sentences that begin with *here* or *there*, the subject follows the verb.

> verb   subject
> There <u>are</u> five **ways** to improve your voice.

> verb   subject
> Here <u>is</u> my **iPod**.

HINT ◄ Ask *Who* or *What*

When you are trying to determine the subject, read the sentence carefully and ask yourself who or what the sentence is about. Do not presume that all nouns are the subjects in a sentence. For example, in the next sentence, *music*, *dance*, and *occasions* are nouns, but they are not the subject.

   Most **cultures** use music and dance to celebrate special occasions.

PRACTICE 3

Circle one or more simple subjects in the next sentences. If the subject is unstated, write "you."

> You (should)
EXAMPLE: Listen to music as often as possible.

1. There are various MP3 players in stores.

2. Many young people listen to loud music on their iPods or smartphones.

3. Marco and Gina constantly wear headphones to listen to songs.

4. Now, the two young students have constant ringing in their ears.

5. Tiny headphones concentrate the sounds in people's ears.

6. Loud noise destroys the hair-like cells inside the ear.

7. A power saw may be quieter than the music from an MP3 player.

8. Avoid prolonged exposure to loud music.

Identifying Prepositional Phrases

A **preposition** is a word that links nouns, pronouns, and phrases to other words in a sentence. It expresses a relationship based on movement or position.

Common Prepositions

about	around	beyond	from	off	to
above	at	by	in	on	toward
across	before	despite	inside	onto	under
after	behind	down	into	out	until
against	below	during	like	outside	up
along	beside	except	near	over	with
among	between	for	of	through	within

A **phrase** is a group of words that is missing a subject, a verb, or both, and it is not a complete sentence. A **prepositional phrase** is made up of a preposition and its object (a noun or a pronoun).

Preposition + Object

in	the morning
over	the rainbow
with	some friends

HINT ◀ Nouns Are Not Always Subjects

Because the object of a preposition is a noun, it may look like a subject. However, the object in a prepositional phrase is never the subject of the sentence.

subject
With her husband, **Carly** composed a hit song.

To help you identify the subject of a sentence, it is a good idea to put parentheses around prepositional phrases, cross them out, or identify them in some other way. In each of the following sentences, the subject is in bold type and the prepositional phrase is in parentheses.

(In most countries,) particular **musical styles** exist.

The **studio** (on Slater Street) is closed.

The **information** (in that magazine) is true.

PRACTICE 4

In each sentence, place parentheses around one or more prepositional phrases. Then circle the simple subject.

EXAMPLE: (According to Kristin Leutwyler of *Scientific American*,) prehistoric (humans) listened to music.

1. In the past, Neanderthals may have had a musical tradition.

2. In 1996, Slovenian archeologist Ivan Turk discovered a small bone flute.

3. Over 50,000 years ago, the sweet-sounding flute was carved from the thigh of a cave bear.

4. With four nearly perfect holes in a row, the wind instrument was quite sophisticated.

5. In a speech, Boston biologist Jelle Atema discussed the technical skills of the ancient people.

6. Early humans, with their friends and family, probably played music together.

7. In other places such as Africa, South America, and China, scientists have found very old wind and stringed instruments.

8. Perhaps ancient people without a common language could communicate with musical sounds.

PRACTICE 5

If the underlined word is the subject, write *C* (for "correct") in the space. If the underlined word is not the subject, then circle the correct subject(s).

EXAMPLES: In 1959, (Michael Jackson) was born. _____

The music star worked throughout his childhood. __*C*__

1. Some young children demonstrate exceptional musical gifts. _____

2. An amazing child prodigy is pianist Emily Bear. _____

3. With intense concentration, seven-year-old Emily plays beautifully. _____

4. The child's father and mother do not force her to perform. _____

5. However, without a doubt, some talented children are exploited. _____

6. At the age of five, Michael Jackson became a part of his family's musical act. _____

7. His days were spent studying and then rehearsing. _____

8. As a child, Jackson had the confidence and poise of an adult. _____

9. As an adult, the musical legend searched for his lost childhood. _____

LO 3 Identify complete verbs, compound verbs, linking verbs, and helping verbs.

Identifying Verbs

Every sentence must contain a verb. The **verb** either expresses what the subject does or links the subject to other descriptive words.

Action Verbs

Action verbs describe the actions that the subject performs.

The musicians performed in Carnegie Hall.

The Irish dancers stamped their heels in time to the music.

Compound Verbs

When a subject performs more than one action, the verbs are called **compound verbs**.

Mr. Gibson makes, polishes, and sells good-quality guitars.

PRACTICE 6

Fill in each space with an appropriate and interesting action verb.

EXAMPLE: The Petersons _____paid_____ for their tickets and

_____entered_____ the theater.

1. Adam, the pianist, _____ the audience.

2. He then _____ beautifully.

3. At the end of the performance, the audience _____ and

_____.

4. The performer _____ to his dressing room.

5. He _____ on his sofa, exhausted.

6. Somebody _____ on the door and

_____.

Linking Verbs

Linking verbs (or state verbs) do not describe an action; instead, they describe a state of being or give information about the subject. The most common linking verb is *be* (*am, are, is, was, were*).

The harp <u>is</u> a lovely instrument.

Those sound systems <u>are</u> unreliable.

Other linking verbs link the subject with descriptive words.

    subject   linking verb   descriptive word
That **music**   <u>sounds</u>   *good.*

    subject   linking verb   descriptive words
Felicia   <u>seems</u>   *quite eccentric.*

Here are some common linking verbs:

act	feel	seem
appear	get	smell
be (am, is, are, was, were)	look	sound
become	remain	taste

PRACTICE 7

Underline the linking verb in these sentences.

EXAMPLE: Jay <u>is</u> small and thin.

1. Jay Greenberg looks very ordinary.

2. However, Jay is a musical genius.

3. He became a Julliard student at the age of ten.

4. Composer Samuel Zyman was shocked at the young boy's abilities.

5. Jay's symphonies sound haunting and powerful.

6. The boy's nickname is "Blue Jay."

7. He appears peaceful and content.

8. He remains a musical prodigy.

HINT ◀ **Infinitives Are Not the Main Verb**

Infinitives are verbs preceded by *to*, such as *to sing*, *to play*, and *to run*. An infinitive is never the main verb in a sentence.

verb infinitive   verb infinitive

Chuck Berry <u>wanted</u> to be famous. He <u>hoped</u> to become a music legend.

PRACTICE 8

Circle the simple subjects and underline the verbs in the following sentences. Some sentences have more than one verb. Write *L* beside any sentence that contains a linking verb.

EXAMPLE: In the nineteenth century, (music) was a local activity.   L

1. Nowadays, many talented amateur musicians are able to find an audience online.

2. Justin Bieber was a YouTube sensation in 2008.

3. Some singers become famous after appearing on talent shows.

4. In 2009, Susan Boyle appeared in a British talent show.

5. The frumpy Scottish woman seemed unattractive and comical.

6. Audience members snickered and rolled their eyes.

7. Then Boyle opened her mouth and sang.

8. The woman with bushy eyebrows became an Internet sensation.

9. During a two-week period, over 100 million people watched her on YouTube.

10. In 2010, the busy Scottish singer released her first album.

Susan Boyle

Helping Verbs

Many verbs contain two or more words: a main verb and a helping verb. The **main verb** expresses what the subject does or links the subject to descriptive words. The **helping verb** combines with the main verb to indicate tense, negative structure, or question structure.

Be, Have, Do

The common helping verbs *be, have,* and *do* combine with the main verb to indicate a tense, negative structure, or question structure.

>   HV   HV   V
> Some songs <u>have been</u> <u>banned</u> from radio station play lists.

Modals

A modal is another type of helping verb. It indicates ability (*can*), obligation (*must*), possibility (*may, might, could*), advice (*should*), and so on.

>   HV   V
> Violent lyrics <u>can</u> <u>influence</u> children.

Questions

In question forms, the first helping verb usually appears before the subject.

>   HV   subject   V
> <u>Should</u> radio **stations** <u>censor</u> song lyrics?

>   HV   subject   V
> <u>Do</u> violent, sexist, or racist **songs** <u>influence</u> young listeners?

> **HINT** ◄ **Interrupting Words and Phrases**
>
> Interrupting words may appear between verbs, but they are *not* part of the verb. Some interrupting words are *always, easily, ever, never, not, often, sometimes,* and *usually*.
>
>   HV   interrupter V
> Blues music <u>can</u> **sometimes** <u>be</u> sorrowful.

PRACTICE 9

Underline each complete verb once. Then underline each main verb twice.

EXAMPLE: Musicians with perfect pitch <u><u>are</u> **envied**</u>.

1. According to an article in *Scientific American,* very few people have achieved perfect pitch.

2. Human beings with absolute pitch will easily sing an F sharp.

3. Most people do not have this ability.

4. Only one person in ten thousand can identify a note perfectly.

5. Do people from some cultures have a superior ability to recognize tones?

6. In languages such as Vietnamese and Mandarin, people can pronounce one word in several different ways.

7. The meaning of each word may depend on the tone of the word.

8. Diana Deutsch of the University of California has discussed the topic in her lectures.

9. According to Deutch, native speakers of tonal languages, even those with no musical training, can recognize and repeat notes perfectly.

10. Perhaps tonal words should be used to teach children about pitch.

FINAL REVIEW

Circle each simple subject and underline each complete verb. Underline each main verb twice. If prepositional phrases confuse you, you can cross them out or put them in parentheses.

EXAMPLE: A (university) in Maryland <u>studied</u> the effects of music on health. The (study) was <u>published</u> in 2009.

1. Across the nation, citizens hope to become famous singers. Television programs have capitalized on this deep-seated desire. There are long line-ups at every *American Idol* audition. The popular program is watched by millions of viewers.

2. Of course, good singing is not a universal skill. Many people do not sing well. For instance, Jamie Orchard and Ryan Woo claim to have horrible voices. But singing may actually be beneficial for our bodies and our overall health. Everybody should sing sometimes.

3. A prominent researcher from George Washington University has published studies about singing and health. Dr. Gene D. Cohen did not expect singing to have a noticeable effect on human bodies. He decided to study two groups of older adults. One group was required to sing every day. The elderly men and women in the singing group felt better and had higher energy than those in the non-singing group. A University of Frankfurt study revealed similar results. Regular singing can stimulate blood circulation and reduce blood pressure.

4. Do you have some musical talent? Are you a good singer? Clearly, there are many good reasons to sing. You should not worry about the quality of your voice. You can always find a private place to create music. Daily singing can become part of your health regime.

THE WRITER'S ROOM   MyWritingLab

MyWritingLab™
Complete these
writing assignments at
mywritinglab.com

Write about one of the following topics. After you finish writing, circle your subjects and underline your verbs. Underline main verbs twice.

1. What qualities does a professional singer need? List at least five qualities.

2. Compare two different singers. How are they similar or different?

Checklist: Subjects and Verbs

☐ To identify **subjects**, look for words that tell you who or what the sentence is about.

☐ To identify **verbs**, look for words that express what the subject does or that link the subject to descriptive words.

☐ To identify **action verbs**, look for words that describe the action that the subject performs.

☐ To identify **linking verbs**, look for words that describe a state of being or that link the subject with descriptive words.

☐ To identify **helping verbs**, look for words that combine with the main verb to indicate tense, negative structure, or question structure.

☐ To identify a **prepositional phrase**, look for words that consist of a preposition and its object. The object of a prepositional phrase cannot be the subject of a sentence.

```
    ┌─── prepositional ───┐              helping
               phrase             ┌─ subject ─┐ verb  verb
                                              ↓      ↓
    With her powerful voice, Jennifer Hudson has found fame.
```

Present and Past Tenses

9

SECTION THEME: Entertainment and Culture

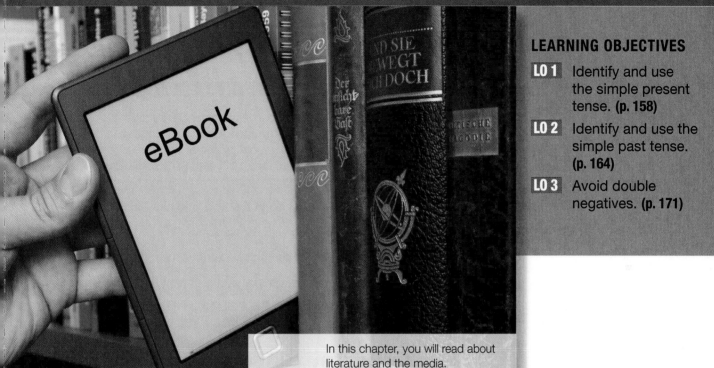

LEARNING OBJECTIVES

LO 1 Identify and use the simple present tense. **(p. 158)**

LO 2 Identify and use the simple past tense. **(p. 164)**

LO 3 Avoid double negatives. **(p. 171)**

In this chapter, you will read about literature and the media.

GRAMMAR SNAPSHOT

Looking at Present and Past Tenses

In 1902, W. W. Jacobs wrote one of the most frightening tales in literature, "The Monkey's Paw." In this excerpt, the past tense verbs are underlined. Which past tense verbs are irregular?

> She <u>noticed</u> that the stranger <u>was</u> well dressed and <u>wore</u> a silk hat of glossy newness. Three times he <u>paused</u> at the gate, and then <u>walked</u> on again. The fourth time he <u>stood</u> with his hand upon it, and then with sudden resolution <u>flung</u> it open and <u>walked</u> up the path.

In this chapter, you will identify and write present and past tense verbs.

Understanding Verb Tense

A verb shows an action or a state of being. A **verb tense** indicates when an action occurred. For example, review the various tenses of the verb *write*.

Past time	J. K. Rowling <u>wrote</u> parts of her first book in a coffee shop.
Present time	She <u>writes</u> every morning.
Future	Perhaps she <u>will write</u> a new book next year.

HINT ◂ **Use Standard Verb Forms**

Nonstandard English is used in everyday conversation and may differ according to the region in which you live. **Standard American English** is the common language generally used and expected in schools, businesses, and government institutions in the United States. Most of your instructors will want you to write using standard American English.

Nonstandard	She **be** busy. She **don't** have **no** time to talk.
	She **ain't** finished with her work.
Standard	She **is** busy. She **doesn't** have **any** time to talk.
	She **isn't** finished with her work.

LO 1 Identify and use the simple present tense.

The Simple Present Tense

The **simple present tense** shows that an action is a general fact or habitual activity.

Fact	Jonathan Safran Foer books <u>sell</u> in countries throughout the world.
Habitual activity	Jonathan Safran Foer <u>writes</u> every morning.

(past) ◂──── | MONDAY MORNING | | TUESDAY MORNING | | WEDNESDAY MORNING | ────▸ (future)

He writes.   He writes.   He writes.

Simple present tense verbs (except *be*) have two forms.

- **Base form.** When the subject is *I, you, we,* or *they,* do not add an ending to the verb.

  They read magazines. We often borrow their magazines.

- **Third-person singular form.** When the subject is *he, she, it,* or the equivalent (*Joe, Anne, New York*), add an *-s* or *-es* ending to the verb.

  The story <u>ends</u> badly. The main character <u>leaves</u> his family.

Look at the two forms of the verb *help.* Notice the *-s* in bold print in the third-person singular form.

Present Tense of *Help*		
	Singular	**Plural**
First person	I help	We help
Second person	You help	You help
Third person	He helps	They help
	She helps	
	It helps	

Subject–Verb Agreement

In the present tense, the subject and verb must **agree** in number. If the subject is third-person singular (*he, she, it*), the corresponding verb must have the singular form, too.

Although plural nouns usually end in -*s*, plural verbs do not. Instead, singular verbs have the -*s* or -*es* ending. Read the following sentences and notice the errors in subject–verb agreement.

GRAMMAR LINK
See Chapter 13 for more detailed information about subject–verb agreement.

> writes appear
> Jan Freeman ~~write~~ for the *Boston Globe*. Her columns ~~appears~~ every Sunday.

PRACTICE 1

George Orwell, the author of *Animal Farm* and *1984*, wrote an essay called "Why I Write." The following sentences summarize his ideas. Underline the correct present tense form of each verb in parentheses.

EXAMPLE: Authors (<u>write</u> / writes) for several reasons.

1. Every writer (want / wants) to seem clever, according to George Orwell.

2. Most human beings (like / likes) to be remembered.

3. Also, a beautiful or moving moment (become / becomes) immortal with writing.

4. A good writer (attempt / attempts) to show others the beauty of certain places.

5. People also (write / writes) to create a historical record of events.

6. Some writers (hope / hopes) to persuade others with their words.

7. Great novels (need / needs) to document political events.

8. Some lies (need / needs) to be exposed.

9. George Orwell's book *Animal Farm* (show / shows) certain injustices, and it (criticize / criticizes) Soviet-style communism.

10. Art (enjoy / enjoys) a relationship with politics.

Irregular Present Tense Verbs: *Be, Have*

Two common present tense verbs are irregular and do not follow the usual pattern for endings. Review the forms of the verbs *be* and *have*.

Present Tense of *Be* and *Have*		
Be	**Singular**	**Plural**
First person	I am	We are
Second person	You are	You are
Third person	He is	They are
	She is	
	It is	
Have		
First person	I have	We have
Second person	You have	You have
Third person	He has	They have
	She has	
	It has	

HINT ◀ **Using the Irregular Verb *Be***

Use the verb *be* to identify age, hunger, thirst, feelings, height, and temperature. Remember that the form of the verb must also agree with the subject of the sentence.

	is
Age	He ~~has~~ forty years old.
	is am
Hunger and thirst	He ~~has~~ thirsty, and I ~~have~~ hungry.
	is
Temperature	It ~~be~~ cold outside.

Do not use *be* to express agreement. I ~~am~~ agree.

PRACTICE 2

Write present tense verbs in the spaces provided. Use the correct forms of *be* and *have*.

EXAMPLE: Stephenie Meyer _____is_____ the author of a successful series.

1. Meyer's book, *Twilight*, _____ a romantic vampire tale. Over
   40 million young adults _____ read the novel. In *Twilight*, Bella
   Swan _____ seventeen years old. She moves to Forks, Washington.
   At school, the other students _____ not very friendly. However,
   one quiet boy with pale skin _____ very sweet to the newcomer.
   He _____ a loner. The other students _____ nothing
   nice to say about him. He _____ odd. For instance, at school he
   _____ never hungry. Soon, Bella _____ a crush on the
   quiet outsider.

2. Over time, Bella discovers that Edward _____ a vampire. He

    _____ thirsty for the taste of blood. However, he and his family

    _____ strong values and will not drink human blood. Small

    animals _____ to be careful, though. The novel _____

    some surprising twists and turns.

3. *Twilight* _____ a huge online fan community. Meyer's book

    follows a Gothic literary tradition. Many horror novels _____

    about a pale creature who drinks human blood. Usually, the vampire

    _____ extremely attractive. The vampire _____ always

    very old, yet he remains young and beautiful forever. The books appeal to our

    human desire for eternal youth and immortality. And, of course, the romance

    _____ an attractive part of the story.

Question Forms: *Do* or *Does*

To create present tense questions, begin each question with *do* or *does*.

He complains a lot.	**Does** he complain a lot?
They read each night.	**Do** they read each night?

In the following chart, notice when to use the third-person singular form *does*.

Question Forms Using *Do* or *Does*		
	Singular	**Plural**
First person	Do I work?	Do we work?
Second person	Do you work?	Do you work?
Third person	**Does** he work?	Do they work?
	Does she work?	
	Does it work?	

Exception: When the main verb is *be* (*is, am, are*), just move *be* before the subject to form a question.

The story is suspenseful.	**Is** the story suspenseful?
They are safe.	**Are** they safe?

PRACTICE 3

Fill in each blank with the correct present tense form of the verb *do* or *be*. Then underline the subject in each question.

EXAMPLES: _____Does_____ it have a happy ending? _____Is_____ it interesting?

1. _____ we have time to discuss the novel?

2. _____ you a fan of murder mysteries?

3. _____ you want to read something else?

Chapter 9

4. _____ the main character about forty years old?

5. _____ you like the author's writing style?

6. _____ she a good storyteller?

7. _____ the characters interesting?

8. _____ you know what the critics think?

9. _____ the newspaper critic fair?

Negative Forms: *Do Not, Does Not*

To form the negative of present tense verbs, place *do* or *does* and the word *not* between the subject and the verb.

We **do not** read her novels.   (Contraction: **don't** read)
Simon **does not** write every day.   (Contraction: **doesn't** write)

Negative Forms of *Do* and *Does*

	Singular Forms	Contraction
First person	I do not work.	don't
Second person	You do not work.	don't
Third person	He does not work.	
	She does not work.	doesn't
	It does not work.	

	Plural Forms	Contraction
First person	You do not work.	don't
Second person	We do not work.	don't
Third person	They do not work.	don't

Exception: When the main verb is *be* (*is, am, are*), just add *not*.

The story **is not** suspenseful.   (Contraction: **isn't**)
They **are not** happy with the ending.   (Contraction: **aren't**)

PRACTICE 4

A. Add *-s* or *-es* to each italicized verb, if necessary. Then, write the negative form and contraction in the spaces provided.

EXAMPLE:

	Negative Form	Contraction
Delphine *do* __es__ many interesting things.	does not do	doesn't do

1. In *One Crazy Summer*, a young girl *move* _____ to California for the summer.   _____ _____

2. Delphine and her sisters *live* _____ with their aunt.   _____ _____

3. Aunt Cecile *treat* _____ her nieces well.   _____ _____

4. The girls *eat* _____ takeout
   dinners.   _____   _____

5. Cecile *send* _____ the girls to
   a special camp.   _____   _____

6. They *learn* _____ about the Black
   Panthers.   _____   _____

7. The book's author,
   Rita Williams-Garcia,
   write _____ every day.   _____   _____

B. Put the correct form of the verb *be* in the spaces. Then write the negative form and contraction.

EXAMPLE:

	Negative Form	Contraction
Delphine's hair __is__ long.	__is not__	__isn't__
8. Cecile _____ a good cook.	_____	_____
9. The young girls _____ brave.	_____	_____
10. The book _____ expensive.	_____	_____

HINT ◀ **Correcting Question and Negative Forms**

In question and negative forms, always use the base form of the main verb even when the subject is third-person singular. Put the *-s* or *-es* ending only on the helping verb (*does*).

> **have**
> Why does the magazine ~~has~~ so many subscribers?

> **contain**
> The magazine does not ~~contains~~ many advertisements.

PRACTICE 5

Correct errors in present tense verb forms.

EXAMPLE: Romance novels ~~be~~ *are* extremely popular.

1. Four Harlequin romance novels sells every second.

2. Romance novels are translated into many languages, but most of the writers be
   from the United States, Canada, or Britain.

3. A typical romance novel follow a formula.

4. Initially, the heroine do not like the hero, and she struggles against her growing
   attraction.

5. Romance novels does not have sad endings.

6. Be chick lit and romance novels the same thing?

7. In so-called "chick lit," the heroine do not always fall in love.

8. Why do Heather Graham write romance novels?

9. According to Graham, each novel express a universal human emotion.

10. Stories about exciting relationships provides readers with an escape from reality.

LO 2 Identify and use the simple past tense.

The Simple Past Tense

The **simple past tense** shows that an action occurred at a specific past time. In the past tense, there are regular and irregular verbs.

Regular Past Tense Verbs

Regular past tense verbs have a standard *-d* or *-ed* ending (*talked, ended, watched*). Use the same form for both singular and plural past tense verbs.

Singular subject	F. Scott Fitzerald **published** his stories in several languages.
Plural subject	Last Friday, we **talked** about the novel.

LAST FRIDAY ▼   TODAY ▼

Last Friday, we **talked** about the novel.

> **GRAMMAR LINK**
> See Chapter 24, "Spelling," for more spelling tips.

HINT   **Spelling of Regular Verbs**

Most regular past tense verbs are formed by adding *-ed* to the base form of the verb.

talk–talk**ed**	mention–mention**ed**

Exceptions

- When the regular verb ends in *-e*, add just *-d*.

hope–hope**d**	bake–bake**d**

- When the regular verb ends in a consonant + *y*, change the *y* to *i* and add *-ed*.

fry–fr**ied**	apply–appl**ied**

Note: if the regular verb ends in a vowel + *y*, add just *-ed*.

play–play**ed**	destroy–destroy**ed**

- When the regular verb ends in a consonant-vowel-consonant combination, double the last consonant and add *-ed*.

stop–stop**ped**	jog–jog**ged**

PRACTICE 6

Write the past tense forms of the following verbs.

EXAMPLE: watch ___watched___

1. care _____
2. try _____
3. stay _____
4. employ _____
5. study _____

6. plan _____
7. rain _____
8. rest _____
9. deny _____
10. ban _____

HINT ◄ *Past* versus *Passed*

Some people confuse *past* and *passed*. *Past* is a noun that means "in a previous time; before now."

> She has many secrets in her <u>past</u>. Her mistakes are in the <u>past</u>.

Passed is the past tense of the verb *pass*, which has many meanings. In the first example, it means "went by" in the second example, it means "to successfully complete."

> Many days <u>passed</u>, and the nights got shorter.

> Celia <u>passed</u> her exams.

PRACTICE 7

Write the simple past form of each verb in parentheses. Make sure that you have spelled your past tense verbs correctly.

EXAMPLE: In 1925, two boys (wonder) ___wondered___ how to enter the comic book industry.

1. In 1933, teenagers Jerry Seigel and Joe Shuster (create) _____ a story about an evil, power-hungry man.

2. Their short story, "The Reign of Superman," (describe) _____ a bald-headed villain who (aim) _____ to take over the world.

3. Nobody (want) _____ to buy their story.

4. Seigel and Shuster (change) _____ their lead character into a noble hero with super powers.

5. Four years later, DC Comics (agree) _____ to publish the first Superman comic.

6. In 1941, Seigel and Shuster (earn) _____ $75,000 for their Superman comics.

7. The pair (battle) _____ their publisher to get a larger share of the immense profits from Superman.

8. The angry publisher then (fire) _____ Seigel and Shuster.

9. In 1948, the writers (accept) _____ a small cash settlement.

10. They (sign) _____ away their rights to any future earnings from the Superman franchise.

11. In the 1950s, both men (watch) _____ the Superman TV series, and they (receive) _____ nothing for it.

12. In 1978, Warner Communications, the makers of *Superman: The Movie*, (offer) _____ to pay the Superman creators a yearly pension.

Irregular Past Tense Verbs

Irregular verbs do not end in any specific letter. Because their spellings can change from the present to the past forms, these verbs can be challenging to remember.

Irregular Verbs

Base Form	Simple Past	Base Form	Simple Past	Base Form	Simple Past
be	was, were	cost	cost	give	gave
beat	beat	cut	cut	go	went
become	became	deal	dealt	grind	ground
begin	began	dig	dug	grow	grew
bend	bent	do	did	hang*	hung
bet	bet	draw	drew	have	had
bind	bound	drink	drank	hear	heard
bite	bit	drive	drove	hide	hid
bleed	bled	eat	ate	hit	hit
blow	blew	fall	fell	hold	held
break	broke	feed	fed	hurt	hurt
breed	bred	feel	felt	keep	kept
bring	brought	fight	fought	kneel	knelt
build	built	find	found	know	knew
burst	burst	flee	fled	lay	laid
buy	bought	fly	flew	lead	led
catch	caught	forget	forgot	leave	left
choose	chose	forgive	forgave	lend	lent
cling	clung	freeze	froze	let	let
come	came	get	got	lie**	lay

*When "hang" means "to suspend by a rope, as in a form of capital punishment," then it is a regular verb. The past form is *hanged*.

**Lie* means "to rest," for example, on a sofa or bed. When *lie* means "tell a false statement," it is a regular verb: *lie, lied, lied*.

Base Form	Simple Past	Base Form	Simple Past	Base Form	Simple Past
light	lit	shoot	shot	strike	struck
lose	lost	shrink	shrank	swear	swore
make	made	shut	shut	sweep	swept
mean	meant	sing	sang	swim	swam
meet	met	sink	sank	swing	swung
mistake	mistook	sit	sat	take	took
pay	paid	sleep	slept	teach	taught
put	put	slide	slid	tear	tore
quit	quit	slit	slit	tell	told
read	read	speak	spoke	think	thought
rid	rid	speed	sped	throw	threw
ride	rode	spend	spent	thrust	thrust
ring	rang	spin	spun	understand	understood
rise	rose	split	split	upset	upset
run	ran	spread	spread	wake	woke
say	said	spring	sprang	wear	wore
see	saw	stand	stood	weep	wept
sell	sold	steal	stole	win	won
send	sent	stick	stuck	wind	wound
set	set	sting	stung	withdraw	withdrew
shake	shook	stink	stank	write	wrote

PRACTICE 8

Write down the correct past form of each verb in parentheses. Some verbs are regular, and some are irregular.

EXAMPLE: In the late 1990s, Jimmy Wales (write) _____ *wrote* _____ the first edit to Wikipedia.

1. In 1993, Rick Gates (think) _____ about the possibility of an online encyclopedia. Soon after, he (make) _____ preliminary plans for his Web site. In the early 2000s, he worked on Nupedia. Only experts (have) _____ the job of writing entries. Each new entry (take) _____ a long time to be peer reviewed. Then philosopher Lawrence Sanger (think) _____ of a better idea. He (propose) _____ another encyclopedia site that anyone could contribute to. In 2001, Wikipedia (hit) _____ the Web.

2. In its first year, Wikipedia contributors (write) _____ over 20,000 articles in eighteen languages. The site (grow) _____ very quickly. In January 2006, it (rise) _____ to prominence with over a million articles. During the first ten years of Wikipedia, many authors (deal) _____ with their favorite topics. Today, there are more entries about *Star Wars* than about World War II.

The Past Form of *Be* (*Was* or *Were*)

The verb *be* has two past forms: *was* and *were*.

Past Tense of *Be*	Singular	Plural
First person	I was	We were
Second person	You were	You were
Third person	He was	They were
	She was	
	It was	

PRACTICE 9

Fill in each blank with *was* or *were*.

EXAMPLE: During the early years of Wikipedia, people _____were_____ curious about how accurate a public encyclopedia could really be.

1. When Wikipedia first appeared in the early 2000s, there _____ many people in the academic community who disliked the site. They believed that contributors _____ not careful about accuracy. Academics thought that Wikipedia _____ a mere distraction and shouldn't be trusted for important information. However, a 2005 study had surprising results. The study _____ the first attempt to find out how accurate Wikipedia _____ compared to more traditional sources of information. The results showed that there _____ almost as many mistakes per entry in the Encyclopedia Britannica as there _____ on Wikipedia.

2. In 2006, many people _____ surprised at the findings of the study. At the time, Wikipedia _____ not a respected site because some users had intentionally put false information on the site. Of course, Encyclopedia Britannica officials _____ upset at the findings of the study. They _____ angry that Wikipedia was presented as a reasonably accurate site.

Negative Forms of Past Tense Verbs

To form the negative of past tense verbs, place *did* and the word *not* between the subject and the verb.

The actress **did not want** to appear in tabloids.	(Contraction: **didn't**)
We **did not buy** that newspaper.	(Contraction: **didn't**)

Exception: When the main verb is *be* (*was, were*), just add *not*.

The story **was not** suspenseful.	(Contraction: **wasn't**)
They **were not** happy with the ending.	(Contraction: **weren't**)

PRACTICE 10

Write the negative forms of the underlined verbs. Use contractions.

EXAMPLE: He <u>worked</u>. _____didn't work_____   They <u>were</u> hungry. _____weren't_____

1. She <u>was</u> busy. _____
2. Joe <u>ate</u> a lot. _____
3. You <u>made</u> it. _____
4. We <u>spoke</u>. _____
5. I <u>lied</u>. _____

6. I <u>did</u> it. _____
7. We <u>washed</u> up. _____
8. They <u>were</u> late. _____
9. Kay <u>went</u> out. _____
10. He <u>opened</u> it. _____

Question Forms of Past Tense Verbs

To create past tense questions, add the helping verb *did* before the subject and change the past tense verb to its base form.

Shuster drew Superman.   **Did** Shuster draw Superman?
They liked the story.   **Did** they like the story?

Exception: When the main verb is *be* (*was, were*), just move *be* before the subject to form a question.

The story was exciting.   **Was** the story exciting?
They were ready.   **Were** they ready?

HINT ◀ **Use the Base Form After *Did***

In question and negative forms, remember to use the base form—not the past form—of the main verb.

      use
Did he ~~used~~ a computer to write his book?

PRACTICE 11

Correct the errors with question or negative forms.

      did he seem
EXAMPLE: Why ~~he seem~~ so surprised by his success?

1. J. R. R. Tolkien don't be born in England.

2. He did not remained in South Africa.

3. When he moved to Birmingham, England?

4. Why did Tolkien wrote about hobbits?

5. His friends not believed in the value of myths.

6. Tolkien wasn't agree with his friends.

7. *The Lord of the Rings* didn't be popular at first.

8. Why the book became popular ten years after its release?

9. Why did the book sold more than 100 million copies?

Common Errors with *Be* and *Have*

Some writers find it particularly difficult to remember how to use the irregular verbs *be* and *have*.

◆ Use *were*, not *was*, when the subject is plural.

> were
> The photographers ~~was~~ extremely persistent.

◆ Use the standard form of the verb (*is* or *was*), not *be*.

> was
> The story about the movie star ~~be~~ shocking.

◆ Use the past form of the verb (*had*), not the present form (*have* or *has*), when speaking about a past event.

> had
> Mike Wallace ~~has~~ to work in dangerous war zones during his early days as a reporter.

PRACTICE 12

If the underlined past tense verb is incorrectly formed or in the wrong tense, write the correct form above it. There are twenty errors.

> wrote
> **EXAMPLE:** In the past, many people <u>writed</u> memoirs.

1. In 2005, I <u>buyed</u> a book called *A Million Little Pieces*, by James Frey. It only

    <u>costed</u> $12. Later, Oprah Winfrey <u>choosed</u> Frey's novel for her televised book

    club. According to Winfrey, the book <u>gived</u> hope to people with addictions.

    The book <u>selled</u> more than 2 million copies.

2. Some investigative reporters <u>be</u> skeptical. According to *The Smoking Gun*,

    Frey's book <u>was</u> not about true events. The author <u>maked</u> up many details. For example, Frey never <u>spended</u> eighty-seven days in jail. Soon, everybody <u>knowed</u> about the scandal.

3. In 2006, Frey <u>taked</u> a big risk and appeared on another episode of *Oprah*. The popular host <u>be</u> very angry with Frey. After the show, Frey <u>thinked</u> that his career was over. Over the next year, he <u>losed</u> many friends. He <u>refunded</u> money to many book buyers.

4. In 2008, another writer <u>called</u> her novel a memoir. Margaret B. Jones <u>wrote</u> about her life as a mixed-race girl from South Central Los Angeles. In the book, the main character <u>becomed</u> a gang member. However, Margaret Jones <u>haved</u> a middle-class life in San Fernando Valley. She never <u>grewed</u> up in South Central Los Angeles.

5. Before his death in 2007, author Norman Mailer <u>speaked</u> about the "memoir" controversies. Frey and Jones never <u>hurted</u> others. They just <u>bended</u> the truth. People <u>readed</u> their books and enjoyed them. According to Mailer, all memoirs are full of lies because writers want to "create an ideal self."

Avoiding Double Negatives

LO3 Avoid double negatives.

A **double negative** occurs when a writer combines a negative word such as *no, nothing, nobody*, or *nowhere* with a negative adverb such as *not, never, rarely*, or *seldom*. The result is a sentence that has a double negative. Such sentences can be confusing because the negative words cancel each other.

Double negative	She **doesn't** give **no** interviews.
	He **never** received **no** royalties.

How to Correct Double Negatives

There are two ways to correct double negatives. Either remove one of the negative forms or change *no* to *any*.

Error	**Corrections**
She doesn't give no interviews.	She **doesn't give** interviews. (Remove *no*.)
	She **gives no** interviews. (Remove *any*.)
	She **doesn't give any** interviews. (Change *no* to *any*.)

Chapter 9

PRACTICE 13

Underline and correct four errors with double negatives. You can correct each error in more than one way.

have nothing or don't have anything

EXAMPLE: I <u>don't have nothing</u> on my Kindle.

1. In 2009, Amazon introduced a new product. The Kindle is an electronic gadget that can hold over 1,500 books. Readers don't need no heavy book bags. Instead, the Kindle fits into a pocket or purse. In 2009, Apple launched the iPad, which can also hold thousands of books.

2. Most reviewers don't say nothing bad about the Kindle or iPad. But will those products help or hurt the publishing industry? Downloaded books cost much less than paper books. A lot of people don't want to pay nothing for their books and newspapers.

3. Book publishers have to adapt to the new technologies. They can't do nothing to stop the changes in the industry.

FINAL REVIEW

Underline and correct twenty errors in this selection. There are present tense, past tense, and double negative errors.

were

EXAMPLE: The books <u>was</u> offensive.

1. On April 4, 2006, Kaavya Viswanathan released her debut novel *How Opal Mehta Got Kissed, Got Wild, and Got a Life*. A few weeks past by. Then someone recognized passages of the novel and argued that Viswanathan's book be unoriginal. On April 23, *The Harvard Crimson* denounced the work as a clear case of plagiarism. The young author feeled humiliated. The publisher quickly payed customers for their novels and destroyed all copies of the book.

2. A few years later, there be another scandal, but this time, the young author have an interesting defense. In 2010, seventeen-year-old Helene Hegemann released *Axolotl Roadkill* to critical acclaim. Her novel about Berlin's club scene

becomed a huge success in Germany. Then someone noticed that parts of her novel was identical to a blogger's posts. Hegemann didn't have no remorse. She didn't see no problem with her writing process. In an interview with the *New York Times*, she said that she remixed ideas like a musician. "True originality doesn't exist, only authenticity," Hegemann argued.

3. Airen, the blogger who originally inspired Hegemann, no longer keeps a blog. He stoped writing after he got a white-collar desk job. When the allegations of plagiarism surfaced, Airen keeped his real name out of the news. He thinked that his employers might find out about his blogging alter ego. Before getting a day job, Airen goed to all the trendy clubs in Berlin, and he writed about his experiences with drugs and casual sex. After Airen found a full-time job and got married, he did not write a blog no more. In an interview, Airen said that Hegemann did not have no reason to plagiarize from his work. Why didn't she just ask for permission?

4. In 2011, Debora Weber-Wulff, a media professor, criticized Hegemann's generation. She said that Hegemann copied the blogger because her generation believes that it is acceptable to copy and paste. These days, Hegemann continue to argue that her past actions was ethical.

THE WRITER'S ROOM

MyWritingLab™
**Complete these
writing assignments at**
mywritinglab.com

Write about one of the following topics. After you finish writing, underline your verbs. Verify that you have formed your present and past tense verbs correctly.

1. What happened in a story, poem, play, or article that you read? Use the past tense in your narration.

2. What was your major source of entertainment during your childhood? Did you read, watch television, or play outside? Describe the main activities that you did.

Chapter 9

Checklist: Present and Past Tenses

When you edit your writing, ask yourself the following questions.

☐ Do I use the correct present tense forms? Check for errors in these cases:

–verbs following third-person singular nouns

–irregular present tense verbs

–question and negative forms

<blockquote>

                      needs

Zoey Cervantes, a young author, ~~need~~ to find a literary agent.

  Do

~~Does~~ you know of anyone she could contact?

</blockquote>

☐ Do I use the correct past tense forms? Check for spelling errors and other mistakes with the following:

–regular past tense verbs

–irregular past tense verbs

–negative and question forms

<blockquote>

                   wrote   **did   decide**

In 1969, Maya Angelou ~~wroted~~ her first novel. Why she ~~decided~~ to write a novel?

</blockquote>

☐ Do my sentences have standard English? Check for errors in the following cases:

–use of *ain't* instead of *is not, am not,* or *are not*

–use of double negatives instead of correct negative forms

<blockquote>

                             any

The author never gives ~~no~~ interviews.

</blockquote>

Past Participles 10

SECTION THEME: Entertainment and Culture

In this chapter, you will read about topics related to television and film.

LEARNING OBJECTIVES

LO 1 Identify and write past participles. (p. 176)

LO 2 Identify and use present perfect tense. (p. 180)

LO 3 Identify and use the past perfect tense. (p. 183)

LO 4 Use the past participle as an adjective. (p. 185)

LO 5 Identify active and passive verbs. (p. 186)

GRAMMAR SNAPSHOT

Looking at Past Participles

Silent film actor George Arliss wrote several autobiographies, including *Up the Years from Bloomsbury*. In this excerpt, Arliss discusses film acting. The past participles of verbs are underlined.

> I had always <u>believed</u> that, for the movies, acting must be <u>exaggerated</u>, but I saw in this one flash that restraint was the chief thing that the actor had to learn in transferring art from the stage to the screen. The art of restraint and suggestion on the screen may be <u>studied</u> by watching the acting of the inimitable Charlie Chaplin.

In this chapter, you will identify and write past participles.

L01 Identify and write past participles.

Past Participles

A **past participle** is a verb form, not a verb tense. You cannot use a past participle as the only verb in a sentence. Instead, you must use it with a helping verb. The most common helping verbs are forms of *have* or *be* (*have, has, had,* or *is, am, are, was, were*).

        helping   past
        verb   participle

My sister and I **were** <u>raised</u> in Austin, Texas.

         helping   past
         verb   participle

Many movies **have been** <u>filmed</u> there.

Regular Verbs

Regular verbs end in *-d* or *-ed*. The past tense and the past participle of regular verbs are the same. Here are some examples.

Base Form	Past Tense	Past Participle
talk	talked	talked
cry	cried	cried
hope	hoped	hoped

PRACTICE 1

Underline each helping verb that appears before the word in parentheses. Then write the past participle of the verb in parentheses.

EXAMPLE: Some consumers <u>have</u> (complain) ___*complained*___ about reality programs.

1. Many viewers have (develop) _____ a taste for reality shows.

2. Reality programming has (appear) _____ on network television since the 1940s.

3. *Wanted*, a show that was (produce) _____ in 1955 by CBS television, contained interviews with fugitives and their families.

4. *Candid Camera*, which was (create) _____ by its host Allen Funt in 1948, showed regular people reacting to surprising events.

5. Many other producers have (copy) _____ Funt's ideas.

6. Today, many reality shows are (base) _____ on singing competitions.

7. Producers have (create) _____ programs such as *The Voice* and *American Idol*.

8. Since 2007, some reality programs have (focus) _____ on the lives of the wealthy, such as the Kardashian sisters.

Irregular Verbs

Certain verbs have irregular past forms and can be challenging to remember. Review the next list of common irregular verbs. Put an *X* next to verbs that you commonly misspell.

Irregular Verbs

Base Form	Simple Past	Past Participle	Base Form	Simple Past	Past Participle
arise	arose	arisen	find	found	found
be	was, were	been	flee	fled	fled
beat	beat	beat, beaten	fly	flew	flown
become	became	become	forbid	forbade	forbidden
begin	began	begun	forget	forgot	forgotten
bend	bent	bent	forgive	forgave	forgiven
bet	bet	bet	freeze	froze	frozen
bind	bound	bound	get	got	got, gotten
bite	bit	bitten	give	gave	given
bleed	bled	bled	go	went	gone
blow	blew	blown	grind	ground	ground
break	broke	broken	grow	grew	grown
breed	bred	bred	hang*	hung	hung
bring	brought	brought	have	had	had
build	built	built	hear	heard	heard
burst	burst	burst	hide	hid	hidden
buy	bought	bought	hit	hit	hit
catch	caught	caught	hold	held	held
choose	chose	chosen	hurt	hurt	hurt
cling	clung	clung	keep	kept	kept
come	came	come	kneel	knelt	knelt
cost	cost	cost	know	knew	known
cut	cut	cut	lay	laid	laid
deal	dealt	dealt	lead	led	led
dig	dug	dug	leave	left	left
do	did	done	lend	lent	lent
draw	drew	drawn	let	let	let
drink	drank	drunk	lie**	lay	lain
drive	drove	driven	light	lit	lit
eat	ate	eaten	lose	lost	lost
fall	fell	fallen	make	made	made
feed	fed	fed	mean	meant	meant
feel	felt	felt	meet	met	met
fight	fought	fought	mistake	mistook	mistaken

*When *hang* means "to suspend by a rope, as in a form of capital punishment," then it is a regular verb. The past forms are *hanged*.

**Lie* means "to rest," for example, on a sofa or bed. When *lie* means "tell a false statement," it is a regular verb: *lie, lied, lied*.

(continued)

Chapter 10

Irregular Verbs (*continued*)

Base Form	Simple Past	Past Participle	Base Form	Simple Past	Past Participle
pay	paid	paid	spread	spread	spread
put	put	put	spring	sprang	sprung
quit	quit	quit	stand	stood	stood
read	read	read	steal	stole	stolen
rid	rid	rid	stick	stuck	stuck
ride	rode	ridden	sting	stung	stung
ring	rang	rung	stink	stank	stunk
rise	rose	risen	strike	struck	struck
run	ran	run	swear	swore	sworn
say	said	said	sweep	swept	swept
see	saw	seen	swell	swelled	swollen
sell	sold	sold	swim	swam	swum
send	sent	sent	swing	swung	swung
set	set	set	take	took	taken
shake	shook	shaken	teach	taught	taught
shoot	shot	shot	tear	tore	torn
show	showed	shown	tell	told	told
shut	shut	shut	think	thought	thought
sing	sang	sung	throw	threw	thrown
sink	sank	sunk	thrust	thrust	thrust
sit	sat	sat	understand	understood	understood
sleep	slept	slept	upset	upset	upset
slide	slid	slid	wake	woke	woken
slit	slit	slit	wear	wore	worn
speak	spoke	spoken	weep	wept	wept
speed	sped	sped	win	won	won
spend	spent	spent	wind	wound	wound
spin	spun	spun	withdraw	withdrew	withdrawn
split	split	split	write	wrote	written

PRACTICE 2

Write the simple past and the past participle of the following verbs.

Base Form	Past Tense	Past Participle
EXAMPLE: lose	lost	lost
1. cost	_____	_____
2. choose	_____	_____
3. drive	_____	_____
4. break	_____	_____
5. ring	_____	_____
6. bring	_____	_____
7. drink	_____	_____

8. think   _____   _____

9. build   _____   _____

10. become   _____   _____

11. grow   _____   _____

12. hit   _____   _____

13. sit   _____   _____

14. go   _____   _____

15. do   _____   _____

PRACTICE 3

The irregular past participles are underlined. Correct the twelve past participle errors, and write *C* above five correct verbs.

learned
EXAMPLE: Many acting students have <u>learn</u> the Stanislavski method.

1. Many people have <u>thinked</u> about becoming famous actors. Most of us believe that acting is very glamorous and easy to do. However, most successful actors have <u>spend</u> years developing their craft. Acting students require proper training.

2. Acting is <u>teached</u> in many colleges and private institutes. In acting classes, students are <u>gived</u> the basic techniques. Acting students are often <u>telled</u> to read novels and plays as well as reference books and biographies. Most actors have <u>read</u> many classic works.

3. According to the late acting teacher Stella Adler, after actors have <u>studied</u> a script, they must visualize different scenes. If an actor has not <u>feeled</u> the reality of the situation, he or she won't be convincing. The audience won't be <u>selled</u> on the performance. Adler also told her students to become "bigger" on stage. Adler and others have <u>finded</u> that many actors are boring when they try to be natural.

4. Lee Strasberg, Adler's former associate, believed that a performance must be <u>based</u> on a real-life experience. However, some actors have <u>falled</u> into the

trap of trying too hard to relate their own life to their acting. Adler, who had <u>breaked</u> away from Strasberg, felt that a situation could be <u>understood</u> with intense study and immersion.

5.   Almost everybody has <u>saw</u> one of Adler's former pupils in the movies. Actors such as Robert De Niro, Salma Hayek, Benicio Del Toro, and Edward Norton have <u>took</u> courses with Adler. Traditionally, good acting jobs have <u>been</u> hard to find. But if students persevere, and get proper training, they have a chance at succeeding.

LO 2 Identify and use present perfect tense.

The Present Perfect Tense: *Have/Has* + Past Participle

A past participle combines with *have* or *has* to form the **present perfect tense**. You can use this tense in two different circumstances.

* Use the present perfect to show that an action began in the past and continues to the present time. Some key words and expressions to look for are *since, for, ever, not yet, so far,* and *up to now.*

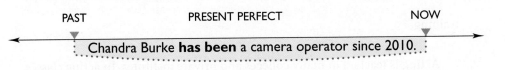

| PAST | PRESENT PERFECT | NOW |

Chandra Burke **has been** a camera operator since 2010.

* Use the present perfect to show that one or more completed actions occurred at unimportant and unspecified past times. Some key words and expressions to look for are *already, once, twice, several times,* and *many times.*

PAST (unspecified past times)   NOW
?   ?   ?   ?

Chandra Burke **has worked** on many different movies.

Look at the difference between the past tense and the present perfect tense in the following examples.

Simple past	In August 2005, three friends <u>launched</u> the Internet site YouTube. (This event occurred at a known past time.)
Present perfect	Since 2005, the YouTube founders <u>have earned</u> a fortune. (The action began in the past and continues to the present moment.)
	J. Junkala <u>has made</u> more than twenty videos. (The repeated past actions have occurred at unspecified past times.)

PRACTICE 4

Write the present perfect form of each verb in parentheses.

EXAMPLE: Horror movies (be) _____have been_____ around for almost a century.

1.   Since its beginning, the Internet (change) _____ people's lives

   in various ways. Recently, with the introduction of video-sharing Web sites,

   people (have) _____ the chance to flirt with fame. In fact, since

   2005, thousands of ordinary men and women (make) _____

   videos for YouTube, Facebook, or other video-sharing sites.

2.   Some of the videos (become) _____ extremely popular.

   For example, more than 30 million people (see) _____ the

   amazing performance of Greyson Michael Chance, a twelve-year-old boy from

   Oklahoma. Many journalists (speak) _____ with him, and

   some record producers (contact) _____ him. Lady Gaga

   (give) _____ him some advice. During an August 2010 taping of

   the show *Ellen*, Gaga told the boy to focus on music, not on girls.

3.   For the last few years, some corporations (be) _____ upset

   with the spread of file-sharing Internet sites. Entertainment industry officials

   object to unauthorized use of film clips or songs. However, they (not, stop)

   _____ the video-sharing Web sites.

HINT ◀ Time Markers

Time markers are words that indicate when an action occurred.

Simple Past Tense
To refer to an incident that occurred at a specific past time, use the following time markers.

yesterday	ago	when I was . . .	last (week, month, year . . .)
in the past	in 1925	during the 1990s	in the early days of . . .

In 2006, Tyler Perry **released** his first film.

Present Perfect Tense
To refer to an action that began in the past and is still continuing, use the following time markers.

since	ever, never	so far	up to now
not yet	for (a period of time up to now)	lately	recently

I have been a Tyler Perry fan since 2006.

To refer to an action that occurred at an unspecified past time or past times, use the following time markers.

many	several times	repeatedly	once, twice, three times

I have watched *Medea Goes to Jail* twice.

PRACTICE 5

Underline the correct past tense or present perfect tense of each verb in parentheses.

EXAMPLE: In 2010, *Avatar* (<u>won</u> / have won / has won) an Oscar for Best Visual Effects.

1. Since movies first began, directors (used / have used / has used) some special effects.

2. In 1902, technicians (built / have built / has built) a miniature model spaceship for the movie *A Trip to the Moon*.

3. Since 1902, special effects (changed / has changed / have changed) a lot.

4. For the 1939 film *The Wizard of Oz*, technicians (built / have built / has built) complicated sets.

5. Since its debut, *The Wizard of Oz* (remained / have remained / has remained) popular.

6. The movie *Avatar* contains some of the greatest special effects that audiences (ever saw / have ever seen).

7. From 2005 to 2009, director James Cameron (created / has created / have created) an entire 3D universe for his movie to inhabit.

8. In 2006, the film studio almost (abandoned / has abandoned / have abandoned) *Avatar* because the movie was costing too much.

9. Since *Avatar*'s release, most action movie directors (choose / have chosen / has chosen) to include 3D effects in their movies.

PRACTICE 6

Fill in the blanks with either the simple past tense or the present perfect tense.

EXAMPLE: I (watch) _____have watched_____ *General Hospital* since I was seven years old.

1. Daytime soap operas (change) _____ a lot since they began. In the 1930s, soap companies (sponsor) _____ daytime radio dramas. For example, the program *The Guiding Light* (begin) _____ in the 1930s as a radio show. Then, in the 1940s, the television network CBS (film) _____ *The Guiding Light*.

2. Since 2000, the audiences (fall) _____ dramatically for soap operas. Why (viewers, leave) _____? Some blame the bad scripts. Also, the workforce (change) _____ over the years, and both men and women work during the day. Additionally, Nielsen ratings don't include people who record programs and watch them later.

3. In 2009, CBS (cancel) _____ *Guiding Light* after a 72-year run. Then in 2010, *As the World Turns* (go) _____ off the air. Today, reality programs and game shows (take) _____ the place of soap operas. Such shows are less expensive to produce. For example, *Let's Make a Deal* (be) _____ on the air since 1968. The show does not require expensive actors and sets.

The Past Perfect Tense: *Had* + Past Participle

LO3 Identify and use the past perfect tense.

Chapter 10

The **past perfect tense** indicates that one or more past actions happened before another past action. To form the past perfect, use *had* plus the past participle.

PAST PERFECT	PAST	NOW
▼	▼	▼

The movie **had started** when Vladimir arrived.

Notice the differences between the simple past, the present perfect, and the past perfect tenses.

Simple past	Last night, I <u>watched</u> *The Hunger Games.* (The action occurred at a known past time: *last night*.)
Present perfect	I <u>have seen</u> many science fiction movies. (The actions have occurred at unspecified past times.)
Past perfect	Last night, I watched *Twilight* again even though I <u>had seen</u> it three times. (The three viewings happened before last night.)

PRACTICE 7

Underline the correct verb tense. Choose either the simple past or the past perfect verb.

EXAMPLE: When Johnny Depp first appeared in a Hollywood film, he (already acted / <u>had already acted</u>) in many smaller productions and TV shows.

1. Johnny Depp was born in Owensboro, Kentucky, on June 9, 1963, and by the time he was sixteen, he (lived / had lived) in twenty different places.

2. When he was twelve, the family lived in a motel because his father (lost / had lost) his job.

3. During high school, Depp (joined / had joined) a rock band, and then he (married / had married) the bass player's sister.

4. When Depp (received / had received) his starring role in the TV series *21 Jump Street*, he (already played / had already played) in over fifteen rock bands.

5. During *21 Jump Street*, Depp (accumulated / had accumulated) a lot of teen fans. At the end of the series, he claimed that he (never wanted / had never wanted) to be a "teen idol."

6. In 1990, Depp played the title character in Tim Burton's *Edward Scissorhands*, and he (received / had received) more critical acclaim than he (ever earned / had ever earned) in his life.

7. Director Tim Burton (developed / had developed) the story based on the alienation he (experienced / had experienced) while growing up in Burbank, California.

8. In 1998, Depp fulfilled a dream that he (had / had had) for several years when he (portrayed / had portrayed) notorious journalist Hunter S. Thompson in *Fear and Loathing in Las Vegas*.

9. Depp was ready for the role because he (lived / had lived) in Thompson's basement for over a month.

10. In 2011, Depp (appeared / had appeared) as Captain Jack Sparrow in a sequel to *Pirates of the Caribbean*. It was a role that he (already did / had already done) three other times.

PRACTICE 8

Underline the correct tense of each verb in parentheses. You may choose the simple past, the present perfect, or the past perfect tense.

EXAMPLE: In 2013, Bollywood (<u>released</u> / had released) over one thousand films.

1. Since 2004, Americans (have become / had become) acquainted with Bollywood films. Before that time, most Americans (never saw / had never seen) an Indian film. The word *Bollywood*, from a mix of Bombay and Hollywood, first (appeared / had appeared) in 1975. Bollywood (has produced / had produced) many superstars. For example, Raj Kapoor was

the Charlie Chaplin of Indian cinema. By the time Kapoor died in 1988, he (has already starred / had already starred) in almost one hundred films.

2.   Film director Danny Boyle (has already seen / had already seen) some Bollywood movies when he (began / had begun) filming *Slumdog Millionaire* in 2006. The film, which has many Bollywood elements, (won / had won) the Oscar for Best Picture in 2009. Even though Bollywood films may seem extremely melodramatic, international audiences enjoy them.

The Past Participle as an Adjective

A past participle can function as an adjective by modifying or describing the noun that follows it.

LO 4 Use the past participle as an adjective.

> He sat near the **broken** window.
>
> (*Broken* modifies *window*.)

PRACTICE 9

Write a logical past participle in each blank. Use the past participle form of the following verbs. Do not use the same word more than once.

delight	enthrall	humiliate	see	~~talent~~
design	hide	seal	shock	tear

EXAMPLE: Every year, Oscars are given to the most _____talented_____ professionals in Hollywood.

1. The first awards were presented on May 16, 1929, in front of an _____ audience.

2. Before each ceremony, women walk down the red carpet in their well-_____ gowns.

3. Every year, the winners' names are placed in _____ envelopes.

4. Then after the winner is announced, the _____ envelope is thrown away.

5. The audience loves to see the _____ and _____ expression of the winners.

6. Cameras also film the _____ losers.

7. Gwyneth Paltrow does not display her award. Her _____ Oscar is kept in a closet.

8. The much-_____ Oscars continue to attract large audiences.

Chapter 10

LO 5 Identify active and passive verbs.

The Passive Voice: *Be* + Past Participle

In sentences with the **passive voice**, the subject receives the action and does not perform the action. To form the passive voice, use the appropriate tense of the verb *be* + the past participle. The helping verb shows the verb tense.

passive

Acting is the art of lying well. I am **paid** to tell elaborate lies.

—Mel Gibson, actor

Look carefully at the following two sentences. Notice the differences between the active and the passive voice.

Active   Woody Allen **released** *Midnight in Paris* in 2011.

(This sentence is active because the subject, Woody Allen, performed the action.)

Passive   The movie **was filmed** in 2012.

(This sentence is passive because the subject, the movie, did not perform the action.)

Active and Passive Voice

Verb Tenses	Active	Passive: *Be* + Past Participle
	The subject performs the action.	The subject receives the action.
Simple present	They produce movies.	Movies are produced by them.
Present progressive	are producing	are being produced
Simple past	produced	were produced
Present perfect	have produced	have been produced
Future	will produce	will be produced
Modals	can produce	can be produced
	could produce	could be produced
	should produce	should be produced

HINT ◀ **Avoid Overusing the Passive Voice**

Generally, try to use the active voice instead of the passive voice. The active voice is more direct and friendly than the passive voice. For example, read the next two versions of the same message.

Passive voice   Your questions about our cable service have been received by us. You will be contacted by our sales representative.

Active voice   We have received your questions about our cable service. Our sales representative will contact you.

PRACTICE 10

Decide whether each underlined verb is active or passive, and write *A* (for "active") or *P* (for "passive") above each verb.

P
EXAMPLE: The story <u>is based</u> on a fictional event.

1. In the early 1940s, a radio <u>was owned</u> by almost every American family. Then,

    in 1941, the first television show <u>was broadcast</u>. In 1942, some veteran radio

    performers <u>predicted</u> that television would never catch on. However, television

    <u>has been</u> a permanent fixture in American homes since then.

2. It is hard for us to imagine the excitement that <u>was felt</u> in the 1940s. In

    those years, one television <u>was watched</u> by many people, including friends and

    relatives of the owners. In fact, TV watching <u>was</u> a social event. For example,

    in 1946, the first TV sports extravaganza <u>was staged</u> by NBC. The program

    <u>featured</u> boxing great Joe Louis. The match <u>was seen</u> by about 150,000 people,

    or about thirty viewers per television. Today, the average television <u>is watched</u>

    by only three people.

HINT ◀ **The *by* . . . Phrase**

In many passive sentences, it is not necessary to write the *by* . . . phrase.

The film was released in 2005 ~~by United Artists~~.

The costumes were made in France ~~by costume designers~~.

PRACTICE 11

A. Complete the following sentences by changing each italicized verb to the passive form. Do not alter the verb tense. In some sentences, you do not have to include the *by* . . . phrase.

EXAMPLE: Producers make movies all over the world.

  Movies are made all over the world (by producers).

1. Fame *attracts* many ordinary people.

    Many ordinary people _____

2. People *view* movie stars as happy, exciting people.

    Movie stars _____

3. In 2013, a producer *offered* Eva Flores a job in a movie.

In 2013, Eva Flores _____

4. The director *filmed* the movie in Texas.

The movie _____

5. Perhaps people *will recognize* Eva in the future.

Perhaps Eva _____

B. The following sentences are in the passive voice. Change the verbs in italics to the active voice, but do not alter the verb tense.

EXAMPLE: Some actors *are paid* too much money by the studios.

Studios pay some actors too much money. _____

6. Famous actors *have been stalked* by overzealous fans.

Overzealous fans _____

7. A few years ago, Jennifer Hudson's privacy *was invaded* by journalists.

A few years ago, journalists _____

8. Many complaints *are made* by actors about their lack of privacy.

Many actors _____

9. Perhaps actors *should not be chased* by paparazzi.

Perhaps paparazzi _____

10. Tabloids *are enjoyed* by some ordinary people.

Some ordinary people _____

HINT **Using the Passive Form**

In the passive voice, sometimes a form of the verb *be* is suggested but not written. The following sentences contain the passive voice.

Be is suggested   Many movies **made** in the 1970s have become classics.

Be is written   Many movies **that were** made in the 1970s have become classics.

PRACTICE 12

Underline and correct fifteen errors with past participles.

               seen
EXAMPLE: I have <u>saw</u> *X-Men Origins: Wolverine* two times.

1. Comic book series, such as *Spiderman*, have been turn into movies. Other

films, such as *The Green Hornet*, took from radio serials of the 1930s, have

become successful films. Of course, great works of literature have also influence

screenwriters.

2. William Shakespeare is the most well-knowed writer of all time. Many movies have been based on his plays. Othello, for example, was transform into the urban drama *O*. The movie starred Mekhi Phifer as Odin, a talented black athlete who is envy by his peers. Odin falls in love with the headmaster's daughter. Hugo, the coach's son, is consume with jealousy, and he eventually causes Odin's downfall.

3. In addition, exceptional books aimed at youths have also been maked into films. For example, *The Hunger Games*, write by Suzanne Collins, became an international bestseller. In 2012, the much-love novel was turned into a film. Jennifer Lawrence received the covet role of Katniss Everdeen. In addition, *The Golden Compass*, from Philip Pullman's *His Dark Materials* trilogy, was also turned into a movie. The two main characters, Mrs. Coulter and Lord Asriel, are play by Nicole Kidman and Daniel Craig.

4. The rights to many best-sellers are hold by film studios. In fact, as soon as a new book is embrace by the public, producers try to determine whether the book should become a movie. Definitely, many great novels will be adapt by screenwriters.

FINAL REVIEW

Underline and correct fifteen errors with past participles, verb tense, or the passive voice.

EXAMPLE: Many companies have <u>payed</u> producers to place products in films and
on television.
$\overset{\text{paid}}{}$

1. Since the 1930s, advertisers found clever ways to promote their products. These days, brands show in films and on television have became pervasive. For example, *The Matrix Reloaded* was release in 2003 and featured only General Motors automobiles. Apple computers and iPods have appear in numerous films and television shows such as *The Office*.

2. Tobacco is the most controversial product placement. By 1984, audiences had saw tobacco product placements in more than five hundred film productions. Health groups have consistently raise concerns about the impact of movie smoking on teenage smoking rates. In fact, according to *CBS News*, films have

Chapter 10

greatly influence teen smoking. In 1990, tobacco companies promised Congress that they would not promote smoking in films. But films have continue to show characters smoking cigarettes. For example, the American Medical Association was anger by scenes from the 2009 movie *He's Just Not That Into You* because the film exhibited tobacco products.

3.   Recently, another trend has develop. It is product displacement. Some companies have decline to grant permission for their products to be connected to certain images. For example, in the movie *Slumdog Millionaire*, some scenes were film in a Mumbai slum. Mercedes-Benz cars could not be shown in shantytown scenes. However, the cars could be use whenever a scene was filmed in a rich neighborhood. Clearly, business and the entertainment industry have a relationship that is base on image and profit.

MyWritingLab™
Complete these writing assignments at mywritinglab.com

MyWritingLab   THE WRITER'S ROOM

Write about one of the following topics. Identify all verbs, and verify that you have used and formed each verb correctly.

1. Some people spend more than four hours a day watching programs on television or online. What steps can people take to reduce their viewing time?

2. Examine this photo. What are some terms that come to mind? Some ideas might be *reality television, talk show, couch potato,* or *sitcom.* Define a term or expression that relates to the photo.

Checklist: Past Participles

When you edit your writing, ask yourself the next questions.

☐ Do I use the correct form of past participles? Check for spelling errors in the following:

–regular past participles
–irregular past participles

> *turned*   *written*
> Novels are often ~~turn~~ into films, and the screenplays are ~~wrote~~ by the author.

☐ Do I use the present perfect tense correctly?

> *have refused*
> Since 2004, I ~~refused~~ to watch television.

☐ Do I use the past perfect tense correctly?

> *had already seen*
> Ursula did not watch the movie because she ~~already saw~~ it.

☐ Do I use the active and passive voice correctly? Check for overuse of the passive voice and errors with verb form and usage.

> *many people watched the documentary*
> Last month, ~~the documentary was watched by many people.~~

11 Progressive Tenses

SECTION THEME: Entertainment and Culture

LEARNING OBJECTIVES

LO 1 Use progressive tenses. **(p. 193)**

LO 2 Use the present progressive tense. **(p. 193)**

LO 3 Use the past progressive tense. **(p. 195)**

LO 4 Use complete verbs with progressive tenses. **(p. 197)**

In this chapter, you will read about well-known artists and issues in the art world.

GRAMMAR SNAPSHOT

Looking at Progressive Tenses

In this excerpt from one of his letters to his brother Theo, Impressionist artist Vincent van Gogh explains his progress in drawing. Notice the underlined progressive verbs.

> Recently I <u>have been drawing</u> from the model a good deal. And I have all kinds of studies of diggers and sowers, both male and female. At present I <u>am working</u> with charcoal and black crayon, and I have also tried sepia and watercolor. Well, I cannot say that you will see progress in my drawings, but most certainly you will see a change.

In this chapter, you will identify and write progressive verb tenses.

Understanding Progressive Tenses

LO 1 Use progressive tenses.

A **progressive tense** indicates that an action was, is, or will be in progress. Progressive verb tenses always include a form of the verb *be* and the present participle (or *-ing* form of the verb).

Past progressive	She <u>was trying</u> to finish her painting when the phone rang.
Present progressive	Right now, Marg <u>is visiting</u> the Louvre.
Present perfect progressive	She <u>has been working</u> as a painter for twelve years.
Future progressive	Tomorrow morning, at eleven o'clock, she <u>will be working</u>.

Present Progressive

LO 2 Use the present progressive tense.

The **present progressive** shows that an action is happening now or for a temporary period of time. Use this tense with key words such as *now, currently, at this moment, this week,* and *this month.*

This month, Tamayo <u>is exhibiting</u> several paintings in an art gallery.

Right now, Tamayo <u>is painting</u> a portrait.

PAST 1 PM　　2 PM　　**RIGHT NOW**　　4 PM　　5 PM　**FUTURE**

Tamayo **is painting** a portrait.

Affirmative, Question, and Negative Forms

Review the present progressive forms of the verb *work*.

Affirmative		Question Form Move *be* before the subject.		Negative Form Add *not*.	
I	am	Am	I	I	am
She	is	Is	she	She	is
He	is	Is	he	He	is
It	is	working.	Is	it	working?	It	is	not working.
We	are	Are	we	We	are
You	are	Are	you	You	are
They	are	Are	they	They	are

Chapter 11

HINT ◄ Spelling of Present Participles (-*ing* Verbs)

To form most regular present participles, add -*ing* to the base form of the verb.

    try–try**ing**   question–question**ing**

Exceptions

- When the regular verb ends in *e*, remove the *e* and add -*ing*.

    realize–realiz**ing**   appreciate–appreciat**ing**

- When the regular verb ends in a consonant + *ie*, change the *ie* to *y* and add -*ing*.

    lie–**ly**ing   die–d**ying**

- When the regular verb ends in a consonant–vowel–consonant combination, double the last consonant and add -*ing*.

    stop–stop**ping**   jog–jog**ging**

- When a verb of two or more syllables ends in a stressed consonant–vowel–consonant combination, double the last consonant and add -*ing*.

    refer–refer**ring**   begin–begin**ning**

Note: If the two-syllable verb ends in an unstressed syllable, add just -*ing*.

    offer–offer**ing**   happen–happen**ing**

PRACTICE 1

Change each verb to the present progressive form.

EXAMPLE: He runs. _____is running_____

1. We fly. _____
2. She studies. _____
3. You worry. _____
4. He writes. _____
5. I drive. _____

6. She plans. _____
7. We open. _____
8. He shops. _____
9. It opens. _____
10. It begins. _____

Compare the Simple Present and the Present Progressive

Use the present progressive when an action is happening right now or for a temporary period of time. Use the simple present tense when the action happens habitually or when the action is a fact.

Ellen **is cleaning** her brushes.   (Action is in progress.)

Ellen **cleans** her brushes.   (Action is habitual or factual.)

HINT ◄ **A Common Tense Error**

Sometimes people overuse the progressive tense. If an action happens on a regular basis, do not use the progressive tense.

complain
Every week, Tamayo's students ~~are complaining~~ about the number of assignments.

PRACTICE 2

In each sentence, underline the correct verb tense. Then identify the action by writing *G* if it is a general fact or habit or *N* if it is happening now.

EXAMPLE: This month, the Museum of Modern Art (exhibits / <u>is exhibiting</u>) the work of Banksy.   <u>N</u>

1. The artist known as Banksy usually (creates / is creating) politically charged graffiti.   ____

2. Right now, he (draws / is drawing) a shocking image.   ____

3. Banksy never (poses / is posing) for photographers.   ____

4. He (doesn't want / isn't wanting) to be a celebrity.   ____

5. Right now, he (sprays / is spraying) paint on a wall.   ____

6. He always (works / is working) very quickly.   ____

7. Right now, some tourists (look / are looking) at a Banksy mural.   ____

8. Look! That building owner (tries / is trying) to sell the wall on his building.   ____

9. A piece of Banksy graffiti often (sells / is selling) for over $300,000.   ____

Past Progressive

L0 3 Use the past progressive tense.

The **past progressive** indicates that an action was in progress at a specific past time. It can also indicate that an action in progress was interrupted.

Yesterday at 1:00 P.M., Tamayo <u>was cleaning</u> his studio.

Tamayo <u>was cleaning</u> his studio when the fire started.

The fire started.   NOW

He **was cleaning** his studio.

Affirmative, Question, and Negative Forms

Review the past progressive forms of the verb *work*.

Affirmative		Question Form Move *be* before the subject.		Negative Form Add *not*.	
I was		Was I		I was	
She was		Was she		She was	
He was		Was he		He was	
It was	working.	Was it	working?	It was	not working.
We were		Were we		We were	
You were		Were you		You were	
They were		Were they		They were	

PRACTICE 3

Fill in the blanks with the past progressive forms of the verbs in parentheses.

EXAMPLE: Michelangelo (sculpt) ___was sculpting___ when he hurt his thumb.

1. Ludovico and Francesca Buonarroti (live) _____ in Florence when their son, Michelangelo, was born in 1475.

2. While Michelangelo and his classmates (draw) _____ sketches of churches, the teacher realized that the young boy had a great gift.

3. The painter Domenico Ghirlandaio (search) _____ for an apprentice when he heard about Michelangelo.

4. While he (work) _____ for Ghirlandaio, Michelangelo noticed the beauty of some statues.

5. Michelangelo (earn) _____ very little when he bought his first piece of marble.

6. In 1496, while the French ambassador and his wife (visit) _____ the Vatican, he commissioned Michelangelo to create a statue.

7. Romans came to see Michelangelo while he (sculpt) _____ *La Pietà*.

8. Spectators realized that the artist (create) _____ a magnificent statue.

Using Complete Verbs

In progressive forms, always include the complete form of the helping verb *be*. Also make sure that the main verb ends in *-ing*.

Right now, the photographer ^{is} examining the scene.

Adam was ~~take~~ ^{taking} a picture when I entered the room.

HINT ◂ A Past Progressive Pitfall

Do *not* use the past progressive to talk about past habits or about a series of past actions.

Renoir ~~was drawing~~ ^{drew} pictures of his friends when he was younger.

PRACTICE 4

Correct ten past progressive errors.

EXAMPLE: Pablo Picasso was ~~listen~~ ^{listening} to the radio when he heard about the attack on Guernica.

1. The Spanish Civil War was fought from 1936 to 1939. Soon after the war was beginning, General Francisco Franco was making a pact with Germany and Italy. On April 26, 1937, German aircraft were destroying Guernica, a small village in the Basque region of Spain.

2. At that time, Pablo Picasso living in Paris. The Spanish government asked him to paint a mural for the Spanish Pavilion at the 1937 World Fair. While he contemplating what to paint, he heard about the bomb attack on Guernica. He was deciding to paint a mural to protest the inhumanity of war. While the painting, *Guernica*, was hang in the Spanish Pavilion, many people came to see it and disliked it. The public wanted to see a clearer denunciation of

Franco. But Picasso responded by saying that as an artist, he was follow his own vision.

3. After the fair, New York's Museum of Modern Art displayed the painting. Picasso was stating that the painting must return to Spain only after the death of Franco. Franco still ruling Spain when Picasso died in 1973. However, in 1981, *Guernica* was returned to Spain and presently hangs in the Reina Sofia Museum in Madrid.

Other Progressive Forms

Many other tenses also have progressive forms. Review the information about the future progressive and the present perfect progressive.

Future Progressive

The future progressive indicates that an action will be in progress at a future time.

Tomorrow morning, do not disturb Tamayo because he <u>will be working</u> in his studio.

Present Perfect Progressive

The present perfect progressive indicates that an action has been in progress, without interruption, from a past time up to the present.

Tamayo <u>has been painting</u> for eight hours, so he is very tired.

HINT ◀ **Nonprogressive Verbs**

Some verbs do not take the progressive form because they indicate an ongoing state or a perception rather than a temporary action.

Perception Verbs	Preference Verbs	State Verbs	Possession
feel*	care*	believe	have*
hear	desire	know	own
look*	dislike	mean	possess
resemble	hate	realize	
see	like	suppose	
seem	love	think*	
smell*	need	understand	
sound	prefer		
taste*	want		

*Some verbs have more than one meaning and can be used in the progressive tense. Compare the following pairs of sentences to see how these verbs are used.

Nonprogressive	**Progressive**
He **has** two Picassos. (Expresses ownership)	He **is having** a bad day.
I **think** it is expensive. (Expresses an opinion)	I **am thinking** about it.
The photo **looks** good. (Expresses an observation)	He **is looking** at the photo.

PRACTICE 5

Examine each underlined verb. Write *C* above correct verbs, and fix any verb errors.
Some verbs may be incomplete or nonprogressive.

has
EXAMPLE: Miguel been living in Austin, Texas, for several years.
^

1. Currently, Miguel working in a contemporary art gallery.

2. Generally, he is loving his job, but this morning something strange happened.

3. Sharon, an installation artist, entered and dropped paper and envelopes on the
   floor while Miguel was cleaning the gallery.

4. Sharon been working as an artist for twelve years.

5. This week, she is exhibit an art project called *Lost Mail*.

6. Miguel is wanting to understand what a work of art is.

7. He is liking abstract paintings, and he sees the value in a lot of contemporary art.

8. However, he is not understanding what Sharon is trying to do.

9. According to Miguel, some contemporary artists are preferring to create art for
   each other rather than for the general public.

10. Sharon, however, is believing in the value of her art, and she treats each exhibit
    seriously.

FINAL REVIEW

Correct fifteen errors with progressive verbs.

has
EXAMPLE: Artist Kittiwat Unarrom been making sculptures of grotesque body
              ^
              parts from bread since 2006.

1. While Judy Chicago was begin her career as an artist in the 1960s, an art critic
   was telling her that women cannot be artists. She was wanting to prove the critic
   wrong. Chicago making minimalist paintings when she became acquainted
   with feminism. While she creating an art piece, she decided to include feminist

symbols in her artwork. In 1974, she was having an inspiration. She fashioned an installation artwork, *The Dinner Party*, to honor great women in history.

2. The sculpture was controversial. While Chicago was design the installation, she realized she could not make the entire piece by herself. So she was hiring about four hundred volunteers to assemble the piece. One day, while one contributor viewing Chicago's installation, he noticed that the contributors' names were not mentioned. The museum director promised to add the contributors' names to a Web site.

3. Many artists regularly are hiring assistants to help make large art pieces. For example, Andy Warhol used assistants while he assembling large installations. Contemporary artists like Jeff Koons and Damien Hirst often use an assembly line of workers to construct large-scale art projects. Art student

Lewis Carey is thinking that artists who design large sculptures should get sole credit for the concept. Presently, Carey planning a ten-foot sculpture for his art class. He is knowing that he will need a few helpers to complete his project. However, some of his classmates disagree with him. In fact, one student is argue with him right now. She says that artists should give credit to helpers.

MyWritingLab™
Complete these
writing assignments at
mywritinglab.com

THE WRITER'S ROOM   MyWritingLab

Write about one of the following topics. Make sure that you have used and formed your verbs correctly.

1. Describe your favorite work of art. It could be a painting, a sculpture, a piece of architecture, or an illustration.

2. Choose a place on campus. You could go to the cafeteria, the lawn outside, a student center, the library, the hallway, or anywhere else on campus. Then, sit and observe what is going on around you. Use your five senses. Write a paragraph describing the things that are happening.

Checklist: Progressive Verbs

When you edit your writing, ask yourself the next questions.

☐ Do I use the correct verb tenses? Check for the overuse or misuse of progressive forms.

> *created*
> Every year, Picasso ~~was creating~~ new types of paintings.

☐ Are my progressive verbs complete? Check for errors in the following:

–the verb *be*
–incomplete *-ing* forms

> *am posing*   *taking*
> Right now, I ~~posing~~ beside a fountain, and Christa is ~~take~~ a picture of me.

12 Other Verb Forms

SECTION THEME: Entertainment and Culture

LEARNING OBJECTIVES

LO 1 Identify and use modals. (p. 203)

LO 2 Differentiate standard and nonstandard English. (p. 207)

LO 3 Identify and use conditional verb forms. (p. 208)

LO 4 Identify and use infinitives and gerunds. (p. 211)

In this chapter, you will read about cultural differences.

GRAMMAR SNAPSHOT

Looking at Other Verb Forms

In this excerpt from their book *Cultural Anthropology*, Carol R. Ember and Melvin Ember discuss body types. Notice the modals in bold print.

> There is a tendency in our society to view "taller" and "more muscled" as better, which **may reflect** the bias toward males in our culture. Natural selection **may have favored** these traits in males but different ones in females. For example, because females bear children, selection **might have favored** earlier cessation of growth, and therefore less ultimate height in females so that the nutritional needs of a fetus **would** not **compete** with the growing mother's needs.

In this chapter, you will identify and write modals, conditionals, gerunds, and infinitives.

Modals

Modals are helping verbs that express possibility, advice, and so on. Review the list of some common modals and their meanings.

Common Modal Forms

Modal	Meaning	Present Form	Past Form
can	Ability	Amir **can draw** very well.	could draw
could	Possibility	He **could sell** his work.	could have sold
may		Amir **may become** famous.	may have become
might		Amir **might become** famous.	might have become
must	Obligation	We **must work** late.	had to work*
	Probability	The buyers **must be** impatient.	must have been
should	Advice	He **should see** a lawyer.	should have seen
ought to		He **ought to see** a lawyer.	ought to have seen
will	Future action or willingness	They **will buy** his products.	would buy
would	Desire	I **would like** to see his designs.	would have liked

*Exception: To show the past tense of *must* (meaning "obligation"), use the past tense of the regular verb *have to*.

HINT ◄ **Modal Forms Are Consistent**

Each modal has a fixed form. When the subject changes, the verb remains the same. In the example, *can* is the modal.

> I **can** go.   You **can** go.   She **can** go.   We **can** go.   They **can** go.

PRACTICE 1

Read the following sentences. In the space, indicate the function of each underlined modal.

> Ability   Possibility   Advice   Obligation   Desire

EXAMPLE: People <u>ought to learn</u> about cultural differences.   *Advice*_____

1. You <u>could say</u> that culture is learned behavior that involves shared language, gestures, arts, attitudes, beliefs, and values.   _____

2. In the United States, people <u>may call</u> you by your first name.   _____

3. Many Americans <u>can speak</u> both English and Spanish.   _____

4. You <u>ought to remove</u> your shoes when you enter a home in India.   _____

5. In Japan, you <u>should bow</u> when you greet someone.   _____

6. In Australia, instead of saying "Good day," you could <u>say</u> "G'day." _____

7. Many people <u>would like</u> to visit Australia. _____

8. In Great Britain, you <u>must drive</u> on the left side of the road. _____

9. In England, some people <u>might say</u> "I shall not" to mean "I will not." _____

10. In Japan, you <u>should not make</u> direct eye contact with people. _____

Present and Past Forms

For some modals, you must use a completely different word in the past tense. Review the differences between *can* and *could*, *will* and *would*.

Can and Could

Use *can* to indicate a present ability.

> Amir **can speak** Arabic.

Use *could* to indicate a past ability.

> When he was younger, he **could write** in Arabic, but he cannot do so now.

Also use *could* to show that something is possible.

> With globalization, some cultures **could disappear**.

Will and Would

Use *will* to discuss a future action from the present perspective.

> Michelle **will visit** Haiti next summer.

Use *would* to discuss a future action from a past perspective.

> Last month, I told her that I **would go** with her.

Also use *would* to indicate a desire.

> Michelle **would like** to visit her ancestral home.

HINT ◀ **Negative Forms of Modals**

Negative Forms
When you add *not* to modals, the full form consists of two words—for example, *could not* and *should not*. However, when you add *not* to the modal *can*, the result is one word.

| **cannot** | should not | could not | would not | will not |

Contracted Forms
You can contract the negative forms of modals. Note that *will* + *not* becomes *won't*.

| can't | shouldn't | couldn't | wouldn't | won't |

PRACTICE 2

Underline the correct modal forms.

EXAMPLE: This year, the Carnival of Venice (<u>will</u> / would) occur during the last
week of Lent.

1. Grazia DeCesare is originally from Italy, so she (can /
could) speak Italian. She (can / could) also speak Spanish.
Next March, she (will / would) travel to Venice to visit
her aunt. Grazia loves the Carnival of Venice, which is a
unique and wonderful celebration.

2. The Carnival of Venice occurs every spring. During the
carnival, people wear elaborate disguises. If Grazia (can /
could) afford it, she will buy a beautiful mask that she (will /
would) wear during the carnival.

3. The first carnival occurred in the twelfth century. At
that time, the celebration (will / would) generally begin about December 26.
Citizens (will / would) wear masks made of leather, papier-mâché, porcelain,
or plaster. They (will / would) also wear brightly colored capes and elaborate
three-cornered hats. Thus, in past centuries, people (can / could) dance in the
streets, drink wine, and gamble in gaming houses without being recognized.
Because the carnival lasted to the end of March, citizens (will / would) spend
several months wearing disguises in public.

4. During the Middle Ages, the Venetian authorities (will / would) sometimes
try to stop the public debauchery, but the people of Venice loved their carnival
and (can / could) not imagine giving it up. People from all over Europe
(will / would) visit Venice because the city was known as an exciting place.

5. In 1797, during the reign of Napoleon, Austria took control of Venice, and
the city fell into decline. For more than two hundred years, citizens (can /
could) not celebrate the carnival. Then, in 1979, a group of Venetians
convinced the city authorities to reintroduce a one-week carnival.
Nowadays, visitors (can / could) buy masks, and they (can / could) enjoy
the special atmosphere in that beautiful city. The festival (will / would)
definitely be fabulous next spring.

Past of *Should, Could,* and *Would*

To form the past tense of *should, could,* and *would,* add *have* + the past participle. Review the following examples.

Before Anik and Richard went to Mexico, they **should have learned** a few words in Spanish. They **could have communicated** with the locals, and they **would have had** a better time.

HINT ◀ Use Standard Past Forms

Some people say *should of* or *shoulda*. These are nonstandard forms, and you should avoid using them, especially in written communication. When you write the past forms of *should, would,* and *could,* always include *have* + the past participle.

should have
Before Jeremy did business in Japan, he ~~shoulda~~ learned about Japanese
have
business etiquette. He would ~~of~~ offended fewer people.

PRACTICE 3

Underline and correct eight errors with modal forms.

have
EXAMPLE: I should of learned about Geisha culture before I went to Japan.

1. In the 1920s, there were over eighty thousand Geishas in Japan, but today there are only a few thousand. Many tourists believe that Geishas are prostitutes, but Geishas are traditional Japanese entertainers. Mitsumi thinks she shoulda trained to become a Geisha when she lived in Tokyo.

2. Mitsumi is now an accountant, but she woulda loved to be a Geisha. She would of acquired many skills in the art of entertainment. Her teacher woulda taught her music, dance, and conversational skills. She could also have learn how to prepare a Japanese tea ceremony. Mitsumi would have know how to wear a kimono and put on the complicated white face makeup.

3. Last summer, my friend and I were in Kyoto in the Geisha district. I shoulda brought my camera because I saw many young Geisha trainees. These student Geishas are called *maiko*. I would of gone to a tea ceremony with Geishas, but I could not afford it.

Nonstandard Forms: *gonna, gotta, wanna*

LO2 Differentiate standard and nonstandard English.

Some people commonly say *I'm gonna, I gotta,* or *I wanna.* These are nonstandard forms, and you should not use them in written communication.

Write *going to* instead of *gonna.*

> *going to*
> My uncle is ~~gonna~~ help me learn Hungarian.

Write *have to* instead of *gotta.*

> *have to*
> I ~~gotta~~ learn to speak with my grandparents.

Write *want to* instead of *wanna.*

> *want to*
> Next year, I ~~wanna~~ go to Hungary.

HINT ◄ **Forming the Main Verb**

When you use modals, make sure to form your main verb correctly. Use the base form of the verb that directly follows a modal.

> *visit*   *go*
> We should ~~visited~~ France. We can ~~going~~ in March.

PRACTICE 4

Underline and correct ten errors with nonstandard verbs and modal forms.

> *going to*
> **EXAMPLE:** You are <u>gonna</u> learn about gestures.

1. If you take a trip to a foreign country, you should studied nonverbal communication. According to experts, humans can expressing up to 80 percent of their thoughts nonverbally.

2. One gesture can had different meanings in various countries. For example, in the United States, if you wanna indicate that you like something, you can join your thumb and forefinger into an "okay" gesture. However, you are gonna insult a waiter in France if you give the okay sign because the gesture means "zero" or "worthless." In Russia, use the okay sign only if you wanna insult someone.

3. If you gotta go on a business trip to Brazil, do not use the thumbs-up gesture because it is highly offensive. If you raise your forefinger and your pinky in Italy, you are gonna make someone very angry because the sign means that a man's wife is cheating on him. In Australia, if you wanna lose friends, make the V for "victory" sign with your palm facing toward you. It is Australia's most obscene gesture.

4. Clearly, if you wanna get along with people from other cultures, it is a good idea to learn about their gestures.

L0 3 Identify and use conditional verb forms.

Conditional Forms

In a **conditional sentence**, there is a condition and a result. This type of sentence usually contains the word *if* and has two parts, or clauses. The main clause depends on the condition set in the *if* clause. There are three conditional forms.

First Conditional Form: Present or Possible Future

Use the "possible future" form when the condition is true or very possible.

If + present tense   ⟶   present or future tense

Condition (*if* clause)	**Result**
If he **needs** help,	he **can call** me.
If you **visit** Mexico,	you **will see** some amazing murals.

Second Conditional Form: Unlikely Present

Use the "unlikely present" form when the condition is not likely and probably will not happen.

If + past tense   ⟶   *would* (expresses a condition)
                                      could (expresses a possibility)

Condition (*if* clause)	**Result**
If **I knew** how to speak Spanish,	I **would live** in Mexico for a year.
If she **were** taller,	she **could be** a runway model.

HINT ◄ If I Were . . .

In informal English, you occasionally hear *was* in the *if* clause. However, in academic writing, when the condition is unlikely, always use *were* in the *if* clause.

If I **were** rich, I <u>would buy</u> a new car.

If my sister **were** rich, she <u>would invest</u> in the stock market.

Third Conditional Form: Impossible Past

Use the "impossible past" form when the condition cannot happen because the event is over.

If + past perfect tense ⟶ *would have* (+ past participle)

Condition (*if* clause)	**Result**
If you **had asked** me,	I **would have traveled** with you.
If Karl **had done** his homework,	he **would have passed** the course.

PRACTICE 5

In each case, identify the type of conditional sentence, and write *A, B,* or *C* in the blank.

A (possible future)	If you ask me, I will help.
B (unlikely present)	If you asked me, I would help.
C (impossible past)	If you had asked me, I would have helped.

EXAMPLE: If I could, I would travel to Spain. ___B___

1. If Raul Morales were younger, he would return to school. _____

2. If he had known how difficult it is to make a career in dance, he would have found a different profession. _____

3. If you want to learn the tango, he will teach it to you. _____

4. According to Raul, the tango is not difficult to master if you practice a lot. _____

5. If he had taken better care of himself, he would not have needed knee surgery. _____

6. Today, if he takes it easy, he can give three dance classes a week. _____

7. He would give more classes if his doctor permitted it. _____

8. If he had never danced, he would have felt unfulfilled. _____

HINT ◄ Avoid Mixing Conditional Forms

Avoid mixing conditional forms. If you are discussing a past event, use the third conditional form. Do not mix the second and third forms.

> had been
> If I ~~were~~ you, I would have done the assignment.

PRACTICE 6

Fill in the blanks with the correct forms of the verbs in parentheses.

EXAMPLE: If you (plan) _____plan_____ to do business abroad, you will benefit from diversity training courses.

1. Eric Zorn went on a business trip to Japan, and, unfortunately, he made some cultural etiquette errors. While there, he made eye contact with his hosts, and

he got down to business immediately. If he (take) _____

more time for small talk, his hosts would have felt more comfortable. Also, if he

had avoided direct eye contact, he (appear) _____

less aggressive. Basically, if he (understand) _____

the cultural differences, he would not have insulted his hosts.

2. Roger Axtell is an international business traveler. He has written a book

   called *Do's and Taboos of Humor Around the World.* If Axtell (travel, not)

   _____ extensively, he would have been unable to write

   about cultural differences.

3. Axtell has had some interesting experiences. A few years ago, when he visited Saudi

   Arabia, he met with an important customer. One day, the customer grabbed his

   hand while they were walking. In Saudi Arabia, hand-holding is a sign of friendship

   and respect. If Axtell (pull) _____ away, he would have

   offended his host. If he (know) _____ in advance about the

   hand-holding, he (feel, not) _____ so uncomfortable.

4. Axtell says that if he (be, not) _____ so busy, he would

   write more books about cultural diversity.

HINT ◀ **Problems with the Past Conditional**

In "impossible past" sentences, the writer expresses regret about a past event
or expresses the wish that a past event had worked out differently. Avoid the
following errors.

- Do not use *would have* . . . in the *if* clause. Instead, use the past perfect tense.

       had asked
  If you ~~would have asked~~ me, I would have traveled with you.

- Do not write *woulda* or *would of*. These are nonstandard forms. When you use
  the past forms of *should*, *would*, and *could*, always include *have* + the past
  participle.

       had done   **have**
  If you ~~would have done~~ the work, you would ~~of~~ passed the course.

PRACTICE 7

Underline and correct nine errors in conditional forms.

                                            have
EXAMPLE: If you had met my grandfather, you wouldn't ~~of~~ liked him.

1. According to the British Broadcasting Corporation, Britain has become a

   "surveillance society." England has one security camera for every fourteen people. If a driver sped, he will receive a ticket because speed cameras are on many roads. Also, cameras are on telephone poles and buildings. For example, there are thirty-five cameras on Oxford Street. Today, if you walk along Oxford Street, you would see a camera.

2. When Liam was in London last year, he littered. If he would have put his candy wrapper into a garbage can, he would not have received a ticket. But a camera spotted his action, and he was identified and charged. If I had been with Liam, I would have warn him about the surveillance cameras, and I woulda said, "Don't litter!"

3. Some British citizens are satisfied with the closed-circuit cameras. Last July, Belinda Reed's car was robbed. Perhaps if she had been in her car, the thief woulda attacked her. Luckily, a camera filmed the action. The thief was identified and arrested. If the camera wouldn't have been there, nobody would of recognized the thief. These days, if I were a criminal in England, I will worry about those cameras!

Gerunds and Infinitives

LO 4 Identify and use infinitives and gerunds.

Sometimes a main verb is followed by another verb. The second verb can be a gerund or an infinitive. A **gerund** is a verb with an *-ing* ending. An **infinitive** consists of *to* and the base form of the verb.

Verb + gerund	We <u>finished</u> **reading** *Wild Swans*.
Verb + infinitive	I <u>want</u> **to write** about it.

Using Gerunds

Some verbs in English are always followed by a gerund. Do not confuse gerunds with progressive verb forms. Compare a progressive verb and a gerund.

Verb	Julie is studying now.
	(*Studying* is in the present progressive form. Julie is in the process of doing something.)
Gerund	Julie <u>finished</u> **studying**.
	(*Studying* is a gerund that follows *finish*. After *finish*, you must use a gerund.)

Some Common Verbs and Expressions Followed by Gerunds

acknowledge	discuss	postpone
adore	dislike	practice
anticipate	enjoy	quit
appreciate	finish	recall
avoid	involve	recollect
can't help	justify	recommend
complete	keep	regret
consider	loathe	resent
delay	mention	resist
deny	mind	risk
detest	miss	tolerate

Using Prepositions Plus Gerunds

Many verbs have the structure **verb + preposition + object**. If the object is another verb, the second verb is a gerund.

> I dream <u>about</u> **traveling** to Greece.

Some Common Words Followed by Prepositions Plus Gerunds

accuse <u>him</u> of*	(be) excited about	(be) good at	prohibit <u>her</u> from*
apologize for	feel like	insist on	succeed in
discourage <u>him</u> from*	fond of	(be) interested in	think about
dream of	forbid <u>him</u> from*	look forward to	(be) tired of
(be) enthusiastic about	forgive <u>me</u> for*	prevent <u>him</u> from*	warn <u>him</u> about*

*Certain verbs must have a noun or pronoun before the preposition. Here, the pronouns are underlined.

Using Infinitives

Some verbs are followed by the infinitive (*to* + base form of verb).

> Helen wants **to travel** with me.
> (*To travel* is an infinitive that follows the verb *wants*.)

Some Common Verbs Followed by Infinitives

afford	decide	manage	refuse
agree	demand	mean	seem
appear	deserve	need	swear
arrange	expect	offer	threaten
ask	fail	plan	volunteer
claim	hesitate	prepare	want
complete	hope	pretend	wish
consent	learn	promise	would like

Using Gerunds or Infinitives

Some common verbs can be followed by gerunds or infinitives. Both forms have the same meaning.

begin	continue	hate	like
love	prefer	start	

LaTasha likes **to live** alone.
LaTasha likes **living** alone.

} Both sentences have exactly the same meaning.

HINT ◀ Used to . . .

You can follow *used to* with a gerund or an infinitive, but there is a difference in meaning.

- *Used to* + infinitive expresses a past habit.

   Rowan does not smoke now, but she used to **smoke**.

- *Be used to* + gerund expresses something you are accustomed to.

   Rowan has been on her own for years, so she is used to **living** alone.

PRACTICE 8

Correct any errors in the underlined gerund and infinitive forms. If the verb is correct, write *C* above it. (Be careful, you may have to change the preposition before the gerund.)

                                                    on reforming
EXAMPLE: Social activist Bhimrao Ambedkar insisted <u>to reform</u> cultural norms.

1. The untouchables of India have been discriminated against for thousands

   of years. Bhimrao Ambedkar was born an untouchable in 1891, but he

   <u>dreamt to change</u> his circumstances.

2. His family was extremely poor, but Ambedkar <u>enjoyed to study</u> and

   <u>wanted to pursue</u> his education.

3. His father <u>agreed sending</u> him to college, and, in 1907, Ambedkar became one

   of the first people from his caste to study at college.

4. Ambedkar <u>disliked to see</u> the way upper-caste Hindus treated untouchables.

5. The young man became a leading political figure and <u>succeeded to fight</u> for

   civil rights of his caste.

6. When India received its independence in 1947, Indian politicians <u>looked forward to work</u> with Ambedkar.

7. He was one of the fathers of the Indian Constitution. It <u>promises to provide</u> civil liberties to all Indian citizens.

8. Today, many Indians are working to eradicate intolerance and <u>deserve having</u> recognition for their efforts.

FINAL REVIEW

Underline and correct fifteen errors in the following blog post.

should have
EXAMPLE: We <u>shoulda</u> stayed in a better hotel.

1. Last year, I found a cheap travel deal to Singapore. Before I left, I shoulda learned more about the city. I could of avoided some problems. For example, I stayed in a cheap hotel, and it was awful! Rainwater trickled into my room, and there was mold on the walls. If I would have read some online reviews before I booked that hotel, I would have avoided a lot of problems.

2. My hotel was dirty, but the city was really clean. In fact, Singapore has some of the strictest anti-littering laws in the world. Back in 1968, Singapore's leader enacted a "Keep Singapore Clean" campaign. Before that, people could littered without a penalty. I would of hated to be in Singapore at that time because the city was very dirty and polluted. Since then, the laws have become very tough. For example, people are prohibited to buy chewing gum. Also, it's good that I stopped to smoke before my trip because it is illegal to throw a cigarette butt on the ground. Citizens really gotta be careful. If they decide littering, they must pay a large fine or do community service.

3. Singapore is a very multilingual city, with four official languages: English, Malay, Mandarin, and Tamil. Also, if you wanna eat interesting food, go to that country. The cuisine is multicultural, and most food is very good. But I had a bad experience at a street stall. I ordered a fried Fuzhou UFO, and I became

sick. It's called a UFO because it resembles a little flying saucer. If I would have

known it contained oysters, I would have chosen something else. I am allergic

to seafood and must avoid to eat oysters.

4. In spite of the problems, I thoroughly enjoyed my stay. If I had the chance to

visit Singapore again, I will do it. Recently, I found another really good travel

deal, so I'm gonna visit Mexico next summer. I promise writing about that trip

on this blog.

THE WRITER'S ROOM — MyWritingLab

Write about one of the following topics. Make sure that you have formed any
modals or conditionals correctly.

1. What can people learn when they interact with other cultures? List some
   things.

2. Think about someone you know who is from another culture. How are
   you and that person similar or different?

MyWritingLab™
**Complete these
writing assignments at
mywritinglab.com**

Checklist: Other Verb Forms

When you edit your writing, ask yourself these questions.

☐ Do I use the correct modal forms? Check for errors in the following:

–*will* vs. *would* and *can* vs. *could*

–past forms

      have
I should ~~of~~ packed an umbrella when I visited Ireland.

☐ Do I use the correct conditional forms? Check for errors in the following:

–possible future forms ("If I meet . . ., I will go . . .")

–unlikely present forms ("If I met . . ., I would go . . .")

–impossible past forms ("If I had met . . ., I would have gone . . .")

      had
If I ~~would have~~ more money, I would stay in good hotels.

☐ Do I use the correct gerund or infinitive form?

      traveling
I recommend ~~to travel~~ during the spring break.

READING LINK

To read more about entertainment and culture, see the following essays:

"What's Your Humor Style?" by Louise Dobson (page 405)

"A Cultural Minefield" by William Ecenbarger (page 408)

"Celanthropists" by Katrina Onstad (page 411)

THE WRITER'S CIRCLE   Collaborative Activity

Work with a group of about three students. You need one sheet of paper for this activity.

STEP 1   Write down as much as you know about the life of a famous entertainer (such as a musician, an artist, an athlete, or an actor). Do not mention the name of the entertainer. Write at least five sentences about the person.

Example: He was born in Philadelphia, and he started rapping at age twelve. In 1990, he played a "prince" on a hit television show. Later, he had several hit movies. He is slender and tall. He has protruding ears. In 2006, he acted in a movie with his son.

STEP 2   Read your sentences aloud to another group of students. They must guess who your mystery person is. If they cannot guess, continue to give them more clues.

Chapter 12

Subject–Verb Agreement 13

SECTION THEME: Beliefs

In this chapter, you will read about mysteries and urban legends.

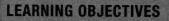

LEARNING OBJECTIVES

LO 1 Practice basic subject–verb agreement. **(p. 218)**

LO 2 Conjugate verbs before the subject. **(p. 221)**

LO 3 Practice subject–verb agreement with more than one subject. **(p. 223)**

LO 4 Practice verb agreement with special subject forms. **(p. 224)**

LO 5 Maintain agreement in sentences with interrupting words and phrases. **(p. 226)**

GRAMMAR SNAPSHOT

Looking at Subject–Verb Agreement

David A. Locher is the author of *Collective Behavior*. In the following excerpt from his book, he describes an urban legend. The subjects are in bold print, and the verbs are underlined.

> An **urban legend** gives specific details about an **event** that has supposedly occurred. For example, there is a **legend** about a **man** who wakes up in a bathtub full of ice. **He** finds a note left by the attractive woman **he** met at a party or bar the night before. **She** has purportedly stolen his kidney. This **urban legend** gives specific **details** that may change every time the **story** is told.

In this chapter, you will practice making subjects and verbs agree.

LO 1 Practice basic subject–verb agreement.

Basic Subject–Verb Agreement Rules

Subject-verb agreement simply means that a subject and a verb agree in number. A singular subject needs a singular verb, and a plural subject needs a plural verb.

	S V
Singular subject	Jay believes in urban legends.
	S V
Plural subject	The **stories** have strange endings.

Simple Present Tense

Writers use **simple present tense** to indicate that an action is habitual or factual. Review the rules for simple present tense agreement.

♦ Add -*s* or -*es* to the verb when the subject is *he, she, it,* or the equivalent (*Mike, Ella, Texas*). This is called the **third-person singular form**.

Ms. Suzuki writes about urban legends.	(one person)
The **museum** displays many exhibits.	(one place)
Perhaps a **giant ape** roams the forests of the northwestern United States.	(one thing)

♦ When the subject is *I, you, we, they,* or the equivalent (*the Smiths, the books, Jay and I*), do not add an ending to the verb.

The moment **we** want to believe something, **we** suddenly see all the arguments for it and become blind to the arguments against it.

—George Bernard Shaw

> **GRAMMAR LINK**
> For more information about present tense verbs, see Chapter 9.

To see how these rules work, review the forms of the verb *run*.

Present Tense of *Run*

	Singular Forms	Plural Forms
First person	I run	We run
Second person	You run	You run
Third person	He **runs**	They run
	She **runs**	
	It **runs**	

PRACTICE 1

In each sentence, underline the subject and circle the correct verb. Make sure that the verb agrees with the subject.

EXAMPLE: Some stories (seem / seems) fantastic.

1. Generally, urban legends (appear / appears) mysteriously.

2. The stories (spread / spreads) rapidly.

3. Usually, the speaker (say / says), "This happened to a friend of a friend."

4. Some people (spread / spreads) urban legends by e-mail.

5. In one message, a man (visit / visits) a tourist resort in Mexico.

6. A tiny dog (beg / begs) for food.

7. The young man (decide / decides) to keep the little Chihuahua.

8. Later, he (bring / brings) his new pet to a veterinarian.

9. The animal doctor (say / says), "Why are you keeping a sewer rat?"

10. Many people (believe / believes) such urban legends.

Troublesome Present-Tense Verbs: *Be, Have, Do*

Some present-tense verbs are formed in special ways. Review the verbs *be*, *have*, and *do*. Be particularly careful when writing these verbs.

	Be	**Have**	**Do**
Singular Forms			
First person	I am	I have	I do
Second person	You are	You have	You do
Third person	He **is**	He **has**	He **does**
	She **is**	She **has**	She **does**
	It **is**	It **has**	It **does**
Plural Forms			
First person	We are	We have	We do
Second person	You are	You have	You do
Third person	They are	They have	They do

PRACTICE 2

Fill in each blank with the correct form of *be*, *have*, or *do*.

EXAMPLE: Some people _____have_____ irrational fears. Max _____is_____ afraid of cats.

1. All people _____have_____ fears. Some fears _____are_____ universal and arise from our human history. They _____are_____ a response to harmful situations. For example, spiders and snakes _____are_____ the potential to harm us. Heights _____are_____ also potentially dangerous, so a fear of heights is common. Basically, fear _____is_____ a healthy response.

2. A phobia _____is_____ an irrational or excessive fear. For example, Shane _____has_____ extremely uncomfortable on a bridge or in a tunnel. Elaine Chen _____has_____ an extreme stress reaction in airplanes. She _____does_____ not enjoy flying, but she still _____does_____ it sometimes. She _____has_____ aware that flying is safer than driving a car. So, in airplanes, Elaine _____has_____ relaxation exercises to overcome her anxiety. According to the Anxiety Disorders Association of America, almost 20 million people _____have_____ specific phobias. Some therapists _____do_____ a good job of helping people overcome their phobias.

PRACTICE 3

In the following paragraphs, the verbs are underlined. Identify and correct ten subject–verb agreement errors. Write *C* above five correct verbs.

                       has
EXAMPLE: Mario <u>have</u> strange opinions about urban legends.

1. Urban legends <u>occurs</u> in every culture. They <u>serve</u> a purpose. They <u>is</u> about

    ordinary people in frightening situations, and each legend <u>warn</u> us about a

    possible danger. Sometimes, a story <u>have</u> a moral. Additionally, when people

    <u>speaks</u> about a scary or traumatic event, they <u>release</u> their collective anxiety.

2. These days, the Internet <u>contribute</u> to the spread of urban myths. For example,

    a popular e-mail <u>advise</u> people about a gang initiation. According to the e-mail,

    gang members <u>drive</u> in cars with the headlights off. If an innocent driver

    <u>flash</u> his lights at the car, a gang member <u>shoot</u> that driver. However, police

    officers <u>insist</u> that the initiation game <u>is</u> a myth. Internet sleuths often <u>exposes</u>

    such legends.

Agreement in Other Tenses

Simple Past Tense

Writers use the **simple past tense** to indicate that an action was completed at a past
time. In the past tense, all verbs except *be* have one form.

Regular   I worked.   He worked.   We worked.   You worked.   They worked.
Irregular   I ate.   He ate.   We ate.   You ate.   They ate.

Exception: In the past tense, the only verb requiring subject–verb agreement is the
verb *be*. It has two past forms: *was* and *were*.

Past Tense of *Be*

Was	Were
I was	You were
He was	We were
She was	They were
It was	

Present Perfect Tense

The present perfect tense is formed with *have* or *has* before the past participle. If the
subject is third-person singular, always use *has*.

    She <u>has</u> <u>finished</u> a book about Native American legends. **I** <u>have</u> <u>read</u> it.

Other Tenses

When writing in most other verb tenses and in modal forms (*can, could, would, may, might,* and so on), use the same form of the verb with every subject.

GRAMMAR LINK
For more information about using the present perfect tense, see Chapter 10.

Future	Past Perfect	Modals
I <u>will</u> read.	I <u>had</u> finished.	I <u>can</u> go.
She <u>will</u> read.	She <u>had</u> finished.	She <u>should</u> go.
He <u>will</u> read.	He <u>had</u> finished.	He <u>might</u> go.
They <u>will</u> read.	They <u>had</u> finished.	They <u>could</u> go.

PRACTICE 4

In each sentence, underline the subject and circle the correct verb. Make sure that the subject and verb agree.

EXAMPLE: Some <u>mysteries</u> (**have** / has) been solved.

1. Most mysteries (is / **are**) not mysterious at all, according to author Benjamin Radford.

2. For example, perhaps giant apelike creatures (**live** / lives) in the mountainous region between British Columbia and California.

3. Radford (have / **has**) visited the sites where Bigfoot sightings were reported, but he (**is** / are) not convinced that the evidence is legitimate.

4. He (give / **gives**) interesting reasons for his opinion.

5. First, when a giant ape (die / **dies**), there should be a dead body, yet no bodies (~~have~~ / has) been found.   *cf). nothing*

6. Second, many people (**claim** / claims) that they have seen Bigfoot, but these eyewitness testimonies (is / **are**) probably unreliable.

7. Finally, believers (**refer** / refers) to sightings of giant footprints, but in 2000, a man named Ray Wallace admitted that he and his son had made fake footprints.

8. They (was / **were**) just having fun, and they (was / **were**) surprised when many people believed them.

9. Many people (**continue** / continues) to believe in Bigfoot.

10. Radford (admit / **admits**) that the legend will probably continue for centuries.

Verb Before the Subject

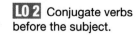 **LO2** Conjugate verbs before the subject.

Usually the verb comes after the subject, but in some sentences, the verb comes *before* the subject. In such cases, you must still ensure that the subject and verb agree.

Sentences Beginning with *There* or *Here*

When a sentence begins with *there* or *here*, the subject always follows the verb. *There* and *here* are not subjects.

            V   S   V   S

Here is a new **book** about Atlantis. There are many new **theories** about it.

Questions

In most questions, the helping verb or the verb *be* appears before the subject. In the next examples, the main verb is *be*.

            V   S   V   S

Where is the mysterious **island**? Was Plato's **story** about Atlantis fictional or factual?

In questions in which the main verb is not *be*, the subject agrees with the helping verb.

           H   S   V H   S   V

Where does the sunken **city** rest? Do **scientists** have any answers?

PRACTICE 5

In each sentence, underline the subject and circle the correct verb.

EXAMPLE: What (is)/ are) Easter Island's most well-known tourist attraction?

1. (Is / Are) there ancient ruins on a Polynesian island?

2. What (do / does) people see on Easter Island?

3. Why (is / are) there over eight hundred statues?

4. How much (do / does) each stone monument weigh?

5. Why (is / are) the expressions on the carved faces so serious?

6. What (do / does) each statue represent?

7. (Do / Does) the Rapanui people still live there?

8. How long (have / has) the island been part of Chile?

PRACTICE 6

Correct any subject–verb agreement errors. If a sentence is correct, write *C* in the blank.

                             is

EXAMPLE: There ~~are~~ a fascinating woman in my neighborhood.   _____

1. There is many stories about Talia Leduc.   _____

2. Do she see the future?   _____

3. There are five customers who want Talia to read their palms.   _____

4. Is her predictions often correct?   _____

5. There is some strange coincidences.   _____

6. Do that woman have a special gift?   _____

7. Does her husband know the truth?   _____

8. There is many possible reasons for her popularity.   _____

More Than One Subject

L03 Practice subject–verb agreement with more than one subject.

There are special agreement rules when there is more than one subject in a sentence.

◆ When two or more subjects are joined by *and*, use the plural form of the verb.

   And   **Florida**, **Bermuda**, and **Puerto Rico** <u>form</u> the Bermuda Triangle.

◆ When two or more subjects are joined by *or* or *nor*, the verb agrees with the subject that is the closest to it.

   Nor   Neither the doctor nor the **nurses** <u>have</u> special powers.
   plural

   Or   Either Chanel or **Vanessa** <u>owns</u> a GPS device.
   singular

PRACTICE 7

In each sentence, underline the subject and circle the correct verb. Make sure the verb agrees with the subject.

EXAMPLE: <u>People</u> (⟨have⟩/ has) too much faith in technology.

1. In 2011, Rita Chretien and her husband, Albert, (was / were) in Nevada.

2. Looking for a shortcut, they (was / were) dependent on their GPS, but the device led them off track.

3. According to Chretien, there (was / were) no houses in the vicinity.

4. After Al Chretien went to find help, Rita (was / were) left alone.

5. Neither Rita's husband nor other rescuers (was / were) nearby.

6. For several days, a tiny piece of chocolate or a fish oil pill (was / were) Rita's only food.

7. Forty-nine days later, Chad Herman and his friends (was / were) Rita's rescuers.

8. Today, there (is / are) many theories about how Rita survived.

9. Either Rita's strong faith or her good health (was / were) responsible for her salvation.

10. Perhaps one or several explanations (is / are) true.

LO 4 Practice verb agreement with special subject forms.

Special Subject Forms

Some subjects are not easy to identify as singular or plural. Two common types are indefinite pronouns and collective nouns.

Indefinite Pronouns

Indefinite pronouns refer to a general person, place, or thing. Carefully review the following list of indefinite pronouns.

Indefinite Pronouns

Singular	another	each	no one	other
	anybody	everybody	nobody	somebody
	anyone	everyone	nothing	someone
	anything	everything	one	something
Plural	both	many	several	
	few	others		

Singular Indefinite Pronouns

In the following sentences, the subjects are singular, so they require third-person singular verb forms.

Almost **everyone** <u>has</u> theories about the Bermuda Triangle.

According to Norm Tyler, **nothing** <u>proves</u> that the Bermuda Triangle is dangerous.

Plural Indefinite Pronouns

Both, few, many, others, and *several* are all plural subjects. The verb is always plural.

The two survivors talked about their journey. **Both** <u>have</u> frequent nightmares.

Many <u>were</u> still on the boat when it mysteriously disappeared.

PRACTICE 8

Underline the subject and circle the correct verb in each sentence.

EXAMPLE: Everybody (has/ have) an opinion on the role of religion in schools.

1. In 1859, Charles Darwin wrote *On the Origin of Species*. In Victorian England, Darwin's ideas (was / were) regarded as a threat to Christianity. Years later, the theory of evolution (was / were) still controversial.

2. In 1925, John Scopes (was / were) accused of violating the Butler Act by teaching Tennessee biology students about evolution. At that time, if anybody (was / were) brave enough to teach evolution, that person could be arrested.

The Scopes Monkey Trial lasted for fifteen days, but nobody (was / were) prepared for defense lawyer Clarence Darrow's decision. He asked the jury to find his client guilty because he wanted to take the case to the Tennessee supreme court.

3. Today, there (is / are) debates about the teaching of religion and science in schools. In this country, one controversial issue (is / are) school prayer. Some (think / thinks) that students should pray every day under the direction of a teacher. Others (disagree / disagrees) and (argue / argues) that parents, not schools, should teach religion and morality.

4. If someone (say / says) that the United States is a multicultural society with a variety of religious beliefs, then someone else (reply / replies) that it was founded on Christian religious principles and that school prayer is necessary. Certainly, everyone (has / have) an opinion about this issue.

Collective Nouns as Subjects

Collective nouns refer to a group of people or things. The group acts as a unit. Here are some common collective nouns.

army	class	crowd	group	population
association	club	family	jury	public
audience	committee	gang	mob	society
band	company	government	organization	team

> **GRAMMAR LINK**
> For more information about using collective nouns with pronouns, see page 128 in Chapter 7.

Generally, each group acts as a unit, so you must use the singular form of the verb.

The **crowd** <u>gathers</u> in the public square.

PRACTICE 9

Underline the subject of each sentence. Then, circle the correct form of the verb.

EXAMPLE: In many communities throughout the world, <u>people</u> (believe / believes) in ghosts.

1. Scientists and other rational thinkers (is / are) likely to question the existence of a spirit world. However, even skeptics (admit / admits) that they may not know the whole truth.

2. In *The Power of Myth*, Joseph Campbell (state / states), "A fairy tale is the child's myth. There (is / are) proper myths for proper times of life. As you (grow / grows) older, you (need / needs) a sturdier mythology." Every society (invent / invents) stories to try to explain basic truths.

3. Each nation (have / has) its own version of ghost stories. In the Chinese lunar tradition, the seventh month (is / are) "ghost month." During ghost month, a gate (open / opens), and spirits (enter / enters) the human world. Buddhist priests (pray / prays) to subdue the spirits. A band (play / plays) music to welcome the spirits, and the crowd (listen / listens) with reverence. In China, a typical family (welcome / welcomes) the ghosts during ghost month.

LO 5 Maintain agreement in sentences with interrupting words and phrases.

Interrupting Words and Phrases

Words that come between the subject and the verb may confuse you. In these cases, look for the subject and make sure that the verb agrees with the subject. To help you see the interrupting words in the following two examples, we have put parentheses around the words that come between the subject and the verb.

Some old **legends** (about vampires and spirits) <u>continue</u> to scare people.

A **student** (in my creative writing class) <u>writes</u> updated vampire stories.

HINT ◄ **Identify Interrupting Phrases**

To make it easier to find errors as you edit for subject–verb agreement, place parentheses around any words that separate the subject and the verb in the sentence. Then you can see whether the subjects and verbs agree.

Many **directors**, (including the late Stanley Kubrick), <u>have made</u> horror films.

When interrupting phrases contain *of the,* the subject generally appears before the phrase.

One (of the neighbors) <u>knows</u> everybody's secrets.

PRACTICE 10

Place parentheses around any words that come between each subject and verb. Then circle the correct form of the verb.

EXAMPLE: Anne Rice,(a popular author,)<u>write</u> /(<u>writes</u>)about vampires.

1. One of this era's most enduring legends <u>is / are</u> the Dracula legend.

2. Tales about vampires <u>was / were</u> common in Eastern Europe and India.

3. The story about the blood-drinking human <u>was / were</u> especially popular after Bram Stoker wrote the novel *Dracula* in 1897.

4. Current myths about vampires <u>emphasize / emphasizes</u> the creature's aversion to sunlight and garlic.

5. Some believers in Eastern Europe <u>surround / surrounds</u> their homes with garlic.

6. Many Internet sites, such as *Vampires.com*, <u>cater / caters</u> to people's interest in vampires.

7. Dracula, with his blood-covered fangs, <u>remain / remains</u> a popular fictional character.

8. Some legends, especially the Dracula legend, <u>last / lasts</u> a long time.

PRACTICE 11

Correct any subject–verb agreement errors. If the sentence is correct, write *C* in the blank.

EXAMPLE: Many of us, in the opinion of Dr. Raoul Figuera, ~~enjoys~~ ^{enjoy} horror stories. _____

"THE FELLOW HAD A KEY"

1. Villains and heroes in most gothic novels is very distinct. _____

2. Evil characters, including Dracula, does not have a good side. _____

3. One novel, *Strange Case of Dr. Jekyll and Mr. Hyde*, show us

   two sides of human nature. _____

4. The hero of the story has a dark side. _____

5. Sometimes Dr. Jekyll, away from the prying eyes of others, drink

   a powerful potion. _____

6. His personality, usually very sweet and friendly, changes completely. _____

7. The doctor, with a lack of control, become the evil Mr. Hyde. _____

8. Both characters, however, resides within the same man. _____

9. In the novel, Robert Louis Stevenson shows us a shocking truth. _____

10. Both good and evil exists within us. _____

Interrupting Words: *Who, Which,* and *That*

Some sentences include a relative clause beginning with the pronoun *who, which,* or *that.* In the relative clause, the verb must agree with the antecedent of *who, which,* or *that.*

In the first example below, the antecedent of *who* is *man.* In the second example, the antecedent of *that* is *books.* And in the third example, the antecedent of *which* is *book.*

There is a man in southern Mexico **who** <u>writes</u> about Aztec beliefs.

Here are some old **books that** <u>discuss</u> unsolved mysteries.

One **book, which** <u>contains</u> stories about crop circles, is very interesting.

PRACTICE 12

The next adapted excerpt is from the H. G. Wells novel, *The Island of Doctor Moreau*. Read the excerpt. Underline each subject and circle the correct verb form.

EXAMPLE: There is <u>something</u> in the starlight that (loosen /(loosens)) one's tongue.

1. The cabin in which I (find / finds) myself (is / are) small and rather untidy. A young man who (have / has) flaxen hair, a bristly straw-colored moustache, and a dropping lip, (is / are) sitting and holding my wrist. For a minute, we (stare / stares) at each other without speaking. His watery grey eyes (is / are) oddly void of expression. Then I hear a sound which (is / are) like the low angry growling of some large animal. The man, who (appear / appears) concerned, (ask / asks), "How do you feel now?"

2. I reply that I (do / does) not recollect how I got here. "You (was / were) picked up in a boat, starving. The name on the boat (is / are) the *Lady Vain*. There (was / were) blood spots on the upper edge of the vessel. You were in luck," he continued, "to get picked up by a ship that (have / has) a medical man aboard. Those who (was / were) with you did not share the same fate."

FINAL REVIEW

Underline and correct fifteen errors in subject–verb agreement.

EXAMPLE: Legends about a magical stork <u>is</u> common.
                                          are

1. In every culture, parents tell their children special stories and pass on particular traditions. Each story have a purpose. For example, a worry doll, which is made of rags, have an important function for Guatemalan children. Before going to bed, the child tell the doll about a particular concern. Then the child carefully leave the doll under his or her pillow. During the night, the doll worries so that the child don't have to.

2. Everybody, at the age of five or six, lose baby teeth. The loss of teeth are an important time in most cultures. The family celebrate the end of babyhood. In Costa Rica, children keep their first tooth after it fall out. Covered in gold, the tooth become an earring. In Japan, when somebody lose a baby tooth from the lower jaw, he or she throws the tooth straight up. The goal is to

have straight permanent teeth. In Mexico, either the child or the parent place the tooth in a special box. El Raton, a magic mouse, exchanges the tooth for money. In parts of Europe and North America, stories about a magical tooth fairy is common.

3. One of the most interesting legends are about leprechauns. The tiny fairy with the face of an old man play tricks on people. Such stories and traditions exist in all cultures.

THE WRITER'S ROOM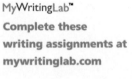

MyWritingLab™
**Complete these
writing assignments at
mywritinglab.com**

Write about one of the following topics. When you finish writing, underline each subject and ensure that all of your subjects and verbs agree.

1. What are the causes of urban legends? Why do people pass along such stories?

2. Many adults tell children stories about magical or mythical people, creatures, or events. For example, they might tell a tale about the tooth fairy, Santa, elves, or a stork that brings babies. Children often believe the stories. Should parents tell such yarns to children? Why or why not?

Chapter 13

Checklist: Subject–Verb Agreement

When you edit your writing, ask yourself these questions.

☐ Do my subjects and verbs agree? Check for errors with the following:

–present tense verbs

–*was* and *were*

>   **were**   **are**
> Dr. Figuera and his associates ~~was~~ surprised; men ~~is~~ more superstitious than women.

☐ Do I use the correct verb form with indefinite pronouns? Check for errors with singular indefinite pronouns such as *everybody, nobody,* and *somebody*.

>   **knows**
> Everybody ~~know~~ about urban legends.

☐ Do my subjects and verbs agree when there are interrupting phrases? Check for errors in these cases:

–when prepositional phrases separate the subject and the verb

–when sentences contain relative pronouns such as *who* or *that*

>   **rents**
> One of our cousins often ~~rent~~ horror movies. She is a girl who
>   **gets**
> never ~~get~~ scared.

☐ Do my subjects and verbs agree when the subject comes after the verb? Check for errors with the following:

–sentences containing *here* and *there*

–question forms

>   **are**
> There ~~is~~ two horror movies on television tonight.

Tense Consistency 14

LO 1   Correct inconsistent verb tense. **(p. 232)**

In this chapter, you will read about religious beliefs, fortune tellers, and astrology.

GRAMMAR SNAPSHOT

Looking at Tense Consistency
In this excerpt from the book *Exploring the Humanities*, the author describes creation myths. The verbs are underlined.

Many myths <u>explain</u> how people <u>came</u> into existence. The ancient Sumerians <u>believed</u> that the Gods <u>were aging</u> and <u>needed</u> servants, so they <u>created</u> people. The Akkadians, who <u>lived</u> in northern Mesopotamia, <u>thought</u> that the first humans <u>came</u> from the blood of rebel Gods. One Greek myth <u>says</u> that Prometheus <u>formed</u> humanity from clay. The Hindus of India <u>believe</u> that people <u>originated</u> from the thigh of a giant.

In this chapter, you will identify and correct tense inconsistencies.

LO1 Correct inconsistent verb tense.

Consistent Verb Tense

When you write, the verb tense you use tells the reader when the event occurred. A **faulty tense shift** occurs when you shift from one tense to another for no logical reason. If you shift verb tenses unnecessarily, you risk confusing your audience. The next sentence begins in the past tense but then shifts to the present tense.

| **Faulty tense shift** | Nostradamus had a great memory and <u>becomes</u> a well-known doctor. |
| **Consistent tense** | Nostradamus had a great memory and <u>became</u> a well-known doctor. |

Sometimes the time frame in a narrative really does change. In those circumstances, you would change the verb tense. The following example accurately shows two different time periods. Notice that certain key words (*In 1550, today*) indicate what tense the writer should use.

                           past

In 1550, Nostradamus <u>wrote</u> a book of prophesies. Today, some

               present

researchers <u>debate</u> his ideas.

PRACTICE 1

Underline the verbs in each sentence, and then correct each faulty tense shift. If a sentence is correct, write *C* in the blank.

EXAMPLE: In 2005, the ABC News program *Primetime* <u>presented</u> a story
                                       watched
       about a family from Louisiana, and I ~~watch~~ the program

       with my brother.   _____

1.   During World War II, a twenty-one-year-old Navy fighter pilot

    was flying over an island when Japanese artillery shoots at the plane.   _____

2.   The plane went down, and the pilot, James Huston, died.   _____

3.   Many years later, a child from Louisiana had vivid dreams

    about the pilot's death, and in 2005, the family tells their

    story to ABC News.   _____

4.   When James Leininger was eighteen months old, he

    becomes fascinated with airplanes.   _____

5. At age two, James began to have severe nightmares, and his
   parents don't understand what was happening. _____

6. One night, James's father, Bruce, listened as his son spoke
   about the fire in his airplane. _____

7. Over time, James revealed details about a specific plane crash
   and was able to describe the type of plane he is flying. _____

8. As James's memories became more detailed, his father decides
   to do some research. _____

9. Bruce Leininger discovered that the details matched James
   Huston's plane crash, which occurs at Iwo Jima, in Japan. _____

10. Today, James Huston's sister, Anna, believes that the boy is the
    reincarnation of her brother, and the Leiningers agreed with her. _____

HINT ◀ *Would* and *Could*

When you tell a story about a past event, use *would* instead of *will*, and use
could instead of *can*.

>   *would*
> Nostradamus predicted that in the year 1999, a great terror ~~will~~ descend
>   *could*
> from the skies, and nobody ~~can~~ stop the event.

PRACTICE 2

Underline and correct the six tense inconsistencies in the following paragraphs.

EXAMPLE: Fortune-tellers and psychics try to predict the future, and some

                     believe
psychics genuinely <u>believed</u> that they have a special gift.

1. A fifteenth-century British woman, Ursula Shipton, made many accurate
   predictions about the future. For example, she predicted that iron boats
   will float on water, and she also said that thoughts will fly around the
   world. She spoke of human flight, modern ships, submarines, and wireless

communications. However, one of her most famous predictions does not come true. She predicted that the world will end in 1881.

2. In 1990, Gordon Stein wrote an article expressing his doubts about Shipton. He said that her predictions were often vague and can be interpreted in many different ways. In addition, Charles Hindley, who edited an 1862 version of Shipton's verses, adds his own verses to make her prophesies seem more accurate. Perhaps readers should be skeptical when they read about ancient prophecies.

Telling a Story

When you narrate, or tell a story, you can describe events using the present, past, or future tense. The important thing is to be consistent. The next two paragraphs tell the same story using different tenses.

Past Tense

Mark Twain **went** to see a magic show. At the show, a hypnotist **made** the audience members do ridiculous things. Twain **asked** to go onstage, and he **did** not fall under the hypnotist's spell. However, he **decided** to act out everything that the hypnotist **asked**.

Present Tense

Mark Twain **goes** to see a magic show. At the show, a hypnotist **makes** the audience members do ridiculous things. Twain **asks** to go onstage, and he **does** not fall under the hypnotist's spell. However, he **decides** to act out everything that the hypnotist **asks**.

PRACTICE 3

The following paragraph shifts between the present and the past tenses. Edit the paragraph to make the tenses consistent. You might choose to tell the story using the present or past tense.

According to Chinese astrology, one day Buddha invites all of the animals in the kingdom to the Chinese New Year's celebration. The rat received an invitation, and he was supposed to invite the cat. However, the rat was jealous of the cat, and he did not pass along the information. On the day of the celebration, only twelve animals can attend; the first to arrive is the rat and the last to arrive is the pig. Buddha assigned each animal a year of its own, and people born in that year will have the characteristics of the animal. The next day, the cat heard about the celebration, and she sent word that she will soon arrive. Later, when the cat met Buddha, she asked to have a year named after her, but Buddha tells her that it is too late. Buddha decides that there will be no year of the cat.

FINAL REVIEW

Underline and correct fifteen tense inconsistencies in the following paragraphs.

EXAMPLE: In 1938, he dieted, but he <u>doesn't</u> lose much weight.

(above "doesn't": didn't)

1. In the past, people had some strange beliefs about medical cures. For example, in the nineteenth century, Bayer Pharmaceuticals produced popular syrups containing morphine and heroin. Many mothers will give them to a sick or overactive child. The child will calm down considerably. Of course, at that time, parents can't know about the addictive properties of those products.

2. In the seventeenth century, many wealthy Europeans use mercury to treat everything from scraped knees to intestinal issues. Afterwards, they can lose weight, or perhaps their hair will fall out. Some people will even die. Many historians believe that Mozart died from ingesting mercury when he tries to cure a venereal disease.

3. For many centuries, bloodletting and skull drilling were common medical practices. Doctors will cut patients and permit the blood to flow in the false belief that it will balance the patient's system. The practice is common until the nineteenth century. Also, doctors had an interesting cure for migraines. They will drill small holes directly into the skull of a patient. Unsurprisingly, the holes will rarely relieve patients' headaches.

4. In the 1930s, some companies marketed miracle diet pills. At that time, many people can't stop taking the pills because they contained dangerous amphetamines. More recently, in the 1990s, dieters took Fen Phen to lose

weight. After scientists linked the pills to heart problems, the government bans the drug. Perhaps in the future, some of our modern medical practices will appear ridiculous.

MyWritingLab
THE WRITER'S ROOM

Write about one of the following topics. When you finish writing, ensure that your verb tenses are consistent.

1. Think of a typical fairy tale, myth, or legend, such as "The Three Little Pigs" or "Little Red Riding Hood." You could also think of a tale that is special in your culture. Retell the story using more modern names and places.

2. Were you superstitious when you were a child? For example, did you consult your horoscope, or did you have a lucky charm? Are your beliefs different today? Compare your past and current beliefs.

Checklist: Tense Consistency

When you edit your writing, ask yourself the following question.

☐ Are my verb tenses consistent? Check for errors with the following:
   –shifts from past to present or from present to past
   –*can, could* and *will, would*

   would
   If a black cat crossed your path, ~~will~~ you have bad luck?

THE WRITER'S CIRCLE Collaborative Activity

Survey an equal number of males and females. Try to survey at least three people of each gender. Ask them if they believe, or do not believe, in the following. Write *M* (for "male") and *F* (for "female") in the spaces.

	Don't Believe	Believe
1. Dead people visit the earth as ghosts.		
2. It is possible to create a society in which everyone has equal wealth.		
3. Some people can contact the dead.		
4. Horoscopes provide useful information about future events.		
5. Capital punishment helps lower the crime rate.		
6. Aliens have visited the earth and kidnapped some people.		
7. Human beings have walked on the moon.		
8. There is life on other planets.		
9. The universe is expanding.		
10. People are safer when they have guns in their homes.		

Next, ask people why they believe a certain thing. Did they read about it? Did someone tell them about it? Keep notes about their answers. Then work with your team members, and write a paragraph about one of the following topics. Ensure that your verb tenses are consistent.

1. Choose one person you asked about his or her beliefs, and write a paragraph about that person. What does he or she believe in? Why does he or she have those beliefs? (Because you are writing about one person, take extra care to ensure that your subjects and verbs agree.)

2. Write a paragraph about the results of the survey. You could discuss any differences between males and females regarding superstitions and beliefs.

READING LINK

To learn more about beliefs, read the following essays:

"The Cult of Emaciation" by Ben Barry (page 414)
"Shopping for Religion" by Ellen Goodman (page 417)

Chapter 14

15 Compound Sentences

SECTION THEME: Trades and Technology

LEARNING OBJECTIVES

LO 1 Compare simple and compound sentences. **(p. 239)**

LO 2 Combine sentences using coordinating conjunctions. **(p. 239)**

LO 3 Combine sentences using semicolons. **(p. 243)**

LO 4 Combine sentences using transitional expressions. **(p. 244)**

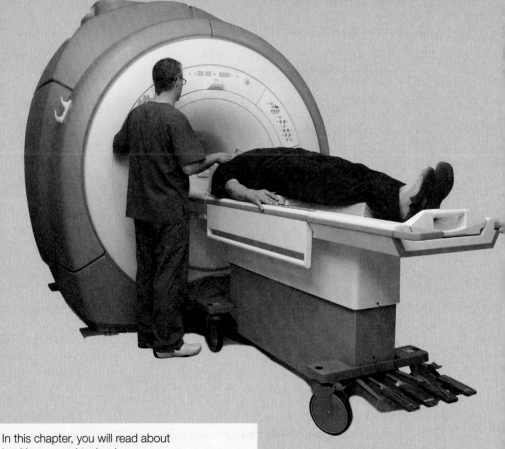

In this chapter, you will read about health care and technology.

GRAMMAR SNAPSHOT

Looking at Compound Sentences

The following excerpt appeared in a radiology journal. This excerpt contains two compound sentences.

> Researchers recently conducted an experiment; they measured radiation exposure of hospital X-ray technicians. The results were interesting, and they were comforting for medical workers. According to the results, the workers received less radiation exposure at work than they did in their homes.

In this chapter, you will practice identifying and writing compound sentences.

Comparing Simple and Compound Sentences

LO 1 Compare simple and compound sentences.

When you write, you can use sentences of varying lengths to make your writing more appealing. One of the easiest ways to create variety is to combine simple sentences to form compound sentences.

A **simple sentence** expresses a complete idea. It has one or more subjects and verbs.

One subject, one verb	**Josh** <u>drives</u> an ambulance.
Two subjects	**Jobs** and **apprenticeships** <u>are</u> important for graduating students.
Two verbs	The **nurse** <u>speaks</u> and <u>writes</u> about hospital procedures.

A **compound sentence** contains two or more simple sentences, and the two complete ideas can be joined in several ways.

	Amir is ambitious. + He hopes to find a job.
Add a coordinator	Amir is ambitious, **and** he hopes to find a job.
Add a semicolon	Amir is ambitious; he hopes to find a job.
Add a semicolon and conjunctive adverb	Amir is ambitious; **therefore**, he hopes to find a job.

Combining Sentences Using Coordinating Conjunctions

LO 2 Combine sentences using coordinating conjunctions.

A **coordinating conjunction** joins two complete ideas and indicates the connection between them. When you combine two sentences with a coordinating conjunction, put a comma before the conjunction.

Complete idea	, **for** , **and** , **nor** , **but** , **or** , **yet** , **so**	complete idea.

The technician examined the X-ray**, and** he placed it in the file.

HINT ◄ Recognizing Compound Sentences

To be sure that a sentence is compound, place your finger over the coordinator, and then ask yourself whether the two clauses are complete sentences.

Simple	Josh is ambitious and hopes to become a paramedic.
Compound	Josh is ambitious, and he hopes to become a paramedic.

Chapter 15

PRACTICE 1

Indicate whether the following sentences are simple (*S*) or compound (*C*). Underline the coordinating conjunction in each compound sentence.

EXAMPLE: During the Civil War, many males worked as nurses, <u>but</u> the
         most famous was the poet Walt Whitman.   *C*

1. Howard Garcia studies nursing and works part time as an
   orderly at the hospital.   _____

2. He wants to specialize in pediatrics, but he is also interested
   in surgery.   _____

3. During the Middle Ages, monks cared for and nursed the
   sick and the elderly.   _____

4. Since that time, nursing has become a female-dominated
   profession, so male nurses have sometimes encountered
   discrimination.   _____

5. Jeremy Woodrow experienced some stereotyping in the
   workplace, for he was one of the first male nurses to be
   employed in a hospital.   _____

6. Today, male nurses receive admiration and respect.   _____

7. Presently, about 5 percent of nurses in the United States are
   males, but this number is growing.   _____

8. Nursing offers a variety of opportunities and provides flexibility
   for career development.   _____

Meanings of Coordinating Conjunctions

Each coordinating conjunction has a specific meaning. Review the next table to see how each coordinator can be used.

Coordinating Conjunction	Function	Example
and	to join two ideas	Florence Nightingale was a nurse, **and** she was a writer.
but	to contrast two ideas	Nightingale was very rich, **but** she cared for the poor.
for	to indicate a reason	She studied nursing, **for** she felt it was a divine calling.
nor	to indicate a negative idea	She did not want to marry, **nor** did she want a family.
or	to offer an alternative	You can read her biography, **or** you can see a documentary.
so	to indicate a cause and effect relationship	Nightingale was wealthy, **so** she didn't need payment for her work.
yet	to introduce a surprising idea	She saw the horrors of war, **yet** she continued to help the sick.

PRACTICE 2

Read each sentence carefully, and decide how the two parts of the sentence are related. Then add a comma and an appropriate coordinating conjunction.

EXAMPLE: Some medical advances occur after years of research _____, but _____ others occur by accident.

1. One day in 1895, Wilhelm Röntgen was bored _____ he decided to work in his lab.

2. He put his hand between a gas tube and a fluorescent screen ___, and___ he saw the bones of his hand.

3. Three days before Christmas, he brought his wife into his lab _____ he didn't tell her about his plan.

4. He took an image of the bones in her hand _____ he watched his wife's expression.

5. He could keep his discovery to himself _____ he could tell others about it.

6. On December 28, he told his colleagues about his discovery _____ they were excited about body-penetrating rays.

7. Röntgen couldn't think of a name for the special ray _____ he called it an X-ray.

8. The news quickly spread around the world _____ everyone was excited about the X-ray images.

PRACTICE 3

Create compound sentences by adding a coordinating conjunction and another complete sentence. Remember that the two ideas must be related. Try to use a variety of coordinating conjunctions.

EXAMPLE: I just got a diploma in surgical nursing, _so now I am looking for a job._

1. Vanessa wants to be a laboratory technician, _but she also wants to do nursing as well._

2. She is a full-time college student, _but she wants to work more hours._

3. Vanessa studies hard, _So she always going to know everyone inside my class._

4. Many students enroll in health science programs, _taker math class_.

5. Vanessa plays basketball well, _and the kids about trying out tennis_.

PRACTICE 4

In the following paragraphs, join at least nine pairs of sentences using coordinating conjunctions. You can keep some of the short sentences so that your paragraph has variety.

EXAMPLE: Godfrey Jones is studying to be a paramedic. ~~He~~ _, but he_ also works part time driving an ambulance.

1.   In 1899, Chicago received the first motorized ambulance. It only reached 15 miles per hour. Patients could not be transported quickly. At that time, workers drove ambulances. They did not treat patients. Since 1900, the job of emergency medical technician, or EMT, has changed a lot.

2.   Today, the role of an EMT is not standard. In some places, ambulance technicians only drive patients. They may give first aid. In other places, EMTs can perform life-saving surgical procedures. Also, rules about transporting patients differ from one country to another. For example, on August 30, 1997, England's Princess Diana was in Paris. She was involved in a major car crash. Soon, rescue workers arrived. Diana could speak. She did not have obvious external injuries. EMTs worked on the princess for 110 minutes. They wanted to stabilize her. They did not want to transport her to the hospital. The emergency team followed the French tradition of treating an accident victim on the scene. On August 31, Diana died.

3.   Many American technicians criticized the French rescue workers. The United States has a "scoop and run"

policy. Patients are transported quickly to a hospital. According to some American rescue workers, Diana should have been transported to a hospital immediately. Maybe nothing could have saved her.

4. Today, ambulances contain specialized equipment. For example, ambulances have computers. Paramedics can send a patient's medical information directly to the hospital. EMTs play a vital role in our society. They should be praised.

Combining Sentences Using Semicolons

LO 3 Combine sentences using semicolons.

A semicolon can join two complete sentences. The semicolon replaces a conjunction.

> Complete idea ; complete idea.

The X-ray clinic is open all day; you don't need an appointment.

PRACTICE 5

Each sentence is missing a semicolon. Put a semicolon in the appropriate place.

EXAMPLE: An MRI gives high-quality imaging of soft tissue ; it can be used to locate tumors in the body.

1. In 1977, some members of the medical community gasped in wonder they had just witnessed an amazing event.

2. Dr. Damadian and his colleagues had worked on an invention for seven years they had developed a magnetic resonance imaging (MRI) machine.

3. The initial MRI image took five hours to develop the images were unclear.

4. The first machine was named "Indomitable" by the inventors it is now exhibited at the Smithsonian Institution.

5. MRI machines have revolutionized modern medicine they use a magnetic field and radio waves to generate body images.

6. MRIs show images of the brain, spine, abdomen, and soft tissue they can detect cancer and other diseases in these areas.

Chapter 15

HINT ◄ **Use a Semicolon to Join Related Ideas**

Do not use a semicolon to join two unrelated sentences.

Incorrect	Karim was in a car crash; he is a medical technician.
Correct	Karim was in a car crash; he lost consciousness.

PRACTICE 6

Create compound sentences by adding a semicolon and another complete sentence to each simple sentence. Remember that the two ideas must be related.

EXAMPLE: Last year, I worked as an intern at a company _; I gained a lot of_ _experience._

1. Students need on-the-job training _____

2. Practical experience is important _; Because they will already know what there going to do_

3. The medical device is expensive _; But I'm going to try and brake it up into monthly_

4. Medical costs are rising _; B cause more and more people are getting hurt or sick_

5. Jamal needs medical insurance _get that he needed to call or go for his insurance to s_

LO 4 Combine sentences using transitional expressions.

Combining Sentences Using Transitional Expressions

A **transitional expression** can join two complete ideas and show how they are related. The next table shows some common transitional expressions.

Transitional Expressions

Addition	Alternative	Contrast	Time	Example or Emphasis	Result or Consequence
additionally	in fact	however	eventually	for example	consequently
also	instead	nevertheless	finally	for instance	hence
besides	on the contrary	nonetheless	later	namely	therefore
furthermore	on the other hand	still	meanwhile	of course	thus
in addition	otherwise		subsequently	undoubtedly	
moreover					

If the second sentence begins with a transitional expression, put a semicolon before it and a comma after it.

| Complete idea | ; | **transitional expression** | , | complete idea. |

The first images were failures; **nevertheless**, Dr. Damadian did not lose hope.
; **still**,
; **however**,
; **nonetheless**,

PRACTICE 7

Punctuate the following sentences by adding any necessary semicolons and commas.

EXAMPLE: Some heart patients must have pacemakers however they are able to
participate in most activities.

1. In 1889, a Scottish doctor made an interesting discovery in fact his find led to the development of the first artificial pacemaker.

2. Other scientists refined Dr. John A. McWilliam's experiments eventually researchers developed a sophisticated pacemaker.

3. In the 1950s, Else-Marie Larsson heard about pacemakers of course she convinced her sick husband Arne to have one implanted.

4. In 1958, Arne Larsson became the first person to have one however his pacemaker lasted just three hours.

5. Mr. Larsson received twenty-six pacemakers in total nevertheless he greatly advocated the technology.

6. Current pacemakers are very sophisticated for instance they can record and adjust a patient's heartbeat patterns.

7. Millions of people wear pacemakers undoubtedly their quality of life has improved.

PRACTICE 8

Create compound sentences using the following transitional expressions. Try to use a different expression in each sentence. Remember to punctuate your sentences by adding semicolons and commas.

consequently	furthermore	however
in fact	nevertheless	~~therefore~~

EXAMPLE: Many students work part time <u>; therefore, they must be very organized.</u>

1. Roy works as a medical assistant _____

_____ .

2. He deals with patients _____

_____.

3. On many days, he is extremely busy _____

_____.

4. Eventually, Roy wants to study health-care management _____

_____.

5. Roy also volunteers at a residence for older adults _____

_____.

PRACTICE 9

Add a transitional expression to join each pair of sentences. Choose an expression from the following list, and try to use a different expression in each sentence.

| consequently | eventually | for example | for instance |
| furthermore | nevertheless | thus | |

; for instance, surgeons

EXAMPLE: Technology has changed the field of health care; Surgeons perform surgery using sophisticated cameras.

1. Telemedicine is a fast-growing health-care network. A nurse may send medical information about a patient to a doctor in another city.

2. Health-care workers can consult colleagues in far locations. The system works very well in remote areas.

3. Telenursing is spreading in the United States. Other long-distance medical systems such as teleradiology are also expanding rapidly.

4. In Sweden, nurses at call centers consult with patients at home. The scheme is cost efficient and timesaving.

thus 5. Telenursing uses highly trained professionals. The system has developed some ethical problems.

6. Telenursing may not provide patients with privacy or face-to-face support. Such issues will have to be dealt with.

FINAL REVIEW

Read the following paragraphs. Create compound sentences by adding semicolons, conjunctive adverbs (*however, therefore,* etc.) or coordinating conjunctions (*for, and, nor, but, or, yet, so*). Try to create at least ten compound sentences.

EXAMPLE: Many disabled people lead active lives due to technology. ~~Computers~~   *; for example, computers* help people with visual, auditory, or manual difficulties.

1. Technology has permeated the field of health care. Computers, digital software, and new inventions have transformed medicine. There are both positive and negative effects of technology on health care.

2. Indeed, new medical innovations help countless people. Michael Price has Parkinson's disease. His hands shake a lot. In the past, he could not type reports at work. Modern technology now enables him to be self-sufficient. He dictates into a microphone attached to a computer. The software allows him to correct mistakes verbally. Some people use electric wheelchairs for mobility. Others with paralysis have battery-powered diaphragm pacers. Such devices allow the users to breathe normally. Journalist Charles Krauthammer uses a computerized van. He was paralyzed in a diving accident many years ago.

3. However, medical technology presents some problems. Health-care workers increasingly rely on machines to diagnose patients. Traditional doctor–patient relationships are changing. MRIs, CT scans, and video surgery help doctors to understand a problem. Machines cannot offer comfort and support to patients. New technology can prolong a person's life. This process can lead to an ethical dilemma. Should a terminal patient be permitted to die in peace? Furthermore, the costs to the public are enormous. In 1960, Americans spent about 5.9 percent of all government revenue on health care. Today, the cost has nearly doubled.

4. Clearly, Americans need to weigh the benefits of technology against the rising costs of health care. Technology can improve people's lives. The ethical questions and the costs have to be assessed.

Chapter 15

MyWritingLab™
Complete these
writing assignments at
mywritinglab.com

MyWritingLab

THE WRITER'S ROOM

Write about one of the following topics. First, write at least ten simple sentences. Then, combine some of your sentences to create compound sentences. When you have finished, edit your writing and ensure that your sentences are combined correctly.

1.   What do you do to keep yourself healthy? Give some examples.

2.   Have you ever been in a hospital? Describe your experience.

Checklist: Past Participles

When you edit your writing, ask yourself these questions.

☐   Are my compound sentences correctly punctuated? Remember to do the following:

–Place a comma before a coordinating conjunction.

> Laboratory technicians may work in hospitals, **or** they may work in industry.

–Use a semicolon between two complete ideas.

> I want to work in emergency services; I need to make a résumé to apply for a job.

–Use a semicolon before a transitional expression and a comma after it.

> The college has a nursing program; **in addition**, it has a hospital management program.

Complex Sentences 16

SECTION THEME: Trades and Technology

LEARNING OBJECTIVES

LO 1 Understand complex sentences. **(p. 250)**

LO 2 Use subordinating conjunctions. **(p. 251)**

LO 3 Use relative pronouns. **(p. 255)**

LO 4 Practice combining questions. **(p. 257)**

In this chapter, you will read about the construction and computer industries.

GRAMMAR SNAPSHOT

Looking at Complex Sentences

The next excerpt appears in *Architectural Drawing and Light Construction* by Grau, Muller, and Fausett. The complex sentences are underlined.

> Baled straw is an inexpensive and environmentally sound material for building construction. The greatest danger to straw bale construction is moisture. <u>If bales become wet and are not permitted to dry out, they will rot.</u> <u>When construction begins, it is important to start with dry bales and to keep them dry.</u>

In this chapter, you will identify and write complex sentences.

LO 1 Understand complex sentences.

Understanding Complex Sentences

A **complex sentence** contains one independent clause (complete idea) and one or more dependent clauses (incomplete ideas).

* An **independent clause** has a subject and a verb and can stand alone because it expresses one complete idea.

    The building has a concrete foundation.

* A **dependent clause** has a subject and a verb, but it cannot stand alone. It "depends" on another clause to be complete.

    Incomplete   Although the solar panel was expensive.

                                                       dependent clause   independent clause

    Complete   Although the solar panel was expensive, Jeremiah installed it on his roof.

Compound-Complex Sentences

You can combine compound and complex sentences. The next example is a **compound-complex sentence**.

                               complex

After the concrete had hardened, the floor cracked, and water poured in.

                                        compound

HINT ‹ **Phrase or Dependent Clause?**

A **phrase** is a group of words that is missing a subject, a verb, or both, and is not a complete sentence. A **clause** always has a subject and a verb.

Phrase	on the weekend	without a doubt
Clause	when we met	because he tried

PRACTICE 1

Decide if the following are phrases or dependent clauses. Put an X in the appropriate space.

	Phrase	Clause
EXAMPLE: while we were working	___	X

	Phrase	Clause
1. after we finish work	___	___
2. near the factory	___	___
3. which he did not ventilate	___	___

4. on September 12   ——   ——

5. although it is late   ——   ——

6. by adjusting the speed   ——   ——

7. because they are exposed to flames   ——   ——

8. at the work site   ——   ——

Using Subordinating Conjunctions

LO 2 Use subordinating conjunctions.

When you add a **subordinating conjunction**—a word such as *after*, *because*, or *although*—to a clause, you make the clause dependent. *Subordinate* means "secondary," so subordinating conjunctions are words that introduce secondary ideas.

Main idea	**subordinating conjunction**	secondary idea.
The tower swayed	**whenever**	the wind blew.

Subordinating conjunction	secondary idea,	main idea.
Whenever	the wind blew,	the tower swayed.

Some Subordinating Conjunctions

after	because	since	until	whereas
although	before	so that	when	wherever
as	even if	that	whenever	whether
as if	even though	though	where	while
as though	if	unless		

Subordinating conjunctions create a relationship between the clauses in a sentence. Review the next table to see how you can use subordinating conjunctions.

Subordinating Conjunction	Usage	Example
as, because, since, so that	To indicate a reason, a cause, or an effect	Romans made concrete because it was a strong building material.
as long as, even if, if, so that, unless	To indicate a condition or result	They mixed milk and blood into cement so that it would bond.
although, even though, though, whereas	To contrast ideas	Although concrete is an old product, it is still useful.
where, wherever	To indicate a location	Wherever you travel, you will find concrete buildings.
after, before, since, until, when, whenever, while	To show a point in time	Visit the Colosseum when you go to Rome.

Chapter 16

PRACTICE 2

Practice identifying dependent and independent clauses. Circle the subordinating conjunction and then underline the dependent clause in each sentence.

EXAMPLE: The restaurant has the shape of a ship (because) it specializes in seafood.

1. When you travel around the United States, you will find some very odd buildings.

2. In 1920, the High Point Chamber of Commerce built a giant chest of drawers because it wanted a distinctive building.

3. After construction workers finished the exterior, they added giant socks to one of the drawers.

4. Designers added giant socks because the town has a hosiery industry.

5. Although the building looks unusual, it has useable office space.

6. If you visit North Carolina, enjoy the architectural marvels.

> **GRAMMAR LINK**
> See Chapter 26 for more information about comma usage.

Punctuating Complex Sentences

If you use a subordinator at the beginning of a sentence, put a comma after the dependent clause. Generally, if you use a subordinator in the middle of the sentence, you do not need to use a comma.

Comma	**Even though** the computer is expensive, she will buy it.
No comma	She will buy the computer **even though** it is expensive.

PRACTICE 3

Underline each subordinating conjunction and add five missing commas.

EXAMPLE: After Utzon finished the drawings, he showed them to city planners.

When architects design buildings, they must consider both form and function. Some amazing architects face criticism because their designs are unusual. When Jorn Utzon presented his designs for the Sydney Opera House, he faced opposition from local citizens. After builders completed the structure journalists criticized it. People phoned and complained whenever radio shows discussed the building. Because the roof looked like broken egg shells some people were confused. After a few years had passed opinions changed. Today, the Sydney Opera House is a World Heritage Site because it has a beautiful and unique style.

PRACTICE 4

The following sentences are missing a subordinating conjunction. Put one of the following conjunctions in each space. Use a different conjunction each time.

although	because	~~before~~	so that
unless	until	when	whenever

EXAMPLE: _____Before_____ she built the cabinet, Selma created a plan.

1. Selma Sussman began building cabinets _____ she turned twelve years old. Later, _____ a faucet leaked or a door handle jammed, Selma did the repairs. She would never ask a man to help her _____unless_____ she needed help lifting very heavy objects.

2. _____although_____ women do a lot of home renovations, most tools are made for men. Recently, some enterprising women have entered the tool business. _____ Barbara Kavovit created a lightweight tool kit, most tools were too large and cumbersome for female hands. In 2000, Mary Tatum and Janet Rickstrew decided to sell small tool belts _____ women could carry their tools easily. Their company, Tomboy Tools, is a great success.

3. These days, _____ women have demanded it, many renovation outlets market to their female customers.

HINT ◄ Putting a Subject After the Subordinator

When you combine sentences to form complex sentences, always remember to put a subject after the subordinator.

                           it
The house collapsed because ˄ was not well built.

PRACTICE 5

Add five missing subjects to this selection. Remember that a subject can be a noun or a pronoun.

EXAMPLE: Mawlid Abdhul was born in Somalia although currently has an *he* American passport.

Mawlid Abdhul wants a career in information technology because wants to earn a good living. He knows that could be a technician. However, many help-desk jobs are being outsourced. He believes the safest option is to become a specialist in anti-virus software. Stores, banks, hospitals, and government offices require secure computer systems. Viruses are dangerous because *they* pose a threat to databases. For example, in February 2009, citizens couldn't enter a Houston courtroom when *they* arrived to pay their traffic tickets. A computer virus had shut down the court's 470 computers. Mawlid wants to be successful, so *will* will study hard. He wants to learn to outsmart hackers.

PRACTICE 6

Combine the sentences by adding a subordinating conjunction. Write each sentence twice: once with the dependent clause at the beginning of the sentence, and once with the dependent clause at the end of the sentence. From the following list, use each conjunction once.

~~even though~~   after   although   when   because

EXAMPLE: The college was far away. Kate enrolled.

Even though the college was far away, Kate enrolled.

Kate enrolled even though the college was far away.

1. Kate loves to draw. She decided to study graphic design.

   _____

   _____

2. She entered a career college. She learned to design Web sites.

   _____

   _____

3. Design software is expensive. Kate had to buy it.

   _____

   _____

4. A company needs a logo. It hires a graphic artist.

   _____

   _____

Using Relative Pronouns

A **relative pronoun** describes a noun or pronoun. You can form complex sentences by using relative pronouns to introduce dependent clauses. Review the most common relative pronouns.

who	whomever	which
whom	whose	that

Use *who* (*whom, whomever, whose*) to add information about a person.

John Aspdin, **who** was a stone mason, invented Portland cement.

Use *that* to add information about a thing.

He made a product **that** would easily harden.

Use *which* to add information about a thing.

Aspdin's cement, **which** contained lime and clay, was a popular building material.

HINT ◀ Punctuating Sentences with Relative Pronouns

Which
Use commas to set off clauses that begin with *which*.

The virus, **which** was created by a young hacker, infected many computers.

That
Do not use commas to set off clauses beginning with *that*.

The computer **that** I own is very old.

Who
When a clause begins with *who*, you may or may not need a comma. If the clause contains nonessential information, use commas. If the clause is essential to the meaning of the sentence, then it does not require commas.

Essential	The woman **who** repairs computers is very friendly.
Not essential	Eli Marcos, **who** used to work as a banker, will study in a technical program.

> **GRAMMAR LINK**
> For more information about punctuating relative clauses, refer to Chapter 26, "Commas."

PRACTICE 7

Underline ten relative clauses. Circle the relative pronouns.

EXAMPLE: People (who) repair computers must continually update their knowledge.

An article that I recently read described ten hot jobs in the computer field. Someone who cares about the environment can become an environment simulations developer. He or she would create programs that predict the effects of global warming. Another job that sounds interesting is in video game development. Video games are not just for people who want to play. Health and education

Chapter 16

industries use video games to train employees. A woman whom I have recently met told me about the benefits of video games in therapy. The animation engages children who are having family problems. She described a boy who was acting violently. The child, who was very shy, would not speak to the therapist. Then the therapist watched the boy play. A video game that had special segments helped the therapist make a diagnosis.

PRACTICE 8

Combine each set of sentences by using the relative pronoun in parentheses. There may be more than one way to combine some sets of sentences.

EXAMPLE: (who) Alvaro is very handy. He often works on night shifts.
Alvaro, who is very handy, often works on night shifts.

1. (which) Computers often break down. They can have complicated problems.

_____

_____

2. (who) People repair computers. They are taken for granted.

_____

_____

3. (that) Alvaro works with computers. The computers need rebuilding.

_____

_____

4. (who) A friend had a computer problem. She asked Alvaro to fix it.

_____

_____

5. (who) Alvaro spent his weekend working on the computer. He did not get paid.

_____

_____

PRACTICE 9

Add dependent clauses to each sentence. Begin each clause with a relative pronoun (*who*, *which*, or *that*). Add any necessary commas.

EXAMPLE: The man <u>who created the virus</u> destroyed many computers.

1. A virus is a program _____.

2. Don't open an attachment _____.

3. Gregor _____ is very skilled.

4. The e-mail _____ contained a funny photo.

5. My friend _____ accidently spread a computer virus.

Combining Questions

LO 4 Practice combining questions.

It is possible to combine a question with a statement or to combine two questions. An **embedded question** is a question that is set within a larger sentence.

Question	How tall was the building?
Embedded question	The tourists wondered <u>how tall the building was</u>.

In questions, there is generally a helping verb before the subject. However, when a question is embedded in a larger sentence, remove the helping verb or place it after the subject. As you read the following examples, pay attention to the word order in the embedded questions.

Combine two questions

Separate	Why **do** humans build skyscrapers? Do you know?
	(In both questions, the helping verb is *do*.)
Combined	Do you know <u>why humans build skyscrapers</u>?
	(The helping verb *do* is removed from the embedded question.)

Combine a question and a statement

Separate	What **should** people do during a fire? I wonder about it.
	(In the question, the helping verb *should* appears before the subject.)
Combined	I wonder <u>what people should do during a fire</u>.
	(In the embedded question, *should* is placed after the subject.)

HINT ◄ Use the Correct Word Order

When you edit your writing, ensure that you have formed your embedded questions properly.

                                   were   he solved
Otis wondered why ~~were~~ elevators unreliable. Do you know how ~~did he solve~~ the problem?

PRACTICE 10

Make a new sentence from each question.

EXAMPLE: Why is the elevator stuck? I wonder <u>why the elevator is stuck</u> .

1. Why is the alarm ringing? Do you know _____

2. When will someone help us? I wonder _____

3. What can we do? Do you know _____

4. Where is the phone? Can you tell me _____

5. What did he say? Can you hear _____

PRACTICE 11

Identify and correct nine errors with embedded questions.

elevators are
EXAMPLE: The writer explains why ~~are elevators~~ safe.

1. Before 1853, elevators were not reliable. Do you know why would people refuse to enter an elevator? The hemp rope could break and the elevator could fall. You can imagine why were people scared of elevators. Then in 1853, Elisha Otis had an insight. Do you know what was his idea? Otis created a safety device out of two hooks and a spring. When an elevator's rope became slack, the hooks would snap into a guide rail and stop the elevator from falling.

2. Otis decided to enter the elevator business. At first, he wasn't successful. He wondered why did nobody buy his elevators. Then, at the 1853 World's Fair in New York, he had the chance to show off his invention. One day, Otis rose to the top of a shaft on his elevator. Then he instructed his helper to cut the cable with an axe. You can imagine why did the spectators scream. Instead of falling, the elevator jolted to a stop. Citizens wondered how did Otis survive. Soon, orders for Otis's safety elevator poured in.

3. Today, elevators are quite safe. In the *New Yorker*, Nick Paumgarten lists some elevator facts. First, do you wonder why does the close button rarely work? In fact, most elevators built since the 1990s have fake close door buttons. Their purpose is to give people the illusion that they can control the elevator. Also, if an elevator falls, most people wonder what should they do. According to Otis spokesman Rick Pulling, jumping just before impact is a bad idea. You cannot jump fast enough to counteract the speed of the descent. Instead, do you know what can you do? Lie flat on the floor to distribute your weight.

FINAL REVIEW

The following paragraphs contain simple sentences. To give the paragraphs more sentence variety, form at least ten complex sentences by combining pairs of sentences. You will have to add some words and delete others.

> *When construction   high rises, they*
> **EXAMPLE:** ~~Construction~~ workers build ~~high rises. They~~ risk injury or death.

1.   People in many fields are responsible for the design and construction of buildings. Architects, engineers, plumbers, electricians, computer programmers, and drywall specialists are just some of the people. They help construct skyscrapers.

2.   Ironworkers have one of the most dangerous jobs. Many people like that job. In the past, high-rise builders had to be very careful. They had no safety equipment. For example, workers built the Empire State building. They had to walk on beams 102 stories high. The ironworkers had no head protection or special boots. The risks were great. Today, all workers wear hard hats and safety harnesses. Construction companies must provide those items.

3.   People study engineering. They have to consider the integrity of structures. Tall buildings must be carefully designed. They have to withstand high winds. The foundations must be solid. They can shift during earthquakes. Modern skyscrapers are made with steel frames. They must bear the weight of hundreds of windows. Sometimes engineers design buildings. They make mistakes. For instance, the John Hancock Tower in Boston has mirrored glass. The glass is not secure during high winds. Huge panels of glass weigh up to 500 pounds. They have fallen to the pavement. Luckily, the glass has not hit pedestrians.

4.   These days, our city is planning to build a tower. It will have over eighty floors. People in many fields will receive jobs.

Chapter 16

MyWritingLab™

Complete these
writing assignments at
mywritinglab.com

MyWritingLab   THE WRITER'S ROOM

Choose one of the following topics and write a paragraph. After you finish
writing, ensure that you have formed and punctuated the complex sentences
correctly.

1. Examine this photo. What are some terms that come to mind? Some
    ideas might be *blue collar*, *manual labor*, *American dream*, *dangerous
    work*, or *idealism*. Define a term or expression that relates to the photo.

2. What are the advantages of doing manual labor? Give examples to
    support your point.

Checklist: Complex Sentences

When you edit your writing, ask yourself the following:

☐ Are my complex sentences complete?

> The basement flooded because
> ~~Because~~ of the storm.

☐ Are my complex sentences correctly punctuated?

> The storm sewer overflowed⫽ after the heavy rains.
>
> ⸴   ⸴
> The wallboards which have gotten wet need to be replaced.
>   ^   ^

☐ Do I have any embedded questions? Check for errors in these cases:
    –Word order
    –Unnecessary helping verbs

>   I will   is
> I don't know what ~~will I~~ study. Do you know what ~~is~~ the tuition rate?
>   ^

Sentence Variety **17**

SECTION THEME: Trades and technology

In this chapter, you will read about infrastructure and technical programs.

LEARNING OBJECTIVES

LO 1 Vary opening words. **(p. 262)**

LO 2 Vary sentence length. **(p. 263)**

GRAMMAR SNAPSHOT

Looking at Sentence Variety

→ In his book *Building Construction*, Michael Smith discusses structural failures. Notice how the sentence lengths are varied.

> A critical error for both residential and commercial construction occurs when key support members are removed before the entire system is stabilized. This mistake often happens during remodeling or renovating. In the early 1970s, the Vendumme Hotel in Boston was being remodeled when a major fire broke out. The building collapsed, and nine firefighters lost their lives.

In this chapter, you will vary the length and structure of sentences in order to produce sentence variety.

Vary the Opening Words

Sentence variety means that your sentences have assorted patterns and lengths. One way to make your sentences more effective is to vary the opening words. Instead of beginning each sentence with the subject, you could try the following strategies.

Begin with an Adverb

An **adverb** is a word that modifies a verb, and it often ends in *-ly*. *Slowly, carefully, clearly,* and *suddenly* are adverbs. Non *-ly* adverbs include words such as *sometimes, often, always,* and *never.*

<u>Eventually</u>, the road collapsed.

<u>Obviously</u>, she should remain in technical college.

<u>Often</u>, colleges have entrance exams.

Begin with a Prepositional Phrase

A **prepositional phrase** consists of a preposition and its object. *After the storm, beside the river,* and *in my lifetime* are prepositional phrases.

<u>In past decades</u>, cities have not invested in highways.

<u>During the election campaign</u>, media coverage was intense.

<u>With a loud bang</u>, the bridge collapsed.

PRACTICE 1

Read the following sentences. Identify and cross out the adverb or prepositional phrase, and rewrite it in the blank at the beginning of the sentence.

EXAMPLE: _____In 2007_____, a surprising event occurred in midtown Manhattan ~~in 2007~~.

1. _____, a one-hundred-year-old steam pipe burst in New York City in July.

2. _____, people heard a loud rumbling noise for ten minutes.

3. _____, thick plumes of ash shot up suddenly.

4. _____, a large crater appeared in the middle of the street.

5. _____, people were undoubtedly quite scared.

6. _____, people saw the smoke for miles around.

HINT ◄ Punctuation Tip

When a sentence begins with an adverb or prepositional phrase, put a comma after the opening word or phrase.

Suddenly, the levee broke.

Without any warning, water gushed into the streets.

PRACTICE 2

To have a variety of sentence openings, place adverbs or prepositional phrases at the beginnings of appropriate sentences. Choose from the list of words and phrases below. Do not repeat your choices. The first one has been done for you.

additionally	eventually	of course	throughout the country
after much debate	~~in 2002~~	over a few years	unexpectedly

1. In 2002,
    ₅Atlanta was losing 20 percent of its drinking water through leaking pipes.

    Altanta's mayor declared herself the "sewer mayor." Atlanta's engineers

    replaced 1,800 miles of pipes. Engineers built a massive underground tank

    to store rainwater. City officials decided to raise water taxes because the tank

    cost $4 billion.

2. Mayor Shirley Franklin had supporters and detractors. Some citizens protested

    about the cost of the projects. However, other citizens wanted the city to do more.

    Atlanta is not alone. Storm sewers overflow and contribute to flooding. Many

    American cities will have to replace old water systems.

Vary the Length of Sentences

LO 2 Vary sentence length.

If a passage contains only simple sentences, it can be quite boring. You can vary the lengths of sentences by combining some short sentences to make compound and complex sentences.

No sentence variety

Aisha will apply to a technical college. She may study computer drafting and design. She is not sure. She has many choices, of course. We are living in difficult economic times. She wants to make a practical choice.

With sentence variety

Aisha will apply to a technical college. Although she may study computer drafting and design, she is not sure. Of course, she has many choices. We are living in difficult economic times, and she wants to make a practical choice.

Chapter 17

GRAMMAR LINK
For more information about comma usage, see Chapter 26, Commas.

HINT ‹ Punctuation Tip

Compound Sentences

When you join two complete sentences with a coordinating conjunction (*for*, *and*, *nor*, *but*, *or*, *yet*, *so*), put a comma before the conjunction.

The levee broke**, and** water gushed into the streets.

Complex Sentences

In complex sentences, place a comma after the dependent clause.

Comma	Because water filled the streets, people evacuated.
No comma	People evacuated because water filled the streets.

PRACTICE 3

Combine some sentences to provide sentence variety. You can keep some long and some short sentences. Also try to vary the opening words in sentences.

1. Orange County is in California. Orange County is turning waste water into drinking water. The idea may seem distasteful. The system really works. Water drains from sinks and toilets. The water is filtered three times. The water is truly safe to drink. It has no odor. It tastes ultimately like regular tap water.

_____

_____

_____

_____

_____

_____

_____

_____

2. Larry Brown works at Cornell University. He has studied fracking. Contaminated fluid is pumped into deep crevices. It lubricates fault lines. Plates of rocks may suddenly shift. Arkansas had one hundred earthquakes during a seven-day period in February 2011. Two fracking wells closed. The number of quakes noticeably dropped.

_____

_____

_____

_____

_____

_____

_____

FINAL REVIEW

Combine some sentences to provide sentence variety. You should have some long and some short sentences. Also try to vary the opening words in sentences. Make at least five modifications to each paragraph.

1.   Napa is a town in California. It usually has a calm river. The river unexpectedly overflowed in 2006. The city decided not to build more levees. Planners worked with the river instead. The river has natural bends. The city built a flood basin. Now, the basin acts as a sink. It can lower the height of the river. Workers also connected two parts of the river. The river no longer overflows, fortunately.

2.   Minneapolis construction workers built an eight-lane bridge in 1967. The bridge spanned the Mississippi River. The bridge had a design flaw. Steel sheets connected the support beams. The sheets were undersized. Some experts issued warnings. Nothing was done. The bridge collapsed on August 1, 2007. It fell during the evening rush hour. Thirteen people lost their lives. It was a tragedy.

WRITER'S ROOM

MyWritingLab

Choose one of the following topics and write a paragraph. Make sure that your paragraph has sentences of varying lengths. Also ensure that the sentences have varied opening words.

1. Describe a district, waterway, or park near you. Use language that appeals to the senses.

2. Is there a problem in your area with roads, bridges, or flooding? Does an area of your town or city need rebuilding? Argue that funds should be spent to improve a specific area. Explain what needs repairing.

MyWritingLab™
Complete these writing assignments at mywritinglab.com

READING LINK

To read more about trades and technology, see the next paragraphs and essays.

"Safety in Welding" by Kelly Bruce (page 61)
"The Allure of Apple" by Juan Rodriguez (page 429)
"The Rewards of Dirty Work" by Linda L. Lindsey and Stephen Beach (page 436)

Chapter 17

Checklist: Sentence Variety

When you edit your writing, ask yourself the following questions.

☐ Do my sentences have varied openings?

> Beside the river, there
> ~~There~~ are steep cliffs ~~beside the river~~.

☐ Are my sentences varied in length and structure? Check for problems in these areas:

– Too many short sentences

– Long sentences that are difficult to follow

> , and it
> The road collapsed. A car drove into the hole. ~~The car~~ was destroyed.

THE WRITER'S CIRCLE Collaborative Activities

Work with a group of three to five students. First, using the words below, create as many new words as possible by combining and moving letters. For example, you can create the word *car*. You can only use the letters given; you cannot add or double any letters.

technological discoveries

Then after you have a list of words, use your list to create sentences. You can add words to make your sentences complete. Make simple, compound, and complex sentences.

SECTION THEME: The Earth and Beyond

LEARNING OBJECTIVES

LO 1 Identify fragments. **(p. 268)**

LO 2 Avoid phrase fragments. **(p. 268)**

LO 3 Avoid explanatory fragments. **(p. 269)**

LO 4 Avoid dependent-clause fragments. **(p. 271)**

In the next chapters, you will read about the world of chemistry and hazardous substances.

GRAMMAR SNAPSHOT

Looking at Fragments

Student writer Lavaughan Williams wrote a paragraph about the famous chemist Dmitri Mendeleev. The underlined errors are called fragments.

> Dmitri Mendeleev. He was a famous Russian chemist. Because he created the periodic table of elements. Before Mendeleev's discovery, there were no common symbols and formulas for elements. For example, the chemical formula H2O. It could mean water for one scientist and something completely different to another scientist. Mendeleev arranged different elements in an understandable manner.

In this chapter, you will identify and correct sentence fragments.

LO 1 Identify fragments.

Understanding Fragments

A **sentence** must have a subject and a verb, and it must express a complete thought. A **fragment** is an incomplete sentence. Either it lacks a subject or a verb, or it fails to express a complete idea. You may see fragments in newspaper headlines and advertisements ("Three-month trial offer"). However, in college writing, it is unacceptable to write fragments.

Sentence	Exposure to radium is very serious.
Fragment	Causes various illnesses.

The following sections explain common types of fragments.

LO 2 Avoid phrase fragments.

Phrase Fragments

Phrase fragments are missing a subject or a verb. In the examples, the fragment is underlined.

No subject	My father did a dangerous job. <u>Worked with hazardous chemicals.</u>
No verb	<u>First, sulfuric acid.</u> It is very dangerous.

How to Correct Phrase Fragments

To correct phrase fragments, add the missing subject or verb, or join the fragment to another sentence.

Add a word(s)	My father did a dangerous job. **He** worked with hazardous chemicals.
Join sentences	First, sulfuric acid is very dangerous.

HINT ◀ **Incomplete Verbs**

If a sentence has an incomplete verb, it is a phrase fragment. The following example contains a subject and part of a verb. However, the helping verb is missing; therefore, the sentence is not complete.

Fragment	Many of the experiments with radium done by Marie Curie.

To make this sentence complete, you must add the helping verb.

Sentence	Many of the experiments with radium <u>were</u> done by Marie Curie.

PRACTICE 1

Underline and correct five phrase fragments.

EXAMPLE: Carver was invited to speak before the United States Congress ~~. About~~ ^{about} his work.

1.   George Washington Carver was a renaissance man. Because of his many

talents, he was often called the black da Vinci. After Leonardo da Vinci. He was born in Missouri. In 1864. His parents had been slaves. Because of his

race, Carver was denied admission at most universities. He was eventually

accepted. At Iowa Agricultural College. He was the first African American to

get a faculty teaching position.

2.   Carver was interested in the chemical composition of soil. He taught

farmers to rotate their crops to stop nutrient depletion in soil. Southern farmers

planted peanuts one year. And cotton the next. Carver also invented over three

hundred products from peanuts, such as shampoo, soap, and peanut butter.

Carver was a great innovator, and he was inducted into the National Inventors

Hall of Fame. For his inventions.

Explanatory Fragments

LO3 Avoid explanatory fragments.

An **explanatory fragment** provides an explanation about a previous sentence and is missing a subject, a complete verb, or both. Such fragments are often written as an afterthought. Explanatory fragments begin with one of the following words.

also	especially	for example	including	particularly
as well as	except	for instance	like	such as

In these two examples, the fragment is underlined.

We did many new experiments. <u>For example, with mercury.</u>

Some new chemical compounds are useful. <u>Particularly in the production of fabrics.</u>

How to Correct Explanatory Fragments

To correct explanatory fragments, add the missing subject or verb, or join the explanation or example to the previous sentence.

Add words   We did many new experiments. For example, **we learned** about mercury.

Join sentences   Some new chemical compounds are useful, particularly in the production of fabrics.

PRACTICE 2

Underline and correct five explanatory fragments.

EXAMPLE: Many electronic products should be recycled. ~~Such~~ as computer batteries.
, such

1.   Hazardous wastes are dangerous for people's safety and very harmful for the

environment. Many types of business generate hazardous wastes. For instance,

the automobile industry, dry cleaning stores, oil refineries, and chemical manufacturing. A leading contributor to hazardous waste is electronic equipment. Especially computers, entertainment gadgets, mobile phones, and so on.

2. Because technology is changing rapidly, e-waste is growing at an incredible rate. In the United States, people throw out 3 tons of electronic products each year. Including over 30 million computers. According to the Environmental Protection Agency, about 70 percent of toxic waste in landfills comes from electronic goods. For example mobile phones. Furthermore, e-waste is transported to developing countries. Such as India. These regions have less strict environmental regulations, so they are the garbage dumps of hazardous materials. We must become aware of the dangers of e-waste and take steps to ensure that it is properly recycled.

PRACTICE 3

Underline and correct five phrase and explanatory fragments.

                  across
EXAMPLE: Water pollution made headlines. ~~Across~~ the nation.

Phosphates are found in the soil, in food, and in chemical fertilizer. Legislators became concerned about phosphate pollution. And decided to act. In 1972, the United States and Canada signed a treaty limiting the amount of phosphates in various products. For example, laundry detergent. The law was successful because it reduced the amount of phosphates entering lakes and rivers. By 50 percent. Presently, however, there is a recurrence of blue algae. In some areas of the country. Experts blame the current outbreak on common products. Such as dishwashing detergent and fertilizers.

Dependent-Clause Fragments

LO 4 Avoid dependent-clause fragments.

A **dependent clause** has a subject and a verb, but it cannot stand alone. It "depends" on another clause to be a complete sentence. Dependent clauses may begin with subordinating conjunctions or relative pronouns. This chart contains some of the most common words that introduce dependent clauses.

Common Subordinating Conjunctions				Relative Pronouns
after	before	though	whenever	that
although	even though	unless	where	which
as	so that	until	whereas	who(m)
because	that	what	whether	whose

In each example, the fragment is underlined.

> Marie Curie had a successful professional life. <u>Although her personal life was plagued with scandal</u>.

> <u>Marie Curie, who won the Nobel Prize for chemistry</u>. She was born in Poland.

How to Correct Dependent-Clause Fragments

To correct dependent-clause fragments, join the fragment to a complete sentence, remove words, or add the necessary words to make it a complete idea.

Join sentences	Marie Curie had a successful professional life, although her personal life was plagued with scandal.
Join sentences and remove words	Marie Curie, who won the Nobel Prize for chemistry, was born in Poland.

Another way to correct dependent-clause fragments is to delete the subordinating conjunction or relative pronoun that makes the sentence incomplete.

Delete *although*	Her personal life was filled with scandal.
Delete comma and *who*	Marie Curie won the Nobel Prize for chemistry.

PRACTICE 4

Underline and correct five dependent-clause fragments.

EXAMPLE: The ancient Greeks liked working with asbestos. ~~Because~~ they could weave the fibers into beautiful tablecloths.
because

Asbestos is a common mineral. That has been used in many household products for approximately four thousand years. Since the Industrial Revolution, asbestos has been used in cement, wall board, putty, paints, hair dryers, vinyl floor tiles, and so on.

However, in the 1980s, legislators implemented regulations limiting the use of asbestos. Because of potential health risks to the public. If people breathe in asbestos fibers, they may contract illnesses such as cancer. Some people may not know that they are exposed to asbestos. Unless they have the material in their homes tested. Homeowners and contractors should be extremely careful. Whenever they are doing home renovations. Older homes may have been built with materials containing asbestos. When removing insulation, replacing vinyl asbestos floor tiles, or sanding plaster that contains asbestos, they should be careful. They should wear masks and goggles. So that they are protected.

PRACTICE 5

Write *C* next to correct sentences and *F* next to fragments.

EXAMPLE: Industrial accidents harm people's health. __C__ As well as the environment. __F__

1. In 1984, a terrible chemical accident happened. _____ In Bhopal, India. _____ Union Carbide was one of the largest chemical companies in the United States. _____ It built a plant in downtown Bhopal in 1969. _____ In 1984, a holding tank leaked toxic gas. _____ Which killed thousands of people. _____ Other victims suffered from health problems. _____ Such as blindness and respiratory diseases. _____ The company refused to take any responsibility for the accident. _____ Even though the Indian government accused it of negligence. _____ The government sued the firm for monetary compensation. _____ For the victims. _____ It wanted billions of dollars. _____ However, the victims' families only received about $2,000. _____

2. In 1986, another human and environmental tragedy occurred. _____ The Chernobyl nuclear power plant. _____ It was built in Ukraine. _____ The reactor exploded and released radioactivity into the atmosphere. _____ It was the largest radioactive fallout in history. _____ For example, greater than the atom bombing of Hiroshima. _____ The accident was such a terrible

catastrophe. _____ That people in the vicinity had to be evacuated. _____

The radioactive particles affected people's health. _____ The accident also

harmed the environment. _____ In particular, contaminated ground water,

soil, rivers, and lakes. _____ Presently, the damaged reactor is covered. _____

In concrete. _____

PRACTICE 6

The next paragraphs contain various types of fragments. Underline and correct ten
fragment errors.

EXAMPLE: Environmental waste can be greatly reduced. ~~By~~ *by* recycling and using
biodegradable products.

1. Nowadays, the public has become very aware of environmental

    pollution. Because of education, urban regulations, and media attention. Many

    citizens recycle household items. Such as plastic containers, newspapers, and

    tin cans. People also try to use biodegradable products. However, this term is

    often misunderstood and misused.

2. The term *biodegradable* means that a product has the ability to break down into

    raw materials. A product can be decomposed. By biological organisms. Such

    products break up into soil. Or water. A flower is a good example of a

    biodegradable product. First, it grows and matures. Then, falls to the ground.

    Finally, it decomposes and fertilizes the soil.

3. There is a difference between products that are biodegradable and recyclable.

    Many common products are biodegradable. For instance, soap and oil.

    However, crude oil spills are an environmental hazard. Because the oil

    spill is usually large, and there are not enough microorganisms to break

    the oil down. Ecologists worry about the 2010 BP oil spill in the Gulf of

    Mexico. Because toxins from the spill continue to affect wildlife in the region.

    The term *recyclable* refers to items that can be turned into other products. For

    example, glass bottles. They can be melted into new glass bottles.

4. Concerned citizens recycle and use biodegradable products. So that environmental damage is minimized. For instance, if a glass bottle is not recycled and reused, it will take approximately one million years to biodegrade. As science advances, people will develop improved ways to cut waste.

FINAL REVIEW

Identify and correct fifteen fragment errors.

EXAMPLE: First, lead poison. ~~It~~ causes people serious harm.

1. Not all scientists develop products beneficial to human beings. For example, Thomas Midgley. He has an interesting reputation. He is known as an inventor. Who caused great damage to the earth's atmosphere.

2. Midgley was born in 1889. In Pennsylvania. He trained as an engineer. Interested in chemistry. In 1921, he developed a compound called tetraethyl lead. While he was working for General Motors. Lead reduced engine knock when added to gasoline.

3. In 1923, General Motors and Standard Oil built a factory to produce lead. Company workers became sick. From lead poisoning. They experienced poor health. Especially confusion and hallucinations. By the 1950s, lead had become a serious problem. Because people's blood-lead levels had significantly increased.

4. At that time, little was known about the effects on people's health from lead in the atmosphere. Until a man named Clair Patterson began to look into the problem. Patterson published his findings. That lead accumulates in the human body. He also showed that there had been no lead in the atmosphere. Before 1923. Patterson began a campaign. Against the lead industry. By 1986, the United States had stopped selling leaded gasoline.

5. Thomas Midgley continued experimenting after his success. With leaded gasoline. The next dangerous product he invented was CFC gas. It was used in many products. Including refrigerators, deodorant sprays, and air conditioners. Eventually, scientists realized that CFCs were destroying the ozone layer. Midgley never knew that his two inventions were possibly the worst discoveries of the twentieth century. He died in 1944. When he accidentally strangled himself.

THE WRITER'S ROOM   MyWritingLab

MyWritingLab™
Complete these writing assignments at mywritinglab.com

Write about one of the following topics. After you finish writing, underline the sentences. Make sure you do not have any sentence fragments.

1. Have modern scientific discoveries made our lives easier? Compare contemporary life with life in a previous era.

2. In your opinion, what is the world's greatest invention? Explain why that invention is so important.

Checklist: Sentence Fragments

When you edit your writing, ask yourself the next questions.

☐ Are my sentences complete? Check for different types of fragments.
   –Phrase fragments
   –Explanatory fragments
   –Dependent-clause fragments

                                                         He also

First, Joseph Priestley. ~~He~~ discovered eight gases. ~~Also~~ drank soda
    , which
water. ~~Which~~ he invented in 1772.

19 Run-Ons

SECTION THEME: The Earth and Beyond

LEARNING OBJECTIVE

LO 1 Identify and correct run-on sentences. (p. 277)

In this chapter, you will read about geology and the diamond trade.

GRAMMAR SNAPSHOT

Looking at Run-Ons

College student Engracia Mendos wrote about calderas. The error in bold print is called a run-on sentence.

A caldera is formed when land collapses under a volcano after a gigantic eruption. A caldera looks like a soup bowl. In the United States, Yellowstone National Park is the most famous caldera. **The Ngorongoro Crater is the world's largest unbroken volcanic caldera, its diameter is about 12 miles across**. It is the home of many wildlife species, such as zebras, lions, elephants, and black rhinoceros.

In this chapter, you will identify and correct run-on sentences.

Understanding Run-Ons

LO 1 Identify and correct run-on sentences.

Sometimes two or more complete sentences are joined together without correct connecting words or punctuation. In other words, a **run-on sentence** "runs on" without stopping. There are two types of run-on sentences.

◆ A **fused sentence** is a run-on sentence that has no punctuation to mark the break between ideas.

Fused sentence	Geologists learn about the origins of the earth they study rocks.
Correct sentence	Geologists learn about the origins of the earth through their study of rocks.

◆ A **comma splice** is a run-on sentence that uses a comma to connect two complete ideas. In other words, the comma "splices" or "splits" the sentence.

Comma splice	Mount St. Helens is an active volcano, it violently erupted on May 18, 1980.
Correct sentence	Mount St. Helens is an active volcano. It violently erupted on May 18, 1980.

HINT ◀ **Identifying Run-Ons**

To identify run-on sentences in your writing, look for sentences that are too long. Such sentences may either lack punctuation or have incorrect comma placement.

PRACTICE 1

Write *C* beside correct sentences and *RO* beside run-ons.

EXAMPLE: Scientists refused to accept the idea that continents drift they laughed at the premise until recently. _____RO_____

1. In 1908, an amateur geologist, Frank Taylor, examined a map of the Earth, Africa and South America seemed to fit together like pieces of a puzzle. _____RO, CS_____

2. A German meteorologist, Alfred Wegener, heard about Taylor's theories he tried to prove them by studying rocks and plants of these regions. _____RO, CS_____

3. Wegener developed a new hypothesis, all the continents had once formed a single mass. _____RO, CS_____

4. Because Wegener was not an expert in geology, geologists dismissed his theory. _____C_____

5. In 1944, a geologist, Arthur Holmes, proposed another theory at some point in the past, continents had drifted apart. _____RO, CS_____

6. Radioactivity caused currents under the earth's crust, forcing continents to move. _____C_____

7. Scientists had difficulty accepting his theory, even Einstein was doubtful.

Ro,Cs

8. By the 1970s, scientists had accepted the idea of moving, continents, today geologists refer to this movement as plate tectonics.

_____

How to Correct Run-Ons

You can correct run-on sentences in a variety of ways.

> **Run-On**   Some volcanoes erupt violently others erupt very slowly.

1. **Make two separate sentences by adding end punctuation, such as a period**.

   Some volcanoes erupt violently. **Others** erupt very slowly.

2. **Add a subordinator** (*after, although, as, because, before, since, when, while, whereas*).

   Some volcanoes erupt violently, **whereas** others erupt very slowly.

3. **Add a coordinator** (*for, and, nor, but, or, yet, so*).

   Some volcanoes erupt violently, **but** others erupt very slowly.

4. **Add a semicolon**.

   Some volcanoes erupt violently; others erupt very slowly.

PRACTICE 2

A.   Correct each run-on by writing two complete sentences.

EXAMPLE: Yellow Stone National Park has a sensitive ecosystem ~~there~~ are *. There* thousands of species of flora and fauna in the park.

1. Yellowstone National Park has unique geological features, it sits on the largest *features It*

   active volcano in the world.

2. The park is often called a supervolcano its vents go down 125 miles to the *Its*

   Earth's mantle.

B.   Correct the run-ons by joining the two sentences with a semicolon.

EXAMPLE: Yellowstone National Park is located on a high plateau its altitude is *;*

   8,000 feet above sea level.

3. The supervolcano last erupted around 640,000 years ago its ash covered half of

   the United States.

4. The ashfall caused the extinction of thousands of species, it also changed

   weather patterns.

C. Correct the run-on by joining the two sentences with a coordinator (*for, and, nor, but, or, yet, so*)

EXAMPLE: Geologists monitor the volcanic activity at Yellowstone they share *, and* information.

5. The volcano holes release heat from the Earth's mantle the heat is the source of the park's geysers and hot springs.

6. Old Faithful blows at regular intervals. it is the most popular site in the park.

D. Correct the run-ons by joining the two sentences with a subordinator such as *after, although,* or *when.*

EXAMPLE: Scientists study the geothermal features of the park they can gather *so that* important geological information.

7. The first men to discover the geyser used it to do their laundry the boiling water washed the clothes thoroughly.

8. The U.S. Congress created Yellowstone National Park in 1872 scientists realized that it was home to many different ecosystems.

PRACTICE 3

Correct eight run-on errors using a variety of correction methods.

EXAMPLE: Extracting rare earth metals is expensive it also damages the environment. *, and*

1. Rare earths are a collection of seventeen elements, manufacturers need these elements to produce numerous items. For example, color televisions, lasers, radar systems, military hardware, and computers contain rare earth elements.

2. Rare earth metals are not really rare they are found mostly in certain countries around the world. China produces 97 percent of world supplies it easily surpasses American production. Many nations are becoming concerned about the Chinese monopoly of rare earth production, the metals are very necessary in the manufacturing of new technological products.

3. Recently, China has used its rare earth reserves as a political weapon. Japan and China had a diplomatic row in 2010 over disputed ownership of islands in the East China Sea. The Japanese arrested Chinese fishers near the islands China

Chapter 19

withheld exports of rare earths to Japan. The elements are crucial for the Japanese electronics industry.

4.   American bureaucrats are worried that China may withhold exports to the United States during a dispute the scarcity would lead to a disaster for the manufacturing sector. Politicians feel that dependence on the Chinese is troublesome, it may lead to both economic and national security risks. The government is looking for other sources of rare earths it is also looking at ways to mine American deposits of the elements in an environmentally safe way.

FINAL REVIEW

Correct ten run-on sentence errors. Use a variety of correction methods.

1.   Diamonds have been a symbol of love and glamour they have also become a symbol of violence and exploitation. In many countries, diamonds are linked to severe human rights abuses. In those countries, diamonds are used to perpetuate wars, they are also used to finance the activities of terrorist groups.

2.   Sierra Leone had a ten-year civil war, it ended in 2001. The cause of the conflict was greed. Sierra Leone has many diamond deposits, antigovernment groups waged military warfare to gain control of the diamonds. Rebel groups in Angola and Liberia have also financed wars, they used money obtained from the diamond trade to do so.

3.   Terrorist groups also benefit from the illegal diamond trade they use diamonds to buy arms and pay informants. *Washington Post* reporter Douglas Farah brought attention to this problem he spoke at a congressional hearing in 2003. Diamonds are small, they are easy to move from one country to another. Therefore, officials find them harder to trace than other contraband items.

4.   Trade in diamonds has come under international scrutiny, to decrease the illicit trade, many countries have agreed to abide by the Kimberley Process. This agreement requires that all international diamonds have a certificate of origin such regulations will curb violence created by the illegal diamond trade.

THE WRITER'S ROOM — MyWritingLab

Write about one of the following topics. After you finish writing, ensure that you do not have any run-on sentences.

1. Describe your jewelry. What is your favorite type of jewelry? If you do not like to wear jewelry, explain why not.

2. Examine this photo, and think of a term that you could define. Some ideas might be *bling bling, costume jewelry,* or *ostentatious.* Write a definition paragraph about any topic related to the photo.

Checklist: Run-Ons

When you edit your writing, ask yourself the next questions.

☐ Are my sentences joined together without punctuation or with incorrect punctuation? Check for fused sentences and comma splices.

Mauna Loa is the world's largest volcano ~~it~~ , and it is located in Hawaii.

Kilauea is the world's most active volcano~~,~~ . It ~~it~~ has been erupting continuously since 1983.

20 Faulty Parallel Structure

SECTION THEME: The Earth and Beyond

LEARNING OBJECTIVES

LO 1 Identify parallel structure. (p. 283)

LO 2 Correct faulty parallel structure. (p. 284)

In this chapter, you will read about our universe.

GRAMMAR SNAPSHOT

Looking at Parallel Structure

President John F. Kennedy's 1962 speech at Rice University was about the U.S. space program. Review the underlined ideas to see how they are parallel.

> For the eyes of the world now look into space, to the moon and to the planets beyond, and we have vowed that we shall not see it governed by a hostile flag of conquest, but by a banner of freedom and peace. We have vowed that we shall not see space filled with weapons of mass destruction, but with instruments of knowledge and understanding.

In this chapter, you will identify and correct faulty parallel structure.

Identifying Parallel Structure

Parallel structure occurs when pairs or groups of items in a sentence are balanced. By using parallel grammatical structure for words, phrases, or clauses, you will make your sentences clearer and your writing smoother.

In the following sentences, the underlined phrases contain repetitions of grammatical structure, but not repetitions of ideas. Each sentence has parallel structure.

The <u>United States</u>, <u>Russia</u>, and <u>Japan</u> have spent funds on the space station.
(The nouns are parallel.)

The astronomer went <u>through the doors</u>, <u>up the stairs</u>, and <u>into the observatory</u>.
(The prepositional phrases are parallel.)

She <u>observes</u>, <u>records</u>, and <u>predicts</u> planet cycles.
(The present tenses are parallel.)

I am <u>awed</u>, <u>excited</u>, and <u>terrified</u> at the prospect of space flight.
(The adjectives are parallel.)

Copernicus was a scientist <u>who took risks</u>, <u>who made acute observations</u>, and <u>who developed new theories</u>.
(The "who" clauses are parallel.)

PRACTICE 1

All of the following sentences contain parallel structures. Underline the parallel items.

EXAMPLE: Dr. Pradhan went <u>into the building</u>, <u>up the elevator</u>, and <u>into the lab</u>.

1. Theoretical physicists desire an elegant, a simple, and a clear understanding of the creation of the universe.

2. To that end, scientists have proposed many theories, collaborated on much research, and built the Large Hadron Collider (LHC).

3. The LHC is the biggest, most advanced, and most expensive particle accelerator in the world.

4. Engineers, physicists, and computer scientists collaborated on its design.

5. The LHC is located in a tunnel, under the French-Swiss border, near Geneva, at the European Organization for Nuclear Research (CERN).

6. Physicists hope to conduct experiments that will expose new particles, that will clarify fundamental theories, and that will give a better understanding of the universe.

7. Scientists are hopeful, anxious, and determined to find the Higgs boson particle, which they call the God particle.

8. Experimentalists at CERN are waiting patiently, enthusiastically, and anxiously for LHC experiment results.

LO 2 Correct faulty parallel structure.

Correcting Faulty Parallel Structure

Faulty parallel structure occurs when you present equivalent ideas with different grammatical structures. The result is a sentence with ideas that are not balanced. To avoid imbalances, use parallel structure.

A Series of Words or Phrases

Use parallel structure when words or phrases are joined in a series.

Not parallel	I like to read articles, watch documentaries, and listening to seminars.
Parallel	I like to read articles, to watch documentaries, and to listen to seminars. (The infinitives are parallel.)
Not parallel	The expanding universe, black holes, and scientists studying matter are all problems relating to the study of cosmology.
Parallel	The expanding universe, black holes, and matter are all problems relating to the study of cosmology. (The nouns are parallel.)

A Series of Dependent Clauses

Use parallel structure with a series of dependent clauses.

Not parallel	The science teacher told the students that they should work in small groups, that they should share equipment, and to present their findings to the class.
Parallel *that* clause	The science teacher told the students that they should work in small groups, that they should share equipment, and that they should present their findings to the class.
Not parallel	He was a scientist who was observant, who was adaptable, and respected.
Parallel *who* clause	He was a scientist who was observant, who was adaptable, and who was respected.

HINT ◀ **Correcting Faulty Parallel Structure**

When you identify faulty parallel structure, correct it by looking carefully at repeated grammatical units and then rewriting the unit that is not parallel.

The cosmologist who built a telescope, who photographed the night sky,

who
and published his photographs received an award.
   ^

PRACTICE 2

Correct the faulty parallel structure in each sentence.

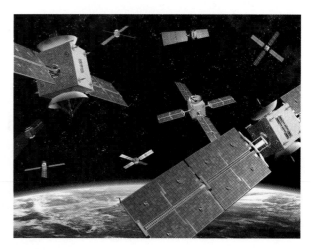

EXAMPLE: Today, amateur astronomers are looking for

satellites, watching the constellations, and
~~to observe~~ *observing* shooting stars.

1. Since the beginning of the space age, scientists have

   observed, have recorded, and discussed the topic of

   space debris.

2. Space debris is man-made objects that are no longer useful, that are flying

   around uncontrollably in space, and *that are* dangerous to spacecraft.

3. Space junk can be parts of dated rockets, obsolete satellites, or metal *eroded*

   ~~that has eroded.~~

4. Scientists, politicians, and people working for the environment *glist* are becoming

   alarmed at the situation.

5. Currently, scientists are trying to gather data on space junk, to analyze their

   statistics, and organize a strategy to deal with the problem.

6. To clean up the space debris, researchers are debating some ideas that are

   practical and some *that are* useless ~~ones.~~

7. For example, people have suggested launching nets, hurling harpoons, or ~~to use~~ *using*

   large brooms to sweep the junk back to Earth.

8. It is difficult to collect space debris because the number of tiny metal

   pieces *are* is large, ~~because~~ no collection method has been completely

   developed, and international rules limit countries to collecting only their

   own debris.

9. NASA scientists are trying to guide objects in space that are large, damaged, or

   ~~that are~~ spinning out of control back to Earth.

10. The United States and other countries need to clean space pollution, to

    establish guidelines for launching satellites, and ~~work~~ together to minimize
    ^to

    the creation of space debris.

Comparisons

Use parallel structure in comparisons containing *than* or *as*.

Not parallel	I wanted a better explanation rather than to remain confused.
Parallel	I wanted to <u>receive</u> a better explanation rather than <u>to remain</u> confused. (The infinitive forms are parallel.)
Not parallel	His raw intelligence was as important as working hard.
Parallel	His raw intelligence was as important as <u>his hard work</u>. (The nouns are parallel.)

Two-Part Constructions

Use parallel structure when comparing or contrasting ideas using these constructions:
either . . . or, not . . . but, both . . . and, or *neither . . . nor.*

Not parallel	My experience was both exciting and a challenge.
Parallel	My experience was both <u>exciting</u> and <u>challenging</u>. (The adjectives are parallel.)
Not parallel	She decided either to publish her research or burning it.
Parallel	She decided either <u>to publish</u> her research or <u>to burn</u> it. (The infinitives are prallel.)

PRACTICE 3

Correct any errors in parallel construction. If the sentence is correct, write *C* in
the blank.

EXAMPLE: Albert Einstein influenced not only how physicists looked at natural
                      how the general public viewed science.
            laws but also ~~the view of science on the general public.~~   _____

1. When Albert Einstein wrote his famous article on the special

   theory of relativity, he was neither a research scientist, nor
                   teacher
   ~~teaching~~ at a university.   _____

2. He worked both as a bureaucrat and evaluating patents.   _____

3. Although he did his job patiently, thoroughly, and with care,

   he was more interested in physics and mathematics.   _____

4. While working at the patent office, he had an idea that was unique

   and full of significance. _____

5. In 1905, he could either send his calculations to a scientific journal,

   or he could publish them independently. _____

6. Einstein's papers caused both surprise and a sense of awe in

   the physics community. _____

7. When they read his theories, some physicists realized that

   Einstein was not only insightful but also had intuition. _____

8. Einstein's contribution to scientific knowledge was more

   important than his work at the patent office. _____

9. In 1921, Einstein accepted the Nobel Prize happily and with pride. _____

PRACTICE 4

Fill in the blanks with parallel and logical words, phrases, or clauses.

EXAMPLE: We studied _____ after class _____ and _____ on weekends _____.

1. At college, I am studying both _____ and

   _____.

2. To get to the college library, you must go _____,

   _____, and _____.

3. My friend is _____, _____, and

   _____.

4. As a child, I _____, _____, and

   _____.

PRACTICE 5

Correct eight errors in parallel construction.

a challenge
EXAMPLE: Living in outer space is both a possibility and ~~challenging~~.

1. Can humans live on other planets? Novelists, movie producers, and people

   who write for television have explored the topic. It is based on the human

   desire to discover and conquer new territories. For example, NASA researchers want to explore space not only for scientific research, but also they want to investigate for possible human habitation on distant planets.

2.   Presently, the International Space Station (ISS) is the only permanent residence for humans in outer space. The construction of the Space Station started in 1998. Astronauts from different countries work at the station. For example, crew members are Russian, American, Canadian, and they also come from Europe.

3.   The ISS is a research laboratory. Scientists conduct both short-term experiments and experiments that last a long period of time. Researchers carry out trials in astronomy, meteorology, and in biological sciences. In addition, scientists investigate the effects of the space environment on bone density, on muscle deterioration, and body fluids. The results help them to evaluate the feasibility of humans living in space.

4.   There are many variables that need to be in place before humans can colonize outer space. For example, engineers must consider how to transport people, how to communicate with them, and keeping them alive. Also, governments will have to determine how much such a project will cost, the colony's size, and how the community will be organized. The possibility of human habitation in outer space is fascinating.

FINAL REVIEW

Correct twelve parallel structure errors.

                                                                doubtful
EXAMPLE: People are either enthusiastic or ~~full of doubt~~ about finding life on
             other planets.

1.   Is there life on other planets? Humans have debated this question sincerely, intellectually, and with passion. Since ancient times, the poor, the middle class,

and people who are rich have believed in extraterrestrial life. Today, scientists are searching for extraterrestrial life by trying to locate exoplanets.

2.   Exoplanets exist in different solar systems from our own. In 1995, Swiss physicists were happy, proud, and full of excitement. They had discovered a planet orbiting a star like our sun. Their discovery was among the first exoplanets to be reported. Since then, around three hundred such planets have been located. Scientists attribute the findings to better instruments, more sensitive electronic sensors, and computer software has become more sophisticated.

3.   Presently, scientists are searching for signs of life, as we know it to be. The exoplanets already discovered have either a mass that is too large or a too short orbit. Thus, these exoplanets are unlike Earth and probably cannot sustain life. On Earth, life requires carbon, oxygen, nitrogen, and life needs hydrogen.

4.   Astrophysicists want to locate, to research, and are mapping exoplanets. On March 6, 2009, NASA engineers marched through the lobby, down the corridor, and then they went into the control room to launch the Kepler Mission. The rocket will spend five and a half years surveying, photographing, and record data from the Cygnus-Lyra region of our Milky Way galaxy. Kepler's camera is both technologically advanced and has a lot of power. From its location, the camera can detect a porch light being turned off on Earth. Kepler will look for planets like Earth. If such planets are found, scientists, philosophers, and people in politics will debate the consequences of the discovery.

5.   We have always wanted to know if other worlds exist, there are other life forms, or if we are alone. The possibility of life on other planets will continue to intrigue scientists.

MyWritingLab™

Complete these writing assignments at mywritinglab.com

MyWritingLab

THE WRITER'S ROOM

Write about one of the following topics. After you finish writing, make sure that you have no faulty parallel structure.

1. How are space explorers comparable to other types of explorers? Compare space explorers with other explorers.

2. Explain why you would or would not travel to outer space.

READING LINK

To read more about the earth and beyond, see the following essays:

"Skydiving" by Touré (page 402)
"The Reverend Evans's Universe" by Bill Bryson (page 421)

Checklist: Parallel Structure

When you edit your writing, ask yourself the next questions.

☐ Are my grammatical structures balanced? Check for errors in these cases:

–When words or phrases are joined in a series

–When independent clauses are joined by *and*, *but*, or *or*

–In comparisons or contrasts

Mars has <u>the largest volcano</u>, <u>the deepest valley</u>, and ~~its weather is very harsh~~ *the harshest weather*

of any planet in our solar system.

THE WRITER'S CIRCLE Collaborative Activity

Form a team with two other students. Imagine that your team has won first-class seats on a space cruise. Each one of you can bring only five small items on the flight. Work together to create a paragraph explaining what items you would bring. You can share the items, so consider what items would be most useful for all of you.

When you finish writing, verify that your paragraph contains no fragments or run-ons. Also, make sure that your sentences have parallel structure.

LEARNING OBJECTIVES

LO 1 Define adjectives. **(p. 292)**

LO 2 Define adverbs. **(p. 296)**

LO 3 Define comparative and superlative forms. **(p. 299)**

In this chapter, you will read about famous couples in history and in literature. You will also read about relationship issues.

GRAMMAR SNAPSHOT

Looking at Adjectives and Adverbs

Comedian Bill Cosby describes a high school romance. Review the underlined adjectives and adverbs.

> During my <u>last</u> year of high school, I fell in love <u>so hard</u> with a girl that it made my love for Sarah McKinney seem like a <u>stupid</u> infatuation with a teacher. Charlene Gibson was the <u>real</u> thing, and she would be Mrs. Charlene Cosby, serving me hot dogs, watching me drive to the hoop, and giving me the <u>full-court</u> press for the rest of my life.

In this chapter, you will identify and use adjectives and adverbs.

Chapter 21

LO 1 Define adjectives.

Adjectives

Adjectives describe nouns (people, places, or things) and pronouns (words that replace nouns). In other words, adjectives add more information and detail to the words they are modifying. They add information explaining how many, what kind, or which one. They also describe how things look, smell, feel, taste, and sound.

> The **proud** parents paid for the **expensive** wedding.
>
> The bride had **four** bridesmaids.
>
> The groom is **nervous** and **excited**.

PRACTICE 1

Underline all of the adjectives in these sentences.

EXAMPLE: Gertrude Stein is an important writer of modern American literature.

1. In 1903, Gertrude Stein, a well-educated, wealthy young female writer, moved from the United States to beautiful and enchanting Paris, France.

2. In Paris, she started a splendid collection of modern art by aspiring and famous artists, such as Pablo Picasso.

3. She also invited many witty intellectuals to her apartment for evenings of intellectual conversations.

4. In 1907, Stein met the short but vivacious Alice B. Toklas, who would become Stein's life partner.

5. Stein and Toklas had a loving and groundbreaking relationship that would last until Stein's death in 1946.

Placement of Adjectives

You can place adjectives either before a noun or after a linking verb such as *be, look, appear*, or *become*.

> **Before the noun**   The **young** Frida Kahlo fell in love with a much older painter.
>
> **After a linking verb**   Their relationship was **passionate** and **volatile**.

HINT ◂ **Problems with Adjective Placement**

In some languages, adjectives can appear directly after nouns. However, in English, never place an adjective directly after the noun that it is describing.

very elegant lady.

Martha Dandridge Washington was a ~~lady very elegant.~~

forty and a half years.

She was married to George Washington for ~~forty years and half.~~

PRACTICE 2

Some of the following sentences have errors in adjective placement. Underline and correct each error. If a sentence is correct, write *C* in the blank.

heavy blue

EXAMPLE: The book <u>heavy blue</u> on my desk is a collection of works by
ˆ Edgar Allan Poe.   _____

1. Edgar Allan Poe, a writer talented young, is considered to be the

   father of the modern short story.   _____

2. He is best known for his wonderful poems such as "The Raven" and

   short stories, such as "The Masque of the Red Death."   _____

3. In 1836, when Poe was twenty-seven years old, he married his

   beautiful cousin thirteen-year-old.   _____

4. Shortly after the marriage, Virginia became an invalid, and in 1847,

   the girl fragile died of tuberculosis.   _____

5. After Virginia's death, Poe became a dark and depressed individual,

   and he died in 1849 under mysterious circumstances.   _____

Order of Adjectives

When using two or more adjectives together, place them in this order: number, quality, size, age, color, origin, and type. The following chart indicates the order of adjectives.

Determiner (number, etc.)		Quality	Size or Shape	Age	Color	Origin	Type	Noun
We bought	two	beautiful		old	red		Persian	rugs.
Santa Fe is	a	lovely	large			New Mexico	desert	town.

HINT ◄ **Punctuating Adjectives**

Place commas between adjectives of equal weight. In other words, if two adjectives describe a quality, place a comma between them.

   Comma   Shah Jahan presented the <u>lovely, rare</u> sculpture to the princess.

Do not place commas between adjectives of unequal weight. For example, if one adjective describes a quality and another describes a place of origin or color, do not put a comma between them.

   No comma   Shah Jahan presented the <u>rare Greek</u> sculpture to the princess.

Chapter 21

PRACTICE 3

Complete these sentences by writing the adjectives in parentheses in the correct order.

EXAMPLE: Henry VIII had (legitimate / three) ___three legitimate___ children.

1. The (seventeen-year-old / charismatic) _____
   _____ Henry VIII married a (Spanish / young / beautiful)
   _____ princess, Catherine of
   Aragon, in 1502. She was a (petite / lovely) _____
   girl.

2. Henry was a (massive / pompous) _____
   king who wanted a son. Unfortunately, Catherine gave birth to an (dark-eyed /
   tiny / adorable) _____ girl. Henry
   grew impatient with his queen and wanted to marry his (slender / new)
   _____ mistress, Anne Boleyn.
   Henry asked his (Roman / gentle / Catholic) _____
   _____ wife for a divorce, but the Pope refused Henry's request.
   The (English / annoyed) _____
   king broke away from the Roman Catholic Church and created the Church
   of England.

3. Henry then married Anne. Over (poor / two thousand) _____
   _____ peasants lined the streets to see Anne in her
   (silk / long / blue) _____ wedding
   dress. Henry and Anne had a (red-haired / chubby) _____
   _____ daughter, Elizabeth. However, Henry wanted
   a son, so he beheaded Anne. All of Henry's (short / six) _____
   _____ marriages were ill-fated.

Problems with Adjectives

You can recognize many adjectives by their endings. Be particularly careful when you use the following adjective forms.

Adjectives Ending in *-ful* or *-less*

Some adjectives end in *-ful* or *-less*. Remember that *-ful* ends in one *l* and *-less* ends in two *s*'s.

Diego Rivera, a **skillful** artist, created many **beautiful** paintings and murals. His work appeared **effortless** because he was so prolific.

Adjectives Ending in *-ed* and *-ing*

Some adjectives look like verbs because they end in *-ing* or *-ed*.

- The *-ed* form generally indicates someone's reaction or feeling.

    The **pleased** and **excited** artist presented his mural to the public.

- The *-ing* form generally describes the quality or characteristic of the person or thing.

    His **exciting, surprising** images are displayed on public buildings in Mexico.

HINT ◀ **Keep Adjectives in the Singular Form**

When a noun describes another noun, always make it singular, even if the noun following it is plural.

> year
> Juliet was a thirteen-~~years~~-old girl when she met Romeo.

> dollar
> We bought several ten-~~dollars~~ tickets to see the play *Romeo and Juliet*.

PRACTICE 4

Correct ten adjective errors in the paragraphs. The adjectives may have the wrong form, or they may be misspelled.

> interesting
EXAMPLE: Men and women can have ~~interested~~ platonic friendships.

1. Can men and women be friends? The thirty-years-old film *When Harry Met Sally* suggests that it is impossible. In the movie, and in most television shows, male–female friendships end in romance. Although psychologists argue that such relationships are beneficial, men and women often have challenged friendships.

2. Don O'Meara published a surprised study in the journal *Sex Roles*. He began the study because his best friend is a wonderfull woman. They have a very rewarded friendship. According to O'Meara, men and women can have pleasants relationships. However, cross-gender friendships are not effortles. Participants must be carefull when they deal with mutual attraction, with the balance of power, and with doubters. Confusing family and friends often ask, "Are you really just friends?" But such friendships are valuable. In fact,

62 percent of men report that they are more truthfull with their female friends than they are with their male friends.

LO 2 Define adverbs.

Adverbs

Adverbs add information to adjectives, verbs, or other adverbs. They give more specific information about how, when, where, and to what extent an action or event occurred.

verb   adverb

Brad Pitt <u>fell</u> in love with Angelina Jolie **quickly**.

adverb verb
of time

Paparazzi **often** <u>take</u> photos of celebrities.

verb adverb adverb

Brad and Angelina's family <u>expanded</u> quite **rapidly**.

adverb adjective

People are **extremely** <u>curious</u> about famous couples.

Adverb Forms

Adverbs often end in -*ly*. In fact, you can change many adjectives into adverbs by adding -*ly* endings.

  Adjective: honest   **Adverb:** honestly

◆ If you add -*ly* to a word that ends in *l*, then your new word will have a double *l*.

    joyful + -ly
  Eros watched **joyfully** as Psyche walked toward him.

◆ If you add -*ly* to a word that ends in *e*, keep the *e*. Exceptions to this rule are *true–truly* and *due–duly*.

             passionate + -ly
  In Greek mythology, Eros, the god of love, fell **passionately** in love with Psyche.

HINT **Some Adverbs and Adjectives Have the Same Form**

Some adverbs look exactly like adjectives. The only way to distinguish them is to see what they are modifying or describing.

Examples	early	fast	high	often	right
	far	hard	late	past	soon

Adjective	In the **early** morning, Eros pierced the heart of a mortal.

Adverb	Psyche arrived **early** at the wedding.

PRACTICE 5

Change each adjective into an adverb. Make sure that you spell the adverb correctly.

EXAMPLE: pure *purely*

1. beautiful _____
2. often _____
3. virtual _____
4. soon _____
5. real _____

6. extreme _____
7. delightful _____
8. heavy _____
9. wonderful _____
10. entire _____

Placement of Frequency Adverbs

Frequency adverbs are words that indicate how often someone performs an action or when an event occurs. They are words such as *always, often, sometimes, usually,* and *ever*.

- Place frequency adverbs before regular present and past tense verbs.

    Zeus **usually** lived on Mount Olympus.
- Place frequency adverbs after the verb *be*.

    The bridegroom is **usually** very dependable.
- Place frequency adverbs after helping verbs.

    Michael has **never** been married before.

PRACTICE 6

Underline and correct six errors with word order or adjective and adverb forms.

often contain
EXAMPLE: Magazines contain often articles about the president.

1.   In 1964, Michelle Robinson was born in Chicago. Her father was a pump operator, and he worked tireless to support his family. He suffered from multiple sclerosis, and he often was in pain. He encouraged his son and daughter to work hard. Nobody in the family ever had been to college. However, Michelle, a very brightly woman, was accepted at Princeton. She graduated with honors.

2.   In 1989, Barack Obama had a job as a summer associate in a Chicago law firm. Michelle Robinson was assigned to be his advisor. Obama asked sometimes his beautiful advisor for a date. The first few times, she rejected him. Eventualy, she agreed, and three years later, the couple married.

Problems with Adverbs

Sometimes people use an adjective instead of an adverb after a verb. Ensure that you always modify your verbs using an adverb.

> *really quietly*
> Samson waited ~~real quiet~~ for the celebrations to begin.
> (*Really* and *quietly* modify the verb *waited*.)

PRACTICE 7

Each sentence has one error with adverb or adjective forms or placement. Correct the errors.

EXAMPLE: Some people ~~sincerelly~~ *sincerely* believe in arranged marriages.

1. Arranged marriages are commonly in many parts of the world.

2. Parents find often a mate for their son or daughter based on criteria such as level of education, job prospects, and family background.

3. Advocates of arranged marriages believe real strongly that love can come later in the relationship.

4. Love marriages happen regular in many countries.

5. In love marriages, people sometimes fall in love quick.

6. In some Western societies, common-law unions have gradualy become popular.

7. The Netherlands officialy recognizes common-law unions.

8. In your opinion, should common-law couples have the same legally rights as married couples?

Good and *Well*, *Bad* and *Badly*

Good is an adjective, and *well* is an adverb.

Adjective   The pastry chef made a **good** wedding cake.

Adverb   The pastry chef cooks **well**.

Exception: Use *well* to describe a person's health.

> **Adverb**   I do not feel **well**.

Bad is an adjective, and *badly* is an adverb.

> **Adjective**   I am a **bad** singer.
> **Adverb**   I sang **badly** at the wedding.

PRACTICE 8

Underline the correct adjectives or adverbs.

EXAMPLE: Generally, couples who communicate (good / <u>well</u>) have successful relationships.

1. Varied wedding traditions exist in the world. In Fiji, it is considered a (good / well) practice to give a whale tooth symbolizing wealth to the bride's father.

2. At Greek weddings, guests throw dishes on the floor for (good / well) luck.

3. In North American Christian weddings, it is (bad / badly) luck for the groom to see the bride before the wedding. There is usually a big wedding feast, and sometimes the food is cooked (bad / badly).

4. At traditional Jewish weddings, an Israeli dance called the hora is performed. Some people dance (good / well) while others dance (bad / badly).

5. Many people consider a community center to be a (good / well) place to hold a wedding reception.

Comparative and Superlative Forms

LO3 Define comparative and superlative forms.

Use the **comparative form** to compare two items.

> **Adjectives**   Michelle is <u>younger</u> than Barack.
>   Michelle became <u>more famous</u> than her best friend.
> **Adverb**   Barack used the Internet <u>more effectively</u> than his opponent.

Use the **superlative form** to compare three or more items.

> **Adjectives**   Michelle Obama became one of the <u>youngest</u> First Ladies.
>   Michelle was the <u>most famous</u> of her high school friends.
> **Adverb**   Barack used the Internet the <u>most effectively</u> of all the presidential candidates.

How to Write Comparative and Superlative Forms

You can write comparative and superlative forms by remembering a few simple guidelines.

Using -er and -est Endings

Add -er and -est endings to one-syllable adjectives and adverbs.

	Comparative	**Superlative**
short	shorter than	the shortest
fast	faster than	the fastest
quick	quicker than	the quickest

Double the last letter when the adjective ends in one vowel + one consonant.

	Comparative	**Superlative**
hot	hotter than	the hottest

Using *More* and *The Most*

Generally add *more* and *the most* to adjectives and adverbs of two or more syllables.

	Comparative	**Superlative**
modern	more modern than	the most modern
clearly	more clearly than	the most clearly
worried	more worried than	the most worried

When a two-syllable adjective ends in *y*, change the *y* to *i* before you add the -er or -est.

	Comparative	**Superlative**
happy	happ**ier** than	the happ**iest**

Using Irregular Comparative and Superlative Forms

Some adjectives and adverbs have unique comparative and superlative forms. Study this list to remember how to form some of the most common ones.

	Comparative	**Superlative**
good, well	better than	the best
bad, badly	worse than	the worst
some, much, many	more than	the most
little (a small amount)	less than	the least
far	farther, further	the farthest, the furthest

HINT *Farther* versus *Further*

- *Farther* indicates a physical distance.

    The wedding reception was **farther** from my home than it was from my fiancé's home.

- *Further* means "additional."

    I need **further** information before I can make a decision.

PRACTICE 9

Write the comparative and superlative forms of each adjective and adverb.

	Comparative	Superlative
EXAMPLE: famous	more famous	most famous
1. dizzy	_____	_____
2. gladly	_____	_____
3. good	_____	_____
4. bad	_____	_____
5. sleepy	_____	_____
6. quickly	_____	_____
7. delightful	_____	_____
8. fast	_____	_____
9. thin	_____	_____
10. lazy	_____	_____
11. red	_____	_____
12. decent	_____	_____

PRACTICE 10

Underline the correct comparative or superlative form of each adjective or adverb.

EXAMPLE: In my opinion, William Shakespeare's tragedy *Romeo and Juliet* is his
(better / <u>best</u>) play.

1. William Shakespeare is considered to be the (greater / greatest) playwright in English literature.

2. During the Renaissance, Shakespeare was (better / best) known than his contemporaries.

3. Queen Elizabeth I regarded him as the (more / most) talented author in her kingdom.

4. His (better / best)-known play is *Romeo and Juliet*.

5. In the play, Romeo thinks that Juliet is the (more / most) beautiful girl in the city.

6. Romeo wants (farther / further) information about Juliet, so he interrogates his cousin.

7. One of the (worse / worst) days of Romeo's life occurs when he realizes that his family is feuding with Juliet's family.

8. The (bigger / biggest) mistake Romeo makes is when he believes that Juliet has died.

9. *Romeo and Juliet* is a (sadder / saddest) play than some of Shakespeare's other tragedies.

10. Critics claim that Shakespeare's plays have been the (more / most) studied works in English literature.

PRACTICE 11

Complete the sentences in this paragraph by writing either the comparative or superlative form of the adjective or adverb in parentheses.

EXAMPLE: Is Valentine's Day the (commercial) _____*most commercial*_____ holiday of the year?

1. For chocolate stores, Valentine's Day is one of the (busy) _____ days of the year. According to a retail survey, males are (generous) _____ than females on February 14. Perhaps women are (angry) _____ than men are if they do not receive a gift. Chocolate and flowers are the (popular) _____ presents.

2. In Japan, Valentine's Day is (important) _____ for men than for women. On that day, women buy "giri" chocolate for their male coworkers and bosses, but women do not receive gifts. For instance, Kaori Kato buys the (good) _____ giri chocolate she can find for the men in her office. Then she buys "Honmei" chocolate for her boyfriend. Such chocolate is usually even (tasty) _____ and (expensive) _____ than giri chocolate. In some stores, green tea chocolate balls sell (quickly) _____ than regular chocolate balls.

3. In Japan, March 14 is White Day. The holiday began in 1965 when a marshmallow company launched an advertising campaign. The company urged men to repay their Valentine's Day gifts by giving women the (soft) _____ marshmallow candies they could find. Nowadays,

white chocolate is (popular) _____ than marshmallows.

According to a survey by a Tokyo department store, flowers are the (good) _____ gift of all for women.

Problems with Comparative and Superlative Forms

In the comparative form, never use *more* and *-er* to modify the same word. In the superlative form, never use *most* and *-est* to modify the same word.

>   better
> His date with Jan was ~~more better~~ than his date with Catherine.

>   best
> It was the ~~most best~~ date of his life.

HINT ◄ **Using "the" in the Comparative Form**

Although you would usually use *the* in superlative forms, you can use it in some two-part comparatives. In this expression, the second part is the result of the first part.

>   action   result
> <u>The more</u> you work at a relationship, <u>the better</u> it will be.

PRACTICE 12

Correct twelve adjective and adverb errors.

                                          most
EXAMPLE: *Pride and Prejudice* by Jane Austen is one of the ~~more~~ famous books of romantic literature.

1.   Mariette Flowers writes romance novels. The plot revolves around the relationship between a beautifull young woman and a handsome man. The couple goes always through a series of conflicts, eventually falls in love, and lives happy ever after.

2.   The English writer Samuel Richardson published the first romance novel called *Pamela: or, Virtue Rewarded* in 1740. The heroine is a poor fifteen-years-old maid. She is seduced by her employer rich. The more he gets to know her, the strongest his feelings become. He falls in love with her very quick and proposes marriage.

3.   The British writer Jane Austen wrote *Pride and Prejudice*, a fascinated romance novel. Published in 1813, the novel revolves around the relationship between the determining protagonist, Miss Elizabeth Bennet, and Mr. Darcy. Elizabeth bad misinterprets Mr. Darcy's actions. After numerous encounters, she realizes he is gracious and eventually marries him.

4.   The romance novel has been a widely read category of literature since the last century. Its popularity grew real quickly during the 1970s and 1980s. Currently, there are historical romances, suspense romances, time-travel romances, science fiction romances, and so on. Romance books have the most largest market share of all fiction genres. Over 55 percent of all paperback books sold in North America belong to this type of novel. It seems that almost everybody loves a good romance.

FINAL REVIEW

Correct twenty adjective or adverb errors.

EXAMPLE: Reporters write ~~surprised~~ surprising articles about same-sex marriage.

1.   Possibly the more controversial issue in contemporary American politics is same-sex marriage. Same-sex marriage refers to a legally union between people of the same sex. People have strong held opinions about this topic.

2.   In the United States, individual states have jurisdiction over marriage. Therefore, the laws are not consistently across the nation. Massachusetts recognized gay marriage more quicker than other states. After the Massachusetts decision, five other states legalized gay marriage. California accepted gay marriage and then rapid reversed the decision. Many states, however, still bar gay marriage, arguing that it is worst for society than heterosexual marriage.

3.   The more this issue remains unsolved, the most divisive it becomes.
Jim and Paul have been together for five years. Paul writes good and runs a
magazine for the gay community. They both work tireless to lobby their state
government to change laws about marriage. They argue that same-sex marriage
is a civil right. Therefore, as citizens, gay couples should have the same
rights as heterosexual couples. The worse mistake a government can make
is to discriminate against a minority group. On the other hand, Edward and
Christabel are opposed to same-sex marriage. They have been married for ten
years and have a seven-years-old daughter. They believe that procreation can
only happen naturaly between a man and a woman. They also feel that families
are the most greatest cornerstones of civilization.

4.   Religious groups have also opinions about the issue. Some conservative
Christians believe that same-sex marriage is real terrible. Other religious groups
support same-sex marriage. They believe that two consented adults should have
the right to form a loving and committed union.

5.   Differents groups voice various opinions. This issue will eventualy be
resolved, but in the meantime, the interested debate continues.

THE WRITER'S ROOM   MyWritingLab

MyWritingLab™
**Complete these
writing assignments at**
mywritinglab.com

Write about one of the following topics. After you finish writing, underline
any adjectives and adverbs. Decide whether your paragraph has enough
descriptive words and phrases.

1.   Describe your ideal partner. What characteristics should he or she have?

2.   Narrate what happened on a funny, boring, or romantic date that you
have had.

Checklist: Adjectives and Adverbs

When you edit your writing, ask yourself the following questions.

☐ Do I use adjectives correctly? Check for errors in these cases:

–Placement of adjectives
–Order of adjectives
–Spelling

> countless
> Throughout history, ~~countles~~ people have enjoyed having
>
> wonderful romances
> ~~romances wonderfull~~.

☐ Do I use adverbs correctly? Check for errors in these cases:

–Spelling of adverbs that end in *-ly*
–Placement of frequency adverbs

> often
> Marriage ceremonies happen ~~often~~ in places of worship.
>   ^

☐ Do I use the correct adverb form? Check for errors in these cases:

–Use of adjectives instead of adverbs to modify verbs
–Use of *good, well* and *bad, badly*

> quickly
> Elizabeth eloped rather ~~quick~~ to escape her father.

☐ Do I use the correct comparative and superlative forms? Check for errors in these cases:

–*more* and *-er* comparisons
–*the most* and *-est* comparisons

> better
> The more you write, the ~~more better~~ writer you become.

Mistakes with Modifiers 22

SECTION THEME: Relationships

LEARNING OBJECTIVES

LO 1 Avoid misplaced modifiers. **(p. 308)**

LO 2 Avoid dangling modifiers. **(p. 312)**

In this chapter, you will read about relationship issues such as Internet dating and workplace romances.

GRAMMAR SNAPSHOT

Looking at Modifiers

As part of an essay on cultural traditions in Japan, college student Malika Jones writes about arranged marriages. In the following excerpt, some of the modifiers are underlined.

In Japan, arranged marriages or *omiai* started in the Samurai class during the sixteenth century. Wanting to make strong alliances, Samurai warlords arranged for their children to wed one another. Today, practicing a modernized version of omiai, Japanese parents may sometimes ask friends and relatives to introduce a son or daughter to a suitable marriage partner.

In this chapter, you will identify and correct misplaced and dangling modifiers.

LO 1 Avoid misplaced modifiers.

Misplaced Modifiers

A **modifier** is a word, phrase, or clause that describes or modifies nouns or verbs in a sentence. To use a modifier correctly, place it next to the word(s) that you want to modify.

modifier   modified noun
Holding her hand, **Charles** proposed.

A **misplaced modifier** is a word, phrase, or clause that is not placed next to the word that it modifies. When a modifier is too far from the word that it is describing, the meaning of the sentence can become confusing or unintentionally funny.

Confusing	I saw the Golden Gate Bridge riding my bike.
	(How could a bridge ride a bike?)
Clear	**Riding my bike**, I saw the Golden Gate Bridge.
Confusing	Boring and silly, Amanda closed the fashion magazine.
	(What is boring and silly? Amanda or the magazine?)
Clear	Amanda closed the **boring and silly** fashion magazine.

Commonly Misplaced Modifiers

Some writers have trouble placing certain types of modifiers close to the words they modify. As you read the sample sentences for each type, notice how they change meaning depending on where a writer places the modifiers. In the examples, the modifiers are underlined.

Prepositional Phrase Modifiers

A prepositional phrase is made of a preposition and its object.

Confusing	Sheila talked to the man in the bar <u>with dirty hands</u>.
	(Can a bar have dirty hands?)
Clear	When Sheila was in the bar, she talked to the man <u>with dirty hands</u>.

PRACTICE 1

In each sentence, underline the prepositional phrase modifier. Then draw an arrow from the modifier to the word that it modifies.

EXAMPLE: <u>With anticipation</u>, Arianne contacted the dating service.

1. Arianne found Cupid Dating Service on a Web site.

2. On the table, a glossy pamphlet contained additional information.

3. Arianne, in a red dress, entered the dating service office.

4. With a kind expression, the interviewer asked Arianne personal questions.

5. Arianne, with direct eye contact, discussed her preferences.

Present Participle Modifiers

A present participle modifier is a phrase that begins with an *-ing* verb.

Confusing	The young man proposed to his girlfriend <u>holding a diamond ring</u>. (Who is holding the diamond ring?)
Clear	While <u>holding a diamond ring</u>, the young man proposed to his girlfriend.

PRACTICE 2

In each sentence, underline the present participle modifier. Then draw an arrow from the modifier to the word that it modifies.

EXAMPLE: <u>Swallowing nervously</u>, Arianne explained her dating history.

1. Hoping to find a soul mate, Arianne described what she wanted.

2. Matching people with similar tastes, Cupid Dating Service is very successful.

3. Some customers using the service express satisfaction.

4. Feeling disappointed, customer Stephen Rooney has never met a suitable companion.

5. However, the owner of Cupid Dating, citing statistics, says that most clients are very satisfied.

Past Participle Modifiers

A past participle modifier is a phrase that begins with a past participle (*walked, gone, known*, and so on).

Confusing	<u>Covered with dust</u>, my girlfriend wiped the windshield of her new car. (What was covered with dust? The girlfriend or the car?)
Clear	My girlfriend wiped the windshield of the car that was <u>covered with dust</u>.

PRACTICE 3

In each sentence, underline the past participle modifier. Then draw an arrow from the modifier to the word that it modifies.

EXAMPLE: <u>Shocked</u>, Arianne met her first blind date.

1. Covered in paint, Stephen sat at Arianne's table.

2. Torn between staying and leaving, Arianne smiled at Stephen.

3. Bored with life, Stephen talked for hours.

4. Trapped in a horrible date, Arianne longed to escape.

5. Stephen, surprised by her actions, watched Arianne stand up and leave.

Other Dependent-Clause Modifiers

Other dependent-clause modifiers can begin with a subordinator or a relative pronoun such as *who, whom, which,* or *that.*

Confusing	I presented Jeremy to my mother <u>who is my boyfriend</u>.
	(How could "my mother" be "my boyfriend"?)
Clear	I presented Jeremy, <u>who is my boyfriend</u>, to my mother.

PRACTICE 4

In each sentence, underline the relative clause modifier. Then draw an arrow from the modifier to the word that it modifies.

EXAMPLE: Arianne complained about the date <u>that had gone horribly wrong</u>.

1. She discussed the date with her friend, Maggie, who was sympathetic.

2. Maggie knew about a place that had many single people.

3. The women went to a club where they met a new friend, Mel.

4. Maggie told Mel, who was also single, about her dating problems.

5. But Mel, whom Maggie really liked, asked Arianne out on a date instead.

PRACTICE 5

Read each pair of sentences. Circle the letter of the correct sentence. Then, in the incorrect sentence, underline the misplaced modifier.

EXAMPLE: a. We read about the love lives of celebrities <u>with curiosity</u>.

(b.) With curiosity, we read about the love lives of celebrities.

1. a. Lara read about a casting call for *The Bachelor* reality show getting a haircut.

   b. While getting a haircut, Lara read about a casting call for *The Bachelor* reality show.

2. a. Wanting to become a contestant, Lara contacted the show's producers.

   b. Lara contacted the show's producers wanting to become a contestant.

Chapter 22

3. a. Ramona helped Lara fill out the application with patience.

   b. With patience, Ramona helped Lara fill out the application.

4. a. Hoping to be selected, Lara greeted the mailman every morning.

   b. Every morning, Lara greeted the mailman hoping to be selected.

5. a. Each season, many people watch *The Bachelor*, known for its moments of suspense.

   b. Known for its moments of suspense, many people watch *The Bachelor* each season.

HINT ◄ Correcting Misplaced Modifiers

To correct misplaced modifiers, do the following:

1. Identify the modifier.
   Ricardo and Alicia found a wedding ring <u>shopping in Dallas</u>.

2. Identify the word or words that are being modified.
   Ricardo and Alicia

3. Move the modifier next to the word(s) that are being modified.
   Shopping in Dallas, **Ricardo and Alicia** found a wedding ring.

PRACTICE 6

Correct the misplaced modifiers in the following sentences.

       Sitting in my car,
EXAMPLE: I listened to the radio ~~sitting in my car~~.

1. The law professor spoke on the radio about marriage laws from Indiana.

2. Mixed-race couples were prohibited from marrying by legislators lacking their basic human rights.

3. Mixed-race couples felt angry who were prohibited from marrying legally.

4. In 1967, allowing interracial couples to marry, a decision was made by the U.S. Supreme Court.

5. The professor explained why these laws were morally wrong last week.

6. My sister married a man of another race who is my twin.

7. The wedding was in a beautiful garden photographed by a professional.

8. My parents welcomed the groom with champagne who supported my sister's choice.

L0 2 Avoid dangling modifiers.

Dangling Modifiers

A **dangling modifier** opens a sentence but does not modify any words in the sentence. It "dangles," or hangs loosely, because it is not connected to any other part of the sentence. To avoid having a dangling modifier, make sure the modifier and the first noun that follows it have a logical connection.

Confusing	<u>Phoning the company</u>, a limousine was booked in advance. (Can a limousine book itself?)
Clear	<u>Phoning the company</u>, **the groom** booked the limousine in advance.
Confusing	<u>Walking down the aisle</u>, many flower petals were on the ground. (Can flowers walk down an aisle?)
Clear	<u>Walking down the aisle</u>, **the bride** noticed that many flower petals were on the ground.

PRACTICE 7

Read each pair of sentences. Circle the letter of each correct sentence, and underline the dangling modifiers.

EXAMPLE: (a.) Having ideas of family honor, some parents force their children to marry at an early age.

     b. <u>Having ideas of family honor</u>, marriage is forced upon children at an early age.

1. a. Placing a high value on a girl's virginity, some cultures consider it good for children to marry at an early age.

     b. Placing a high value on a girl's virginity, marriage at an early age is considered good by some cultures.

2. a. To protect their daughters, parents often encourage girls to marry older men.

     b. To protect their daughters, encouragement is often given to girls to marry older men.

3. a. Feeling frightened, the future is unknown to the child bride.

     b. Feeling frightened, the child brides worries about her unknown future.

4. a. Having to marry very young, many physical and psychological consequences are experienced.

     b. Having to marry very young, girls experience many physical and psychological consequences.

5. a. Forced into sexual relations at a very young age, girls can suffer complications from childbirth and sometimes die.
   b. Forced into sexual relations at a very young age, complications from childbirth and sometimes death can occur.

6. a. Recognizing the violation of human rights, child marriages are banned.
   b. Recognizing the violation of human rights, many governments ban child marriages.

HINT ◄ Correcting Dangling Modifiers

To correct dangling modifiers, follow these steps.

1. Identify the modifier.

   <u>Walking down the aisle</u>, many flower petals were on the ground.

2. Decide who or what should be modified.

   the bride

3. Add the missing subject (and in some cases, also add or remove words) so that the sentence makes sense.

   Walking down the aisle, the bride noticed that many flower petals were on the ground.

PRACTICE 8

Correct the dangling modifiers in the following sentences. Begin by underlining each dangling modifier. Then rewrite the sentence. You may have to add or remove words to give the sentence a logical meaning.

EXAMPLE: <u>Making films with older male leads and young female costars,</u> stereotypes were perpetuated.

Making films with *older male leads and young female costars,*

Hollywood film *directors perpetuated stereotypes.*

1. Discussing the importance of age in a relationship, many ideas were exchanged.

   _____

   _____

2. Conducting a survey, questions were asked about age differences between couples.

   _____

   _____

3. Accepting a double standard, older men with younger women are depicted in many Hollywood films.

   _____

   _____

4. Depicting old men as sex symbols, different standards are applied to Hollywood actors.

_____

_____

5. Marrying the much younger Catherine Zeta-Jones, praise was given to Michael Douglas.

_____

_____

PRACTICE 9

Underline each dangling or misplaced modifier, and correct the mistakes. Remember that you may have to add or remove words to give some sentences a logical meaning. If a sentence does not have modifier errors, simply write *C* to indicate it is correct.

whom I like

EXAMPLE: I met a man at my workplace ~~whom I like~~. _____
     ^

1. Some personnel department employees are debating the

   subject of workplace relationships in their meetings. _____

2. Two employees can have a lot of problems with their

   superiors who fall in love. _____

3. Some people believe that companies should develop

   policies prohibiting workplace romance. _____

4. Debating sexual harassment, discussions have been heated. _____

5. Couples can develop antagonistic feelings who work

   together. _____

6. Policies can cause problems in people's lives that prohibit

   workplace romance. _____

7. Workplace romance in the future is a topic that will be

   debated. _____

8. Dealing with the issue, humane policies should be implemented. _____

FINAL REVIEW

Correct ten errors with dangling or misplaced modifiers.

EXAMPLE: Divorcing her husband, ~~her lawyer earned a lot of money~~.

she paid her lawyer a lot of money

1. Living in difficult economic times, weddings are becoming more modest. Nonetheless, there are still many people who indebt themselves with expensive weddings. Karla Gowan admits that she was a "bridezilla" during her 2010 wedding. Her parents gave her a fancy and impressive wedding who paid the expenses.

2. Karla Gowan made many unreasonable demands. She asked her parents to pay for crystal champagne glasses in a huff. She asked guests to avoid wearing blue or black because the colors would clash with the tablecloths in the invitations. The bridesmaids had to buy identical dresses made of pink Chinese silk who could not afford them. Getting more and more stressed, feelings were hurt. Taking out a loan, an antique Aston Martin was rented for the wedding day.

3. The wedding occurred on July 31. Then three months later, Gowan's father lost his job. Feeling very guilty, apologies have been made to her family. Gowan has offered to repay her parents in tears. The money spent on the wedding could have gone to much better use. Making the relationship a priority, huge debts can be avoided.

THE WRITER'S ROOM

MyWritingLab

Write about one of the following topics. Take care to avoid writing misplaced or dangling modifiers.

1. How are romance movies unrealistic? List examples of some movies or scenes that are not realistic.

2. Can men and women be friends? Give some steps to have a successful friendship with someone of the opposite gender.

3. What causes people to search for love on the Internet? Explain why people visit online dating sites.

MyWritingLab™
**Complete these
writing assignments at
mywritinglab.com**

READING LINK

To read more about relationships, see the following essays:

"Fish Cheeks" by Amy Tan (page 393)

"Birth" by Maya Angelou (page 395)

"Fat Chance" by Dorothy Nixon (page 399)

Chapter 22

Checklist: Modifiers

When you edit your writing, ask yourself the following questions.

☐ Are my modifiers in the correct position? Check for errors with the following:

–prepositional phrase modifiers
–present participle modifiers
–past participle modifiers
–*who, whom, which,* or *that* modifiers

> Eating chocolate, the
> ~~The~~ young couple looked at the sportswear ~~eating chocolate~~.

☐ Do my modifiers modify something in the sentence? Check for dangling modifiers.

> my girlfriend created
> Reading love poetry, a romantic atmosphere ~~was created~~.

THE WRITER'S CIRCLE Collaborative Activity

Work with a group of students on the following activity.

STEP 1   Choose one of the following topics. Brainstorm and come up with adjectives, adverbs, and phrases that describe each item in the pair.

  a. A good date and a bad date
  b. A great relationship and an unhappy relationship
  c. A good romance movie and a bad romance movie

EXAMPLE: A good friend and a bad friend.

  A good friend: smart, makes me laugh, good talker

  _____

  A bad friend: ignores my calls, insults me, rude

  _____

STEP 2   For each item in the pair, rank the qualities from most important to least important.

STEP 3   As a team, write a paragraph about your topic. Compare the good with the bad.

STEP 4   When you finish writing, edit your paragraph. Ensure that you have written all adjectives and adverbs correctly. Also, ensure that you have no dangling or misplaced modifiers.

Exact Language

SECTION THEME: Creatures Large and Small

23

LEARNING OBJECTIVES

LO 1	Use a dictionary and thesaurus. **(p. 318)**
LO 2	Use specific vocabulary. **(p. 320)**
LO 3	Avoid clichés. **(p. 322)**
LO 4	Distinguish slang from Standard American English. **(p. 323)**

In this chapter, you will read about animal behavior and careers with animals.

GRAMMAR SNAPSHOT

In his book *Animal Watching*, Desmond Morris describes the action of a skunk. The descriptive language is underlined.

> Before actually firing its spray, the skunk must revert to a position in which all four feet are on the ground, the tail is raised, and the back is <u>fully arched</u>. Then, looking back over its shoulder at the enemy behind it, it aims and shoots. As it does so, it <u>swings its body slightly from side to side, like a machine-gunner raking the enemy ranks</u>. This gives its <u>nauseating, pungent</u> spray a wider range—an arc of about 45 degrees—and greatly increases the defender's chances of covering its target.

In this chapter, you will identify and correct clichés and slang.

L0 1 Use a dictionary and thesaurus.

Using a Dictionary and Thesaurus
Dictionary

A dictionary provides more than just a word's meaning. It also provides information about the part of speech, pronunciation, and even the word's history. Review the following tips for proper dictionary usage.

- Look at the preface and notes in your dictionary. The preface contains explanations about the various symbols and abbreviations. Find out what your dictionary has to offer.

- If the difficult word has a prefix such as *un-* or *mis-*, you may have to look up the root word.

- When you write a word in your text, ensure that you use the correct part of speech!

Incorrect	I hope to become a veterinary.
	(*Veterinary* is an adjective.)
Correct	I hope to become a **veterinarian**.
	(*Veterinarian* is a noun.)

For example, the word *sensible* has the following definitions.

Word-Break Divisions
Your dictionary may use heavy black dots to indicate places for dividing words.

Stress Symbol (') and Pronunciation
Some dictionaries provide the phonetic pronunciation of words. The stress symbol (') lets you know which syllable is stressed.

Parts of Speech
This means that *sensible* is an adjective. If you don't understand the "parts of speech" symbol, look in the front or the back of your dictionary for a list of symbols and their meanings.

sen•si•ble /(sen′sə-bəl)/ *adj* 1. reasonable. 2. aware; cognizant. 3. perceptible through the senses. 4. capable of sensation.

From *The New American Webster Handy College Dictionary,*
New York: Signet, 2000 (606)

HINT ◄ Cognates

Cognates are English words that may look and sound like words in another language. For example, the English word *graduation* is similar to the Spanish word *graduacion*, but it is spelled differently.

If English is not your first language, and you see an English word that looks similar to a word in your language, check how the word is being used in context. It may or may not mean the same in English that it means in your language. For example, in English, *deception* means "to deliberately mislead someone." In Spanish, *decepcion* means "disappointment." Both English and German have the word *fast*, but in German it means "almost." If you are not sure of a word's meaning, you can always consult a dictionary.

PRACTICE 1

Part A: Look at the front of your dictionary to find the abbreviations key. Then write down the abbreviations that your dictionary uses for the following parts of speech.

EXAMPLE: verb _____*v*_____

1. adjective _____
3. preposition _____

2. adverb _____
4. pronoun _____

Part B: Using a dictionary, write two brief definitions beside each word. (Note that some words have multiple definitions. Just choose two.) Beside each definition, indicate the part of speech in parentheses.

EXAMPLE: ticket *(n): a printed document indicating a price or fare*

(v): to give a summons for a traffic or parking violation

1. fan _____

_____

2. mean _____

_____

3. suit _____

_____

4. grave _____

_____

> ## HINT ◄ Online Dictionaries and Thesauruses
>
> Many dictionaries are available online. Some Web sites may provide definitions from multiple sources, and they may indicate stress marks differently from regular dictionaries. For instance, on *Dictionary.com*, the stressed syllable is indicated in bold, and by clicking on the loudspeaker, you can hear the word being pronounced. (Note that *Dictionary.com* also has a "Thesaurus" tab.)
>
> **co·op·er·a·tion** ◁》 [koh-op-*uh*-**rey**-sh*uh*n]
>
> From *Dictionary.com*

PRACTICE 2

Use your dictionary to determine which syllable is accented in each word. Underline the accented syllable.

EXAMPLE: r e c e p t i o n i s t

1. l a b o r a t o r y
3. e q u i t a b l e

2. s e c r e t a r y
4. i n v e n t

Chapter 23

5. inventory   8. filtration
6. psychiatrist   9. motivate
7. cooperate   10. motivation

Thesaurus

To avoid repeating the same word over and over in a text, use a thesaurus. A thesaurus provides you with a list of synonyms, which are words that have close to the same meaning as the word you looked up. However, be careful to pick a word that means what you intended. Sometimes synonyms are similar but not exactly the same in meaning. For example, look at the various synonyms for the word *serious*. Some of the words have particular nuances, or shades of meaning.

> **Serious**, adj. austere, contemplative, downbeat, grim, humorless, poker-faced, somber, thoughtful, unsmiling, weighty

PRACTICE 3

Using a thesaurus, find a minimum of five synonyms for each word.

1. shy _____
2. interesting _____
3. sad _____
4. terrible _____
5. hot _____

LO 2 Use specific vocabulary.

Using Specific Vocabulary

When you revise your writing, ensure that your words are exact. Replace any vague words with more specific ones. For example, the following words are vague.

> good   bad   nice   interesting   great   boring

Look at the following example. The second sentence creates a very clear image.

| **Vague** | The bird is beautiful. |
| **More precise** | The bird has a brilliant turquoise head and red breast, with black and white stripes on its wings. |

How to Create Vivid Language

When you choose the precise word, you convey your meaning exactly. To create more vivid and detailed vocabulary, try these strategies:

Modify your nouns. If the noun is vague, make it more specific by adding one or more adjectives. You could also rename the noun with a more specific term.

| **Vague** | the woman |
| **Vivid** | the agreeable trainer   the nervous marine biologist |

Modify your verbs. Use more vivid, precise verbs. You could also use adverbs.

Vague	said
Vivid	whispered commanded yelled spoke sharply

Include more details. Add more information to make the sentence more complete.

Vague	She yelled at the bad dog.
Precise	The obedience trainer spoke firmly to the aggressive black Doberman.

PRACTICE 4

Read the excerpt from George Orwell's story "Shooting an Elephant." In the story, a police officer must shoot an elephant that had killed someone. Underline words or phrases that help you imagine the scene. Look for vivid language that describes the sights and sounds. The first sentence has been done for you.

When I pulled the trigger, I heard the <u>devilish roar of glee</u> that went up from the crowd. In that instant, a mysterious, terrible change had come over the elephant. He looked suddenly stricken, shrunken, immensely old, as though the frightful impact of the bullet had paralysed him without knocking him down. At last, after what seemed a long time, he sagged flabbily to his knees. His mouth slobbered. An enormous senility seemed to have settled upon him. One could have imagined him thousands of years old. I fired again into the same spot. At the second shot he did not collapse but climbed with desperate slowness to his feet and stood weakly upright, with legs sagging and head drooping. I fired a third time. You could see the agony of it jolt his whole body. But in falling he seemed for a moment to rise, for as his hind legs collapsed beneath him, he seemed to tower upward like a huge rock toppling, his trunk reaching skyward like a tree. He trumpeted, for the first and only time. And then down he came, his belly toward me, with a crash that seemed to shake the ground.

PRACTICE 5

In each of the following sentences, replace the words in parentheses with more precise words or add more vivid details.

EXAMPLE: My puppy (looks cute) <u>has expressive eyes, large</u>

<u>paws, and soft caramel-colored fur</u>.

1. A shark (looks scary) _____

_____.

2. Great white sharks (are dangerous) _____

_____.

3. Their numbers are declining (for many reasons) _____

_____.

4. In China, shark fin soup is sold (everywhere) _____

_____.

5. (Someone) _____ should focus

on the problem and (do something) _____

_____.

LO 3 Avoid clichés.

Avoiding Clichés

Clichés are overused expressions. Because they are overused, they lose their power and become boring. You should avoid using clichés in your writing. In each example, the underlined cliché has been replaced with a more direct word.

	clichés	direct words
The dog trainer was	as cool as a cucumber.	relaxed
It was	raining cats and dogs.	pouring

Some Clichés and Their Substitutions

Cliché	Possible Substitution	Cliché	Possible Substitution
a dime a dozen	common	as luck would have it	fortunately
apple of my eye	my favorite	axe to grind	a problem with
as big as a house	very big	under the weather	sick
in the blink of an eye	quickly	rude awakening	shock
bear the burden	take responsibility	slowly but surely	eventually
break the ice	start the conversation	top dog	boss
busy as a bee	very busy	tried and true	experienced
finer things in life	luxuries	true blue	trustworthy

PRACTICE 6

Underline each clichéd expression and replace it with words that are more direct.

EXAMPLE: The Great Dane was as big as a house.
huge

1. Langston was stuck in a rut, and he wanted to find a new job.

2. He wanted a career with animals, but changing fields was easier said than done.

3. Online, he found information about veterinarians, wildlife biologists, and

    animal control officers, and in the blink of an eye he came to a conclusion.

4. It dawned on him that he should start by working in an animal shelter.

5. He was hired, and on his second day, he saw something that

    made his blood boil.

6. A group of dogs from a puppy mill had been brought to the shelter, and some

    of the puppies really pulled at the heartstrings.

7. Throwing caution to the wind, Langston adopted four of the dogs.

8. Langston probably bit off more than he can chew because the dogs have

   destroyed his furniture.

Slang versus Standard American English

LO 4 Distinguish slang from Standard American English.

Most of your instructors will want you to write using Standard American English. The word "standard" does not imply better. Standard American English is the common language generally used and expected in schools, businesses, and government institutions in the United States.

Slang is nonstandard language. It is used in informal situations to communicate common cultural knowledge. In any academic or professional context, do not use slang. Read the following examples.

Slang

Alex is a marine mammal trainer. She <u>hangs</u> with killer whales and dolphins. One particular dolphin was <u>miffed</u> when another trainer tried working with it. The dolphin <u>freaked</u> <u>cuz</u> it was scared. It refused to obey anyone but Alex.

Standard English

Alex is a marine mammal trainer. She works extensively with killer whales and dolphins. One particular dolphin was upset when another trainer tried working with it. The dolphin panicked because it was scared. It refused to obey anyone but Alex.

PRACTICE 7

In the sentences that follow, the slang expressions are underlined. Substitute the slang with the best possible choice of Standard American English. You may have to rewrite part of each sentence.

                      easy
EXAMPLE: Finding a good job is not <u>a cakewalk</u>.

1. On YouTube, some animal videos <u>go viral</u>.

2. A <u>lame</u> video called "Funny Animal Clips" has been viewed more than

   20 million times.

3. In one segment, a lady is <u>chilling</u> when her dog knocks her over.

4. In another clip, a dog is lying on a couch when it gets <u>all riled up</u> and attacks its

   own foot.

5. In a popular video that <u>really creeped me out</u>, an eagle grabs the legs of a baby

   mountain goat and throws the goat to its death.

6. There is also <u>a touchy-feely</u> video called "Christian the Lion."

7. In the video, John Rendall and Anthony Bourke raise a baby lion, but then it <u>trashes</u> their apartment.

8. A year later, Bourke and Rendall <u>ditch</u> their lion at a Kenyan animal reserve.

9. Viewers are <u>blown away</u> when they see the owners reunite with the fully grown lion.

10. When Christian sees his former owners, the lion looks <u>really stoked</u> as he runs to embrace the humans.

FINAL REVIEW

Edit the following paragraphs. Change fifteen clichés and slang expressions into standard English words.

EXAMPLE: Masson's book really ~~opened a can of worms~~. *caused some controversy*

1.   Do animals have feelings? Some zoologists and wildlife specialists freak out when others attribute human emotions to animals. Nonetheless, Jeffrey Masson decided to knuckle down and learn about feelings in the animal kingdom. Masson's book *When Elephants Weep* is filled with way cool stories about wildlife.

2.   Masson provides examples of animals showing compassion. The book has some stuff about apparent friendships across animal species. For example, some racehorses get all mopey and refuse to run when they are separated from their goat friends. A captive chimpanzee named Lucy got all mushy and gently kissed and groomed a pet kitten. In another example, a young female elephant had a badly broken leg. Other elephants in the herd refused to ditch their wounded companion. Instead, they showed the patience of a saint as they traveled slowly and waited for the injured friend to catch up.

3.   Masson also raps about possible altruism in animals. In one example, researcher Geza Teleki was playing it cool and observing some Gombe chimps. The chimps were stuffing their faces with fruit. When Teleki realized that he had forgotten his own lunch, he stood under a tree and tried to knock down

some fruit with a stick. After ten minutes of unsuccessful efforts, he gave up.
In the blink of an eye, an adolescent male chimpanzee collected some fruit,
climbed down a tree, and handed the fruit to Teleki. Feeling extremely grateful,
Teleki chowed down on the food.

4. Many in the scientific community accuse Masson of "anthropomorphism,"
which means "attributing human traits to nonhumans." Basically, Masson can
argue until he's blue in the face about this theory, but he is still dissed by other
scientists.

MyWritingLab™
**Complete these
writing assignments at
mywritinglab.com**

WRITER'S ROOM   MyWritingLab

Choose one of the following topics and write a paragraph. Make sure that your
paragraph has sentences of varying lengths. Also ensure that the sentences
have varied opening words.

1. Tell a story describing how you or someone you know acquired an animal.

2. Argue that animals do, or do not, display emotions. Use examples to
    support your point of view.

Checklist: Exact Language

When you edit your writing, ask yourself the following questions.

☐ Do I use clear and specific vocabulary? Check for problems with these elements:
   −vague words
   −clichés
   −slang

               unhappy   screamed
   The child was ~~bummed~~ when he couldn't have a pet, and he ~~kicked up a stink~~.

Chapter 23

24 Spelling

SECTION THEME: Creatures Large and Small

LEARNING OBJECTIVES

LO 1 Improve your spelling. (p. 327)

LO 2 Understand when to write *ie* or *ei*. (p. 327)

LO 3 Practice adding prefixes and suffixes. (p. 328)

LO 4 Practice spelling two-part words. (p. 333)

LO 5 Review 120 commonly misspelled words. (p. 334)

In this chapter, you will read about zoos and the conservation of endangered species.

GRAMMAR SNAPSHOT

Looking at Spelling
In this excerpt from the novel *The Life of Pi*, writer Yann Martel discusses the characteristics of zoos. The underlined words are sometimes difficult to spell.

> A house is a <u>compressed</u> territory where our basic needs can be <u>fulfilled</u> close by and safely. Such an enclosure is <u>subjectively</u> neither better nor worse for an animal than its condition in the wild; so long as it <u>fulfills</u> the animal's needs, a territory, natural or constructed, simply *is*, without <u>judgment</u>, a given, like the spots on a leopard.

In this chapter, you will identify and correct misspelled words.

Improving Your Spelling

It is important to spell correctly. Spelling mistakes can detract from good ideas in your work. You can become a better speller if you always proofread your written work and if you check a dictionary for the meaning and spelling of words about which you are unsure.

> **HINT** ◀ **Reminders About Vowels and Consonants**
>
> When you review spelling rules, it is important to know the difference between a vowel and a consonant. The vowels are *a, e, i, o, u,* and sometimes *y.* The consonants are all of the other letters of the alphabet.
>
> The letter *y* may be either a consonant or a vowel, depending on its pronunciation. In the word *happy,* the *y* is a vowel because it is pronounced as an *ee* sound. In the word *youth,* the *y* has a consonant sound.

PRACTICE 1

Answer the following questions.

1. Write three words that begin with three consonants.

   Example: strong _____ _____ _____

2. Write three words that begin with *y* and contain at least two vowels.

   Example: yellow _____ _____ _____

3. Write three words that have double vowels.

   Example: moon _____ _____ _____

4. Write three words that end with three consonants.

   Example: birth _____ _____ _____

Writing *ie* or *ei*

Words that contain *ie* or *ei* can be tricky. Remember to write *i* before *e* except after *c* or when *ei* is pronounced *ay,* as in *neighbor* and *weigh.*

i before *e*	chief	patient	priest
ei after *c*	conceit	perceive	deceive
ei pronounced as *ay*	weigh	neighbor	freight
Exceptions	ancient	height	society
	efficient	leisure	species
	either	neither	their
	foreigner	science	weird

PRACTICE 2

Write *ie* or *ei* in the blanks.

EXAMPLE: ch_ie_f

1. rel___f
2. for___gn
3. f___ld
4. sc___nce

5. rec___ve
6. ach___ve
7. n___ther
8. br___f

9. h___ght
10. dec___ve
11. effic___nt
12. w___rd

LO 3 Practice adding prefixes and suffixes.

Adding Prefixes and Suffixes

A **prefix** is added to the beginning of a word, and it changes the word's meaning.

<u>re</u>organize   <u>pre</u>mature   <u>un</u>fair   <u>mis</u>understand

A **suffix** is added to the ending of a word, and it changes the word's tense or meaning.

amuse<u>ment</u>   sure<u>ly</u>   offer<u>ing</u>   watch<u>ed</u>

When you add a prefix to a word, keep the last letter of the prefix and the first letter of the main word.

u**n** + **n**erve = u**nn**erve   di**s** + **s**imilar = di**ss**imilar

When you add the suffix *-ly* to a word that ends in *l*, keep the *l* of the root word. The new word will have two *l*'s.

beautiful + ly = beautiful**l**y   real + ly = real**l**y

HINT   **Words Ending in -ful**

Although the word *full* ends in two *l*'s, when *-full* is added to another word as a suffix, it ends in one *l*.

wonder**ful**   peace**ful**

Exception: Notice the unusual spelling when *full* and *fill* are combined: *fulfill*.

PRACTICE 3

Underline the correct spelling of each word.

EXAMPLE: <u>awful</u>   awfull

1. unecessary   unnecessary
2. dissolve   disolve
3. personally   personaly
4. irational   irrational
5. immature   imature
6. mispell   misspell
7. plentiful   plentifull

8. universaly   universally
9. fullfilled   fulfilled
10. usually   usualy
11. disrespectfull   disrespectful
12. joyfuly   joyfully
13. useful   usefull
14. ilogical   illogical

PRACTICE 4

Underline and correct the spelling error in each sentence. If the sentence is correct, write *C* in the blank.

EXAMPLE: Lions are <u>beautifull</u> creatures.   _____beautiful_____

1. In Kenya's wildlife parks, animal life is plentifull.   _____

2. It is ilegal to hunt for lions in the reserves.   _____

3. Lions have roamed African plains since anceint times.   _____

4. Most cat species live a solitary existence.   _____

5. However, lions have a complex social system and usualy live in large groups.   _____

6. Kenya's lions are very efficient hunters.   _____

7. They hunt every three days, and pateintly follow their prey.   _____

8. A baby lion cub wieghs about three pounds.   _____

9. Naturaly, it is important to preserve the lion's habitat.   _____

Adding -s or -es Suffixes

Generally, add -s to nouns and to present tense verbs that are third-person singular. However, add -es to words in the following situations.

♦ When a word ends in s, sh, ss, ch, or x, add -es.
   Noun: porch–porch**es**   **Verb:**   mix–mix**es**
♦ When a word ends in the consonant y, change the y to i and add -es.
   Noun: lady–lad**ies**   **Verb:**   carry–carr**ies**
♦ Generally, when a word ends in o, add -es.
   Noun: tomato–tomato**es**   **Verb:**   go–go**es**
   Exceptions: piano–pianos, radio–radios, photo–photos
♦ When a word ends in f or fe, change the f to a v and add -es.
   Nouns: calf–cal**ves**   wife–wi**ves**
   Exceptions: roof–roofs, belief–beliefs

PRACTICE 5

Add an -s or -es ending to each word.

EXAMPLE: reach _reaches_

1. piano _____   3. fax _____
2. watch _____   4. leaf _____

5.	box _____	9.	kiss _____
6.	berry _____	10.	belief _____
7.	volcano _____	11.	vanish _____
8.	potato _____	12.	baby _____

Adding Suffixes to Words Ending in *-e*

When you add a suffix to a word ending in *e*, make sure that you follow the next rules.

* If the suffix begins with a vowel, drop the *e* on the main word. Some common suffixes beginning with vowels are *-ed, -er, -est, -ing, -able, -ent,* and *-ist*.

    create–creating   move–movable

    Exceptions: For some words that end in the letters *ge*, keep the *e* and add the suffix.

    courage–courageous   change–changeable

* If the suffix begins with a consonant, keep the *e*. Some common suffixes beginning with consonants are *-ly, -ment, -less,* and *-ful*.

    definite–definitely   improve–improvement

    Exceptions: Some words lose the final *e* when you add a suffix that begins with a consonant.

    argue–argument   true–truly   judge–judgment

PRACTICE 6

Rewrite each word by adding the suggested ending.

EXAMPLE: use + ed *used* _____

1.	advertise + ment _____	6.	produce + er _____
2.	convince + ing _____	7.	believe + ing _____
3.	complete + ly _____	8.	move + ing _____
4.	give + ing _____	9.	use + able _____
5.	cure + able _____	10.	late + er _____

PRACTICE 7

Correct ten spelling mistakes in the underlined words. Write *C* over two correct words.

                                                             really
EXAMPLE: The story of Shaun Ellis is <u>realy</u> amazing.

1. Shaun Ellis, a British naturalist, felt <u>disatisfied</u> with his life. He wanted

    to do something <u>completly</u> different. In 2008, he made the decision to try liv-

    ing in the wild with <u>wolfs</u>. He arrived at a research center in the Rockies. After

    a short <u>arguement</u> with the man who ran the center, Ellis ventured alone into

    the woods.

Chapter 24

2. Ellis didn't bring along <u>usefull</u> items such as a gun or sleeping bag. Instead, using his army training, he <u>believed</u> that he could survive by making traps and catching rabbits. He also planned to eat wild <u>berrys</u> and to sleep in beds of <u>leafs</u>.

3. After four months, Ellis saw his first wolf. Soon, <u>groupes</u> of the animals <u>clearly</u> accepted his presence. Sometimes, a young female wolf would carry a <u>peice</u> of meat to Ellis. Ellis described his <u>truely</u> remarkable experiences in his book, *My Life as a Wolf.*

Adding Suffixes by Doubling the Final Consonant

Sometimes when you add a suffix to a word, you must double the final consonant. Remember these tips when spelling words of one or more syllables.

One-Syllable Words

♦ Double the final consonant of one-syllable words ending in a consonant–vowel–consonant pattern.

    stop–sto**pp**ing   drag–dra**gg**ed

Exception: If the word ends in *w* or *x*, do not double the last letter.

    snow–snowing   fix–fixed

♦ Do not double the final consonant if the word ends in a vowel and two consonants or if it ends with two vowels and a consonant.

    look–looking   list–listed

Words of Two or More Syllables

♦ Double the final consonant of words ending in a stressed consonant–vowel–consonant pattern.

    confer–confe**rr**ing   omit–omi**tt**ed

♦ If the word ends in a syllable that is not stressed, then do not double the last letter of the word.

    open–opening   focus–focused

PRACTICE 8

Rewrite each word with the suggested ending.

	Add *-ed*		**Add *-ing***
EXAMPLE: park	*parked*	open	*opening*
1. answer	_____	**6.** happen	_____
2. clean	_____	**7.** run	_____
3. prod	_____	**8.** drag	_____
4. mention	_____	**9.** refer	_____
5. prefer	_____	**10.** question	_____

Adding Suffixes to Words Ending in -y

When you add a suffix to a word ending in *y*, follow the next rules.

- If a word has a consonant before the final *y*, change the *y* to an *i* before adding the suffix.

    heavy–heavily   angry–angrily   easy–easily

- If a word has a vowel before the final *y*, if it is a proper name, or if the suffix is -*ing*, do not change the *y* to an *i*.

    play–played   fry–frying   Kennedy–Kennedys

    Exceptions: Some words do not follow the previous rule.

    day–daily   lay–laid   say–said   pay–paid

PRACTICE 9

Rewrite each word by adding the suggested ending.

EXAMPLE: say + ing = _saying_

1. justify + able   _____
2. fly + ing   _____
3. enjoy + ed   _____
4. Binchy + s   _____
5. beauty + ful   _____

6. lively + hood   _____
7. day + ly   _____
8. mercy + less   _____
9. duty + ful   _____
10. pretty + est   _____

PRACTICE 10

Underline and correct ten spelling mistakes in the next selection.

EXAMPLE: The wolves were thriveing in the national park.   *thriving*

1. As mentionned in Practice 7, Shaun Ellis lived with wolves for one year and developed a close relationship with some of the beasts. In his book, he describes a beautyful moment. One day, something unusual happenned. Ellis was alone with a young wolf. Ellis was begining to feel very thirsty, so he decided to walk to a nearby stream to drink. The wolf suddenly jumped up and knocked Ellis to the ground. Then the wolf angryly bared its teeth and stood over the cowering man. Ellis was confused by the unecessary violence.

2. Later, when the sun was setting, the tension abruptly dissolved. The wolf walked toward the stream and looked back, which meant that it wanted to be followed. At one point, the animal stoped and sniffed some scratch marks on the ground. Near the stream, Ellis noticed grizzly bear dropings and deep claw marks in some nearby trees. The wolf had not wanted to hurt Ellis. In fact, it had tryed to protect the human from a dangerous predator!

Writing Two-Part Words

LO 4 Practice spelling two-part words.

The following indefinite pronouns sound as if they should be two separate words, but each is a single word.

Words with _any_	anything, anyone, anybody, anywhere (Exception: no one)
Words with _some_	something, someone, somebody, somewhere
Words with _every_	everything, everyone, everybody, everywhere

---

HINT ◀ **Writing _Another_ and _A lot_**

• _Another_ is always one word.

  <u>Another</u> gorilla has escaped from the zoo.
• _A lot_ is always two words.

  <u>A lot</u> of people are looking for the animal.

PRACTICE 11

Underline and correct twelve spelling errors in the next paragraph.

EXAMPLE: <u>Every one</u> should be concerned about the destruction of animal species.
        Everyone

In the last century, some amazeing animals have become extinct. Some times animals are overhunted. Other times they lose their habitat. In Indonesia, the beautifull Bali tiger has disappearred from the jungles. An other animal that no longer exists is the golden toad. The last time any one saw the toad was in 1989. Alot of bird species have also vanished. You will not find Hawaiian crows any where in the wild. The only remaining birds are in zoos. Additionaly, the Brazilian Macaw has not been seen since 2000. Like many other species, macaws have been ilegally captured. According to *Scientific American* magazine, many more species will disappear in the next ten years. Every body knows the problem is serious. But maybe no thing can stop the extinctions.

120 Commonly Misspelled Words

The next list contains some of the most commonly misspelled words in English. Learn how to spell these words. You might try different strategies, such as writing down the word a few times or using flash cards to help you to memorize the spelling of each word.

absence	curriculum	loneliness	responsible
absorption	definite	maintenance	rhythm
accommodate	definitely	mathematics	schedule
acquaintance	desperate	medicine	scientific
address	developed	millennium	separate
aggressive	dilemma	mischievous	sincerely
already	disappoint	mortgage	spaghetti
aluminum	embarrass	necessary	strength
analyze	encouragement	ninety	success
appointment	environment	noticeable	surprise
approximate	especially	occasion	sympathy
argument	exaggerate	occurrence	technique
athlete	exercise	opposite	thorough
bargain	extraordinarily	outrageous	tomato
beginning	familiar	parallel	tomatoes
behavior	February	performance	tomorrow
believable	finally	perseverance	truly
business	foreign	personality	Tuesday
calendar	government	physically	until
campaign	grammar	possess	usually
careful	harassment	precious	vacuum
ceiling	height	prejudice	Wednesday
cemetery	immediately	privilege	weird
clientele	independent	probably	woman
committee	jewelry	professor	women
comparison	judgment	psychology	wreckage
competent	laboratory	questionnaire	writer
conscience	ledge	receive	writing
conscientious	legendary	recommend	written
convenient	license	reference	zealous

HINT ◄ **Using a Spell Checker**

Most word processing programs have spelling and grammar tools that will alert you to some common errors. They will also suggest ways to correct them. Be careful, however, because these tools are not 100 percent accurate. For example, a spell checker cannot differentiate between *your* and *you're*.

PRACTICE 12

Underline the correctly spelled words in parentheses.

EXAMPLE: Many interest groups (campaine / <u>campaign</u>) to raise public awareness.

1. Ever since the (legendary / ledgendary) French actress Brigitte Bardot photographed herself with a baby harp seal in 1977, the Canadian seal hunt has been (aggresively / aggressively) debated. The sight of celebrities on ice floes protecting baby seals from being killed has become a (familar / familiar) scene. It has raised public (sympathie / sympathy) for the seals. Yet there are two (oposite / opposite) views in this debate.

2. Animal rights activists claim that the seal hunt is cruel to animals and must be stopped (immediately / imediately). The seal hunt is (unnecesary / unnecessary) for the economy. People who rely on the (business / buisness) can make their money elsewhere. For instance, activists are (encourageing / encouraging) the Canadian (goverment / government) to develop the northern region for ecotourism. Animal rights groups also (recommand / recommend) that (foriegn / foreign) countries ban seal product imports.

3. According to the pro-sealing movement, animal welfare activists have greatly (exaggerated / exagerrated) the claim that sealing is inhumane. Moreover, sealers have a (responsibility / responsability) to support their families in a region where jobs are scarce. In addition, sealers also point out that it is (convenient / convienient) to accuse hunters of cruelty to animals simply because baby harp seals are cute.

4. Clearly, each group will continue to influence the other's (jugement / judgment) about the seal hunt, and the seal hunt issue will remain a (dilemma / dillema).

HINT ◄ Becoming a Better Speller

These are some useful strategies to improve your spelling.

• In your spelling log, which could be in a journal, binder, or computer file, keep a record of words that you commonly misspell. (See Appendix 5 for more on spelling logs.)

• Use memory cards or flash cards to help you memorize difficult words.

• Write down the spelling of difficult words at least ten times to help you remember how to spell them.

• Always check a dictionary to verify the spelling of difficult words.

Chapter 24

FINAL REVIEW

Underline and correct twenty spelling errors in the following selection.

EXAMPLE: Historically, zoos have displayed <u>thier</u> collections of wild animals for public entertainment and profit.

their

1. Since the begining of civilization, human beings have always enjoyed viewing animals. Originaly, wild animals were captured and displayed for the pleasure of the upper classes. By the early twentieth century, zoos were openned to the general public. Today, the role of zoos is a hotly debated subject in our soceity.

2. Supporters of zoos argue that in the past two decades, zoos have tried to acheive different goals and objectives. Zoos in the Western world have spent millions of dollars creating truely natural enviroments for the animals. Furthermore, zoos are neccesary and educational. Zoo breeding programs have helped bring about a noticable increase in the population of alot of threatened species, such as the panda and the red wolf.

3. Zoo opponents from countrys around the world beleive that zoos are imoral prisons for wild animals. A zoo's only function is to entertain the public and run a profitable buisness. Displaying animals in cages is cruel, unatural, and unethical. Furthermore, zoo opponents have questionned the validity of breeding statistics released by zoos. Animal Aid, an animal rights group in the United Kingdom, argues that only 2 percent of endangered animals are bred in zoos.

4. Conservationist Gerald Durrell, who started the Jersey Zoological Park, stated that a zoo is successfull if it can contribute to the conservation of forests and feilds. However, others think that zoos should be banned. Everyone should consider whether zoos are helpfull or harmfull.

MyWritingLab™
**Complete these
writing assignments at
mywritinglab.com**

THE WRITER'S ROOM

MyWritingLab

Write about one of the following topics. After you finish writing, circle any words that you may have misspelled.

1. If you could live in a natural environment, what type of environment would you prefer: a forest, a seashore, a mountain, a desert, a lakefront, or a prairie? Explain your answer.

2. Examine this photo. What are some terms that come to mind? Some ideas might be *conservation, ivory, illegal trade,* or *poaching.* Define the term or expression that relates to this photo.

Chapter 24

Checklist: Spelling Rules

When you edit your writing, ask yourself the next questions.

☐ Do I have any spelling errors? Check for errors in words that contain these elements:

–an *ie* or *ei* combination
–prefixes
–suffixes

         species   disappearing
Many ~~speices~~ of animals and plants are ~~dissappearing~~ from our planet.

☐ Do I repeat spelling errors that I have made in previous assignments? (Each time you write, check previous assignments for errors or consult your spelling log.)

GRAMMAR LINK
Keep a list of words that you commonly misspell. See Appendix 5 for more about spelling logs.

25 Commonly Confused Words

SECTION THEME: Creatures Large and Small

LEARNING OBJECTIVE

LO 1 Review commonly confused words. (p. 339)

In this chapter, you will read about pet ownership and exotic animals.

GRAMMAR SNAPSHOT

Looking at Commonly Confused Words

In his book *Animal Wonderland*, Frank W. Lane examines experiments with animals. In this excerpt, commonly confused words are underlined.

> A feeding apparatus was installed in a cage whereby a pellet of food fell <u>through</u> a slot when a lever was pressed. Lever and slot <u>were</u> side by side. Three rats were placed one at a time in the cage, and soon each learned <u>to</u> use the lever. <u>Then</u> Mowrer put the lever on the side of the cage opposite the food slot, thus making it necessary for a rat to run from one end of the cage to the other for every <u>piece</u> of food. Again the rats learned, separately, how to obtain <u>their</u> food.

In this chapter, you will identify and use words that sound the same but have different spellings and meanings.

Commonly Confused Words

LO 1 Review commonly confused words.

Some English words can sound the same but are spelled differently and have different meanings. For example, two commonly confused words are *for*, which is a preposition that means "in exchange," and *four*, which is the number. Dictionaries will give you the exact meaning of unfamiliar words.

Here is a list of some commonly confused words.

Commonly Confused Words

	Meaning	**Examples**
accept	to receive; to admit	Presently, the public accepts the need for wildlife preservation.
except	excluding; other than	Everyone in my family except my sister wants a pet.
affect	to influence	Pollution affects our environment in many ways.
effect	the result of something	Deforestation has bad effects on global climate.
aloud	spoken audibly; out loud	Please read the story aloud so others can hear you.
allowed	permitted	Tenants are not allowed to keep snakes.
been	past participle of the verb *be*	Joy Adamson has been a role model for conservationists.
being	present progressive form (the *-ing* form) of the verb *be*	She was being very nice when she agreed to give a speech.
by	next to; on; before	Gerald Durell sat by the rocks to film the iguana. He hoped to finish filming by next year.
buy	to purchase	Many people buy exotic animals for pets.
complement	to add to; to complete	The book will complement the library's zoology collection.
compliment	to say something nice about someone or something	Ann Struthers receives many compliments on her book about snakes.

PRACTICE 1

Underline the appropriate word in each set of parentheses.

EXAMPLE: Owners of exotic pets must (<u>accept</u> / except) responsibility for the behavior of these creatures.

1. Many people (buy / by) exotic animals for pets. Stop (buy / by) some pet stores, and you will see monkeys, snakes, and wild cats. For example, a capuchin monkey is (been / being) displayed at our local pet shop. The monkey has (being / been) on display for three weeks. Evan, a good friend of mine, wants to buy the monkey to (complement / compliment) his menagerie of exotic pets. Everyone, (accept / except) me, supports Evan's plan. I don't think that Evan would make a good monkey owner.

Chapter 25

2. Capuchin monkeys are tiny and appealing creatures, but they are difficult to care for. Owners must (accept / except) a change in lifestyle because the monkeys require a great deal of attention. Capuchins bond with their owners and are badly (affected / effected) (buy / by) change. They can suffer negative (effects / affects) if the original owner decides to sell the animal.

3. Certainly, people (compliment / complement) monkeys because the creatures are so cute and human-like. However, monkeys are expensive to house and feed. Those wanting to own monkeys must (accept / except) that they are making a serious long-term commitment. Perhaps people should not be (aloud / allowed) to own such animals.

Commonly Confused Words

	Meaning	Examples
conscience	a personal sense of right or wrong	Poachers have no <u>conscience</u>.
conscious	to be aware; to be awake	The poacher was <u>conscious</u> of his crime.
considered	thought about; kept in mind; judged	Dian Fossey was <u>considered</u> a leader in her field. She never <u>considered</u> leaving Africa.
considerate	thoughtful; understanding; selfless	She was very <u>considerate</u> and patient with the gorillas.
die	to stop living or functioning	I wonder what will happen after I <u>die</u>.
dye	to color; a coloring compound	Those women <u>dye</u> their hair.
everyday	ordinary; common	Poaching is an <u>everyday</u> occurrence.
every day	during a single day; each day	Government officials search <u>every day</u> for poachers.
find	to locate	Biologists are trying to <u>find</u> the nesting grounds of parrots.
fine	of good quality; a penalty of money for a crime	A robin prepares a <u>fine</u> nest. Poachers must pay a <u>fine</u> when caught.
its	possessive case of the pronoun *it*	The baby elephant was separated from <u>its</u> herd.
it's	contraction for *it is*	<u>It's</u> known that elephants are very intelligent.
knew	past tense of *know*	We <u>knew</u> that the lioness had three cubs.
new	recent; unused	We used a <u>new</u> camera to film the cubs.
know	to have knowledge of	Photographers <u>know</u> that the public loves pictures of animals.
no	a negative	I have <u>no</u> photos of Bengal tigers.

PRACTICE 2

Underline the appropriate word in each set of parentheses.

EXAMPLE: (<u>Every day</u> / Everyday), people do extreme things to their pets.

1. Many people love their pets, but some spoil their animals. New York pet owners can (fine / find) designer jackets for their dogs. With no (conscience / conscious), some citizens walk past the unemployed to go buy Louis Vuitton carriers for their Chihuahuas. Did you (no / know) that in Naples, Florida, dog owners can take their pooches to a therapist? At Elite Pet Haven in New Jersey, a dog can engage in (fine / find) dining and then have (its / it's) back massaged. And of course, when pets (die / dye), they can be buried in private pet cemeteries.

2. In dog salons, (new / knew) grooming trends are an (everyday / every day) occurrence. In some dog competitions, (it's / its) (considerate / considered) normal for dogs to have colored fur. However, in the town of Boulder, Colorado, pet owners are not (aloud / allowed) to color their pets. Salon owner Joy Douglas paid a $1,000 (fine / find) for using beet juice to (die / dye) her poodle pink. Officials want pet owners to be (conscious / conscience) of the risks that (dye / die) poses to animals.

3. Basically, people should be gentle and (considered / considerate) pet owners. But they should also remember that (no / know) animal needs luxuries.

Commonly Confused Words

	Meaning	Examples
lose	to misplace or forfeit something	If we <u>lose</u> a species to extinction, we will <u>lose</u> a part of our heritage.
loose	too big or too baggy; not fixed	They wear <u>loose</u> clothing at work.
loss	a decrease in an amount	The <u>loss</u> of forests is a serious problem.
past	previous time	In the <u>past</u>, people shot big game for fun.
passed	accepted or sanctioned; past tense of *to pass*	Recently, governments have <u>passed</u> laws forbidding the killing of endangered species.
peace	calmness; an end to violence	I feel a sense of <u>peace</u> in the wilderness.
piece	a part of something else	I found a <u>piece</u> of deer antler in the woods.
personal	private	My professor showed us her <u>personal</u> collection of snake photographs.
personnel	employees; staff	The World Wildlife Fund hires a lot of <u>personnel</u>.
principal	main; director of a school	The <u>principal</u> researcher on snakes is Dr. Alain Leduc.
principle	rule; standard	I am studying the <u>principles</u> of ethical research techniques. Stealing is against my <u>principles</u>.

Chapter 25

PRACTICE 3

Commonly confused words are underlined. Correct twelve word errors. Write *C* above four correct words.

piece
EXAMPLE: Edwin ate a peace of whale meat.

1. In the past, marine parks bought dolphins that had been captured in the wild. Since 1993, many laws have been past to protect dolphins. Today, American parks rely on captive breeding to replenish their stocks. They cannot except wild dolphins. But overseas, there is a booming "swimming with the dolphins" industry, and the rules are much loser.

2. Christopher Porter, a former dolphin trainer, owns a piece of property in the Solomon Islands. The dolphin trade is his principle source of income. He captures wild dolphins and then sells them to resorts. Porter says that he has strong principals and would never hurt the mammals. However, he may loose a percentage of his stock. Animals can dye from stress during transportation. Also, Porter can suffer a lost if the dolphins become ill.

3. Many tourists do not know or care about the controversy. For example, Kaya Wilson had a personnel experience with dolphins. In 2008, she swam with dolphins in Mexico. The resort personnel encouraged her to gently touch the mammals. She went into the water wearing a lose top over her bathing suit, and a dolphin past by and pulled at her shirt. Kaya says that she felt happy and at piece with the dolphins.

Commonly Confused Words

	Meaning	Example
quiet	silent	It was quiet in the woods.
quite	very	The herd was moving quite fast.
quit	stop	The zoo director quit after receiving a bad report.
sit	to seat oneself	I will sit on this rock to watch the birds.
set	to put or place down	He set his book about birds on the grass.
taught	past tense of *to teach*	Dr. Zavitz taught a class on sharks.
thought	past tense of *to think*	His students thought that he was a good teacher.

	Meaning	Example
than	word used in comparisons	Whales are larger <u>than</u> dolphins.
then	at a particular time; after a specific time	The grizzly entered the river, and <u>then</u> it caught some salmon.
that	word used to introduce a clause	Some people do not realize <u>that</u> grizzlies are extremely dangerous.
their	possessive form of *they*	Anita and Ram went to see <u>their</u> favorite documentary on bird migration.
there	a place; something that exists	<u>There</u> are many birds in the park. The students went <u>there</u> by bus.
they're	contraction of *they are*	<u>They're</u> both very interested in falcons.

PRACTICE 4

Underline the appropriate word in each set of parentheses.

EXAMPLE: (<u>There</u> / Their) are many types of exotic birds.

1.   One hundred years ago, parrots were (quiet / quite) common in tropical countries. Today, (there / their / they're) are about 350 different types of parrots, each with a distinct size and appearance. With (there / their / they're) beautiful colors, parrots have become one of the most sought-after exotic animals.

2.   Some people think (than / then / that) parrots are easy to maintain. In fact, parrots are more difficult to care for (than / then / that) many other bird species. For one thing, some types of parrots love to vocalize, so (there / their / they're) not ideal for owners who want peace and (quite / quiet). Parrots are social creatures (than / then / that) mate for life, and they become very attached to (there / their) owners. They do not like to (sit / set) in one place for long periods of time. Instead, (there / their / they're) happiest when being caressed or permitted to fly around a room. When owners ignore parrots, the birds can develop (quiet / quite) strange behavior. For instance, a neglected parrot might pull out (its / it's) own feathers.

3.   In the (past / passed), people (taught / thought) that parrots simply mimicked human sounds. In fact, recent research has shown (than / then / that) parrots are capable of complex thinking. Irene Pepperberg began studying African gray parrots thirty years ago. (Than / Then / That), after many experiments, she published articles about them. She (taught / thought) a parrot named Alex to recognize about one hundred objects. Nowadays, gray parrots are (considered / considerate) the most intelligent bird species.

Commonly Confused Words

	Meaning	Examples
through	in one side and out the other; finished	The monkeys climbed through the trees. Although they were still active, we were through for the day.
threw	past tense of *throw*	The monkeys threw fruit down from the tree.
thorough	complete	The biologist did a thorough investigation of monkey behavior.
to	indicates direction or movement; part of an infinitive	I want to go to Africa.
too	*very* or *also*	Kenya is too hot in the summer. It is hot in Somalia, too.
two	the number after one	Africa and the Amazon are two places that intrigue me.
write	to draw symbols that represent words	I write about conservation issues for the newspaper.
right	correct; the opposite of *left*	Is this the right way to go to the village? The jeep's right turn signal does not work.
where	question word indicating location	Where did the zoo keep the gorillas?
were	past tense of *be*	The gorillas were in the enclosure.
we're	contraction of *we are*	We're going to see a film about gorillas.
weather	atmospheric conditions	The weather is sunny and hot.
whether	term used to introduce alternatives	I don't know whether he won or lost.
who's	contraction of *who is*	Makiko, who's a friend of mine, is doing research on lemurs.
whose	pronoun showing ownership	Animals whose habitat is disappearing need to be protected.
you're	contraction of *you are*	You're going on the field trip, aren't you?
your	possessive adjective	Your sister went to the pet store.

PRACTICE 5

Underline the appropriate word in each set of parentheses.

EXAMPLE: (We're / Were) going to see some whales.

1. Last week, we (we're / were) at Marineland (were / where) there are (to / two / too) killer whales. What (were / where) the whales doing? They were leaping (threw / thorough / through) hoops and jumping in unison. One trainer (threw / through) fish to the whales whenever they completed a trick. He stroked the whales' bellies, (to / two / too). The (whether / weather) was beautiful, and we had a great time.

2. Carolyn Thomson and others often (write / right) about the benefits of marine parks. The parks do a very (thorough / through / threw) analysis of a whale's needs,

and they provide the basic necessities. However, marine park opponents believe that the parks are immoral places. (Who's / Whose) (right / write) about this issue?

3.   John Holer, (who's / whose) the owner of Marineland in Niagara Falls, supports the parks. Captive whales educate children about marine life. A scientist (who's / whose) working with whales can learn valuable information about the species. Other experts (who's / whose) work centers around animal (rights / writes) disagree. Carter Dillard, a lawyer for the Animal Legal Defense Fund, points out that whales are usually (to / too / two) large for their enclosures. Also, they have a high death rate in captivity. In the wild, Orcas can live for sixty years, but in marine parks, (it's / its) rare for an Orca to live (passed / past) ten years. Often, one well-known whale is really many different whales. After a whale (dyes / dies), another whale is given (it's / its) name. Furthermore, the whales are generally kept in separate enclosures, and they cannot pass (threw / thorough / through) the gates. Yet whales are social mammals that benefit from contact with others.

4.   (Were / We're / Where) planning to take another vacation when the (weather / whether) gets warmer. We must decide (weather / whether) or not we should visit a marine park again. I'm not sure (weather / whether) such parks are harmful or beneficial. What is (you're / your) opinion? Maybe (you're / your) more likely to care about whales if you get a chance to see one.

FINAL REVIEW

Underline and correct fifteen errors in word choice.

EXAMPLE: The parrot escaped <u>thorough</u> the window.
through

1.   Some states ban the ownership of exotic pets. In other states, people are aloud to buy lions, monkeys, and other exotic creatures. Ownership of exotic animals has become a passionately debated subject.

2.   Animal activists argue than it is cruel to capture and cage exotic animals. Furthermore, such animals can have diseases that are considerate dangerous for humans. Additionally, exotic animals are often released into the wild when there owners become tired of them. For example, in Florida, many snake

owners release their Burmese Pythons into the wild. Skip Snow, whose a snake expert, dissected a 16-foot-long python in the Everglades. The snake had a fully formed deer in it's belly. Unfortunately, many owners of exotic pets do not really no how to take care of their animals because they have never been thought. For example, 90 percent of pet snakes dye within the first year of captivity because they have been mistreated.

3.   Owners of exotic pets state that it's perfectly reasonable to keep such animals. Proponents say that accept for the occasional case, most exotic pet owners are very responsible and have strong principals. Owners with a strong conscious would never neglect their pets. Moreover, many business owners would loose their income if the sale of exotic pets were prohibited.

4.   More states may past laws that limit the exotic animal market. Do you know weather or not you would support such legislation?

MyWritingLab™
Complete these writing assignments at mywritinglab.com

MyWritingLab™   **THE WRITER'S ROOM**

Write about one of the following topics. After you finish writing, proofread your paragraph for spelling or word-choice errors.

1. What are some reasons that people own pets? How can pet ownership affect a person's life? Write about the causes or effects of owning pets.

2. Would you ever own an exotic pet such as a snake, an alligator, a monkey, or a tiger? Explain why or why not.

Checklist: Commonly Confused Words

When you edit your writing, ask yourself whether you have used the correct words. Check for errors with commonly confused words.

My friend Patricia, ~~whose~~ (who's) a veterinarian, believes ~~than~~ (that) pet owners

should take courses on how to take care of ~~they're~~ (their) pets.

READING LINK

To read more about creatures large and small, see the following essays:

"Saving Animals" by Tom Spears (page 423)
"Is It Love or a Trick?" by Jon Katz (page 425)

THE WRITER'S CIRCLE Collaborative Activity

Work with a partner. You will have two minutes to come up with as many homonyms as possible. A homonym is a word that sounds exactly like another word, but the spelling and meaning differ. Write your homonyms beside each word.

EXAMPLE: write _right_

hair _____	pale _____	flower _____
cents _____	nose _____	missed _____
wait _____	medal _____	patience _____
ate _____	whale _____	see _____
bare _____	foul _____	board _____
disgust _____	cruise _____	waste _____
gorilla _____	pear _____	witch _____

Chapter 25

26 Commas

SECTION THEME: The Business World

LEARNING OBJECTIVES

LO 1 Define the purpose of a comma. **(p. 349)**

LO 2 Use commas in a series. **(p. 349)**

LO 3 Use commas after introductory words and phrases. **(p. 350)**

LO 4 Use commas around interrupting words and phrases. **(p. 351)**

LO 5 Use commas in compound sentences. **(p. 353)**

LO 6 Use commas in complex sentences. **(p. 354)**

LO 7 Use commas in business letters. **(p. 357)**

In this chapter, you will read about business-related topics, including job searching and unusual jobs.

GRAMMAR SNAPSHOT

Looking at Commas

The next introductory excerpt is from a *Christian Science Monitor* article about student debt by Stacy Teicher Khadaroo. Notice the use of commas in the excerpt from her article.

> College costs are not only what you pay up front, but also what debt you carry into the future. The class of 2009 graduated with an average of $24,000 in debts from student loans, up 6 percent from the previous year, according to a report from *The Project on Student Debt* in Oakland, California.

In this chapter, you will learn how to use commas correctly.

Understanding Commas

LO 1 Define the purpose of a comma.

A **comma** (,) is a punctuation mark that helps keep distinct ideas separate. Commas are especially important in series, after introductory words and phrases, around interrupting words and phrases, and in compound and complex sentences.

Some jobs, especially those in the service industry, pay minimum wage.

Commas in a Series

LO 2 Use commas in a series.

Use a comma to separate items in a series of three or more items. Remember to put a comma before the final *and* or *or*.

item 1	,	item 2	,	and or	item 3
Series of nouns		The conference will be in Dallas, Houston, Galveston, or Austin.			
Series of verbs		During the conference, guests will eat, drink, and network.			
Series of phrases		She dressed well, kept her head up, and maintained eye contact.			

HINT ◂ Punctuating a Series

In a series of three or more items, do not place a comma after the last item in the series (unless the series is part of an interrupting phrase).

His mother, father, and sister, were at the ceremony.

Do not use commas to separate items if each item is joined by *and* or *or*.

The audience clapped <u>and</u> cheered <u>and</u> stood up after the speech.

PRACTICE 1

Each sentence contains a series of items. Add the missing commas.

EXAMPLE: John L. Holland, a psychology professor from Johns Hopkins University, has taught students, done research, and published books.

1. According to John L. Holland, the six basic types of jobs include realistic jobs conventional jobs investigative jobs artistic jobs social jobs and leadership jobs.

2. When trying to choose a career, you should try a variety of jobs work in different places and volunteer for various tasks.

3. Realistic jobs involve working with tools large machines or other types of equipment.

4. People who work with tools or machines are usually strong competitive and physically healthy.

5. Bank tellers secretaries office managers and accountants have conventional jobs.

Chapter 26

6. People who describe themselves as outgoing cooperative helpful and responsible have social jobs.

7. Eric Townsend wants to be a teacher nurse or social worker.

8. Investigative workers often do market surveys develop military strategies or tackle economic problems.

9. Adela Sanchez is energetic self-confident and ambitious.

10. Sanchez hopes to get a leadership job in sales politics or business.

LO3 Use commas after introductory words and phrases.

Commas After Introductory Words and Phrases

Place a comma after an **introductory word**. The word could be an interjection such as *yes* or *no*, an adverb such as *usually*, or a transitional word such as *therefore*.

| Introductory word(s) | , | sentence | . |

Yes, I will help you finish the project.

Honestly, you should reconsider your promise.

However, the job includes a lot of overtime.

Introductory phrases of two or more words should be set off with a comma. The phrase could be a transitional expression such as *of course* or a prepositional phrase such as *in the morning*.

As a matter of fact, the manager explained the new policy.

In the middle of the meeting, Nancy decided to leave.

After his speech, the employees asked questions.

PRACTICE 2

Underline the introductory word or phrase in each sentence. Add fifteen missing commas.

EXAMPLE: Each morning, I read the careers section in the newspaper.

1. In 2009 the tourism department in Queensland, Australia, wanted to promote the Great Barrier Reef as a tourist site. Therefore department officials hired

a publicity firm to launch a campaign. After much discussion the publicity team developed an interesting way of advertising the Great Barrier Reef. To attract attention the team created a job posting called "The Best Job in the World."

2.   First the team created a Web site, showing the natural beauty of the islands in the Great Barrier Reef. Furthermore the publicists advertised a "Caretaker of the Islands" job on the tourism website. Certainly it was one of the most unique jobs in the world. In addition the job had great benefits such as a high salary and free housing in a magnificent mansion overlooking a beautiful beach. Yes the job recipient had some duties to perform. Primarily the caretaker had to make videos of the islands, write blog entries, and post photos to attract visitors to the area.

3.   Naturally thousands of people from all over the world applied for the job. After interviewing sixteen finalists the hiring committee offered Ben Southall the job as caretaker of paradise. With a six-month contract Southall started his new job. After a great deal of success as caretaker Southall was offered another job in Australia. Currently he is the ambassador of Queensland tourism.

Commas Around Interrupting Words and Phrases

LO 4 Use commas around interrupting words and phrases.

Interrupting words or phrases appear in the middle of sentences. Such interrupters are often asides that break the sentence's flow but do not really affect the meaning.

| Noun | , | interrupting word(s) | , | rest of sentence. |

My coworker, for example, has never taken a sick day.
Kyle, frankly, should never drink during business lunches.
The company, in the middle of an economic boom, went bankrupt!

> ## HINT Using Commas with Appositives
>
> An appositive comes before or after a noun or pronoun and adds further information about the noun or pronoun. The appositive can appear at the beginning, in the middle, or at the end of the sentence. Set off appositives with commas.
>
>   beginning
> <u>An ambitious man</u>, Donald has done well in real estate.
>
>   middle
> Cancun, <u>a coastal city</u>, depends on tourism.
>
>   end
> The hotel is next to Alicia's, <u>a local restaurant</u>.

PRACTICE 3

Underline any interrupting phrases and add commas where needed to the following sentences.

EXAMPLE: Some young entrepreneurs, <u>for instance</u> are very successful. _____

1. Young entrepreneurs, showing ingenuity continue to develop interesting products. _____

2. Mark Zuckerberg, for example was a young college student when he and his friends developed Facebook. _____

3. Facebook a social Internet site, was first aimed at Harvard undergraduates. _____

4. Evan Williams another young entrepreneur, created one of the first Web applications for blogs. _____

5. Google bought Williams's Web site, *Blogger* in 2003. _____

6. YouTube one of the fastest growing Web sites, was bought by Google in 2006. _____

7. Three young friends, former PayPal employees created this popular site. _____

8. Risk takers, with insight and skill are finding creative ways to profit from the Internet. _____

PRACTICE 4

Add ten missing commas to the following passages.

EXAMPLE: Life coaches, funeral directors and square dance callers are people who have out-of-the-ordinary careers.

1.   Many people have interesting, fulfilling and unique jobs. Newton Proust is a freelance greeting card writer. He writes verses for birthday cards graduation cards, and sympathy cards. He feels that the sentiments expressed in a greeting card bring people together. To express accurate emotions Mr. Proust studies the latest cultural trends. In fact he constantly reads magazines, comic strips and pulp fiction to acquire knowledge of what people are thinking and feeling.

2.   Angelica Pedersen a master coffee taster, travels to coffee-producing regions around the world. She works for Blue Coffee a small business. However the company is a supplier to some of the biggest coffee retailers in North America. Ms. Pedersen, an experienced professional must develop the perfect blend of coffee for her clients. She smells and tastes about three hundred cups of coffee per day. Clearly she loves her job and would not consider doing anything else.

Commas in Compound Sentences

L0 5 Use commas in compound sentences.

A **compound sentence** contains two or more complete sentences joined by a coordinating conjunction (*for, and, nor, but, or, yet, so*).

Sentence	, and	sentence.

The job is interesting, **and** the pay is decent.

The job requires fluency in Spanish, **so** maybe I will be hired.

Michael works as a bank teller, **but** he is looking for a better position.

HINT ◄ Commas and Coordinators

You do not always have to put a comma before coordinating conjunctions such as *and*, *but*, or *or*. To ensure that a sentence is truly compound, cover the conjunction with your finger and read the two parts of the sentence.

• If each part of the sentence contains a complete idea, then you need to add a comma.

   Comma   Anna does marketing surveys**,** and she sells products.

• If one part is incomplete, then no comma is necessary.

   No Comma   Anna does marketing surveys and sells products.

PRACTICE 5

Add the missing commas to the next compound sentences.

EXAMPLE: Charles Schulz created the comic strip *Peanuts*, and it was one of the most popular comics of all time.

1. As a child, the cartoonist Charles Schulz loved to draw so he often drew his dog Spike.

Chapter 26

2. Young Charles sent a drawing of Spike to *Ripley's Believe It or Not* and the picture was published in the magazine.

3. The boy drew cartoon figures every day for he wanted to be a cartoonist.

4. In the late 1940s, Schulz began sending his comic strips to newspapers but he was rejected seventeen times.

5. Schultz continued his efforts to be a cartoonist and eventually, *Peanuts* became an international success.

PRACTICE 6

Add six missing commas to the following letter.

EXAMPLE: I like to travel, so I volunteer overseas.

Hi Leeann,

I know I haven't written in a long time but I have been busy getting used to my daily life here. As you know, I volunteer with the Human Connections Foundation. Last week I arrived in Honduras. I was met by Fredo my supervisor. We traveled to the village together. After a couple days of training, I started work on the project. The volunteers build houses, install water pumps and repair roads. My job actually, is to dig holes for the pumps. I start work very early so I usually take a siesta in the afternoon. I will send you some photos and videos in a couple days.

Cheers,

Antonio

LO 6 Use commas in complex sentences.

Commas in Complex Sentences

A **complex sentence** contains one or more dependent clauses (or incomplete ideas). When a **subordinating conjunction**—a word such as *because*, *although*, or *unless*—is added to a clause, it makes the clause dependent.

independent clause   dependent clause

When opportunity knocks, you should embrace it.

Use a Comma After a Dependent Clause

If a sentence begins with a dependent clause, place a comma after the clause. Remember that a dependent clause has a subject and a verb, but it cannot stand alone. When the subordinating conjunction comes in the middle of the sentence, it is not necessary to use a comma.

Dependent clause	**,**	main clause.

Comma   Because she loves helping people, she is studying nursing.

Main clause	**dependent clause.**

No comma   She is studying nursing because she loves helping people.

PRACTICE 7

Edit the following sentences by adding or deleting commas. If a sentence is correct, write *C* in the blank.

EXAMPLE: Before she went to the interview, Ellen removed her

eyebrow ring.   _____

1. Because first impressions count, it is important to dress well for

   an interview.   _____

2. Before you leave the house review your wardrobe.   _____

3. Although your current boss may accept casual clothing, your

   future boss may object.   _____

4. Monica Zacharias wants to work as a restaurant manager,

   because she is ambitious.   _____

5. Although she loves her tattoos she will cover them with clothing

   during the interview.   _____

6. After she gets the job Zacharias will dress to show her personality.   _____

7. When Clayton Townsend wore a T-shirt and baggy pants to the

   interview he was not hired.   _____

8. Because Townsend wanted to be hired, he should have tried to

   make a better impression.   _____

9. After she left her job as a personnel director Amy Rowen started

   an employment consulting business.   _____

10. According to Rowen, unless job applicants want to work in

    an artistic milieu they should wear conservative clothing to interviews.   _____

Chapter 26

Use Commas with Nonrestrictive Clauses

Clauses beginning with *who*, *that*, and *which* can be restrictive or nonrestrictive. A **restrictive clause** contains essential information about the subject. Do not place commas around restrictive clauses.

No commas	The woman <u>who invented the windshield wiper</u> never became wealthy. (The clause is essential to understand the sentence.)

A **nonrestrictive clause** gives nonessential information. In such sentences, the clause gives additional information about the noun, but it does not restrict or define the noun. Place commas around nonrestrictive clauses.

Commas	The restaurant, <u>which is on Labelle Boulevard</u>, has excellent seafood. (The clause contains extra information. If you removed it, the sentence would still have a clear meaning.)

HINT ◂ Using *Which*, *That*, and *Who*

which

Use commas to set off clauses that begin with *which*.

> Apple Computer, **which** started in 1976, was co-founded by Steve Wozniak and Steve Jobs.

that

Do not use commas to set off clauses that begin with *that*.

> One product **that** changed the world was the personal computer.

who

When a clause begins with *who*, you may or may not need a comma. If the clause contains nonessential information, put commas around it. If the clause is essential to the meaning of the sentence, then it does not require commas.

Essential	The man **who** employs me uses Apple computers.
Not Essential	Steve Jobs, **who** had four children, was a billionaire.

PRACTICE 8

Underline the clause in each sentence that begins with *who*, *which*, or *that*. Add commas if necessary.

EXAMPLE: The sea captain <u>who was hijacked by pirates</u> appeared in the news.

1. Jobs that are interesting are often the subject of news articles.

2. Ranvir Shah who likes to travel is the captain of a merchant ship.

3. His ship which is named *Prospector* is a medium-sized cargo vessel.

4. The ship which carries dry goods often sails near the Horn of Africa.

5. The vessel that Shah sails has been a target of pirates.

6. In 2011, about two hundred ships that were near the Somali coast were hijacked.

7. Pirates who plunder the waters off the Horn of Africa are considered to be the most dangerous in the world.

8. Last year, an experience that Shah had was memorable.

9. Somali pirates who were in small boats tried to capture Shah's vessel.

10. Only the crew members who had weapons fought with the pirates.

Commas in Business Letters

LO 7 Use commas in business letters.

When you write or type formal correspondence, ensure that you use commas correctly in all parts of the letter.

Addresses

In the address at the top of a business letter, put a comma between these elements.

- The street and apartment number
- The city and state or country

Do not put a comma before the zip code.

> Anita Buchinsky
>
> XYZ Company
>
> 11 Maple Lane, Suite 450
>
> Brownfield, Texas 79316

If you include an address inside a complete sentence, use commas to separate the street address from the city as well as the city from the state or country. If you include only the street address, do not put a comma after it.

Commas	The building at 1600 Pennsylvania Avenue, Washington, D.C., is called the White House.
No comma	The building at 1600 Pennsylvania Avenue is called the White House.

Dates

In the date at the top of the letter, put a comma between the full date and the year. If you write just the month and the year, then no comma is necessary.

> January 28, 2015   January 2015

If you include a date inside a complete sentence, separate the elements of the date with commas.

We flew to Dallas on Friday, March 14, 2014.

HINT ◂ **Writing Numbers**

In business letters, do not write ordinals, which are numbers such as *first* (1*st*), *second* (2*nd*), *third* (3*rd*), and *fourth* (4*th*). Instead, write just the number *1*, *2*, *3*, *4*, and so on.

  May 13, 2013   September 25, 1961

Salutations

Salutations are formal letter greetings. The form "To Whom It May Concern" is no longer used regularly. The best way to address someone is to use the recipient's name followed by a comma.

Dear Ms. Cheng,   Dear Mrs. Kulkarni,   Dear Sir or Madam,

Dear Miss Kim,   Dear Mr. Copely,   Dear Claims Department,

Complimentary Closings

Capitalize the first word of a complimentary closing, and place a comma after the closing. Here are some formal complimentary closings.

Respectfully,   Sincerely,   Yours truly,

Respectfully yours,   Yours sincerely,   Many thanks,

PRACTICE 9

Add nine missing commas to the following business letter.

Trudy Fossey
Zephyr Montgolfier
2397 West Barrow Avenue
Miami FL 33112

October 5 2015

Roger Danberry
Sors Communications Group
Miami FL 33170

Dear Mr. Danberry

We are happy to inform you that Zephyr Montgolfier is moving its head office to a new location at 4519 Main Street. Please join us for our grand opening on Friday   November 1   2015   from 3:00 p.m. to 6:00 p.m.

Please let us know if you would like us to send a car for you by Wednesday   October 30. We look forward to seeing you.

Thank you very much.

Yours truly

Trudy Fossey

Trudy Fossey

FINAL REVIEW

Edit the following essay by adding or removing commas. There are twelve missing commas and three unnecessary commas.

EXAMPLE: Many actors, musicians , and artists hire personal coaches.

1.   Last month Hanna Brandon hired a life coach. She wanted to make changes in her life. After graduating from college Hanna worked as a social worker but she quit her job last year. Since then Hanna has been working with Bram Connor her life coach, to help her realize her aims.

2.   Connor, who has been a life coach since April 1 2006, works for a company called Ready, Set, Go. His firm, which is a respected organization has many clients. The company has offices in Houston, Boston and Fort Lauderdale. Connor works with clients to set personal, business or career objectives. According to Connor clients want help to clarify goals, to make a plan to achieve those goals, and to overcome any obstacles in their way. People, who have hired Connor claim to be very satisfied with his advice.

3.   A life coach initially assesses the client through a series of tests. The tests, that Connor uses help him to understand his client's personality. Each week,

Connor gives Hanna homework. The assignment, for example may require Hanna to compare her future goals to her present reality. Indeed Hanna is getting closer to her target, because the homework helps her take practical steps toward her objectives.

MyWritingLab™

Complete these writing assignments at mywritinglab.com

MyWritingLab

THE WRITER'S ROOM

Write about one of the following topics. After you finish writing, make sure that you have used commas correctly.

1. Have you, or someone you know, ever had an interesting or unusual job? Describe the job.

2. What are some types of Facebook users?

Checklist: Commas

When you edit your writing, ask yourself the following questions.

☐ Do I use commas correctly in series of items?

   The store sells bikes, inline skates, and skateboards.

☐ Do I use commas correctly after introductory words or phrases?

   In fact, many sportswear companies hire athletes to promote their products.

☐ Do I use commas correctly around interrupting words and phrases?

   The campaign, in my opinion, is extremely creative.

☐ Do I use commas correctly in compound sentences?

   The advertisement is unusual, and it is quite shocking.

☐ Do I use commas correctly in complex sentences?

   When the commercial airs, the company will track viewer responses.
   The company, which was founded in 1998, is very successful.

The Apostrophe   27

SECTION THEME: The Business World

In this chapter, you will read about controversies in the business world.

GRAMMAR SNAPSHOT

Looking at Apostrophes

The following excerpt is taken from an *LA Times* article, "Preying on the Unwary with Official-Looking Letters" by David Lazarus. Review the underlined words.

> "I've had more than 50 clients contact me to ask if the letter was real," said Scott Kelley, a Woodland Hills patent attorney. "It seems to say that if you don't pay the money, you'll lose your trademark. That's just not true."

In this chapter, you will learn to use apostrophes correctly.

LO 1 Define the purpose of apostrophes.

Understanding Apostrophes

An **apostrophe** (') is a punctuation mark. It shows that two words have been contracted into one word, or it shows ownership.

> **Richard's** business is new, but **it's** growing.

LO 2 Use apostrophes in contractions.

Using Apostrophes in Contractions

A **contraction** is two words joined into one. When you contract two words, the apostrophe generally indicates the location of the omitted letter(s).

> is + not = isn't   I + am = I'm

HINT ◄ Formal Writing

Do not use contractions when you write a formal academic paper. For example, in a literary analysis, you would not use contractions.

Common Contractions

There are two types of common contractions. You can join a verb with *not;* you can also join a subject and a verb.

Verb + *not*

When a verb joins with *not*, the apostrophe replaces the letter *o* in *not*.

Common Contractions

is + not = isn't	did + not = didn't
are + not = aren't	has + not = hasn't
was + not = wasn't	have + not = haven't
were + not = weren't	must not = mustn't
could + not = couldn't	should + not = shouldn't
do + not = don't	can + not = can't
does + not = doesn't	would + not = wouldn't

Exceptions: *am + not* cannot be contracted. The contraction for *I am not* is *I'm not*, and the contraction for *will not* is *won't*.

PRACTICE 1

Write contractions for the underlined words in the next sentences.

aren't
EXAMPLE: Since the 2008 economic crisis, many Americans <u>are not</u> having too much success in finding jobs.

1. In 2012, politicians wondered why more corporations <u>could not</u> manufacture

   their products in the United States.

2. For example, Apple used to manufacture in the United States, but today most

   Apple products <u>are not</u> made in this country.

3. Like Apple, many companies manufacture overseas, and those jobs <u>will not</u> be coming back to America.

4. Because they make more money by outsourcing, <u>it is</u> hard for businesses to create manufacturing jobs in the United States.

5. In the past, corporations felt an obligation to the United States even if such a strategy <u>was not</u> profitable.

6. Today, most manufacturers feel they <u>should not</u> be judged by how many jobs they create in the United States.

7. Many business leaders feel that it <u>is not</u> their job to cure unemployment levels; <u>it is</u> their job to make profits.

Subject + Verb

When you join a subject and a verb, you must remove one or more letters to form the contraction.

Contractions with *be*	**Contractions with *will***
I + am = I'm	I + will = I'll
he + is = he's	he + will = he'll
it + is = it's	it + will = it'll
she + is = she's	she + will = she'll
they + are = they're	they + will = they'll
we + are = we're	we + will = we'll
you + are = you're	you + will = you'll
who + is = who's	who + will = who'll

Contractions with *have*	**Contractions with *had* or *would***
I + have = I've	I + had *or* would = I'd
he + has = he's	he + had *or* would = he'd
it + has = it's	it + had *or* would = it'd
she + has = she's	she + had *or* would = she'd
they + have = they've	they + had *or* would = they'd
we + have = we've	we + had *or* would = we'd
you + have = you've	you + had *or* would = you'd
who + has = who's	who + had *or* would = who'd

Exception: Do not contract a subject with the past tense of *be*. For example, do not contract *he + was* or *they + were*.

she was
When you asked her about the product, ~~she's~~ not helpful.

They were
The sales staff were in a meeting. ~~They're~~ discussing new products.

HINT ◄ **Contractions with Proper Nouns**

You can contract a proper noun with the verb *be* or *have*.

Shania is   Deiter has
Shania's late for work. **Deiter's** been waiting for her since 9:00 a.m.

PRACTICE 2

Add eight missing apostrophes to the underlined words in this selection.

          I've
EXAMPLE: Ive been reading about the Swiss banking scandal.

1.   Mark Schyler's great grandparents perished in the Holocaust. These

     days, <u>Marks</u> tracing their financial records in Switzerland. When

     he uncovers enough information, <u>hell</u> forward it to the authorities.

     <u>Hed</u> like to see the property of his great grandparents restored

     to his family.

2.   In the 1930s, the Nazis started to persecute German Jews, so they deposited

     their money in Swiss banks. Jews <u>whod</u> try to escape to Switzerland were

     turned away. After the war, Jewish survivors knew about family deposits in

     Swiss banks. Swiss bankers were secretive and required death certificates. The

     victims, however, had died in concentration camps. <u>Theyd</u> left no death or

     bank records.

3.   The U.S. government pressured Swiss banks for information. The Swiss

     government agreed to help resolve the issue. <u>Its</u> already released some bank

     details. Many people have found documents concerning family property.

     <u>Theyve</u> already received some money. Mark Schyler is one person <u>whos</u>

     working hard to uncover facts about his family so that he can reclaim his great

     grandparents' legacy.

> **HINT** ◂ **Contractions with Two Meanings**
>
> Sometimes one contraction can have two different meanings.
>
> **I'd** = I had *or* I would   **he's** = he is *or* he has
>
> When you read, you can usually figure out the meaning of the contraction by looking at the words in context.
>
> *He is*   *He has*
> **He's** starting up a new company. **He's** had three successful businesses.

PRACTICE 3

Look at each underlined contraction, and then write out the complete word.

EXAMPLE: <u>He'd</u> like to hire more people.   He would

1. <u>Hanif's</u> a chocolatier.   _____

2. <u>He's</u> been working at his present job for three years. _____

3. His <u>company's</u> been providing chocolate fountains
    to catering services.   _____

4. <u>He'd</u> like to expand the business.   _____

5. When we met last year, I was impressed because
    <u>I'd</u> never seen such a hardworking person before.   _____

Using Apostrophes to Show Ownership

LO3 Use apostrophes to show ownership.

Possession means that someone or something owns something else. Nouns and indefinite pronouns such as *anyone* and *everyone* use an apostrophe to show ownership.

the office of the businessman = the businessman's office

Singular Nouns: To show possession of singular nouns, add -'s to the end of the singular noun.

Sheila's mother works as a dispatcher.

Everyone's computer was upgraded.

Even if the noun ends in *s*, you must still add -'s.

Dennis's dad helped him find a job.

My **boss's** assistant arranges her schedule.

Plural Nouns: To show possession when a plural noun ends in -*s*, add just an apostrophe.

Many **employees'** savings are in pension plans.

Taxi drivers' licenses are regulated.

Add -'s to irregular plural nouns to indicate ownership.

That **men's** magazine is very successful.

The **children's** toy department is on the main floor.

Compound Nouns: When two people have joint ownership, add the apostrophe to the second name only.

> joint ownership
> Mason and **Muhammad's** restaurant is successful.
> (They share ownership of a restaurant.)

When two people have separate ownership, add apostrophes to both names.

> separate ownership
> **Mason's** and **Muhammad's** cars are parked in the garage.
> (They each own a car.)

PRACTICE 4

Write the possessive forms using apostrophes.

EXAMPLE: the office of Nicolas   _Nicolas's office_ _____

1. the laptop of Iris _____
2. the committee of the ladies _____
3. the company of Matt and Chris _____
4. the promotion of the manager _____
5. the desks of Marcia and Lewis _____
6. the building of the company _____
7. the club of the women _____
8. the field trip of the class _____
9. the workforce of China _____
10. the lawyers of the Smiths _____

PRACTICE 5

Correct nine errors in possessive forms.

                         Group's
EXAMPLE: The Occupy ~~Groups~~ protests are getting global attention.

1.   In the fall of 2011, activists occupied New York Citys Zuccotti Park. They

wanted to protest growing economic inequalities. The protest campaign

is called Occupy Wall Street. The Occupy Movements slogan, "We are

the 99 percent," brings attention to the gap between the top 1 percent

earners and everybody else. In 2011, the Congressional Budget Offices

report disclosed that the top 1 percent of income earners have tripled their wealth in the past thirty years. The bottom 99 percent of earners income

has declined. The activists were especially opposed to Wall Street financial

companies profits.

2.   The Occupy Movement has many organizers. The organizers inspiration came

from the Arab Spring demonstrations. The demonstrators reliance on social media

led to much of their international success. For example, Facebook's and Twitters

interactive technologies enabled people to organize events. Critics said that the

Occupy campaigns lack of specific goals was a major weakness to the cause. Yet

the Occupy Movement has gained a lot of support in cities around the world.

Using Apostrophes in Expressions of Time

LO 4 Use apostrophes in expressions of time.

If an expression of time (year, week, month, or day) appears to possess something, you can add an apostrophe plus -*s*.

My mother won a **month's** supply of groceries.

Eve Sinclair gave **three weeks'** notice before she left her job.

When you write out a year in numerals, you can use an apostrophe to replace the missing numbers.

The graduates of the class of '04 often networked with each other.

However, if you are writing the numeral of a decade or century, do not put an apostrophe before the final *s*.

In the **1800s**, many farmers took factory jobs in nearby towns.

Many investors lost money in the **1990s**.

HINT ◄ Common Apostrophe Errors

- Do not use apostrophes before the final *s* of a verb.

          wants
    Zaid ~~want's~~ to start a new business.

- Do not confuse contractions with possessive pronouns that have a similar sound. For example, the contraction *you're* sounds like the pronoun *your*. Remember that possessive pronouns never have apostrophes.

             Its
    The corner store is new. ~~It's~~ owner is very nice.

               theirs
    That is our account. It is not ~~their's~~.

PRACTICE 6

Correct the apostrophe mistakes in each sentence.

> *your*
> **EXAMPLE:** I saw ~~you're~~ friend at the meeting.

1. Its well known that many clothing manufacturers receive criticism for the poor working conditions of employees in Third World countries.

2. Theres documented evidence that these workers are usually underpaid.

3. For example, Nikes directors have admitted that there was a problem in Indonesia in the late 1990's.

4. As recently as 2011, Nike admitted that its' Indonesian plant mangers were abusing workers.

5. Kathie Lee Giffords clothing line for Walmart was manufactured in Honduras.

6. In 1995, reports revealed that the plants employees were working under terrible conditions.

7. Gifford publicly acknowledged that working condition's had to be improved.

8. Mitsumi work's as a buyer for an internationally known clothing company.

9. Her companys official policy is to buy clothing from manufacturers who pay fair wages.

10. As a consumer, Ill always try to be well informed about the things that I buy.

FINAL REVIEW

Correct fifteen apostrophe errors. Apostrophes may be used incorrectly, or there may be errors with possessive nouns.

> *should've*
> **EXAMPLE:** The government ~~shouldve~~ known about the bonuses.

1. In 2009, American Insurance Group (AIG) became the most hated business in the United States. AIG is one of the worlds largest insurance companies. During the 08 world economic crisis, AIG lost a lot of money. It's credit rating was downgraded. The companys coffers emptied. To prevent AIGs collapse, the United States government offered to loan it more than $100 billion.

2.   Soon after receiving the governments money, AIG executives were accused of spending over $400,000 from the bailout at a California spa. Apparently, the trip was a reward for managers whod been promised it before the bailout. The firm had also paid over $165 million in bonuses to senior executives. Theyd received the money because the company wanted to retain top managers. The public was outraged.

3.   These days, theres a growing demand by Americans to regulate business. The public want's the government to develop policies so that the situation wont happen again. Executives whove accepted government money shouldnt have the right to keep the bonuses. Managers mustnt feel entitled to rewards if their businesses fail. Certainly, many companies business practices need to be reexamined.

THE WRITER'S ROOM

MyWritingLab™
Complete these writing assignments at mywritinglab.com

Write about one of the following topics. After you finish writing, underline any words with apostrophes, and verify that you have correctly used the apostrophes.

1. Think about at least three types of jobs. Divide your topic into categories and find a classification principle. For example, you could write about jobs that are high stress, medium stress, and low stress.

2. Define a term or expression that relates to the photo. Examples are *plugged in*, *drone*, or *workaholic*.

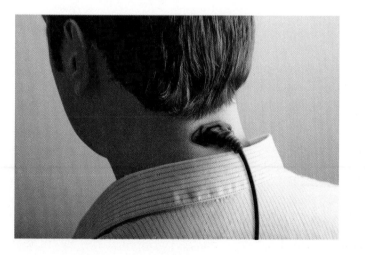

Chapter 27

Checklist: Apostrophes

When you edit your writing, ask yourself the next questions.

☐ Do I use the apostrophe correctly in contractions? Check for errors in these cases:

–contractions of verbs + *not*
–contractions with subjects and verbs

>   shouldn't   Weston's
> You ~~should'nt~~ be surprised that ~~Westons'~~ going to be a consultant in China.

☐ Do I use the apostrophe correctly to show possession? Check for errors in these possessives:

–singular nouns (*the student's*)
–plural nouns (*the students'*)
–irregular plural nouns (*the women's*)
–compound nouns (*Joe's and Mike's motorcycles*)

>   Chris's
> ~~Chris'~~ company gave him the use of a car.

☐ Do I place apostrophes where they do not belong? Check for errors in these cases:

–possessive pronouns
–spelling of third-person singular present tense verbs

>   looks   its
> It ~~look's~~ like my company is moving ~~it's~~ headquarters to Tokyo.

Quotation Marks and Capitalization

28

SECTION THEME: The Business World

In this chapter, you will read about business success stories.

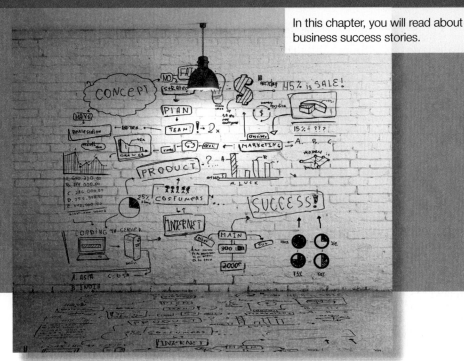

LEARNING OBJECTIVES

LO 1 Distinguish direct and indirect quotations. **(p. 372)**

LO 2 Define the purpose of quotation marks. **(p. 372)**

LO 3 Review capitalization rules. **(p. 376)**

LO 4 Punctuate titles correctly. **(p. 378)**

GRAMMAR SNAPSHOT

Looking at Quotation Marks

This excerpt is taken from Ben Carson's autobiography, *Gifted Hands*. The quotation marks and associated capital letters are underlined.

> One of the counselors at our high school, Alma Whittley, knew my predicament and was very understanding. One day I poured out my story, and she listened with obvious concern. "I've got a few connections with the Ford Motor Company," she said. While I sat next to her desk, she phoned their world headquarters. I particularly remember her saying, "Look, we have this young fellow here named Ben Carson. He's very bright and already has a scholarship to go to Yale in September. Right now the boy needs a job to save money for this fall." She paused to listen, and I heard her add, "You have to give him a job."

In this chapter, you will learn how to use direct quotations correctly. You will also learn about capitalization and punctuation of titles.

LO1 Distinguish direct and indirect quotations.

Direct and Indirect Quotations

A **direct quotation** reproduces the exact words of a speaker or writer. An **indirect quotation**, however, simply summarizes someone's words. Indirect quotations often begin with *that*.

Direct quotation	Mrs. Delaware said, "I'm moving to a new office."
Indirect quotation	Mrs. Delaware said that she was moving to a new office.

The next sections discuss proper capitalization and punctuation of direct quotations.

LO2 Define the purpose of quotation marks.

Quotation Marks

Use **quotation marks** (" ") to set off the exact words of a speaker or writer. If the quotation is a complete sentence, there are some standard ways that it should be punctuated.

- Capitalize the first word of the quotation.
- Place quotation marks around the complete quotation.
- Place the end punctuation inside the closing quotation marks.

Generally, attach the name of the speaker or writer to the quotation in some way.

> . . . said,   "Complete sentence."

Mrs. Delaware said, "You are hired."

Using Quotation Marks with an Introductory Phrase

When the quotation is introduced by a phrase, place a comma after the introductory phrase.

> . . . says,   "_____."

Miguel Lanthier says, "You should feel passionate about your work."

PRACTICE 1

Place quotation marks around the direct quotations in the following sentences. Add capitals and other punctuation where necessary.

EXAMPLE: According to businessman George Van Valkenburg , "Leadership is doing what is right when no one is watching."

1. Martha Stewart once said   life is too complicated not to be orderly.

2. Author Henry David Thoreau stated   success usually comes to those who are too busy to be looking for it.

3. Businessman Peter Schutz said   hire character and train skill.

4. Henry Ford reflected   failure is the opportunity to begin again, more intelligently.

5. Walt Disney declared   a man should never neglect his family for business.

Using Quotation Marks with an Interrupting Phrase

When the quotation is interrupted, do the following:

◆ Place a comma after the first part of the quotation.
◆ Place a comma after the interrupting phrase.

> " _____," . . . says,   " _____."

"To cultivate kindness," said essayist Samuel Johnson, "is a valuable part of business life."

PRACTICE 2

Place quotation marks around the direct quotations in the following sentences. Add other punctuation marks where necessary.

EXAMPLE: "Yesterday's homeruns," stated Babe Ruth, "don't win today's games."

1. Your most unhappy customers   remarked Bill Gates   are your greatest source of learning.

2. A budget tells us what we can't afford   observed publisher William Feather   but it doesn't keep us from buying it.

3. All lasting business   stated author Alfred A. Montapert   is built on friendship.

4. Every young man would do well to remember   declared abolitionist Henry Ward Beecher   that all successful business stands on the foundation of morality.

5. I rate enthusiasm   acknowledged Nobel Prize–winning physicist Edward Appleton   even above professional skill.

Using Quotation Marks with an End Phrase

When you place a phrase at the end of a quotation, end the quotation with a comma instead of a period.

> " _____,"   says . . . .

"There's no business like show business," said Irving Berlin.

If your quotation ends with another punctuation mark, put it inside the ending quotation mark.

> " _____?"   says . . . .

"Don't do that!" he yelled.

"Why did you hire her?" she asked.

PRACTICE 3

Place quotation marks around the direct quotations in the following sentences. Add other punctuation marks where necessary.

EXAMPLE: "Anything is possible if you've got enough nerve," says J.K. Rowling.

1.   Don't be afraid to give up the good to go for the great   stated entrepreneur John D. Rockefeller.

2.   If people believe in themselves, it is amazing what they can accomplish   reflected Sam Walton, founder of Walmart.

3.   If you want more, you have to require more from yourself   advises Dr. Phil.

4.   It is neither wealth nor splendour, but tranquillity and occupation which give happiness   stated Thomas Jefferson.

5.   When you undervalue who you are, the world will undervalue what you do and vice versa   counsels financial advisor Suze Orman.

Using Quotation Marks with an Introductory Sentence

You can introduce a quotation with a complete sentence. Place a colon (:) after the introductory sentence.

> **He explains his views: "_____."**

Writer William Feather explains his views on parenthood: "Setting a good example for children takes all the fun out of middle age."

PRACTICE 4

Place quotation marks around the direct quotations in the following sentences. Add capital letters and other punctuation marks where necessary.

EXAMPLE: Philosopher Friedrich Nietzsche explained perseverance : "W what doesn't kill us makes us stronger."

1.   Entrepreneur P. D. Armour expressed his views   anybody can cut prices, but it takes a brain to produce a better article.

2.   Malcolm Forbes, a magazine publisher, discusses how to succeed   try hard enough.

3.   Spanish writer Miguel deCervantes referred to his success   to be prepared is half the victory.

4. We discussed the words of Norman Vincent Peale   it's always too soon to quit.

5. Philanthropist Thomas Dewar discusses human minds   they only function

   when open.

HINT ◄ **Integrating Partial Quotations**

Sometimes, you may want to use only a small part of a quotation in your own sentence because the full quotation is unnecessary. Add quotation marks only around the words that you are using. The first word of the quotation does not need to be capitalized.

Direct Quotation   Bill Cosby says, "In order to succeed, your desire for success should be greater than your fear of failure."

Partial Quotation   Comedian Bill Cosby states that "your desire for success should be greater than your fear of failure."

PRACTICE 5

Place quotation marks around the direct quotations in bold print. Add capital letters and punctuation marks to the direct quotations.

EXAMPLE: Coco Chanel often said   , "A   **a fashion that does not reach the streets is**

   not fashion."

1.   Coco Chanel was a risk taker. People often heard her say   **I have never done**

   anything by halves. Chanel was born in 1883 into an extremely impoverished

   family in Samur, France. Her mother died when Coco was young, so her father

   sent her to a convent school where the nuns taught her to sew. After graduating

   from school, Chanel worked as a seamstress in a tailor's shop. During that

   period, she began designing hats. By 1913, she had opened her first fashion

   store in Paris. She wanted women to look elegant. **fashion fades, but style**

   remains   she once stated.

2.   Chanel was one of the first women designers to introduce fashionable wear

   for women. She designed clothes by following her values **a girl should be**

   two things: classy and fabulous. Many celebrities began to wear her clothes.

   For example, the Chanel jacket has been worn by generations of women. She

Chapter 28

often declared **luxury must be comfortable; otherwise it is not luxury.**   In an interview, the designer expressed her philosophy **one cannot be forever innovating. I want to create classics.** Her clothes were known for their timeless simplicity.

3.   Chanel's designs liberated women from the earlier corset and lace fashions. **In fashion, you know you have succeeded** she stressed **when there is an element of upset.** She claimed that she was **not a feminist,** but she brought out the femininity in women. She was ahead of her time because she became a successful businesswoman when women were mostly housewives.

LO 3 Review capitalization rules.

Capitalization

Remember to always capitalize the following:

* The pronoun *I*
* The first word of every sentence

    My coworkers and **I** share an office.

There are many other instances in which you must use capital letters. Always capitalize the following:

* **Days of the week, months, and holidays**

Wednesday	January 1	New Year's Eve

    Do not capitalize the seasons: summer, fall, winter, spring.

* **Titles of specific institutions, departments, companies, and schools**

IBM	U.S. Department of Defense	Pinewood Elementary School

    Do not capitalize general references.

the company	the department	the school

* **Names of specific places, such as buildings, streets, parks, cities, states, countries, and bodies of water**

Dale Street	Times Square	Los Angeles, California
Central Park	Mississippi	Lake Erie

    Do not capitalize general references.

the street	the state	the lake

* **Names of specific languages, nationalities, tribes, races, and religions**

Portuguese	Mohawk	Buddhist	an Italian restaurant

Chapter 28

+ **Titles of specific individuals**

General Eisenhower	President Kennedy	Dr. Marcos
Professor Wong	Prime Minister Blair	Mrs. Eleanor Roosevelt

If you are referring to the profession in general, or if the title follows the name, do not use capital letters.

a senator	my professor	the doctors

+ **Titles of specific courses and programs**

Mathematics 201	Civil Engineering 100	Beginner's Spanish

If you refer to a course but do not mention the course title, then it is not necessary to use capitals.

He is in economics.   I study hard for my civil engineering class.

+ **The major words in titles of literary or artistic works**

The Lord of the Rings   *The Bourne Identity*   *War and Peace*

+ **Names of historical events, eras, and movements**

the Korean War   Impressionism   the Industrial Revolution

HINT ◄ Capitalizing Computer Terms

Always capitalize the following computer terms.

Internet   World Wide Web

Capitalize software titles as you would any other published work.

Netscape   Microsoft Office

PRACTICE 6

Add any necessary capital letters to the following sentences.

                                        W
EXAMPLE: The creation of the World Wide web has allowed many new
                entrepreneurs to become successful.

1. In 1996, Larry Page and Sergey Brin started out as graduate students at

   Stanford university but ended up founding google inc.

2. They created an internet search engine, which is one of the most used products

   in america.

3. The company headquarters are located in googleplex, 1600 amphitheatre

   Parkway, Mountain view, california.

4. The search engine is so popular that the verb "to google" can be found in the *Merriam webster collegiate dictionary*.

5. Another successful product is Google earth, which allows users to see aerial maps through satellite imaging.

6. In december 2006, Google bought youTube, an online video site.

7. For the past few years, i have mainly used Google to research many subjects.

8. In my political science 201 class, my instructor, professor Warner, asked us to find out about criticism directed against Google.

9. Google has been criticized for infringing copyright laws, violating privacy laws, and complying with censorship rules in china.

10. In march 2010, Google shut down its service in beijing to protest internet censorship in China.

LO 4 Punctuate titles correctly.

Titles
Punctuating Titles

Place the title of a short work in quotation marks. Italicize the title of a longer work. If you are handwriting your text, underline the title.

Short Works		Long Works	
Short story	"The Bear"	**Novel**	*The Da Vinci Code*
Chapter	"Abbreviations"	**Book**	*MLA Handbook for Writers of Research Papers*
Newspaper article	"Missing in Action"	**Newspaper**	*New York Times*
Magazine article	"History's Fools"	**Magazine**	*Newsweek*
Web article	"Music Artists Lose Out"	**Web site**	*Blackbeat.com*
Essay	"Neighborhoods of the Globe"	**Textbook**	*Essentials of Sociology*
TV episode	"Fixed"	**TV series**	*The Good Wife*
Song	"Naughty Girl"	**CD**	*Dangerously in Love*
Poem	"The List of Famous Hats"	**Collection**	*Reckoner*

Capitalizing Titles

When you write a title, capitalize the first letter of the first word and all the major words. Do not capitalize the letters *.com* in a Web address.

    The Hunger Games   *Monster.com*   "Lucy in the Sky with Diamonds"

Chapter 28

Also, do not capitalize the following words, except as the first or last word in a title.

Articles	a, an, the
Coordinators	but, and, or, nor, for, so, yet
Short prepositions	of, to, in, off, out, up, by

PRACTICE 7

Add ten capital letters to the next paragraphs. Also, add quotation marks or underlining to eight titles. If you were typing this essay, you would put titles of long works in italics.

EXAMPLE: When I was a child, I loved to read <u>Horton ~~h~~ears a Who.</u>

1. Who hasn't read a book by Dr. Seuss? He is mainly known for writing children's books such as Green eggs and ham. He is considered to be one of America's most successful writers of children's books.

2. Theodor Seuss Geisel was born in Springfield, Massachusetts, in 1904. After finishing college, he submitted humorous articles to magazines such as Vanity fair. Dr. Seuss's first book was And to Think I Saw It on mulberry street. The manuscript was rejected twenty-six times but was eventually published in 1937.

3. In the 1950s, Americans felt that schoolchildren were falling behind in their reading skills. Geisel's editor asked him to write a children's book using only 250 words. Geisel wrote The Cat in the hat, which contains only 236 words. The book gained instant fame.

4. Most critics view Dr. Seuss's books favorably. In a Web article called Dr. Seuss's Five lessons for PR Pros for the Web site PR daily, writer Daniel Cohen stated that Dr. Seuss cleverly shows children a world that makes them want to read. In the New York times, in an article called The Children's Authors Who Broke the rules, Pamela Paul suggests that Dr. Seuss's books are popular because he wrote about children who did not always behave as their parents wished them to. Many of Dr. Seuss's characters broke the rules.

Chapter 28

FINAL REVIEW

A. Add three missing capital letters, and properly punctuate the two quotations in bold print.

EXAMPLE: After graduating from college, Jeff Bezos worked on Wall street.
<small>S</small>

1.   Since the creation of the world Wide Web, many businesses have been selling products to customers online. One of the largest internet companies in the world is Jeff Bezos's book-selling business. In 1994, Bezos founded his firm in his garage. **I am going to do a crazy thing** he recalls saying **by selling books online**. Bezos, unlike other businesspeople, did not expect to make a profit for a few years. **What we wanted to be was something completely new** Bezos reminisced. His business plan proved to be excellent, and the company has slowly grown. When the dot-com bubble burst, and many online companies failed, amazon posted profits.

B. Add seven missing capital letters and properly punctuate three titles. If you were typing the essay, the titles of long works would be in italics.

EXAMPLE: There are many articles in the *New York times* about Jeff Bezos's company.
<small>T</small>

2.   The first book sold by Amazon was titled Fluid Concepts and Creative analogies: Computer Models of the Fundamental Mechanisms of thought. Soon after, Bezos's company became very successful, and, in 1999, he was named Person of the year by *Time*.

3.   Nowadays, Amazon does not sell just books. It sells electronics, food, toys, and other products. While its headquarters is in seattle, Washington, the company has also expanded its business in China, the United Kingdom, canada, and other countries. In 2008, in an article called America's best Leaders, the magazine U.S. News and world Report included Bezos for his innovative approach to business.

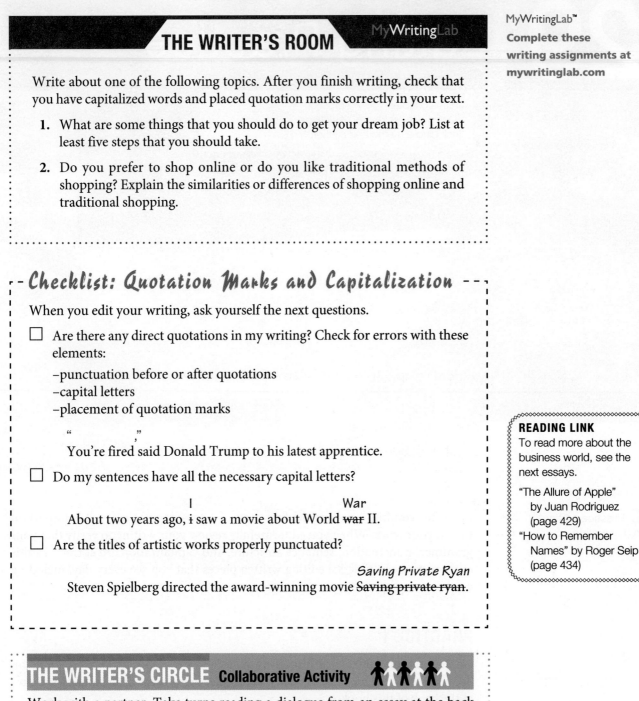

THE WRITER'S ROOM

MyWritingLab™

Complete these
writing assignments at
mywritinglab.com

Write about one of the following topics. After you finish writing, check that
you have capitalized words and placed quotation marks correctly in your text.

1. What are some things that you should do to get your dream job? List at
   least five steps that you should take.

2. Do you prefer to shop online or do you like traditional methods of
   shopping? Explain the similarities or differences of shopping online and
   traditional shopping.

Checklist: Quotation Marks and Capitalization

When you edit your writing, ask yourself the next questions.

☐ Are there any direct quotations in my writing? Check for errors with these
   elements:

   –punctuation before or after quotations
   –capital letters
   –placement of quotation marks

   "   "
   You're fired said Donald Trump to his latest apprentice.

☐ Do my sentences have all the necessary capital letters?

                    I   War
   About two years ago, ~~i~~ saw a movie about World ~~war~~ II.

☐ Are the titles of artistic works properly punctuated?

                                            Saving Private Ryan
   Steven Spielberg directed the award-winning movie ~~Saving private ryan~~.

Chapter 28

> **READING LINK**
> To read more about the
> business world, see the
> next essays.
> "The Allure of Apple"
>   by Juan Rodriguez
>   (page 429)
> "How to Remember
>   Names" by Roger Seip
>   (page 434)

THE WRITER'S CIRCLE Collaborative Activity

Work with a partner. Take turns reading a dialogue from an essay at the back
of this book. Write down everything that your partner says. When you are both
finished, exchange papers, compare them with the original essays, and mark any
misspelled words or incorrectly placed punctuation or quotations marks. Here
are some suggested readings.

"Birth" (page 395), paragraphs 3 to 8 (stop at the word *condemnation*)

"Your World's a Stage" by Josh Freed (page 397), paragraph 3

In a dialogue, begin a new paragraph every time the speaker changes.

29 Editing Practice

LEARNING OBJECTIVES

LO 1 Practice editing everyday writing. (p. 382)

In this chapter, you will practice editing different types of writing, including a memo and a letter.

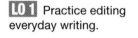
LO 1 Practice editing everyday writing.

After you finish writing the first draft of a paragraph or essay, it is important to edit your work. When you edit, carefully review your writing to verify that your grammar, punctuation, sentence structure, and capitalization are correct. In this chapter, you can practice editing written pieces that you see every day, including e-mail, paragraphs, essays, and business correspondence.

PRACTICE 1

Correct fifteen underlined errors. An editing symbol appears above each error. To understand the meaning of each symbol, refer to the revising and editing symbols at the back of this book.

1. Salem, Massachusetts, is a small <u>beautifull</u> ^sp city located a short distance north

   of <u>boston</u> ^cap. Salem was founded in 1626 ^p and it immediately became a center

   of shipping. It was also home to the American writer Nathaniel Hawthorne.

But nowadays, tourists come to Salem because it was the location of the witch

frag
trials. Of 1692.

2. In the seventeenth century, the majority of <u>persons</u> believed in the supernatural.
   pl

   Some experimented with charms and spells because they <u>were wanting</u> good
   vt

   weather for farming. Over time, people became suspicious of magic <u>they</u> blamed
   ro

   the power of spells for general misfortunes.

3. In the winter of 1692, two girls started to have fits <u>who were cousins</u>. The
   m

   villagers thought that black magic was the cause for <u>your</u> symptoms. The
   shift

   authorities could not find <u>no</u> reasonable explanation for the hysteria. They
   wc

   accused three <u>real</u> poor village women of black magic. Over the next months,
   ad

   many villagers accused <u>they're</u> neighbors of performing witchcraft.
   wc

4. Soon afterwards, the witch trials began. The court <u>accepts</u> evidence that could
   vt

   not be proven. All in all, nineteen people <u>was</u> hanged for being witches, and five
   agr

   others died in prison. By the following year, the witch hysteria had died down,

   and the trials were stopped. Today, tourists visit the memorial for the victims

   <u>who come to Salem</u>.
   m

PRACTICE 2

There are no editing symbols in the next paragraph. Proofread it as you would your own writing, and correct ten errors.

People often wonder what do motivational speakers do. In fact, they inspire audience members to achieve particular goals. Many companies hire motivational speakers to encourage its employees and to give keynote speeches at conferences. Companies look for speakers who has a positive message and who are engaging. Much people who have achieved success have become motivational speakers, including General Norman Schwarzkopf and former New York City mayor, mr. Rudolph Giuliani. Actors, former presidents, and sports heroes also inspires audiences. Some times, a motivational speaker can earn more than fifty-thousands for an appearance. The best motivational speakers encourages the audience members to analyze their own beliefs, and goals.

PRACTICE 3

In the next memo, there are no editing symbols. Identify and correct ten errors.

Memo

Subject: A Warm Welcome to Chef Gilbert Rodriguez

I am pleased to announce that Chef Gilbert Rodriguez will be joining our companys food services team next Wenesday. Chef Rodriguez has a international reputation. He is senior chef at the Parisienne Restaurant for much years. He also collaborated very close with senior White House chefs during previous administrations.

Chef Rodriguez will manage, train, and to recruit a team of young chefs. He also wanna create a more healthier menu. He will appreciate to get your suggestions for a variety of dishes. Please join me in welcoming Chef Rodriguez.

PRACTICE 4

Identify and correct fifteen errors in the next letter.

Dear Maya,

I have being at the police training center for two weeks. It is real hard. Every day, we have to get up at 5:30 and go for a ten-mile run in the dark. It is very likely than I will get into great shape by the end of my training.

Each morning, we receive our schedule. For the rest of the day. We don't have no time to relax. Their is no time for leisure activities. The older students have said that there used to the long hours.

Last week, we visited a police department and learned some investigative techniques. In one workshop, we pretended to arrest thiefs. I prefered target shooting to any other activity on our visit. I am more better at shooting than the other students in my class.

I imagine that your busy this summer. Did you go to Puerto Rico last april? Did your mother go to? I hear that your brother and his friend are local heroes, they rescued a boy. Who was drowning.

I have to go, but I will write again soon.

Your friend,

Christine

PRACTICE 5

Identify and correct twelve errors.

There is several things you should do to avoid credit card fraud. First, make sure that you sign your credit card as soon as it arrive. Keep a record of your card number, the expiration date, and the phone number, of the credit card company. When you give your credit card to a cashier, watch the transaction, then get your card back immediatly. Keep your receipt untill you get your credit card bill. Check each months bill carefully, and report any suspicious transactions. Do not throw away receipts who contain your credit card information. Criminals go often through recycling bins and garbage cans to find old receipts. It is adviseable to burn receipts or tear it into very small peaces.

PRACTICE 6

Identify and correct fifteen errors.

To have a healthy diet, ensure that you make the good choices. First, avoid to eat red meat. It is preferable having lean meat such as pork or chicken. Also, proteins can be found in fish, wich has less calories than meat and contains omega-3 fatty acids. Moreover, you should have five to ten portion of fruits and vegetables per day. Try to eat a variety of vegetables. Such as carrots, spinach, broccoli, and peppers. Cut the amount of sugar you eat because it can leads to belly fat. Which is bad for blood pressure. For example, instead eating cake, choose fruit salad. Also, sugar. Do you know what is the recommended amount of sugar? You should have only four to six teaspoons per day. Finally, remember that too much salt it can cause high blood pressure in some adults. According to the Web site *HealthCastle.com*, you should "reduce the amount of salt called for in recipes". Always remember that eating good is important.

PRACTICE 7

Identify and correct twenty editing errors in this student essay.

1.   Many people and events have influenced my life and changed my way of thinking. For exemple, sports were important to me when I was a child. At the age of seventeen, I had problems with my back, so my doctor recomended that I start weight lifting. Weight lifting has changed my life in a profound way. In fact, if I would have known the benefits of exercise, I would have started weight lifting sooner.

2.   Before becoming a weight lifter, I did not like how I looked physicaly. When I started lifting weights, I learned to like my appearance and to respect my body. I realized that I only have one body, so I gotta take care of it. Now that I am more conscience of my health, I make an effort to eat good. As a result, I am more stronger and more energetic. I am finally treating my body with the respect he deserves.

3.   Furthermore, weight lifting has taught me to persevere, to work hard, and having confidence. At the beginning of my fitness program, I consulted my cousin who showed me how to do the exercises correctly, the more I trained, the better the effects were. I could lift heavy weights more easy than before. Now I no longer wonder how can I do something. I make goals and stay with them.

4.   Moreover, weight lifting it has also changed my personallity and helped me be more confident. I am able to accept each success and failures with grace. I am also more focused, and I do not loose my temper as easily as I used to.

5.   Fitness training, wich has both physical and psychological benefits, has improved my body, my health, and my self-esteem. I have been practicing this sport since ten years, and I will continue to do so. People should choose activities. That motivate them.

Part III

Reading Strategies and Selections

In Chapter 30, you will learn strategies that can help you improve your reading skills. Then you will read a number of thought-provoking essays that present a wide range of viewpoints about topics related to lifestyles and relationships; entertainment, culture, and beliefs; the earth and its creatures; and trades, technology, and the business world. The predominant writing pattern of each essay is shown in parentheses.

LIFESTYLES AND RELATIONSHIPS

30

Reading Strategies and Selections

LEARNING OBJECTIVES

LO 1 Practice reading strategies. **(p. 390)**

LO 2 Analyze reading selections. **(p. 393)**

Aspiring sculptors study historical and contemporary works to learn about composition, technique, and material. In the same way, by reading different types of writing, you can observe how other writers develop their essays.

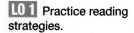

LO 1 Practice reading strategies.

Reading Strategies

Reading helps you develop your writing skills. Each time you read, you accomplish these goals:

- Expand your vocabulary.
- Learn how other writers develop topics.
- Learn to recognize and use different writing patterns.
- Find ideas for your own paragraphs and essays.

The strategies discussed in this chapter can help you become a more successful reader and writer.

Previewing

When you **preview** a passage, you quickly look at key points. You can get a general sense of a passage's topic and main ideas by checking visual clues.

- Read the title and the main headings.
- Look at the first and last sentence of the introduction.
- Look at the first sentence of each paragraph.

♦ Look at the concluding sentences in the essay.
♦ Review any photos, graphs, or charts, and read the captions that accompany them.

Previewing helps you prepare for the next step, which is reading the essay.

Taking Notes

To help you remember and quickly find the important points in a text, you can highlight key ideas and make annotations. An **annotation** is a comment, question, or reaction that you write in the margin of a passage.

Highlighting and Making Annotations

Each time you read a passage, do the following:

♦ Look at the introductory and concluding paragraphs, and underline sentences that sum up the main idea.
♦ Using your own words, write the main idea in the margin.
♦ Underline or highlight supporting ideas. You might even want to number the arguments or ideas. This will allow you to understand the essay's development.
♦ Circle words that you do not understand.
♦ Write questions in the margins if you do not understand the author's meaning.
♦ Write notes beside passages that are interesting or that relate to your own experiences.
♦ Jot down possible writing topics.

If you are reading a library book, or if you have borrowed a book from somebody else, use sticky notes to make annotations. Do not write in the book!

> **An Annotated Passage**
>
> In Sydney, Australia, I simply hailed a taxi, opened the door, and jumped in the back seat. The driver narrowed his eyes. "Where to, mate?" he asked in a voice that could chill a refrigerator. In Marrakech, Morocco, I crossed my legs during an interview with a government official. Immediately, a hush fell over the room. In a restaurant in Mumbai, India, all I did was reach for the naan. A diner at the next table shot me a look that stuck two inches out my back.

◅ Why? I don't get it.

◅ main point?
offended his hosts?

◅ What is naan?

Understanding Unfamiliar Words

When you read, you will sometimes come across an unfamiliar word. You can try to guess the word's meaning, or you can circle it and look it up later.

Use Context Clues

Context clues are hints in the text that help define a word. To find a word's meaning, try the next steps.

1. **Determine the word's function.** For example, is it a noun, a verb, or an adjective? Sometimes you can understand a word if you know how it functions in the sentence.
2. **Look at surrounding words.** Try to find a relation between the difficult word and the words that surround it. Maybe there is a **synonym** (a word that means the same thing) or an **antonym** (a word that means the opposite). Maybe other words in the sentence help define the word.

3. **Look at surrounding sentences.** Look at the sentences, paragraphs, and punctuation surrounding the word. If you use logic, you may understand what the word means.

PRACTICE 1

Can you define the word *heed*?   ____ Yes ____ No

Can you define *yearn*?   ____ Yes ____ No

If you do not understand the meaning of those two words, then read the words in context in the next example. You will notice that it is much easier to guess their meanings in context.

> Travel makes it impossible to pay no **heed** to the suffering of others, simply because they are far away. It erases distance, and makes you a more sensitive citizen of the world, **yearning** for peace everywhere.
>
> —Arthur Frommer, "How Travel Changed My Life"

Now write your own definitions of the words.

1. heed: _____

2. yearn: _____

HINT ◀ Using a Dictionary

Some words have many definitions. When you look up a word in a dictionary, do not stop after you read the first meaning. Keep reading, and look for the meaning that best fits the context of your sentence. To learn more about dictionary usage, see Chapter 23, "Exact Language."

Writing About the Reading

After you finish reading a text, you may have to answer questions about it or write about it. There are several steps you can take to help you better understand a reading passage.

- **Summarize** the reading. When you summarize, you use your own words to write a condensed version of the reading. You leave out all information except for the main points.

- **Outline** the reading. An outline is a visual plan of the reading. First, write the main idea of the essay, and then write the most important idea from each paragraph. Under each idea, you can include a detail or an example.

Respond to the Reading

Before you make a written response to the reading, ask yourself the next questions.

- What is the writer's main point?

- What is the writer's purpose: to entertain, to persuade, or to inform?

- Who is the intended reader? Is the writer directing the message at someone like me?

- What is my opinion of the reading?
- What aspects of the topic can I relate to?

Reading Selections

LO 2 Analyze reading selections.

Theme: Lifestyles and Relationships

READING 1

Fish Cheeks

Amy Tan

Amy Tan, the author of the best-selling novel *The Joy Luck Club,* wrote this essay for an issue of *Seventeen* magazine. Using vivid detail, Tan describes a family dinner. As you read, notice how the author uses mainly description but also elements of narration and illustration.

1   I fell in love with the minister's son the winter I turned fourteen. He was not Chinese but as white as Mary in the manger. For Christmas, I prayed for this blond-haired boy, Robert, and a slim new American nose.

2   When I found out that my parents had invited the minister's family over for Christmas Eve dinner, I cried. What would Robert think of our shabby Chinese Christmas? What would he think of our noisy Chinese relatives who lacked proper American manners? What terrible disappointment would he feel upon seeing not a roasted turkey and sweet potatoes but Chinese food?

3   On Christmas Eve, I saw that my mother had outdone herself in creating a strange menu. She was pulling black veins out of the backs of fleshy prawns. The kitchen was littered with appalling mounds of raw food: a slimy rock cod with bulging eyes that pleaded not to be thrown into a pan of hot oil; tofu, which looked like stacked wedges of rubbery white sponges; a bowl soaking dried fungus back to life; and a plate of squid, their backs crisscrossed with knife markings so they resembled bicycle tires.

4   And then they arrived—the minister's family and all my relatives in a clamor of doorbells and rumpled Christmas packages. Robert grunted hello, and I pretended he was not worthy of existence.

5   Dinner threw me deeper into despair. My relatives licked the ends of their chopsticks and reached across the table, dipping them into the dozen or so plates of food. Robert and his family waited patiently for platters to be passed to them. My relatives murmured with pleasure when my mother brought out the whole steamed fish. Robert grimaced. Then my father poked his chopsticks just below the fish eye and plucked out the soft meat. "Amy, your favorite," he said, offering me the tender fish cheek. I wanted to disappear.

6   At the end of the meal, my father leaned back and belched loudly, thanking my mother for her fine cooking. "It's a polite Chinese custom to show you are satisfied," explained my father to our astonished guests. Robert was looking down at his plate with a reddened face. The minister managed to muster up a quiet burp. I was stunned into silence for the rest of the night.

7   After everyone had gone, my mother said to me, "You want to be the same as American girls on the outside." She handed me an early gift. It was a miniskirt in beige tweed. "But inside you must always be Chinese. You must be proud you are different. Your only shame is to have shame."

8 And even though I didn't agree with her then, I knew that she understood how much I had suffered during the evening's dinner. It wasn't until many years later—long after I had gotten over my crush on Robert—that I was able to fully appreciate her lesson and the true purpose behind our particular menu. For Christmas Eve that year, she had chosen all my favorite foods.

Vocabulary and Comprehension

MyWritingLab™

Complete additional reading comprehension questions for this selection at **mywritinglab.com**

1. What is the meaning of *muster* in paragraph 6?
   a. to summon up or create
   b. to gather
   c. a yellow sauce

2. What three reasons does Tan give for her embarrassment when Robert comes for dinner? Use your own words.

   _____

   _____

   _____

3. What lesson was the writer's mother trying to teach her?

   _____

   _____

4. On the surface, Tan's purpose is to entertain, but what is her deeper purpose?

   _____

   _____

5. Tan uses descriptive imagery. Imagery includes active verbs, adjectives, and other words that appeal to the senses (sight, smell, touch, sound, taste). Highlight at least five examples of imagery.

Grammar

GRAMMAR LINK
For more information on adjectives, see Chapter 21. For more information on past tense, see Chapter 9.

6. Underline six adjectives in paragraph 3. Then circle the nouns that the adjectives modify. Discuss how the adjectives make the writing more vivid.

7. In the essay, identify six irregular past tense verbs not including the verb *be*. Write the present- and past-tense forms of each verb on the lines provided.

   _____ _____

   _____ _____

   _____ _____

Discussion and Writing

8. Think about a time when you felt different from others. Explain what happened. Try to use some descriptive vocabulary.

9. What are the possible causes for a person to give up his or her own cultural traditions (language, dress, food, ceremonies, etc.)? What are the effects when people lose their cultural distinctiveness? Discuss the causes or effects of losing cultural traditions.

READING 2

Birth

Maya Angelou

Maya Angelou is an award-winning author. In this selection from her best-known autobiographical work, *I Know Why the Caged Bird Sings*, Angelou writes about the birth of her son. As you read, notice how the author uses mainly narration but also elements of description and cause and effect writing.

1   Two days after V-Day, I stood with the San Francisco Summer School class at Mission High School and received my diploma. That evening, in the bosom of the now-dear family home, I uncoiled my fearful secret, and in a brave gesture left a note on Daddy Clidell's bed. It read, "Dear Parents, I am sorry to bring this disgrace upon the family, but I am pregnant. Marguerite."

2   The confusion that ensued when I explained to my stepfather that I expected to deliver the baby in three weeks, more or less, was **reminiscent** of a **Molière** comedy. Daddy Clidell told Mother that I was "three weeks gone." Mother, regarding me as a woman for the first time, said indignantly, "She's more than any three weeks." They both accepted the fact that I was further along than they had first been told but found it nearly impossible to believe that I had carried a baby, eight months and one week, without their being any the wiser.

3   Mother asked, "Who is the boy?" I told her. She recalled him, faintly.

4   "Do you want to marry him?"

5   "No."

6   "Does he want to marry you?" The father had stopped speaking to me during my fourth month.

7   "No."

8   "Well, that's that. No use ruining three lives." There was no **overt** or subtle **condemnation**.

9   Daddy Clidell assured me that I had nothing to worry about. He sent one of his waitresses to I. Magnin's to buy maternity dresses for me. For the next two weeks, I whirled around the city going to doctors, taking vitamin shots and pills, buying clothes for the baby, and except for the rare moments alone, enjoying the imminent blessed event.

10   After a short labor, and without too much pain (I decided that the pain of delivery was overrated), my son was born. Just as gratefulness was confused in my mind with love, so possession became mixed up with motherhood. I had a baby. He was beautiful and mine. No one had bought him for me. No one had helped me endure the sickly gray months. I had had help in the child's conception, but no one could deny that I had had an immaculate pregnancy.

11   I was afraid to touch him. Home from the hospital, I sat for hours by his bassinet and absorbed his mysterious perfection. His extremities were so dainty they appeared unfinished. Mother handled him easily with the casual confidence of a baby nurse, but I dreaded being forced to change his diapers. Wasn't I famous for awkwardness? Suppose I let him slip or put my fingers on that throbbing pulse on the top of his head?

12   Mother came to my bed one night bringing my three-week-old baby. She pulled the cover back and told me to get up and hold him while she put rubber sheets on my bed. She explained that he was going to sleep with me.

reminiscent: similar to

Molière: a French playwright (1622–1673)

overt: evident, open

condemnation: criticism; disapproval

13   I begged in vain. I was sure to roll over and crush out his life or break those fragile bones. She wouldn't hear of it, and within minutes the pretty golden baby was lying on his back in the center of my bed, laughing at me.

14   I lay on the edge of the bed, stiff with fear, and vowed not to sleep all night long. But the eat-sleep routine I had begun in the hospital, and kept up under Mother's dictatorial command, got the better of me. I dropped off.

15   My shoulder was shaken gently. Mother whispered, "Maya, wake up. But don't move."

16   I knew immediately that the awakening had to do with the baby. I tensed. "I'm awake."

17   She turned the light on and said, "Look at the baby." My fears were so powerful I couldn't move to look at the center of the bed. She said again, "Look at the baby." I didn't hear sadness in her voice, and that helped me to break the bonds of terror. The baby was no longer in the center of the bed. At first I thought he had moved. But after closer investigation, I found that I was lying on my stomach with my arm bent at a right angle. Under the tent of blanket, which was poled by my elbow and forearm, the baby slept touching my side.

18   Mother whispered, "See, you don't have to think about doing the right thing. If you're for the right thing, then you do it without thinking."

19   She turned out the light, and I patted my son's body lightly and went back to sleep.

MyWritingLab™

**Complete additional
reading comprehension
questions** for this selection at
mywritinglab.com

Vocabulary and Comprehension

1. Find a word in paragraph 9 that means "soon to arrive; forthcoming."

   _____

2. How does Angelou's family react to the pregnancy?

   _____

3. In paragraph 11, the author says that she was afraid to touch her own baby. Why did she feel this way?

   _____

4. Were her fears well-founded? Why or why not?

   _____

   _____

5. What does the reading suggest about becoming a parent?

   _____

GRAMMAR LINK
For more information
on quotations, see
Chapter 28. For more
information on vivid
language, see
pages 320–323 in
Chapter 23.

Grammar

6. In paragraph 2, the author writes the following sentence: Daddy Clidell told Mother that I was "three weeks gone." Why is there no comma before the beginning of the quotation marks?

   _____

7. Angelou uses the following vivid verbs. Look at the verbs in the paragraphs. Then write two or three synonyms next to each verb.

whirled (paragraph 9) _____

handled (paragraph 11) _____

dreaded (paragraph 11) _____

begged (paragraph 13) _____

Discussion and Writing

8. In paragraph 18, the author's mother says, "See, you don't have to think about doing the right thing." Do you agree that people instinctively know how to become parents? Explain your answer and provide examples.

9. The author acted impulsively when she was an adolescent. Write about an impulsive act that you did when you were an adolescent. What happened, and what were the consequences? Try to use some descriptive language in your writing.

READING 3

Your World's a Stage

Josh Freed

Josh Freed is an award-winning columnist for the *Montreal Gazette*. Freed has published many books, including *Fear of Frying and Other Fax of Life*. In the next essay, Freed compares and contrasts two items. As you read, also notice how the author uses definition writing.

1   The next time I'm tempted to barbecue on the front balcony in a Speedo swimsuit, I will think twice—because the whole world might be watching. Google Street View is the latest camera to spy on us in our camera-crazed world. Google offers a view of cities from space—but it also has cameras traveling our city streets, offering shots of our houses, our cars, and any of us who happen to be in the neighborhood yelling at our dogs or our neighbors' kids. For young cyber-fans, it's another fun addition to our growing on-stage lives where the whole world can see what we're doing while we're doing it. But to many older types, it's another possible small invasion of our privacy, one more stray chance to get filmed walking into an AA meeting or a sexual dysfunction clinic. It's also a symptom of the biggest generation split in decades: "Generation Parent" vs. "Generation Transparent." One generation guards its privacy obsessively, while the other barely knows what privacy is.

2   Generation Transparent members are largely young people who have lived their whole lives on stage, ever since their embryo was photographed by a womb-cam at eight weeks old. They love to share their experiences with the whole planet on sites likes My Face or Space Book—everything from their personal diaries and dating history to their latest holiday snaps. For instance, my family recently returned from a holiday, and minutes after we'd stepped through our door, my Generation Transparent son had posted all his pictures of us—in our bathing suits—online for the world to see. But when his Generation Parent mother found out, she took them down faster than a Chinese government censor.

Big Brother: In George Orwell's novel *1984*, Big Brother is the dictator and face of the state. Today, Big Brother means mass surveillance of citizens by the government.

3   Generation Transparent loves publicity and spends its days on sites like Twitter, sending their friends brief "tweet" messages about what they're doing as they do it.

–Hi. I'm at Metro buying tofu (see attached photo.) Where r u?

–Cool! I'm buying yogurt right down the aisle from u—I'm in the photo u just took.

–Oh yeah! Cool—Wave, wave. Kiss, Kiss. :-)

–OK, bye for now. Let's tweet again when we're at the cash.

4   Generation Parent is older people who see all this transparency as a nightmare. Members of Generation Parent grew up in the wake of McCarthyism, Nixon wire tappers, and CIA spies—and they are paranoid about spreading any bit of personal information about themselves or their families. Many are frightened to bank online or even buy a book on Amazon. They'd never share their credit card number online, let alone their personal diary or photos. To them, our camera-crazed culture is right out of George Orwell's **Big Brother**. But to Generation Transparent, *Big Brother* is just the name of a cool reality show.

5   From Generation Parent's perspective, members of the Transparent Generation are also naive—they're exposing themselves with embarrassing information that could eventually cost them a job or an identity theft. The older generation thinks the younger one confuses virtual friends with real ones—and will eventually get burned by them.

6   But from Generation Transparent's perspective, it's the older generation who's naive and uptight. For many young people, public embarrassment and fame often come together, à la Kim Kardashian, and that's just what they want. They figure the worst that can happen is that someone will show an embarrassing photo of them ten years down the line. The important thing is to make sure they look good in that photo—because it's one more chance to get an audience. And is life really happening if no one is watching?

7   Generation Transparent can hardly wait for the next stage in their ever more public lives. They already dream of Google Home View where people will all watch each other watching TV or slurping spaghetti in the kitchen—with optional Google "Bedroom and Bathroom View," or Google Anatomy, where they'll check out their friends' X-rays, MRI scans, and colonoscopies. Or they dream of Google Ogle, which will let them take a more private peek at their favorite friends, which is already happening on popular new "sexting" sites.

8   Generation Parent's concerns may eventually be proven to be right, and young people will become more private over time, once they're job- or spouse-hunting. But it's more likely that privacy will just become a forgotten term—a relic of the twentieth century before public and private life blurred. Meanwhile, I think I'll go out and do some barbecuing—in my jacket and tie.

MyWritingLab™

Complete additional reading comprehension questions for this selection at **mywritinglab.com**

Vocabulary and Comprehension

1. Find a word in paragraph 8 that means "an object or idea associated with the past."

   _____

2. Underline the thesis statement.

3. In paragraph 2, why did Freed's wife insist that her son remove photos from the Internet? Make a guess.

   _____

   _____

4. Contrast Generation Parent and Generation Transparent. What are at least three major differences?

Generation Parent   **Generation Transparent**

_____   _____

_____   _____

_____   _____

_____   _____

5. Why does Freed call Generation Transparent *naive*?

_____

_____

_____

6. How does Freed conclude the essay?
   a. a prediction   b. a suggestion   c. a quotation

Grammar

7. The first sentence of paragraph 2 contains the phrase "young people who have lived their whole lives on stage." Why is the verb *have lived* instead of *lived*?

_____

8. Freed uses dialogue in paragraph 3. What idea does the dialogue support?

_____

_____

> **GRAMMAR LINK**
> For more information about the present perfect tense, see Chapter 10.

Discussion and Writing

9. Compare and contrast two addictive items. For instance, you can compare two communication devices, Web sites, types of food or drinks, and so on.

10. Should typing instead of handwriting be taught in schools? Is handwriting an obsolete skill? Support your ideas with specific evidence.

READING 4

Fat Chance

Dorothy Nixon

Dorothy Nixon, a freelance writer, has written for *Salon.com*, *Chatelaine*, and *Today's Parent* magazine. She has also published *Threshold Girl* on Kindle. In this text, she ponders about parental responsibility. As you read this cause and effect essay, also look for elements of argument and definition.

1   Being a parent, these days, can make me feel like a fish. I feel like a splish-splashing salmon, to be specific, forced to gamely swim upstream against the currents of society to guarantee the safe propagation of the species. Lately, there have been a spate of studies, widely reported in the press, telling us how North American kids are getting fatter and fatter—and claiming it's mostly up to

parents to do something about it. This kind of news puts more stress on my cardiovascular system than a daily dose of cheeseburger and fries. What can I do, I wonder. I'm only one person. I didn't invent the car or the computer—or those delicious double-chunk-chocolate-chip cookies.

2 True, the researchers behind the most recently published studies don't directly blame parents for this so-called "epidemic of childhood obesity." They point fingers at our sedentary modern lifestyle. But they do say that it is up to parents to get kids moving again, one family at a time. I must admit, these social scientists serve up some convincing reasons for reversing the trend. Overweight kids suffer from poor self-esteem. Overweight kids become overweight adults, predisposed to heart disease and diabetes. However, the solution isn't a simple matter of slapping a padlock on the fridge door, as my mother always threatened to do. Kids aren't eating more, anyway. They are just exercising less, much less. And dieting has never been the answer, as experts have shown.

3 Obesity, (I simply hate that word—what exactly is "obese," compared to kinder, gentler cousins like chunky or chubby?) is a side effect of a technological society. We've moved indoors, en masse, and pulled up a soft, comfy chair in the process. Most of us would rather watch just about any sport on cable, even one-armed alpine unicycle racing, than participate in it. Even would-be jocks like my sons can't help but be sidetracked—or, dare I say, seduced—by the siren call of TV, video games, and online chat rooms.

4 Besides, it's costly to counteract this slothful societal trend: I've spent hundreds of dollars outfitting my boys for tennis and skiing. Do you know that credit card commercial? Tennis shoes: 100 dollars. Tennis whites: 80 dollars. Tennis racquet and lessons: 300 dollars. The look on your face when your son says he doesn't want to go to tennis anymore: PRICELESS.

5 I can lead my sons to the courts, but I can't make them serve. And neither can I make society rewind to a time where free play and arduous physical activity were woven into the cloth of everyday life, a time before remote controls, microwaves, indoor plumbing, and the Internet. I can't even go back to the sixties, when girls skipped and boys rode bikes with no brakes.

6 I shouldn't have to put my sons through this kind of humiliation. They are average children, genetically wired to move, jump, and play, play, play 'til they drop. But nobody plays outside most of the time—and when the neighborhood kids do have some down time, they spend ten minutes outside skateboarding and three hours inside playing *Final Fantasy*.

7 I read somewhere that male brains are designed to "hit the target," which is why some boys can spend hours taking slap shots at a garbage can or tossing basketballs into a hoop. But for about a decade now, they've had video games to gratify this primal urge. Modern boys don't have to budge a muscle to get a testosterone buzz.

8 The experts have a point when they say it's up to parents to act as role models in this regard. It sure wouldn't hurt us oldsters to get off our duffs, too. I have noticed, over the years, that the active couples I know have active kids. But then I ask my son, "Why don't you come exercise to *Sweatin' to the Oldies* with me?" He just stares at me in horror.

9 If childhood obesity is as big a problem in North America as these researchers say, it's likely we have to do something more to help our kids and to help society. We should lobby school boards and governments. We need to demand more gym classes and more money for subsidized sports programs in communities.

We need to do one more thing, as well. Let our kids engage in more free play—unstructured, inexpensive, creative play beyond the toddler years, even if it entails some misguided bravura, a steep hill, and a bike with no brakes.

Vocabulary and Comprehension

1. Find a word in paragraph 1 that means "large number of."

   _____

2. Why is the writer anxious?

   _____

   _____

3. What is causing the childhood obesity epidemic?

   _____

   _____

4. According to the writer, what are some negative aspects of being overweight?

   _____

   _____

5. Why do parents fail to make their children more active?

   _____

   _____

   _____

6. What suggestions does the writer give to get children to exercise more?

   _____

   _____

   _____

MyWritingLab™

Complete additional reading comprehension questions for this selection at **mywritinglab.com**

Grammar

7. The first sentence in paragraph 5 contains a comma. Why is there a comma before *but*?

   _____

   _____

8. In paragraph 6, underline the verb that follows *nobody*. Why does the verb end in *s*?

   _____

   _____

> **GRAMMAR LINK**
> For more information on commas, see Chapter 26. For more information about subject–verb agreement, see Chapter 13.

Discussion and Writing

9. What advice would you give to the government to combat obesity?

10. Parents should be blamed for their children's obesity. Argue for or against this statement.

READING 5

....

Skydiving

....

Touré

Touré is a novelist, cultural critic, and host of *Hip Hop Shop* and *On the Record*. The next essay is from his book *Who's Afraid of Post-Blackness? What It Means to Be Black Now*. As you read this descriptive essay, also note elements of narrative writing.

1   Once, I went skydiving. For about four minutes in 2007, I was above— and plummeting rapidly toward—a small town in the middle of the Florida panhandle. I jumped out of the plane solo at 14,000 feet for a TV show called *I'll Try Anything Once*. On the way to the skydiving center, the production team stopped for lunch at a restaurant where three middle-aged black men who worked there recognized me from TV and came over to our table to say hi. They asked what I was doing there, and I told them I was on my way to go skydiving. They were stunned. One of them said, in a conspiratorial tone and at a volume meant to slide under the sonic radar of the white people sitting right beside me, "Brother, black people don't do that." The other two nodded in agreement. They quickly glanced at the rest of my team and then back at me as if that clinched their point: The only people doing this life-risking crazy foolishness are some loony white boys and you. As they saw it, I was breaking the rules of blackness. I was afraid, but not about breaking the invisible rulebook.

2   The plane was old, with only a seat for the pilot and barely enough room for five adults to sit on the floor. There was one clear thin plastic rickety door that didn't look strong enough to keep people from falling through it. In order to be heard, we had to yell. The plane did not move with efficiency and grace. In fact, it reminded me of an old dying car that sputters and wheezes. If I hadn't been scheduled to jump out for the sake of television, I would have listened to the voice inside me yelling, "Bail!"

3   At 14,000 feet, the thin plastic door—similar to a grandmother's couch protector—was pushed up. Through the open maw, the oppressively fast hard wind slashed by. We could barely see the Earth below: large buildings smaller than ants and acre-sized fields tinier than a baby's palm. My eyes were saucer wide, my palms were soaked, and my heart was banging in my chest as if looking for a way out. The breathless terror enveloping me as a jump virgin was not assuaged by my macho divemaster Rick, a former cop and Marine with a military-style buzzcut who owns the drop zone, jumps twenty times a day, and finds the fear of newbies funny. Rick thought gallows humor was appropriate at that moment. With the door open he said, "Just remember, no matter what happens . . . I'm going to be all right." He laughed. I did not. He was going to jump out after me, but he wasn't going to be on my back. I was going solo. Or as he put it, I was going to have the chance to save my own life.

4   As I scooted on my butt toward the open door, the wind vacuumed angrily like horror movie vortices that suck people into another world. I was directly violating my constitution as a human, which places a very high value on survival. Still, I got in the doorway and grabbed hold of the sides of the plane. I could feel the wind smacking me in the face. I could barely see the ground and could not imagine letting go. Then Rick began to

count down from three. I told myself, "You will let go when he says go. You will not hesitate." My body was semi-paralyzed. Rick said two. My frontal lobe tried to veto the whole thing. Can't we just wimp out and let the plane take us back to the ground? Then Rick said go. And I just let go. And I was falling.

5   Freefall does not feel like falling. It feels like floating but without the peace we associate with floating. Things move at supersonic speed and the virgin skydiver's mind can't process all that's going on, so it's a chaotic blur. The wind was so loud, I couldn't hear myself; I was screaming for about ten seconds before I even realized it. I kept trying to grab on to something, anything, but there was nothing, just air.

6   Rick told me to keep my head bent upward because the weight of my head would send me into a spin or at least into the wrong dive position. But I looked down; the view of the earth was awesome. That sent me spinning heels overhead and then hurtling down for a tumultuous forty-five seconds of twisting and turning and upside-down plunging. Everything happened too fast to realize how screwed up it was and how terrified I should've been. I pulled the cord, but because I was in the wrong dive position—still falling on my back—part of the parachute coiled around my arm and did not unfurl. I saw a thread wrapped twice around my right forearm as I kept falling to the ground. If I did nothing, I would die eight or nine seconds later. But I was calm. I did not panic one bit. The voice in my mind was cool. With the same inner tone I might use to say to myself, "Hmm, we're out of pretzels," I said to myself, "Hmm, the chute's wrapped around my arm."

7   The day before my dive, during my eight-hour training class, Rick told me what to do if this happened: just shake my arm and the cord should come loose. So at about 5,000 feet from the ground, which skydivers know is next to nothing, I shook my arm as if shooing off a fly. The cord came loose and the chute went free and unfurled above me, breaking my fall.

8   Suddenly, I was floating gently like a snowflake. All was quiet. I could look up and see the sun playing peek-a-boo amidst the clouds, and below, I saw tiny cars and buildings and fields. I felt like a speck of dust blowing in the cosmos at the whim of a much, much larger force conducting a massive, magnificent opera. And in that moment, the perspective I gained from being thousands of feet in the air made me fully grasp how small a part of this world I am. That bird's eye view of Earth, and the soul-stirring meditative quiet I was wrapped up in, made me feel like a tiny dot in our awesomely sculpted world, a minute particle floating through a gigantic universe that will outlast me by a long way. If I'd turned down the opportunity to skydive because "black people don't do that," I would've cheated myself out of an opportunity to grow as a human.

Vocabulary and Comprehension

1. Find a word in paragraph 1 that means "falling rapidly."

   _____

2. Why did Touré go skydiving?

   _____

3. In paragraph 3, the writer describes his "breathless terror." What are some images he uses to show his terror?

   _____

   _____

MyWritingLab™

Complete additional reading comprehension questions for this selection at **mywritinglab.com**

4. In paragraph 3, why does he call the instructor's remark *gallows humor*?

_____

_____

5. What dangerous event happened during his skydive?

_____

_____

_____

6. How was skydiving a positive experience for the writer?

_____

_____

_____

GRAMMAR LINK
For more information about commas, see Chapter 26. For more information about commonly confused words, see Chapter 25.

Grammar

7. In paragraph 6, why does the second sentence contain a semicolon instead of a comma?

_____

8. Paragraph 7 contains the word *loose*. What is the difference between *lose* and *loose*?

_____

Discussion and Writing

9. Go for a walk in a new place. Use your senses and give details about what you see, hear, smell, and touch.

10. Describe a time when you felt frightened or excited. Use details that appeal to the senses.

MyWritingLab™
Complete these writing assignments at mywritinglab.com

MyWritingLab   **THE WRITER'S ROOM**   Images of Lifestyles and Relationships

Writing Activity 1: Photo Writing

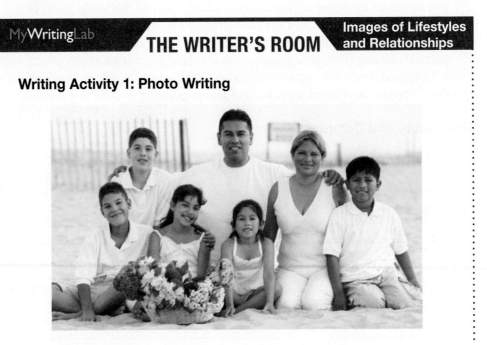

1. Would you prefer to have a large or small family? Give your reasons.

2. Compare and contrast a large family and a small family.

3. Why do most people decide to have small families? List some reasons and give examples to support your points.

Writing Activity 2: Film Writing

1. Find a movie about obsession. For instance, you can watch *W.E.*, *Martha Marcy May Marlene*, *The Master*, *Like Water*, or another film of your choice. Define a particular obsession, and give examples of how it is portrayed in the film.

2. Find a movie about a family. You can watch one of Tyler Perry's Madea films such as *Madea's Big Happy Family*. You can also watch a film such as *The Descendants*, *Trouble with the Curve*, or *Friends with Kids*. Compare and contrast two characters in the film.

Theme: Entertainment, Culture, and Beliefs

READING 6

What's Your Humor Style?

Louise Dobson

Louise Dobson has written for *Psychology Today*. As you read this text, look for patterns of classification and illustration.

1   In today's personality stakes, nothing is more highly valued than a sense of humor. We seek it out in others and are proud to claim it in ourselves, perhaps even more than good looks or intelligence. If someone has a great sense of humor, we reason, it means that he or she is happy, socially confident, and has a healthy perspective on life.

2　　This attitude would have surprised the ancient Greeks, who believed humor to be essentially aggressive. And in fact, our admiration for the comedically gifted is relatively new, and not very well founded, says Rod Martin, a psychologist at the University of Western Ontario who studies the way people use humor. Being funny isn't necessarily an indicator of good social skills and well-being, his research has shown; it may just as likely be a sign of personality flaws.

3　　He has found that humor is a double-edged sword. It can forge better relationships and help us cope with life, or it can be corrosive, eating away at self-esteem and antagonizing others. "It's a form of communication, like speech, and we all use it differently," says Martin. We use bonding humor to enhance our social connections—but we also may wield it as a way of excluding or rejecting an outsider. Likewise, put-down humor can at times be an adaptive, healthy response: Employees suffering under a vindictive boss will often make the office more bearable by secretly ridiculing their tyrant.

4　　Though humor is essentially social, how people use it says a lot about their sense of self. Those who use self-defeating humor, making fun of themselves for the enjoyment of others, tend to maintain that hostility toward themselves even when alone. Similarly, those who are able to view the world with amused tolerance are often equally forgiving of their own shortcomings.

Put-down Humor

5　　This aggressive type of humor is used to criticize and manipulate others through teasing, sarcasm, and ridicule. When it's aimed against politicians, it's hilarious and mostly harmless. But in the real world, it has a sharper impact. Put-down humor, such as telling friends an embarrassing story about another friend, is a socially acceptable way to deploy aggression and make others look bad so the storyteller looks good.

6　　When challenged on their teasing, put-down jokers often turn to the "just kidding" defense, allowing the aggressors to avoid responsibility even as the barb bites. Martin has found no evidence that those who rely on this type of humor are any less well adjusted. But it does take a toll on personal relationships.

Bonding Humor

banter: exchange of light teasing remarks

7　　People who use bonding humor are fun to have around; they say amusing things, tell jokes, engage in witty **banter**, and generally lighten the mood. These are the people who give humor a good name. They're perceived as warm, down-to-earth, and kind, good at reducing the tension in uncomfortable situations, and able to laugh at their own faults.

8　　Talk show host and comedian Ellen DeGeneres embraces her audience by sharing good-natured, relatable humor. Her basic message is that we're alike, we find the same things funny, and we're all in this together.

9　　Nonetheless, bonding humor can have a dark side. After all, a feeling of inclusion can be made sweeter by knowing that someone else is on the outs. J.F.K. and his brothers would often invite a hated acquaintance to vacation with them; they'd be polite to his face, but behind his back, the brothers would unite in deriding the hapless guest.

Hate-me Humor

10   In this style of humor, the funny person is the butt of the joke for the amusement of others. Often **deployed** by people eager to ingratiate themselves, it's the familiar clown or "fat guy" playfulness that we loved in John Belushi and Chris Farley—both of whom suffered for their success. A small dose of it is charming, but a little goes a long way: Routinely offering oneself up to be humiliated erodes self-respect, fostering depression and anxiety. It also can backfire by making other people feel uncomfortable, finds Nicholas Kuiper of the University of Western Ontario. He proposes that it may remind others of their own tendency toward self-criticism.

deployed: used strategically

11   Farley, who died at age thirty-three from an overdose, had a streak of self-loathing. "Chris chose the immediate pleasure he got in pleasing others over the long-term cost to himself," his brother wrote after his death. The bottom line: Excelling at this style of humor may lead to party invitations but can ultimately exact a high price.

Laughing at Life Humor

12   When we admire someone who "doesn't take himself too seriously," this is the temperament we're talking about. More than just a way of relating to other people, it's a prism that colors the world in rosier shades. Someone with this outlook deploys humor to cope with challenges, taking a step back and laughing at the absurdities of everyday life. *The Onion* is a repository of this benign good humor. The columnist Dave Barry has perfected it with quips like this: "Fishing is boring, unless you catch an actual fish, and then it is disgusting."

The Onion: a satirical online newspaper

13   Studies that link a sense of humor to good health are probably measuring this phenomenon; when people have a wry perspective, it's hard to remain anxious or hostile for long. Martin calls it "self-enhancing humor," because they don't need other people to entertain them—if something peculiar or annoying happens, they're perfectly capable of laughing at it on their own.

Vocabulary and Comprehension

1. In paragraph 10, what is the meaning of *erodes*?
    a. improves   b. adds to   c. slowly destroys

2. In your own words, state the writer's main point.

    _____

    _____

3. What is the difference between put-down humor and hate-me humor?

    _____

    _____

    _____

MyWritingLab™

Complete additional reading comprehension questions for this selection at **mywritinglab.com**

4. Which type of humor is the most positive? Support your answer with evidence from the text.

_____

_____

_____

5. How has contemporary society's attitude toward humor changed from ancient times?

_____

_____

6. The author uses different types of support to develop her ideas. For each type of support listed, find an example from the text.

expert opinion: _____

example: _____

GRAMMAR LINK
For more information on combining sentences using semicolons, see Chapter 15. For more information on punctuating quotations, see Chapter 28.

Grammar

7. There is a sentence in paragraph 2 that uses a semicolon. Explain why the writer uses a semicolon in this sentence.

_____

8. The last sentence in paragraph 12 contains a quotation. Why is a colon instead of a comma before the quotation marks?

_____

_____

Discussion and Writing

9. Think of another emotion such as pride, boredom, anger, or happiness. Then divide that emotion into categories, and list types of that emotion. Give examples to support each type.

10. What type of humor do you have? Describe your sense of humor.

READING 7

A Cultural Minefield

William Ecenbarger

William Ecenbarger is an award-winning journalist. He has written numerous articles for magazines such as _Reader's Digest_. In the next essay, Ecenbarger gives many examples of international business etiquette. As you read this illustration essay, also look for elements of narration, cause and effect, and comparison and contrast.

1   In Sydney, Australia, I simply hailed a taxi, opened the door, and jumped in the back seat. The driver narrowed his eyes. "Where to, mate?" he asked in a voice that could chill a refrigerator. In Marrakech, Morocco, I crossed my legs during an interview with a government official. Immediately, a hush fell over the

room. In a restaurant in Mumbai, India, all I did was reach for the naan. A diner at the next table shot me a look that stuck two inches out my back.

2   It took years before I realized what I'd done. It turns out that in each case I had, unwittingly, committed a **faux pas**. To varying degrees, I had offended my hosts. My only comfort is my ignorance. I take solace in Oscar Wilde's observation that a gentleman is someone who never gives offense—unintentionally. And after nearly twenty-five years of travel on six continents, I have learned the hard way that getting through customs is a lot more difficult than just filling out a declaration form. It means navigating a series of cultural booby traps. It means understanding that although people everywhere are the same biologically, they can be worlds apart in their habits and traditions.

faux pas: a socially embarrassing act

3   Here's my advice for anyone visiting another country: Eat, drink—and be wary. My Australian taxi driver was offended because I sat in the back seat rather than up front next to him. His attitude is not uncommon, according to *Kiss, Bow or Shake Hands*, a book on business behavior. It stems from Australians' disdain of class distinctions. My interview with the Moroccan bureaucrat was cut short because, in crossing my legs, I had showed him the sole of one of my shoes, a grave affront to Muslims who see the foot as unclean. I reached for the bread in Mumbai. There's nothing wrong with this **per se**, but I did it with my left hand. Indians eat with their hands, in particular their right; their left hands are reserved for other matters, including after-toilet cleansing, and are therefore unacceptable for use at the dining table.

per se: by itself

4   When I curled my thumb and index finger into a circle and pointed the other three fingers upward, my intention was to tell the Brazilian hotel clerk that everything had been "OK." That would have worked fine at home in the U.S., but in Brazil it's considered vulgar. The OK sign is not OK in many other places too, including most of the rest of Latin America, plus Germany, Malta, Tunisia, Greece, Turkey, Russia, and the Middle East.

5   There are many hand gestures that don't travel well. The "V" for victory sign was immortalized by Winston Churchill in the early, dark days of World War II, and the proper form is with the palm facing outward. A simple twist of the wrist puts you in dangerous cultural waters. Throughout much of Her Majesty's realm, the palm-in V sign is the equivalent of the more infamous middle-digit salute. During the Middle Ages, it was thought that French soldiers would permanently disarm English bowmen by cutting off their middle and index fingers, the ones they used to draw the bowstring. Consequently, the English were said to celebrate battlefield victories and taunt the French by displaying these two digits intact.

6   Even though the "thumbs up" (meaning everything is fine) has worldwide acceptance among many pilots, it can get you in big trouble outside the cockpit. If you're hitchhiking in Nigeria, for example, your upraised thumb may be interpreted as a take-this-and-shove-it insult to passing motorists. The rule of thumb there is, don't do it.

7   Sometimes I think the solution is to tie my hands behind my back, but there are countless other ways to offend while traveling. The entire area of food and drink is a cultural minefield. In Asia, for example, you would never leave your chopsticks upright in your food. As Chin-ning Chu, author of *The Asian Mind Game*, advises, "In the ceremony to honor the dead, many Asians offer food to their deceased ancestors by placing incense in the bowl and burning it as a way to carry the food to the other world. It is a common Asian superstition that to

place your chopsticks in such a way is bad luck and means that this meal is for the dead rather than the living." Furthermore, if you show up with flowers at Asian homes, you'll probably be welcomed warmly, unless, of course, you take white chrysanthemums (they're used only for funerals) or you offer an odd number (considered unlucky in some cultures).

8   When drinking with others in Prague, Czech Republic, before the first sip, the Czechs deem it important to look their companions in the eye and lightly clink glasses. But less than 300 miles away in Budapest, Hungary, that identical gesture can get you deep in goulash. The clink is considered unpatriotic because it was once the signal for a coup.

9   Travel won't broaden you unless your mind is broad to begin with. After all, a foreign country isn't designed to make the traveler comfortable; it's designed to make its own people comfortable.

MyWritingLab™

Complete additional reading comprehension questions for this selection at **mywritinglab.com**

Vocabulary and Comprehension

1. In paragraph 8, what is the meaning of *deem*?

   _____

2. In paragraph 2, what are "cultural booby traps"?

   _____

   _____

3. In your own words, what is the main thesis of this essay?

   _____

   _____

4. The author gives examples of what he did wrong in different countries. What was the author's mistake, and why was it a mistake?

   Australia: _____

   _____

   Morocco: _____

   _____

   India: _____

   _____

5. Which North American hand gestures may possibly offend people of other cultures? Give three examples.

   _____

   _____

6. In some Asian countries, why should a person never place chopsticks sticking up in a bowl?

   _____

   _____

7. What is the difference in custom when drinking a beer in Prague and drinking a beer in Budapest?

_____

_____

8. How did the author acquire his information on cultural mistakes?

_____

_____

Grammar

9. *Kiss, Bow or Shake Hands* (paragraph 3) and *The Asian Mind Game* (paragraph 7) are in italics. Why are they italicized?

_____

10. The author uses contractions in his essay. Write out the long form for the following contractions.

> **GRAMMAR LINK**
> For more information on punctuating titles, see Chapter 28. For more information on contractions, see Chapter 27.

paragraph 2: I'd = _____   paragraph 7: they're = _____

paragraph 3: there's = _____   paragraph 9: won't = _____

paragraph 6: don't = _____   paragraph 9: it's = _____

Discussion and Writing

11. Think of some social and professional situations. Then give examples of good and bad manners particular to that situation. Explain why the manners are considered good or bad.

12. What kinds of skills does travel give a person? Give some examples of those skills, and explain why they are important to have.

READING 8

Celanthropists

Katrina Onstad

Katrina Onstad is a journalist and author. Her novels include *How Happy to Be* and *Everybody Has Everything*. In the following essay, Onstad reflects on celebrity philanthropy. As you read this definition essay, also look for elements of illustration and cause and effect.

1   Elizabeth Taylor, all rounded edges and violet eyes, held the hands of children with AIDS at a point in history when such a touch was still considered courageous. She spent much of her post-cinematic life crusading for HIV/AIDS research. When she died, Democrat Jim Graham said of her charity work, "There [are] so many celebrities that get involved but never really get *deeply* involved. But she really did." Within days of Taylor's death, another celebrity philanthropist—arms like anchor lines, eyes in sunglasses—found herself at the center of a scandal: Madonna's $18-million (U.S.) charity, Raising Malawi, had failed to erect a school for girls in the African country of her adopted children's births. Auditors found Raising Malawi in a riot of fiscal mismanagement,

citing the spending of $3.8 million on a school that doesn't exist. The project's managers reportedly enjoyed huge salaries and pricey cars while nary a brick was laid. "Ha! This is what happens when you put a seemingly good idea in the hands of egomaniacal celebrities," wrote a commenter on the *New York Times* Web site, just one of numerous online raspberries.

2   It's easy to be cynical about celebrity philanthropy when, so often, the good intentions of the rich and famous seem to go awry. According to *Forbes*, the Justin Timberlake Foundation spent $146,000 (U.S.) on operating costs in 2006 but distributed only $32,500. In 2010, Lindsay Lohan tweeted that she had personally helped rescue forty Indian children from child trafficking, but she wasn't actually in India at the time. Even Oprah, celebrated for well-managed, generous philanthropy, spent months tending to a rash of molestation accusations [against staff] at her South African school for girls.

3   Such stories paint a picture of celebrities blundering, like Jimmy Choo-wearing Big Foots, into delicate issues, doing more harm than good. As Zambia-born economist Dambisa Moyo, author of the trade-not-aid screed *Dead Aid*, told *Newsweek*, "If there is a criticism I would level against celebrities, [it's that] they have tended to perpetuate negative stereotypes. Taking a picture with a starving African child—that doesn't help me raise an African child to believe she can be an engineer or a doctor."

Kangol: Kangol is a hat brand

4   Still, in the past few years, perhaps guided by the light of Bono and Brangelina's big stars, charity has become a celebrity fashion. This is preferable to the **Kangol** hat trend, but it's hard not to raise an eyebrow when altruism seems like another checked box on a Make-A-Star marketing plan: first a cosmetics contract, then a foundation supporting . . . some afterthought. This me-so-sensitive posture makes for an awkward barrage of self-promotion: "Go see *Transformers 3*! And support stray badgers!"

5   In their book *Philanthrocapitalism*, authors Matthew Bishop and Michael Green applaud "celanthropists" who use their fame to drive change in an era when cash-strapped governments are doing less for social equity and the private sector is expected to do more. The assumption behind celanthropy is that the same fandom that gets people to endure *The Tourist* will also generate curiosity about Angelina Jolie's work as Goodwill Ambassador for the U.N. Yet it's a paradox that the very thing that makes celebrities successful charity spokespeople—their intoxicating, otherworldly status—is precisely what makes us suspicious of them: How can those who are inhuman be humanitarians? Isn't a star's every gesture in service of his stardom?

6   In spiritual terms, charity is linked to humility, which is close to anonymity. And anonymity is the enemy of celebrity. However, it seems that anonymity may be at odds with all charity. For nine months, researchers at Yale monitored an alumni fundraising "phone-athon" and found that, when solicitors mentioned donors might be listed in a "giving circle" or even mentioned in a newsletter, people were more inclined to give. They concluded that social recognition motivates charitable giving, a finding in line with earlier research by other scholars suggesting people gain utility from giving in three ways: as a material benefit (perhaps a tax break, or a free pen), as a burnished social reputation, or as the generator of a "warm glow." This may be called "impure altruism," but a warm glow happens to look great on a red carpet, though all of us can wear it well.

7   If we're all impure altruists, then maybe celebrities deserve room to use their inhuman, self-promotional powers for good. Interestingly, Madonna's recent charitable woes may ultimately benefit the impoverished country of

Malawi: Instead of funding the building of a school, the money is now going to be distributed across several NGOs with up-and-running education initiatives. This cleanly removes the ego from a project that seemed a little Oprah wannabe, but imagine the effect if one day Madonna does start that school for girls, setting her Madonna-patented ferocity and discipline to real, well-managed change, not symbolic, self-serving posturing. There's a greater good waiting if she becomes, like Liz, "deeply involved." The question is, will we, the unfamous, follow?

Vocabulary and Comprehension

MyWritingLab™

Complete additional reading comprehension questions for this selection at **mywritinglab.com**

1. In your own words, describe a celanthropist.

   _____

   _____

   _____

2. What introduction style does this essay have?
   a. general   b. definition   c. anecdote   d. contrasting position

3. List three examples of ineffective attempts at celanthropy.

   _____

   _____

   _____

   _____

4. In paragraph 3, the author writes that celebrities involved in overseas charities "do more harm than good." How does celanthropy sometimes do more harm than good? Give three reasons.

   _____

   _____

   _____

   _____

   _____

5. In paragraph 5, the author writes that using celebrities to promote a cause is a *paradox*. In your own words, explain what she means.

   _____

   _____

   _____

   _____

6. In paragraphs 6 and 7, the author refers to *impure altruism*. Explain what she means by this term.

   _____

   _____

   _____

GRAMMAR LINK
For more information about titles, see Chapter 28. For more information about contractions, see Chapter 27.

Grammar

7. In paragraph 3, why are *Dead Aid* and *Newsweek* italicized?

_____

8. Circle four contractions in the text. Then write out the long form of each contraction.

_____   _____

_____   _____

Discussion and Writing

9. In a paragraph, define one of the following terms: *public image*, *damage control*, *political philanthropy*, *paparazzi*, and *celebrity*.

10. Should all high school students be forced to do volunteer work? Argue for or against this topic.

READING 9

The Cult of Emaciation

Ben Barry

Ben Barry is CEO of Ben Barry Agency, a model consultancy in Toronto. A graduate of Cambridge University, Barry is the author of *Fashioning Reality*. As you read this argument essay, notice how the author also uses cause and effect, illustration, narration, and description.

1   On this final day of L'Oreal Fashion Week, Canada's top models are strutting their stuff in Toronto. For some, this will have been their first chance to walk the runway. Others will be veterans of the global catwalk circuit. But they will all have one thing in common: extreme, some would say freakish, thinness.

2   Models are the stars of every fashion week. Sure, designers create the outfits, but the models bring those clothes to life. Their faces and bodies saturate our televisions, newspapers, and computer screens. Models are the ones with glamour on tap, the kind of glamour we all supposedly want to taste.

3   For the past nine years, since I was fifteen years old, I have attended countless fashion shows. I was initially an up-and-coming modeling agent sneaking into the shows through back doors. I eventually became established, and I was officially invited to sit among the fashion elite. "Ben, you're so lucky," my friends bemoan, "going to fashion shows and meeting the models. It must all be so glamorous." That sad truth is that I have always found fashion modeling to be a tragic and demeaning experience.

4   In the days before a fashion week begins, models rush to meet with designers for castings. The designers flip through models' portfolios, ask them to walk the length of the room, have them try on articles of clothing, and of course, take their pictures. The models are in and out without saying anything more than "yes" and "thank you." When asked what they remember about the models, designers respond, "her size." Physical attributes constitute the only job requirement.

5   Things start going wrong for many models right away. At one casting, "Ashley," nineteen years old, size zero, 5'10", is asked to try on a pair of trousers. After a couple of minutes of struggling to close the top button, the designer marches over.

"Your hips are too big, you need to make them smaller," he says in front of all the other models before shooing her out the door. Ashley leaves, humiliated and confused, wondering how she is supposed to alter the size of her hips.

6   The girls who do get booked for shows aren't allowed to leave their body stress behind them. Backstage is where things get really frightening. At London Fashion Week in 2007, I took it all in. One model, "Jennifer," was trying to close a zipper on her designer jacket. The designer stood before her, shaking his head. "You've gotten fat," he said to the eighteen-year-old, size zero model. "I'll need to let this jacket out. It will ruin the cut. They're not made for big girls like you." Jennifer turned red. She managed to hold back her tears as the designer made his adjustments, and everyone stopped to gawk.

7   On another occasion, I witnessed an equally thin model get even worse treatment when she couldn't fit into her size zero dress. The designer pointed to another model and proclaimed, "She'll wear the dress instead. Your stomach has gotten too big. Dismissed!" The girl tried to hide between the racks of clothing while she peeled off the tiny dress. She was later escorted out as everyone stared.

8   The situation is worse for mature models; we are talking about anyone older than twenty. Most begin their careers at a time when their body shape is still pre-pubescent. They get older, they develop curves, and bye-bye sample sizes. I met Rena, twenty-two years old, size two, backstage at London Fashion Week. She told me that this had to be her last season. "I can't handle it any more. Every time I do a show now, I get so anxious. There are so many teenage girls. I'm on Slim-Fast, but there's no way I can compete any longer." I offered her an apple. "No, thanks," she replied. "My agent said fruit causes bloating." I assured her that there is no fat in fruit, but she didn't care.

9   Megan, sixteen years old, put it this way: "No matter how skinny you are, you always think you can be skinnier, and there are other girls that are going to be skinnier than you." If the very women representing the beauty ideal feel excluded from it, how can anyone feel included?

10   Agents are always there to make sure a model's weight remains first and foremost in her mind. Rebecca, eighteen years old, dropped by her agency before a casting to surprise her hard-working booker with a latte. Her kindness was repaid by her being unexpectedly weighed and measured in front of everyone who happened to be there.

11   Constant public humiliation—whether at the casting, the fashion show, or the agency—is the norm in the so-called glamorous life of a model. Everyone in the fashion world, from the agents to the designers to the make-up artists, feels he or she has a God-given right to comment on a model's appearance. And everyone is prepared to tell painfully thin models that they need to be thinner. Such comments would amount to harassment in any other profession.

12   It is no wonder that many models develop eating disorders. No one values their thoughts, personalities, or feelings. Everyone values them for their bodies alone. In time, models internalize the dangerous idea that they are worth what they look like. I have met many models who had a passion for politics or writing or basketball when they first started. Two or three years later, any other interests are squelched to make way for a deep and abiding obsession with weight and appearance. The sad irony is the qualities that make supermodels—the ones who rise to the very top of the industry exude energy, attitude, and character with every strut and pose—are progressively stripped away by the casting process when it comes to most girls.

13   Fashion industry insiders claim that they are not to blame for any deaths by malnutrition. Those are isolated incidents. The ways models are treated and valued supposedly has nothing to do with the tragedies. I beg to differ. Just YouTube any episode of *Top Model* and watch how girls are transformed in front of your eyes from multifaceted, confident young women to weight-obsessed, insecure wrecks. The heartrending incidents are the result of working within an industry that objectifies women, which, in turn, teaches them to objectify themselves.

14   This must sound very hypocritical coming from a modeling agent. But I do things differently. My models span all ages, sizes, colors, and abilities. They are accepted, promoted, and hired based on their natural physical attributes. I don't represent any models full-time. They go to school, work as doctors and sales clerks, and run their own businesses. Modeling is something they do on the side for a few days every month—a performance to which they bring their varied experiences to bear.

15   I don't expect our entire "glamorous" modeling industry to follow my example overnight. What can we do to protect the well-being of models in the short term? L'Oreal Fashion Week needs to follow the lead of event organizers in Madrid and Milan by mandating medical tests for each model to ensure they are of healthy weight. Let them feel like they can get away with eating an apple now and then.

16   Any major fashion house choosing such a strategy would receive international attention. For those worried about the bottom line, diversity would allow consumers to relate to the models, relate to the brand, and demonstrate that positive relationship through spending power. Most significantly, women reading magazines and watching fashion television who say, "I could never look like that," will be free to rediscover themselves. Then, and only then, will modeling truly be a glamorous life.

MyWritingLab™

Complete additional reading comprehension questions for this selection at **mywritinglab.com**

Vocabulary and Comprehension

1. Using context clues, define *bemoan* as it is used in paragraph 3.

   _____

2. Underline the thesis statement of the essay. Remember that it may not be in the first paragraph of the text.

3. How does the writer support his point that modeling is demeaning?

   _____

   _____

4. How does life in the modeling industry affect the models?

   _____

   _____

   _____

5. What is the main problem that Ben Barry identifies in the fashion industry?

   _____

   _____

6. What solution does Barry suggest to help solve the problem?

   _____

   _____

Grammar

7. In the first sentence of paragraph 3, the author writes *have attended*, using the present perfect form of the verb. Why does he use the present perfect instead of the simple past (*attended*)?

_____

_____

GRAMMAR LINK
For more information on the present perfect tense, see Chapter 10. For more information on the apostrophe, see Chapter 27.

8. In the second sentence in paragraph 4, why does the word *models'* have an apostrophe after the final *s* rather than before the final *s*?

_____

_____

Discussion and Writing

9. Barry suggests that the modeling industry has contributed to the rise in eating disorders. What other factors cause people to develop eating disorders?

10. What can the fashion industry and the media do to provide viewers with more positive body images? Give examples to support your point.

READING 10

Shopping for Religion

Ellen Goodman

Ellen Goodman is a columnist for the *Boston Globe*. She has also authored many books. In 1980, she received a Pulitzer Prize for distinguished commentary. As you read this argument essay, also look for elements of comparison and contrast.

1   Just below the text there was a Google ad inviting me to take a quiz. "Christian? Jewish? Muslim? Atheist? See Which Religion is Right for You." Aside from the eccentricity of listing atheism as a religion, I couldn't help wondering what my grandparents would make of this religious matching service. For that matter, what would they make of the idea that they could choose their religion at all? To them, religion was part of their identity, if not their DNA. They were born into it, grew up in it, and died with its prayers.

2   I noticed this ad because it was attached to the story of a new report on religion in America released by the Pew Forum on Religion and Public Life. The researchers interviewed 35,000 Americans. Their figures show that Protestants now comprise a bare majority—51 percent—of the population, and that the fastest-growing group is the 16 percent now self-described as "unaffiliated." But what is most fascinating is that 44 percent of Americans have left the religious traditions in which they grew up. They left the religion of their parents with the frequency that they left their old neighborhood.

3   In my grandparents' day, Americans were divided between the big three religions, sort of like TV networks: Catholic, Protestant, and Jew. Now they have fragmented across a spectrum more like cable TV with satellite radio thrown in. The researchers describe a "vibrant marketplace where individuals pick and choose religions that meet their needs." They surf their options. "We are shopping for everything else, why wouldn't we shop for religion?" asks religion professor Donald Miller of the University of Southern California. Pew's John Green adds, "It's not surprising that we have a marketplace in religious or

spiritual ideas." What's qualitatively different these days, he says, is that we have much more religious diversity.

4   I realize that, for many Americans, the idea of shopping for eternal truths is still jarring, even contradictory. The movement from one "tradition" to another may even suggest a kind of promiscuity—a faithless pursuit of faith. Yet the idea of religion as a personal choice seems thoroughly American—as American as religious tolerance. And increasingly these two ideas may be related.

5   America has long been regarded as the most religious of Western nations. Six in ten Americans say that religion plays a very important role in our lives. Polls show that Americans are more willing to vote for a woman, a black, or a Jew than an atheist. **Secular** Europeans who look at those figures regard Americans as unthinking believers—conservatives following orders delivered from the pulpit.

secular: not connected with religion

6   At home the culture wars are often polarized between the religious right and the secular left. Leaders of both sides often characterize—perhaps **caricature**—religious members as people rooted in old ways and immutable ideas. But a huge number of Americans are mobile in pursuit of the immutable. "We are, as a country, people who want to choose their own identity in a lot of areas of life, and religion is one more part of it," says Alan Wolfe of Boston College. There's a difference between an identity that's achieved rather than **ascribed**. Those who leave their childhood religions largely regard themselves as making their own individual choice. In this cultural context, even staying becomes an active decision.

caricature: a portrait that exaggerates certain characteristics

ascribed: given to someone

7   When religion was cast in stone, we were more likely to cast stones. It may be the new pluralism and the framing of religion as a choice that make us more accepting. "You are the artist of your own life when it comes to religion," says Miller. "This enables people to be more thoughtful about what they perceive to be true and right rather than inheriting what passes down to them."

8   Indeed, if we've left our childhood traditions, if our children may leave ours, there is good reason to nurture what Wolfe calls "intolerance insurance." The Pew study also shows that 40 percent of all marriages are of mixed religious traditions—including "none of the above." We take coexistence pretty literally.

9   I don't think Americans are just shopping for their beliefs in a trivial sense, trying on creeds like this year's **vestment**, searching for the latest spiritual fashion. But we are a people on the move. About 40 million of us move to another home every year. So too, we drop in and out of church, U-Hauling our beliefs off in search of a better fit. Today, we may shop in a spiritual mall but with the good fortune to find the mall paved over the old religious battlefields.

vestment: clothing

MyWritingLab™

Complete additional reading comprehension questions for this selection at **mywritinglab.com**

Vocabulary and Comprehension

1. Find a word in paragraph 6 that means *unchanging*.

    _____

2. Which sentence best expresses the main idea of this essay?

    a. In the past, Americans were divided between the big three religions.

    b. People shop for religion as casually as they shop for socks; they do not consider the consequences.

   c. In America, many people now choose their religion, leading to more religious diversity than in the past.

   d. There are many religious options available for people, but most are undecided and do not know what religion to follow.

3. According to the author, what is the difference between the present generation and past generations in terms of practicing a religion?

   _____

   _____

4. According to a report on religion in America, what percentage of people claim to have changed religious views?

   _____

5. Does the author support the notion of shopping for religion? Explain your answer and provide examples from the text.

   _____

   _____

   _____

   _____

Grammar

6. In paragraph 3, why are Catholic, Protestant, and Jew capitalized?

   _____

   _____

7. In paragraph 3, the author writes, "my grandparents' day" and in paragraph 9, she writes "this year's vestment." Why does she place the apostrophe after the *s* in the first example and before the *s* in the second example? Explain the rule about possession.

   _____

   _____

> **GRAMMAR LINK**
> For more information on capitalization, see Chapter 28. For more information on the apostrophe, see Chapter 27.

Discussion and Writing

8. Have you ever rejected your own religion or tried "shopping for religion"? Narrate some of your experiences.

9. Should high schools teach courses about comparative religion? Would it help to promote religious tolerance? Explain your views.

10. In 2007, Governor Sonny Perdue of Georgia led a public prayer for rain. In many states, politicians publicly oppose abortion on religious grounds. Should there be a more strict separation of church and state? Explain why or why not?

MyWritingLab

THE WRITER'S ROOM

Images of Entertainment,
Culture, and Beliefs

Writing Activity 1: Photo Writing

1. Describe a music concert
   or performance that you
   have seen. Use imagery
   that appeals to the
   senses.

2. Do you think music
   lessons should be
   compulsory in school?
   Explain why or why not.

3. Does a song bring back
   specific memories for
   you? Describe the song
   and the memories that
   it evokes.

Writing Activity 2: Film Writing

1. Watch *The Intouchables*, *Silver Linings Playbook*, or *The Vow*. Choose
   one of the characters, and describe the process the character goes through
   to achieve his or her goals.

2. View a film biography about a real-life person. For example, watch *Marley*,
   Lincoln, or *My Week with Marilyn*. Write about the causes or effects of the
   character's actions.

3. Watch a film clip from *The Artist* or another silent film, and then invent
   dialogue for the film.

Theme: The Earth and Its Creatures

READING 11

The Reverend Evans's Universe

Bill Bryson

Bill Bryson has written many humorous and very popular books on science such as *A Walk in the Woods*. In the next essay, Bryson writes about a man with a very unusual talent. As you read this narrative essay from *A Short History of Nearly Everything*, also look for elements of definition and comparison and contrast.

1   When the skies are clear and the Moon is not too bright, the Reverend Robert Evans, a quiet and cheerful man, lugs a bulky telescope onto the back deck of his home in the Blue Mountains of Australia, about fifty miles west of Sydney, and does an extraordinary thing. He looks deep into the past and finds dying stars. Looking into the past is of course the easy part. Glance at the night sky and what you see is history and lots of it—the stars not as they are now but as they were when their light left them. For all we know, the North Star, our faithful companion, might actually have burned out last January or in 1854 or at any time since the early fourteenth century and news of it just hasn't reached us yet. The best we can say—can ever say—is that it was still burning on this date 680 years ago. Stars die all the time. What Bob Evans does better than anyone else who has ever tried is spot these moments of celestial farewell. By day, Evans is a kindly and now semiretired minister in the Uniting Church in Australia, who does a bit of freelance work and researches the history of nineteenth-century religious movements. But by night he is, in his unassuming way, a titan of the skies. He hunts supernovae.

2   Supernovae occur when a giant star, one much bigger than our own Sun, collapses and then spectacularly explodes, releasing in an instant the energy of a hundred billion suns, burning for a time brighter than all the stars in its galaxy. "It's like a trillion hydrogen bombs going off at once," says Evans. If a supernova explosion happened within five hundred light-years of us, we would be goners, according to Evans. "It would wreck the show," as he cheerfully puts it. But the universe is vast, and supernovae are normally much too far away to harm us. In fact, most are so unimaginably distant that their light reaches us as no more than the faintest twinkle. For the month or so that they are visible, all that distinguishes them from the other stars in the sky is that they occupy a point of space that wasn't filled before. It is these anomalous, very occasional pricks in the crowded dome of the night sky that the Reverend Evans finds.

3   To understand what a feat this is, imagine a standard dining room table covered in a black tablecloth and someone throwing a handful of salt across it. The scattered grains can be thought of as a galaxy. Now imagine fifteen hundred more tables like the first one—enough to fill a Walmart parking lot, say, or to make a single line two miles long—each with a random array of salt across it. Now add one grain of salt to any table and let Bob Evans walk among them. At a glance he will spot it. That grain of salt is the supernova.

4   Evans's is a talent so exceptional that Oliver Sacks, in *An Anthropologist on Mars*, devotes a passage to him in a chapter on autistic savants—quickly adding

that "there is no suggestion that he is autistic." Evans, who has not met Sacks, laughs at the suggestion that he might be either autistic or a savant, but he is powerless to explain quite where his talent comes from. "I just seem to have a knack for memorizing star fields," he told me, with a frankly apologetic look, when I visited him and his wife, Elaine, in their picture-book bungalow on a tranquil edge of the village of Hazelbrook, out where Sydney finally ends and the boundless Australian bush begins. "I'm not particularly good at other things," he added. "I don't remember names well."

5   "Or where he's put things," called Elaine from the kitchen. He nodded frankly again and grinned, then asked me if I'd like to see his telescope. I had imagined that Evans would have a proper observatory in his backyard—a scaled-down version of a Mount Wilson or Palomar, with a sliding domed roof and a mechanized chair that would be a pleasure to maneuver. In fact, he led me not outside but to a crowded storeroom off the kitchen where he keeps his books and papers and where his telescope—a white cylinder that is about the size and shape of a household hot-water tank—rests in a homemade, swiveling plywood mount. When he wishes to observe, he carries them in two trips to a small deck off the kitchen. Between the overhang of the roof and the feathery tops of eucalyptus trees growing up from the slope below, he has only a letter-box view of the sky, but he says it is more than good enough for his purposes. And there, when the skies are clear and the Moon not too bright, he finds his supernovae.

MyWritingLab™

Complete additional reading comprehension questions for this selection at **mywritinglab.com**

Vocabulary and Comprehension

1. Find a word in paragraph 2 that means "unusual."

   _____

2. Who is Robert Evans?

   _____

   _____

3. Why is spotting supernovae so difficult?

   _____

   _____

4. How does the author demonstrate that Evans's ability is really quite amazing?

   _____

   _____

   _____

5. What is a supernova?

   _____

6. In paragraphs 4 and 5, what do the Reverend's words demonstrate about his personality?

   _____

   _____

Grammar

7. In paragraph 2, the author writes, "But the universe is vast, and supernovae are normally too far away to harm us." Is this a simple, compound, or complex sentence? Also explain why there is a comma in the sentence.

_____

_____

GRAMMAR LINK

For more information about compound sentences, see Chapter 15. For more information on *good* and *well*, see Chapter 21.

8. In paragraph 5, the author writes, "I don't remember names well." Why does he use "*well* instead of *good*?"

_____

_____

Discussion and Writing

9. Do you or someone you know have an unusual talent? Write about your talent or about that person's talent.

10. Would you ever want to explore outer space? Why or why not?

READING 12

Saving Animals

Tom Spears

Tom Spears is a science writer for the *Ottawa Citizen*. In the next essay, he discusses the politics of saving endangered species. As you read this comparison and contrast essay, also look for elements of cause and effect and argument.

1   For endangered species, it pays to be a large mammal with sad eyes that cuddles its babies. Glamorous animals, big predators and, above all, the extremely cute and fuzzy stand a chance of getting people to protect them and their habitats. Ugly animals—as judged by human eyes—are far more likely to be left aside when humans draw up conservation plans. Would anyone care to save Ontario's rattlesnakes? Ecology experts say such thinking means we're in danger of re-shaping nature to beautify it according to human notions of what's pretty, saving the mammals but letting the reptiles and amphibians disappear.

2   Ernie Small, veteran research scientist, produced a research paper, recently published in the science journal *Biodiversity*, called "The New Noah's Ark." But while Noah rescued everything in sight, Small says today's conservation is for "beautiful and useful species only." There's broad support for "marquee and poster species," he writes: whales, pandas, polar bears, and elephants. We also protect commercially important species, such as salmon stocks. Bluefin tuna are the object of efforts to prevent overfishing. And farmers are desperate to save the honeybee from whatever mysterious threats are wiping out colonies. But that's where our efforts often stall. "Aesthetic and commercial standards have become the primary determinants of which species in the natural world deserve conservation," Small concludes. The losers in the competition for protection are mostly reptiles and amphibians, even though these—especially frogs and toads—are probably the most endangered groups of animals in the world.

3   Cost estimates for protecting individual species can be big business. The joint Canada-U.S. recovery plan for the whooping crane, for instance, costs the two countries a total of $6.1 million a year now and will cost nearly $125 million through 2035. Meanwhile, many less spectacularly endangered plants and creatures have no budget at all for conservation. That means there are no satellites to search for homes for the Lake Erie water snake. Coca-Cola, meantime, will contribute $2 million to the World Wildlife Fund over five years to protect polar bears and will match consumers' donations up to a further $1 million. But corporate donors aren't lining up to save toads.

4   There are haves and have-nots among these plants (and animal species, too). The haves are lucky enough to live in national parks, where the staff has a legal duty to protect them under the National Parks Act. The have-nots live elsewhere, and they're on their own. "Look at the money that has been put into conservation of the Gulf of St. Lawrence population of beluga whales," Dan Brunton, a researcher, says. "The St. Lawrence beluga population is not even one percent of the global population of beluga whales," he points out, adding that the St. Lawrence belugas are protected as if they were the world's whole supply of belugas. Political winds blow differently in different places. It's legal to hunt and eat Arctic belugas, even though they are the same animal.

5   What are the attributes that make animals attractive to humans? According to Small, the successful candidates exhibit usefulness and have human-like traits, such as having a high forehead and expressive eyes. Also, for some reason, we like dangerous animals, and are fascinated with their weapons, from teeth to horns. Small thinks this may explain the fact that tigers are the kings of global conservation efforts. We prefer animals with adorable cubs or kittens. Bright colors also help, while being covered with scales or a slimy skin is bad. We don't like scavengers and carrion-pickers, and we have little urge to conserve animals with warts, irregular teeth or a habit of drooling.

MyWritingLab™

Complete additional reading comprehension questions for this selection at **mywritinglab.com**

Vocabulary and Comprehension

1. In paragraph 5, what is the meaning of *attributes*?
    a. symbols   b. results   c. assigns   d. characteristics

2. What is the author comparing?

    _____

3. Underline the thesis statement.

4. List at least three characteristics of "ugly" animals and at least three characteristics of "beautiful" animals.

    Ugly animals: _____

    _____

    Beautiful animals: _____

    _____

5. Besides beautiful animals, what other types of animals do humans protect?

    _____

6. What does the author mean when he says that there are "the haves and the have-nots"? See paragraph 4.

_____

_____

Grammar

7. The first sentence in the essay contains the verb *cuddles*. What is the subject of that verb? Also, why does the verb end in *s*?

_____

_____

8. In paragraph 2, why is the title *Biodiversity* in italics whereas the title "The New Noah's Ark" is in quotation marks?

_____

_____

GRAMMAR LINK
For more information on subject–verb agreement, see Chapter 13. For more information on quotation marks, see Chapter 28.

Discussion and Writing

9. Compare and contrast one of the following topics: weeds to flowers, life for animals in zoos to life for animals in the wild, or two animals that are endangered.

10. Compare your attitude about the environment with that of somebody you know.

READING 13

Is It Love or a Trick?

Jon Katz

Jon Katz is the author of *A Good Dog: The Story of Orson, Who Changed My Life*. As you read this cause and effect essay, also look for elements of argument.

1   My friend and fellow dog lover Edie, an occupational therapist in Massachusetts, has been looking for a mate for nearly ten years. She finally thought she'd found one in Jeff, a nice guy, generous and funny, who teaches high school. They dated for several months, and just as there was talk about a future, it occurred to Edie that Jeff hadn't really bonded with her yellow Lab, Sophie. In fact, as she thought more about it, she wasn't sure Jeff was a dog guy at all.

2   She confronted him about this issue at dinner one night, and he confessed, in some anguish, that he didn't love Sophie, didn't love dogs in general, and never had. They broke up the next week. More accurately, she dumped him. "What can I say?" Edie told me, somewhat defensively. "Sophie has been there for me, day in and day out, for years. I can't say the same of men. She's my girl, my baby. Sooner or later, it would have ended."

3   Having just spent two months on a book tour talking to dog lovers, I can testify that this story isn't unusual. The lesson Edie gleaned, she says, was that she should have asked about Sophie first, not last. In North America, we love our dogs a lot. We love them so much that we rarely wonder why anymore.

benighted: unenlightened

Darwinian: adjective referring to Darwin's theory of evolution.

Charles Darwin (1809–1882): an English naturalist who developed the theory of natural selection.

4   This feeling, perhaps, is why God created academics. John Archer, a psychologist at the University of Central Lancashire, has been puzzling for some time over why people love their pets. In evolutionary terms, love for dogs and other pets "poses a problem," he writes. Being attached to animals is not, strictly speaking, necessary for human health and welfare. Studies show that people with pets live a bit longer and have better blood pressure than **benighted** non-owners, but in the literal sense, they don't really need all those dogs and cats to survive.

5   Archer has an alternative **Darwinian** theory: Pets manipulate the same instincts and responses that have evolved to facilitate human relationships, "primarily (but not exclusively) those between parent and child." It is no wonder Edie ditched Jeff. She was about to marry the evil stepfather, somebody who wasn't crazy about her true child.

6   Or, to look at it from the opposite direction, Archer suggests, "consider the possibility that pets are, in evolutionary terms, manipulating human responses. Consider that they are the equivalent of social parasites." Social parasites inject themselves into the social systems of other species and thrive there. Dogs are masters at that strategy. They show a range of emotions—love, anxiety, curiosity—and thus trick us into thinking they possess the full range of human feelings. They dance with joy when we come home, put their heads on our knees, and stare longingly into our eyes. Ah, we think, at last, the love and loyalty we so richly deserve and so rarely receive. Over thousands of years of living with humans, dogs have become wily and transfixing sidekicks with the particularly appealing characteristic of being unable to speak. We are therefore free to fill in the blanks with what we need to hear. What the dog may really be telling us, much of the time, is, "Feed me."

7   It's a good deal for the pets, too, since we respond by spending lavishly on organic treats and high-quality health care. Psychologist Brian Hare of Harvard has also studied the human-animal bond and reports that dogs are astonishingly skilled at reading humans' patterns of social behavior, especially behaviors related to food and care. They figure out our moods, what makes us happy, and what moves us. Then they act accordingly, and we tell ourselves that they're crazy about us. "It appears that dogs have evolved specialized skills for reading human social and communicative behavior," Hare concludes, which is why dogs live so much better than moles.

8   These are interesting theories. Raccoons and squirrels don't show recognizable human emotions, nor do they trigger our nurturing "She's my baby" impulses. So, they usually don't move into our houses, get their photos taken with Santa, or even get names. Thousands of rescue workers aren't standing by to move them lovingly from one home to another.

insinuate: to integrate slyly

9   If the dog's love is just an evolutionary trick, is it diminished? I don't think so. Dogs have figured out how to **insinuate** themselves into human society in ways that benefit us both. We get affection and attention. They get the same, plus food, shelter, and protection. To grasp this exchange doesn't trivialize our love; it explains it.

10   I'm surrounded by dog love, myself. When I stir to make tea, answer the door, or stretch my legs, my three dogs move with me. They peer out from behind the kitchen table or pantry door, awaiting instructions, as border collies do. If I return to the computer, they resume their previous positions. If I analyzed it coldly, I would admit that they're probably checking to see if they will get a walk outside or some beef jerky. But I would rather believe that they **can't bear** to let me out of their sight.

can't bear: hate; do not want

Vocabulary and Comprehension

MyWritingLab™

Complete additional reading comprehension questions for this selection at **mywritinglab.com**

1. What is the meaning of *gleaned* in paragraph 3?

   a. removed   b. added   c. discovered

2. Which sentence best expresses the main idea of the essay?

   a. Our pets, and dogs in particular, have learned to manipulate humans to the benefit of both species.

   b. People love their pets too much and spend extravagantly, paying for items such as their pets' organic food and health care.

   c. Most animals, including raccoons and squirrels, do not trigger our nurturing response.

   d. Dogs trick humans into loving them, which is beneficial for the dogs but not for their human owners.

3. Explain how dogs are *social parasites.*

   _____

   _____

4. How do dogs manipulate their owners? List at least three actions.

   _____

   _____

   _____

5. According to the writer, what is the real reason that dogs trick humans?

   _____

   _____

6. How is the behavior of dogs different from wild animals?

   _____

   _____

7. How do human beings benefit from their pets?

   _____

   _____

Grammar

8. Adverbs modify verbs, adjectives, and other adverbs. In paragraph 6, underline three adverbs and circle the words they modify.

9. In paragraph 10, what is the difference in meaning of the words *they're* and *their*?

   _____

   _____

> **GRAMMAR LINK**
> For more information on adverbs, see Chapter 21. For more information on commonly confused words, see Chapter 25.

Discussion and Writing

10. In America, many people enter their pets in pet shows. They spend a lot of time and money grooming their pets and training them for the competitions. Why do

people do that? What are the effects on the pets? Give the causes and/or effects of pet shows.

11. Define pet obsession. Give examples of people who are obsessed with their pets.

12. Sometimes pets attack their owners or harm other people. Should certain types of pets such as Pitt Bulls or snakes be banned?

MyWritingLab™

Complete these writing assignments at mywritinglab.com

MyWritingLab

THE WRITER'S ROOM   Images of the Earth and Its Creatures

Writing Activity 1: Photo Writing

1. What animal scares you the most? Explain why.

2. How do animals contribute to humans' lives? Think about products or services that animals provide for humans. List specific examples.

3. What can humans learn by watching animals? List specific examples.

Writing Activity 2: Film Writing

1. Watch a science fiction film about the future or about a fantasy world. For example, view *Men in Black III*, *The Hunger Games*, *Dredd*, or any of the *Iron Man* or *Star Wars* movies. Describe the time and place. Include descriptions that appeal to the senses.

2. Watch a classic film about a fear of animals. For example, watch

Spielberg's *Jaws*, Hitchcock's *The Birds*, or Cronenberg's *The Fly*. Classify the types of animal fears that people have. You might also choose one of the movies and describe the most frightening scene. Include details that appeal to the senses.

3. View a film such as *The Grey* or *The Impossible*. What are the causes and effects of the main characters' struggle?

Theme: Trades, Technology, and the Business World

READING 14

The Allure of Apple

Juan Rodriguez

Juan Rodriguez writes about popular culture and music for various publications in Canada and the U.S. He writes a weekly column and feature essays for *The Montreal Gazette*. As you read this definition essay, also look for elements of comparison and contrast.

1   Born to shop, and looking for nirvana in an iMac or iPod or iPhone or iPad, I enter an ultra-sleek Apple Store anticipating a quasi-spiritual experience. It is a place of glass and mirrors and wood and stainless steel that acts as a shrine to the cult of Apple Computer. The store is like a gleaming interdenominational church offering a Grand Design for Living that Apple co-founder Steve Jobs called the "digital lifestyle." The **buzz** around Apple products is intense, but the **furtive murmur** inside the store is pure postmodern prayer. No doubt, the cult of Apple is a transformative experience. I've been hooked for twenty years without knowing the first thing about the science behind the computer revolution.

buzz: excitement

furtive murmur: secretive whispering

2   Part of the "Apple ecosystem," encompassing 360 outlets in twenty-nine countries, the Apple store is très chic. The ceiling appears higher than it is. The sky's the limit! Customers don't merely browse the goods in this sacred space. It's more like stargazing: hardware as **objets d'art**. A pale sea-green glass staircase (patented by Jobs) leads up to where accessories are sold. Apple personnel wear T-shirts over a simple cotton jersey to go with their open no-pressure faces. When we walk into the Apple Store, we feel like we will be taken care of in a cool no-pressure way, and that the experience could potentially turn out to be something akin to . . . enlightenment!

objets d'art: works of art

3   Those cute PC versus Mac ads on the tube remind me of my first encounter with the cult of Apple. My journey in life had taken me, on a whim, to Berkeley, California to hook up with a teenage flame whom I hadn't seen in twenty-three years. One of the first things that she advised me to do was dump my PC and get a Macintosh Classic, the beginner computer that even an idiot—or an East Coaster—could operate hassle-free. She took me to BMUG (Berkeley Macintosh Users Group) meetings on the University of California campus that she attended religiously.

The large auditorium in the round science building—the Mac cult's church of nerds—was populated by geeks speaking in exotic codes and futuristic tongues.

4   From the get-go, she set up the contrasts: The PC, then typified by IBM, was old, stuffy and hierarchical, *sooo* East Coast. Apple was the West, embodying the American frontier spirit—the digital frontier! Then there was the name itself: IBM refers to International Business Machines, the anonymous and crass anything-at-all-costs business. Apple, on the other hand, is a whole earth digital food inviting you to take a creative bite, like so many artists and designers did. Besides, Steve Jobs was way cooler than Bill Gates, head geek of the Evil Empire. It mattered little that Gates was the same age as Jobs (both were born in 1955), talked the same future-shock lingo and, like Steve, wore a modified Beatles hairdo.

portly: heavy; slightly overweight

smug: self-satisfied

5   Gates went ballistic over Apple's great campaign, PC versus Mac, in which the pompous **portly** PC's attempt to prove the superiority of his product is frustrated every time while the unassuming, polite, boy-next-door Mac looks on, trying not to be **smug**. Gates told tech reporter Steven Levy, "I don't know why they're acting superior. I don't even get it. I mean, do you get it? What are they trying to say? There's not even the slightest shred of truth to it!"

6   For years, Steve Jobs was Apple's Svengali-like digital shaman, and we were hooked on his aura. One columnist joked that Americans more keenly anticipated Steve's announcement of the brand-new iPad than they did Barack Obama's State of the Union the night before. Magician David Blaine described Jobs as "the ultimate showman who keeps the audience excited the whole way leading up to the reveal." Just as cult leaders are cloaked in secrecy, Apple employees are sworn to it 24/7. Indeed, media columnist David Carr compares Apple's disciplined way of managing the message to "corporate omerta."

7   Of course, Apple's iconic introductions of new products are a kind of "news theater" that generates hundreds of millions of dollars in free advertising. "Our secret marketing program for the iPhone (prior to the launch) was none. We didn't do anything," Steve explained. In an interview with *Business Week*, he said, "A lot of times, people don't know what they want until you show it to them." Those words were spoken like a true cult leader.

8   Jobs's ultimate cultural appropriation was music. The iPod spread sounds in the service of mankind—and, at the same time, stabilized Apple Computer and reinvented the music industry. A simple catchphrase—"1000 songs in your pocket"—was all it took. Of course, Apple has also released the iPad, which could be considered a savior for the book and newspaper industries. Now call me a spiritualist or a sucker, but I'm possessed by a tingling feeling that my iLife is about to change again. Another visit to the Apple Store is certain.

MyWritingLab™

Complete additional reading comprehension questions for this selection at **mywritinglab.com**

Vocabulary and Comprehension

1. Find a word in paragraph 5 that means "irrationally angry."

    _____

2. What is Rodriguez defining in this essay?

    _____

3. What are some examples he uses to support his definition? List at least three examples.

   _____

   _____

   _____

4. What is the introductory style of the essay?
   a. historical background   b. contrasting position   c. anecdote

5. Rodriquez compares and contrasts PCs and Macs. What are the major differences?

   PC   Mac

   _____   _____

   _____   _____

   _____   _____

6. Why does Rodriguez mention Obama's State of the Union address?

   _____

   _____

   _____

   _____

7. What is the writer's opinion of Apple? Does he like the brand? Support your answer with evidence from the text.

   _____

   _____

   _____

Grammar

8. Paragraph 7 contains the following sentence: "His iconic introductions of new products are a kind of 'news theater' that generates hundreds of millions of dollars in free advertising." Why does *generates* end in *s*?

   _____

   _____

> **GRAMMAR LINK**
> For more information on subject–verb agreement, see Chapter 13. For more information on compound and complex sentences, see Chapters 15 and 16.

9. Identify and underline a simple, compound, and complex sentence. Why does the writer use different types of sentences?

   _____

   _____

Discussion and Writing

10. Define *news theater*. Explain how an Apple announcement, or any other advertisement, becomes news theater. Give examples to support your definition.

11. Some people identify strongly with brands such as Harley Davidson or Apple. Are you loyal to certain brands, or do you have no brand loyalty? Explain your answer.

12. What is your approach to new technologies? Do you plunge in and learn the new systems? Are you more cautious? Does a new gadget scare you? Write about your relationship to technology.

READING 15

How to Handle Conflict

P. Gregory Smith

P. Gregory Smith writes for *Career World*. In the next essay, he describes some steps a person can take to avoid conflict. As you read this process essay, notice how the author also uses elements of argument writing.

1   "Hey, college boy," Mr. Jefferson smirked as Ramon walked into the supermarket, "a lady just dropped a bottle of grape juice in aisle six. Do you think you could lower yourself enough to mop it up?" Ramon was seething inside as he grabbed the mop and headed off to clean up the spill. Ever since he told some of his coworkers that he had applied to the state university, Mr. Jefferson, the night manager, had teased and taunted him. As Ramon returned to the front of the store, he remembered the presentation his guidance counselor, Mrs. Chang, had given last week on something called assertiveness. It is a way of standing up for one's rights without creating conflict. As Ramon walked toward Mr. Jefferson, the main points of the presentation started to come back to him.

2   Find the right time and place. Mr. Jefferson was talking with a customer when Ramon reached the front of the supermarket. Ramon waited until Mr. Jefferson was finished and then asked, "Can I talk with you in your office when you have a moment?" By waiting for the right time, Ramon was likely to have Mr. Jefferson's attention. Also, by asking to speak with him in private, Ramon reduced the chances that Mr. Jefferson would feel that he had to impress others, protect his reputation, or save face.

stance: manner; position

3   Maintain good posture, eye contact, and a relaxed **stance**. Before Ramon said the first word, he reminded himself of a few important things. If he wanted to stand up for himself, he would need to stand up straight! He knew that it was important to make eye contact. Ramon also knew the importance of relaxing his hands and keeping a comfortable distance from Mr. Jefferson. He did not want to appear hostile or threatening. Even though he was angry, Ramon reminded himself that he must speak calmly, clearly, and slowly in order to get his point across. If he let his anger creep in, he would probably get an angry or defensive response from Mr. Jefferson. Even worse, if he hid his feelings behind a quiet tone or rapid speech, then Mr. Jefferson would probably doubt his seriousness.

4   Use *I* statements. Mr. Jefferson closed the office door, folded his arms, and looked at Ramon questioningly. Ramon took a deep breath and began, "Mr. Jefferson, I really feel embarrassed when you call me 'college boy.' I like it a lot better when people call me Ramon. I don't mind doing my fair share of the dirty jobs around here," Ramon continued, "but I feel like I'm getting a lot more mop time than anyone else." By using a statement that began with *I*, Ramon was able to state his feelings honestly, without accusing Mr. Jefferson. *I* statements usually can't be considered false or cause an argument because they're simple statements of feelings.

5   Then introduce cooperative statements. Ramon said, "We used to get along fine until everybody started talking about me going to college next year. I haven't changed, and I'd like to go back to the way things were." Cooperative statements—or statements that connect you with the other person—create common ground for further discussion. They also serve as a subtle reminder that you share experiences and values with the other person.

6   "Remember that standing up for your personal rights, or being assertive, is very important," explains Betty Kelman of the Seattle University School of Nursing. "Standing up for your rights involves self-respect—respect for your rights and the other person's rights. Respecting yourself is the ability to make your own decisions involving relationships, how you spend your time, and whom you spend it with." Kelman also explains what assertiveness is not. "Standing up for yourself does not mean that you express yourself in an aggressive, angry, or mean way." She sums it up this way: "Think of standing up for yourself as being in a win-win situation. You win, and they win."

Vocabulary and Comprehension

MyWritingLab™
Complete additional reading comprehension questions for this selection at **mywritinglab.com**

1. What are *cooperative statements* (paragraph 5)?

   _____

   _____

2. What introduction style does the essay have?
   a. anecdote   b. historical
   c. general   d. contrasting position

3. What is Smith's main point?

   _____

   _____

4. List the steps in the process that Smith describes.

   _____

   _____

   _____

   _____

5. How does the quotation from Betty Kelman (paragraph 6) support the author's point of view?

   _____

   _____

   _____

Grammar

6. Underline the verbs in the first sentences of paragraphs 2 through 5. Who or what is the subject in each sentence?

   _____

> **GRAMMAR LINK**
> For more information on subjects and verbs, see Chapter 8. For more information on contractions, see Chapter 27.

7. In paragraph 5, the author says, "I <u>haven't</u> changed, and <u>I'd</u> like to go back to the way things were." Write out the long form of each contraction.

Discussion and Writing

8. Can you think of a time when you should have been more assertive? Describe what happened.

9. Explain the steps that you take when you are faced with a major problem. What do you usually do?

READING 16

How to Remember Names

Roger Seip

Roger Seip is the president of Freedom Speakers and Trainers, a company that specializes in memory training. In this process essay, he describes how to remember people's names. As you read, notice how the author uses elements of argument and cause and effect writing.

1   If you live in fear of forgetting people's names, sometimes within mere seconds of being introduced to them, you are not alone. Surveys show that 83 percent of the population worries about an inability to recall names. While common, this frustrating phenomenon can be relatively easy to overcome. The most important key to really effective learning of any kind is to understand that there are three learning styles: visual, auditory, and kinesthetic (physically interactive). The more you can apply all three of these styles to a task, the more quickly and solidly you will learn anything. Practice each of the following steps to improve your name recollection in every sales and social situation.

2   When you are first introduced to someone, look closely at his or her face and try to find something unique about it. Whether you find a distinctive quality or not is irrelevant; by really looking for a memorable characteristic in a new face, you are incorporating the visual learning style. And a word of advice: If you do find something that really stands out about someone's face, don't say anything!

3   The next step utilizes both auditory and kinesthetic learning styles. When you meet someone, slow down for five seconds, and concentrate on listening to him or her. Focus on the person, and repeat his or her name back in a conversational manner, such as "Susan. Nice to meet you, Susan." Also make sure to give a good firm handshake, which establishes a physical connection.

4   Creating a mental picture of someone's name incorporates the visual sense again. Many people have names that already are pictures: consider Robin, Jay, Matt, or Dawn, to name just a few. Some names will require you to play with them a bit to create a picture. Ken, for example, may not bring an immediate image to your mind, but a "can" is very close. Or you might envision a Ken doll. The point is not to create the best, most creative mental image ever, so don't get caught up in your head during this step of the process, thinking, "Oh, that's not a very good picture. What is a better one?" The worst thing you can do when learning is to stress yourself out and overthink the process. If an image does not come to you right away, skip it and do it later. You will undo all of your good

efforts if you are staring dumbly at the person, insisting, "Hey. Hold still for a minute while I try to turn your name into a picture!"

5   Once you have identified a mental image that you associate with a person's name, the next step is to "glue" that image to the person's face or upper body. This bridges that gap many people experience between being able to recall faces but not the names that belong to those faces. If you met a new prospect named Rosalind, for example, you might have broken her name down into the memorable image of "rose on land." Now you must create a mental picture that will stick with you as long as you need it and pop into your head every time you meet her; this should be something fun, even a little odd, that will bring "rose on land" to mind when you see her face. You might imagine her buried up to her neck in earth, with roses scattered around her, for example. Because you created the image, it will come up next time you see her and enable you to recall her name.

6   At the end of the conversation, integrate auditory learning by repeating the prospect's name one more time, but don't ever overuse someone's name in an effort to place it more firmly in your mind. For example, in formal situations, use the person's name only at the beginning of the conversation, and then again at the end. If you feel that you can do so naturally, you might insert someone's name once or twice in a natural fashion during the course of the conversation, too.

7   Writing is a form of kinesthetic learning—you are getting a part of your body involved in the learning process—so if you are really serious about wanting to remember people's names for the long term, keep a name journal or a log of important people you meet, and review it periodically.

8   People can't remember names for one main reason: they are just not paying attention. This process forces you to think. If, for example, you struggle with the step of creating a mental picture, the other steps—looking at the person closely, shaking his or her hand confidently, and repeating the name a few times—are easy to do, will solidify the name in your memory, and will ultimately convey a positive image of you to others.

Vocabulary and Comprehension

1. In the first paragraph, the writer mentions three learning styles. Using your own words, define each style:

   a. visual _____

   b. auditory _____

   c. kinesthetic _____

2. Why does the writer mention learning styles?

   _____

3. Who is the audience for this essay?

   _____

4. Underline the thesis statement.

5. Underline the topic sentences in paragraphs 2 through 6.

MyWritingLab™

Complete additional reading comprehension questions for this selection at **mywritinglab.com**

Grammar

6. In paragraph 1, circle the first five commas. Then write three rules about comma usage.

_____

_____

_____

GRAMMAR LINK
For more information on commas, see Chapter 26. For more information on pronouns and antecedents, see Chapter 7.

7. The second sentence in paragraph 3 contains *him or her*. What is the antecedent for those pronouns? In other words, whom do the pronouns refer to?

_____

Discussion and Writing

8. Describe a process that people can follow to remember details such as birthdays, exam deadlines, appointments, telephone numbers, or computer passwords.

9. Think about a time when you forgot a person's name. What strategy did you use to deal with the situation?

10. Describe the first time you met your best friend, spouse, or colleague. Why did you decide to keep that person in your life?

READING 17

The Rewards of Dirty Work

Linda L. Lindsey and Stephen Beach

Linda L. Lindsey teaches sociology at Maryville University of St. Louis, and Stephen Beach teaches at Kentucky Wesleyan College. In the next essay, they list some surprising rewards of dirty work. As you read, notice how the authors mainly use the illustration writing pattern but also use elements of description and argument.

1   As sociologist Everett Hughes once pointed out, in order for some members of society to be clean and pure, someone else must take care of unclean, often taboo work, such as handling dead bodies and filth. In India and Japan, such jobs were, and to some extent still are, relegated to the Dalits (or Untouchables) and the Eta, respectively. Both groups were regarded as ritually impure. Our society does not have formal taboos against dirty work, but some jobs are rated near the bottom of the scale of occupational prestige and are viewed as not quite respectable and certainly not something to brag about. Garbage collection is a good example. Why would anyone choose to become a garbage collector? Stewart Perry asked this question to sanitation workers for the Sunset Scavenger Business in San Francisco. For a job that requires little training or education, the pay is relatively good. But pay was not what drew men to the job.

2   One attraction of becoming a garbage collector was variety. The job involves many different activities. Collecting garbage also means being outdoors and moving around. On another level, variety means the unexpected. For the sanitation workers, every day brought something different: witnessing a robbery, calling in a fire alarm and getting residents out of the building before the fire truck arrived, and responding to FBI requests to save all the rubbish from a house under surveillance.

3   Also, the garbage itself was full of surprises. Almost every day the men found something of interest, whether a good book, a child's toy, or a fixable radio. Almost inevitably, garbage men became collectors. In the course of his research, Perry himself acquired a rare seventeenth-century book of sermons and a sheepskin rug.

4   Garbage men got to know intimately the neighborhoods in which they worked. Watching children grow up, couples marry or separate, or one house or block deteriorating while another was being renovated had the appeal of an ongoing story, not unlike a soap opera on TV. They witnessed not just public performances, but also what Erving Goffman called the "backstage" of life. The respectable facades in affluent neighborhoods cannot hide the alcoholism a garbage man detects from cans full of empty liquor bottles or the sexual longings symbolized by bundles of pornographic magazines.

5   Another attraction of garbage collection was a sense of camaraderie among workers. The friendships people make on the job are a major source of satisfaction in any occupation. Many Sunset workers came from the same ethnic background (Italian) and in some cases from the same neighborhood. All of the men hoped that their own sons would go to college and make something better of themselves. But at least thirty were following in their fathers' footsteps. These intergenerational family ties and friendships made the company a familiar and welcome place and a stronghold of tradition for members of ethnic communities that were beginning to break apart.

6   The garbage collectors liked working at their own pace, scheduling their own breaks, deciding when to do their paperwork—in short, being their own bosses. Collecting garbage may be "dirty work" in many peoples' eyes, but these men were proud of what they did for a living.

Vocabulary and Comprehension

1. What is a *taboo*? See paragraph 1 for clues.

   _____

   _____

2. How is Western society different from other societies regarding garbage collecting or other dirty work?

   _____

   _____

   _____

   _____

3. How do Western societies judge the profession of garbage collecting?

   _____

   _____

   _____

   _____

MyWritingLab™

Complete additional reading comprehension questions for this selection at **mywritinglab.com**

4. The writers give a positive spin on garbage collecting. List the main points.

    _____

    _____

    _____

    _____

    _____

5. How do garbage collectors see the "backstage" of life?

    _____

    _____

    _____

6. In this essay, the main idea is suggested but is not written. Write your own thesis statement for the essay.

    _____

    _____

    _____

    _____

> **GRAMMAR LINK**
> For more information on irregular past tense, see Chapter 9. For more information on reflexive pronouns, see Chapter 7.

Grammar

7. Underline five irregular past tense verbs in paragraphs 3 and 4. Then write the present and past forms of each verb.

    _____

    _____

8. In paragraph 5, who does the word *themselves* refer to?

    _____

Discussion and Writing

9. List some jobs that might be considered dirty. What do the jobs have in common?

10. What are some stereotypes that we have about other professions? These professions could be prestigious or nonprestigious. Give some examples.

11. Think of another job that lacks prestige. Explain why that job has value and is rewarding.

12. What steps should people take to find a job? Explain at least three steps.

MyWritingLab   **THE WRITER'S ROOM**   Images of Trades, Technology, and the Business World

MyWritingLab™
**Complete these
writing assignments at
mywritinglab.com**

Writing Activity 1: Photo Writing

1. Define videogame addiction, or explain the causes or effects of a videogame addiction.

2. Classify computer dangers into three categories. For instance, there are dangers with hackers, online gambling, viruses, cyberstalkers, cyber bullying, and so on. Give examples to support the categories.

3. Explain some ways that your life has changed because of technology.

Writing Activity 2: Film Writing

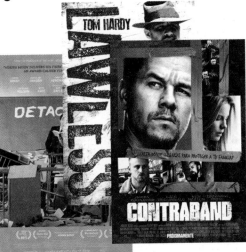

1. View a film about the business world such as *Arbitrage* or *Wall Street: Money Never Sleeps.* Explain the causes or effects of the main character's greed.

2. Watch *Lawless, You've Been Trumped, Contraband,* or a film of your choice. Then focus on a central character and explain the process he or she goes through to overcome a crisis.

3. Watch *Detachment, Bernie, Goon,* or another movie of your choice. Compare and contrast two characters in the film.

Term	Meaning	Examples
Active voice	• Form of the verb when the subject does the action	Maria <u>will mail</u> the letter.
Adjective	• Adds information about the noun	quiet, clear, decent
Adverb	• Adds information about the verb; expresses time, place, or frequency	quietly, clearly, decently, easily; sometimes, often, usually, never
Base form of verb	• The main form of a verb that is found in a dictionary	eat, go, feel, listen, whisper
Clause	• An independent clause has a subject and a verb and expresses a complete idea. • A dependent clause has a subject and a verb but cannot stand alone. It "depends" on another clause to be complete.	The athlete was thrilled. because she won a gold medal
Conditional sentence	• Explains possible, imaginary, or impossible situations; each type of conditional sentence has a condition clause and a result clause.	Possible future: If I win, I will fly to Morocco. Unlikely present: If I won, I would fly to Morocco. Impossible past: If I had won, I would have flown to Morocco.
Conjunctive adverb	• Shows a relationship between two ideas	also, consequently, finally, however, furthermore, moreover, therefore, thus
Conjunction	• **Coordinating conjunction:** connects two ideas of equal importance • **Subordinating conjunction:** connects two ideas when one idea is subordinate (or inferior) to the other idea	but, or, yet, so, for, and, nor after, although, because, before, unless, until, when
Determiner	• Identifies or determines whether a noun is specific or general	a, an, the; this, that, these, those; any, all, each, every, some, one, two
Indirect speech	• Reports what someone said without using the person's exact words	Mr. Simpson said that he would never find a better job.
Infinitive	• *To* plus the base form of the verb	He wants <u>to think</u> about it.
Interjection	• A word expressing an emotion; interjections usually appear in quotations	ouch, yikes, wow, yeah, oh
Irregular verb	• A verb that does not have an -*ed* ending in at least one of its past forms	ate, broke, swam, went
Linking verb	• A verb that describes a state of being; joins the subject with a descriptive word	is, am, are, was, were, act, appear, look, seem
Modal	• A type of helping verb that indicates willingness, possibility, advice, and so on	<u>may</u> help, <u>can</u> go, <u>should</u> deliver
Noun	• A person, place, or thing	Singular: man, dog, person Plural: men, dogs, people

Term	Meaning	Examples
Passive voice	• Form of the verb when the subject does not perform the action (formed with *be* + the past participle)	The letter will be mailed shortly.
Preposition	• Shows a relationship between words (source, direction, location, etc.)	at, to, for, from, behind, above
Pronoun	• Replaces one or more nouns	he, she, it, us, ours, themselves
Regular verb	• A verb that has a standard *-d* or *-ed* ending in the past tense	walked, looked, checked, carried, moved
Sentence types	• A **simple sentence** has one independent clause that expresses a complete idea.	Some food is unhealthy.
	• A **compound sentence** has two or more independent clauses joined together.	Some restaurants serve junk food, and others serve healthy meals.
	• A **complex sentence** has at least one dependent and one independent clause joined together.	Although the food is not healthy, it is very tasty.
	• A **compound–complex sentence** has at least two independent clauses joined with at least one dependent clause.	Although the food is not healthy, it is very tasty, and I enjoy eating it.
Transitional word or expression	• Linking words or phrases that show the reader the connections between ideas	in addition, however, furthermore, in fact, moreover, for example
Verb	• Expresses an action or state of being	go, run, have, wear, believe

PRACTICE 1

Label each word with one of the following terms.

adjective	conjunction	noun	pronoun
adverb	interjection	preposition	verb

EXAMPLE: carried _____verb_____

1. but _____
2. them _____
3. below _____
4. believe _____
5. famous _____
6. slowly _____
7. although _____
8. ouch _____

9. student _____
10. pretty _____
11. yikes _____
12. behind _____
13. laugh _____
14. we _____
15. never _____
16. people _____

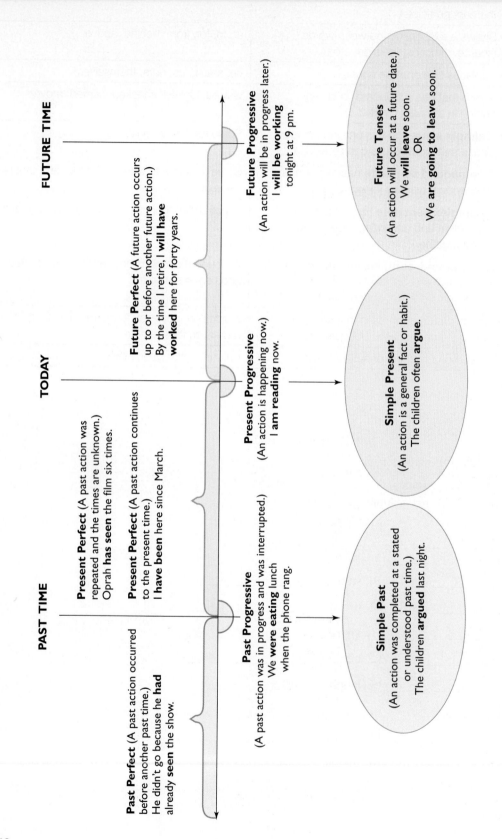

PAST TIME

TODAY

FUTURE TIME

Past Perfect (A past action occurred before another past time.)
He didn't go because he **had** already **seen** the show.

Present Perfect (A past action was repeated and the times are unknown.)
Oprah **has seen** the film six times.

Present Perfect (A past action continues to the present time.)
I **have been** here since March.

Future Perfect (A future action occurs up to or before another future action.)
By the time I retire, I **will have worked** here for forty years.

Past Progressive (A past action was in progress and was interrupted.)
We **were eating** lunch when the phone rang.

Present Progressive (An action is happening now.)
I **am reading** now.

Future Progressive (A future action will be in progress later.)
I **will be working** tonight at 9 pm.

Simple Past (An action was completed at a stated or understood past time.)
The children **argued** last night.

Simple Present (An action is a general fact or habit.)
The children often **argue.**

Future Tenses (An action will occur at a future date.)
We **will leave** soon.
OR
We **are going to leave** soon.

Combining Ideas in Sentences

Making Compound Sentences

A.

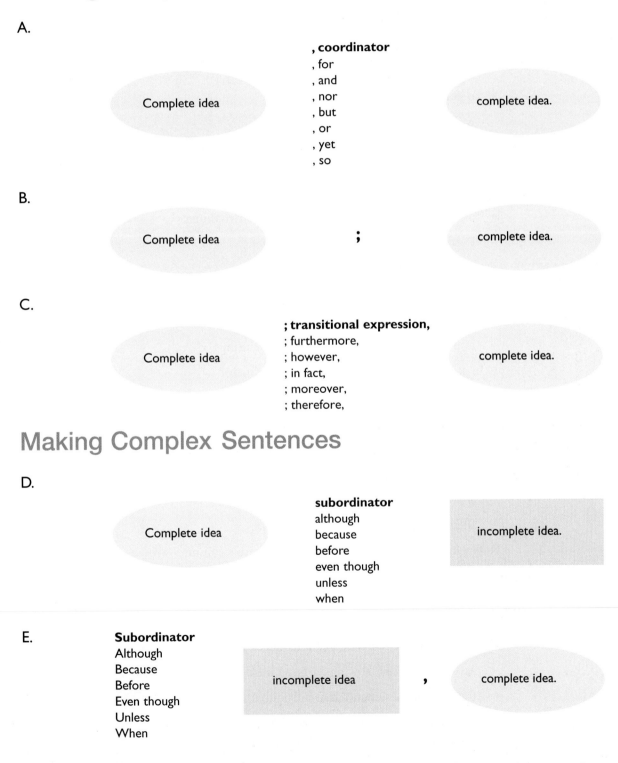

Complete idea

, coordinator
, for
, and
, nor
, but
, or
, yet
, so

complete idea.

B.

Complete idea

;

complete idea.

C.

Complete idea

; transitional expression,
; furthermore,
; however,
; in fact,
; moreover,
; therefore,

complete idea.

Making Complex Sentences

D.

Complete idea

subordinator
although
because
before
even though
unless
when

incomplete idea.

E.

Subordinator
Although
Because
Before
Even though
Unless
When

incomplete idea

,

complete idea.

Apostrophe (')

Use an apostrophe for the following reasons.

- To join a subject and a verb

    She's tired.

- To join a helping verb with *not*

    You **shouldn**'t smoke.

- To indicate possession

    Mike's camera is new.

Comma (,)

Use a comma in the following cases.

- To separate words in a series of more than two things

    Everyone needs food, water, and shelter.

- After an introductory word or phrase

    After the election, the candidate rested.

- Around interrupting phrases that give additional information about the subject

    Isabelle, an artist, makes astonishing paintings.

- In compound sentences before the coordinator

    The job is easy, but it does not pay well.

- Around relative clauses containing *which*

    The files, which are in my office, contain important information.

- In quotations, after an introductory phrase or before an end phrase

    Durrell said, "Personality is an illusion."

    "Personality is an illusion," Durrell said.

Note: Do not join two complete sentences with a comma.

Colon (:)

Use a colon in the following cases.

- After a complete sentence that introduces a list or after *the following*

    An essay has the following parts: an introduction, a body, and a conclusion.

- After a complete sentence that introduces a quotation

    Durrell's point was clear: "Personality is an illusion."

- Before an explanation or example

    Kaitlin realized what she really needed: time alone.

- To separate the hours and minutes in expressions of time

    The college bookstore opens at 8:30 a.m.

Semicolon (;)

Use a semicolon to join two independent and related clauses.

    Many Brazilian tribes are isolated; they do not interact with the outside world.

Quotation Marks (" ")

Use quotation marks around direct speech. When a quotation is a complete sentence, do the following:

- Capitalize the first word in the quotation.

- Place the end punctuation mark inside the closing quotation marks.

    In her essay, Dorothy Nixon said, "I am the television addict."

Integrated Quotation

If you integrate a quotation into your sentence, just add quotation marks.

    Dorothy Nixon calls herself a "television addict."

"Inside" Quotation

If one quotation is inside another quotation, use single quotation marks (' ') around the inside quotation.

    Maya Angelou describes the moment: "She turned on the light and said, 'Look at the baby.' "

Citing Page Numbers

Put the page number in parentheses. Place the final period *after* the parentheses.

    In her novel, Maya Angelou says, "I didn't feel lonely or abandoned" (127).

Capitalization

Always capitalize the following:

- The pronoun *I* and the first word of every sentence

    The doctor and **I** discussed the problem.

- The names of days of the week, months, and specific holidays

    Wednesday   **A**pril 14   **L**abor **D**ay

- The names of specific places, such as buildings, streets, parks, public squares, lakes, rivers, cities, states, and countries

    Elm **S**treet   **M**ississippi **R**iver   **M**iami, **F**lorida

- The names of languages, nationalities, tribes, races, and religions

    Greek   Mohawk   Christian

- The titles of specific individuals

    General Smith   President Bush   Mrs. Sloan

- The major words in titles of literary or artistic works

    War and Peace   *The Last Supper*   *Django Unchained*

- The names of historical events, eras, and movements

    Boer War   Dadaism   the Depression

Punctuating Titles

Capitalize all of the major words in a title. Place quotation marks around the titles of short works (songs, essays, short stories, poems, newspaper articles, magazine articles, etc.).

Chopin's most famous story was called "The Storm."

Italicize the titles of longer works (television series, movies, plays, books, works of art, magazines, newspapers, etc.). If you are handwriting a text, underline titles of long works.

I read the classic novel *The Awakening*.

Spelling, Grammar, and Vocabulary Logs

The goal of keeping spelling and grammar logs is to help you stop repeating errors. When you do new writing assignments, you can consult the lists and hopefully break some ingrained bad habits. The vocabulary log can provide you with interesting new terms that you can incorporate into your writing.

Spelling Log

Every time you misspell a word, record both the mistake and the correction in your spelling log. Then, before you hand in a writing assignment, consult your list of misspelled words. The goal is to stop repeating the same spelling errors.

EXAMPLE:

Incorrect	Correct
alot	a lot
responsable	responsible

Grammar Log

Each time a writing assignment is returned to you, identify one or two repeated errors and add them to your grammar log. Consult the grammar log before you hand in writing assignments to avoid making the same errors. For each type of grammar error, follow these steps.

◆ Identify the assignment, and write down the type of error.

◆ In your own words, write a rule about the error.

◆ Include an example from your writing assignment.

EXAMPLE: <u>Narration Paragraph</u> (Sept. 28): Run-on

Do not connect two complete sentences with a comma.

pole. The
We hit a telephone ~~pole, the~~ airbags burst open.

Vocabulary Log

As you read, you will learn new vocabulary words and expressions. Keep a record of the most interesting and useful vocabulary words and their meanings. Write a synonym or definition next to each new word.

EXAMPLE:

Term	Meaning
reminisce	to recollect in an enjoyable way

Spelling Log

Grammar Log

_____

_____

_____

_____

_____

_____

_____

_____

_____

_____

_____

_____

_____

_____

_____

_____

_____

_____

_____

_____

_____

_____

_____

_____

Vocabulary Log

Credits

TEXT

Page 8: "Zion Market" by Jinsuk Suh. Used by permission of the author; **p. 13:** Thomas, Veena "College Culture". Used by permission of the author; **p. 23:** Norman Christensen "A Requiem for the Po'ouli" *The Environment and You.* Published by Benjamin Cummings, © 2012; **p. 26:** Hosseini, Khaled. From *A Thousand Splendid Suns.* Published by Riverhead Books, © 2007; **p. 34:** "Zion Market" by Jinsuk Suh. Used by permission of the author; **p. 39:** "Zion Market" by Jinsuk Suh. Used by permission of the author; **p. 45:** Cornelius, Steven and Mary Natvig. *Music: A Social Experience.* Copyright © 2011 by Pearson Education; **p. 50:** Campbell, Bebe Moore. *Dancing With Fear;* **p. 61:** Bruce, Kelly. Used by permission of the author; **p. 66:** From *Invitation to Psychology* 2nd Ed. by Carole Wade and Carol Tavris, Published by Pearson, Upper Saddle River, © 2001; **p. 71:** Hines, Tiffany. "Cooks Have the Advantage"; **p. 82:** From *Criminal Justice Today* by Frank Schmalleger; **p. 87:** Cage, Kyle. "Concealed Carry on College Campuses". Used by permission of the author; **p. 95:** Allard, Renaud. "Bad Habits" Used by permission of the author; **p. 104:** "How to Get Rich Quickly" by Veronique Benard-Jimenez. Used by permission of the author; **p. 110:** From "Yoga Y'all" by Elizabeth Gilbert; **p. 126:** From "Chicken Hips" by Catherine Pigott, *Globe and Mail,* March 20, 1990. Used by permission of Catherine Pigott; **p. 157:** W. W. Jacobs, *The Monkeys Paw.* Harper's Magazine Company; **p. 175:** Arliss, George. From *Up the Years From Bloomsbury: An Autobiography;* **p. 192:** Vincent van Gogh, His Letters. **p. 202:** From *Cultural Anthropology* by Ember et al; **p. 217:** From *Collective Behavior* by David A. Locher; **p. 218:** George Bernard Shaw; **p. 225:** From *The Power of Myth* by Joseph Campbell; **p. 228:** H. G. Wells, The Island of Doctor Moreau; **p. 231:** From *Exploring the Humanities* by Laurie Schneider Adams; **p. 249:** From *Architectural Drawing and Light Construction* by Phillip A. Grau, Edward J. Muller, and James G. Fausett. Upper Saddle River, New Jersey: Pearson Prentice Hall, 2009; **p. 261:** From *Building Construction:* Methods and Materials for the Fire Service by Michael Smith. Upper Saddle River, NJ: Pearson Prentice Hall; **p. 282:** John F. Kennedy, 1962 Speech at Rice University. John F. Kennedy Presidential Library and Museum; **p. 317:** From *Animal Watching:* A Field Guide to Animal Behavior by Desmond Morris. London: Jonathan Cape, Ltd, Copyright © 1990; **p. 318:** From *New American Webster's Handy College Dictionary* by Phillip D. Morehead and Andrew T. Morehead, copyright 1951 (renewed), © 1955, 1956, 1957, 1961 by Albert H.Morehead, 1972, 1981, 1985, 1995 by Philip D. Morehead and Andrew T. Morehead. Used by permission Dutton Signet, a division of Penguin Group (USA) LLC; **p. 319:** "Pronunciation of Cooperation" from dictionary.reference.com. Copyright © by Dictionary.com. Used by permission of Dictionary.com, LLC; **p. 321:** From *Shooting an Elephant* by George Orwell. Published by Penguin Group (USA) Inc., © 2009; **p. 326:** From *Life of Pi* by Yann Martel. (Harcourt 2001). Copyright © 2001 by Yann Martel; **p. 338:** From *Animal Wonderland* by Frank Walter Lane. New York: Sheridan House, Copyright © 1951; **p. 371:** From *Gifted Hands* by Ben Carson, M.D. Copyright © 1990 by Review and Herald Publishing Association and Zondervan; **pp. 393–394:** "Fish Cheeks" by Amy Tan. Copyright ©1987 by Amy Tan. First appeared in Seventeen Magazine. Used by permission of Amy Tan and the Sandra Dijkstra Literary Agency; **pp. 395–396:** "Birth" from *I Know Why the Caged Bird Sings* by Maya Angelou. Copyright © 1969, and renewed 1997 by Maya Angelou. Used by permission of Random House, Inc; **pp. 397–398:** "Your World's a Stage" by Josh Freed from (Montreal) Gazette, Copyright © March 28, 2009 by Josh Freed. Used by permission of Josh Freed; **pp. 399–401:** "Fat Chance" by Dorothy Nixon. Copyright © by Dorothy Nixon. Used by permission of Dorothy Nixon. Dorothy Nixon is the author of "Threshold Girl"; **pp. 402–403:** "Skydiving" by Touré. Reprinted and abridged with the permission of Atria Publishing Group from the Free Press edition of *Who's Afraid of Post-Blackness:* What It Means to Be Black Now by Touré. Copyright © 2011 by Touré. All rights reserved; **pp. 405–407:** Dobson, Louise. "What's Your Humor Style" from *Psychology Today Magazine.* July 1, 2006. *Reprinted with Permission from Psychology Today Magazine,* (Copyright © 2006 Sussex Publishers, LLC.); **pp. 408–410:** "A Cultural Minefield" "Innocent gestures can translate poorly, traveler warns" by William Ecenbarger. Los Angeles Times, April 20, 2008. Used by permission of the author; **pp. 411–413:** "Celanthropists" by Katrina Onstad from Globe and Mail, September 10, 2012 . Used by permission of the author; **pp. 414–416:** "The Cult of Emaciation" by Ben Barry originally published in National Post, March 17, 2007. Used by permission of the author; **pp. 417–418:** "Shopping for Religion" by Ellen Goodman from Boston Globe, Feb. 29, 2008. Used by permission of the author; **pp. 421–422:** "Reverend Evan's Universe" from *A Short History of Nearly Everything* by Bill Bryson. Copyright © 2003 by Bill Bryson. Used by permission of Broadway Books a division of Random House, Inc; **pp. 423–424:** "Saving Animals" by Tom Spears from Postmedia News; Ottawa Citizen, Montreal Gazette, April 23, 2012. Used by permission of Ottawa Citizen, a division of Postmedia Network Inc; **pp. 425–426:** "Why People Love Dogs" by Jon Katz from Slate.com. Jan. 30, 2007. Used by permission of Jon Katz; **pp. 429–430:** "The Allure of Apple" by Juan Rodriguez from (Montreal) Gazette, Feb. 20, 2010. Used by permission of Montreal Gazette, a division of Postmedia Network Inc; **pp. 432–433:** "How to Handle Conflict" by P. Gregory Smith from *Career World,* November 1, 2003. Copyright © by The Weekly Reader Corporation. Reprinted by permission of Scholastic Inc; **pp. 434–435:** "How to Remember Names" by Roger Seip, co-founder of Freedom Personal Development and best selling author of *Train Your Brain for Success.* Copyright © by Roger Seip. Used by permission; **pp. 436–437:** "Rewards of Dirty Work" by Lindsey, Linda L.; Beach, Stephen, *Essentials of Sociology,* 1st, © 2003. Printed and Electronically reproduced by permission of Pearson Education, Inc., Upper Saddle River, New Jersey.

PHOTOS

Page 4: Sugar0607/Fotolia; **p. 11:** © Ralph Hagen/www.CartoonStock.com; **p. 12:** Alex Hubenov/fotolia; **p. 30:** Photos.com; **p. 31:** Yuri Arcurs/Fotolia; **p. 32 (tr):** JupiterImages/Photos.com; **p. 32 (bl):** Dbvirago/Fotolia; **p. 34:** Photos.com; **p. 35:** Pixtal/SuperStock; **p. 36:** Photos.com; **p. 38:** Ron Niebrugge/Alamy; **p. 44:** Zakaz/Fotolia; **p. 49:** Brian Jackson/Fotolia; **p. 54:** Greg Blomberg/Fotolia; **p. 60:** Joe Gough/Fotolia; **p. 65:** Photos.com; **p. 70:** ArenaCreative/Fotolia; **p. 75:** Kuvien/Fotolia; **p. 81:** Radius Images/JupiterImages; **p. 86:** Eric Isselée/Fotolia; **p. 92:** iStock/Thinkstock; **p. 93:** Photos.com; **p. 107:** Monkey Business/Fotolia; **p. 110:** Christopher

Pillitz/Dorling Kindersley, Ltd.; **p. 116:** Oliver Taylor/Fotolia; **p. 126:** Marco Mayer/Fotolia; **p. 145:** Alexandre Zveiger/Fotolia; **p. 147:** Paul Buck/EPA/Newscom; **p. 152:** AFP Photo/Newscom; **p. 154:** Biker3/Fotolia; **p. 157:** Markus Bormann/Fotolia; **p. 165:** SuperStock; **p. 172:** Kaczor58/Shutterstock; **p. 175:** Deklofenak/Fotolia; **p. 182:** 20TH CENTURY FOX/Album/Newscom; **p. 184:** Toshifumi Kitamura/AFP/Newscom; **p. 185 (tr):** Darkfreya/Fotolia; **p. 185 (br):** Gary Hershorn/Reuters; **p. 190:** Alessandrozocc/Fotolia; **p. 192:** Giuliano Maciocci/Fotolia; **p. 197:** Guernica/© Castrovilli/Fotolia 49842960; **p. 200** AFP Photo/Stan Honda/Newscom; **p. 202:** Brandon Bourdages/Shutterstock; **p. 205:** Selitbul/Fotolia; **p. 206:** Apeiron/Fotolia; **p. 209:** Jose AS Reyes/Shutterstock; **p. 214:** Salvador Manaoi/Fotolia; **p. 217:** Tero Hakala/Shutterstock; **p. 227:** Photos.com; **p. 229:** Victorian Traditions/Shutterstock; **p. 231:** Thomas Francois/Fotolia; **p. 232:** JaxPix5/Fotolia; **p. 235:** lynea/Shutterstock; **p. 238:** James Steidl/Fotolia; **p. 241:** EAlisa/Fotolia; **p. 242:** Jason Winter/Fotolia; **p. 249:** Steven Chiang/Shutterstock; **p. 252 (t):** Johnny Stockshooter/Alamy; **p. 252 (b):** Simone80/Fotolia; **p. 260:** Michael Doolittle/Alamy; **p. 261:** p. Seydel/Shutterstock; **p. 262:** Fernando Pacheco/Fotolia; **p. 267:** Karramba Production/Fotolia; **p. 270:** Stephen Gibson/Shutterstock; **p. 276:** EastVillageImages/Fotolia; **p. 278:** Delphimages/Fotolia; **p. 281:** Gautam Narang/Getty Images; **p. 282:** AbleStock.com/GettyImages/Thinkstock; **p. 285:** Paul Fleet/Fotolia; **p. 291:** Freesurf/Fotolia; **p. 292:** Rook76/Fotolia; **p. 294:** Georgios Kollidas/Shutterstock; **p. 307:** Thinkstock/Getty Images; **p. 313:** Pictorial Press Ltd/Alamy; **p. 317:** Dmitry Pichugin/Fotolia; **p. 321:** Faup/Fotolia; **p. 324:** Bierchen/Fotolia; **p. 326:** JohanSwanepoel/Fotolia; **p. 335:** Vladimir Melnik/Fotolia; **p. 337:** Nataliya Hora/Fotolia; **p. 338:** Santi Rodriguez/Shutterstock; **p. 340:** Peter Kim/Shutterstock; **p. 343:** MiroArt/Shutterstock; **p. 345:** Dave King/Dorling Kindersley, Ltd.; **p. 348:** Donna/Fotolia; **p. 350:** Regien Paassen/Shutterstock; **p. 361:** Zoe/Fotolia; **p. 369:** Kutay Tanir/Photos.com; **p. 371:** Shutterstock; **p. 382:** Pixsooz/Fotolia; **p. 390:** Rnl/Fotolia; **p. 398:** Rukanoga/Fotolia; **p. 400:** Stefanolunardi/Fotolia; **p. 402:** Germanskydive110/Fotolia; **p. 404:** Jack Hollingsworth/Photodisc/Thinkstock; **p. 405 (tl):** AF Archive/Alamy; **p. 405 (tm):** Locomotive/Album/Newscom; **p. 405 (tr):** *Malpaso Productions*/Album/Newscom; **p. 409:** "V for victory"/© Peter factors/Fotolia 1845121; **p. 414:** Stefanos Kyriazis/Fotolia; **p. 420 (tr):** Philip Dvorak; **p. 420 (ml):** Photos 12/Alamy; **p. 420 (mr):** Photos 12/Alamy; **p. 420 (m):** Mirage Enterprises/Album/Newscom; **p. 423:** Alan Lucas/Fotolia; **p. 425:** Muro/Fotolia; **p. 428 (t):** Steve Byland/Fotolia; **p. 428 (bl):** PRNewsFoto/Lionsgate/AP Images; **p. 428 (bm):** DNA Films/Album/Newscom; **p. 428 (br):** Amblin Entertainment/Album/Newscom; **p. 429:** Anatol/Fotolia; **p. 439 (t):** SanjMur/Fotolia; **p. 439 (bl):** Kingsgate Films/Album/Newscom; **p. 439 (bm):** Piero Oliosi/PolarisImages/Newscom; **p. 439 (br):** Universal Pictures/Album/Newscom.

Index

Revising Checklist for a Paragraph

Does the topic sentence

- ☐ make a point about the topic?

- ☐ express a complete thought?

- ☐ make a direct statement and not contain expressions such as *I think that* or *I will explain*?

Does the body

- ☐ have **adequate support**? Are there enough details to support the topic sentence?

- ☐ have **coherence**? Are ideas presented in an effective and logical manner?

- ☐ have **unity**? Is the paragraph unified around one central topic?

- ☐ have **style**? Are sentences varied in length? Is the language creative and precise?

Does the concluding sentence

- ☐ bring the paragraph to a satisfactory close?

- ☐ avoid introducing new or contradictory information? (Note: Not all paragraphs have concluding sentences.)

Revising Checklist for an Essay

Does the introduction

- ☐ contain a clearly identifiable thesis statement?

- ☐ build up to the thesis statement?

Does the thesis statement

- ☐ convey the essay's controlling idea?

- ☐ make a valid and supportable point?

- ☐ appear as the last sentence in the introduction?

- ☐ make a direct point and not contain expressions such as *I think that* or *I will explain*?

Do the body paragraphs

- ☐ have **adequate support**? Does each body paragraph have a topic sentence that clearly supports the thesis statement? Are there enough details to support each paragraph's topic sentence?

- ☐ have **coherence**? Are ideas presented in an effective and logical manner? Do transitional words and phrases help the ideas flow smoothly?

- ☐ have **unity**? Is the essay unified around one central topic? Does each body paragraph focus on one topic?

- ☐ have **style**? Are sentences varied in length? Is the language creative and precise?

Does the conclusion

- ☐ bring the essay to a satisfactory end?

- ☐ briefly summarize the ideas that the writer discusses in the essay?

- ☐ avoid introducing new or contradictory ideas?

- ☐ possibly end with a quotation, suggestion, or prediction?